Voice of Concern

Indian Geography
VOICE OF CONCERN

ANU KAPUR

NATIONAL ASSOCIATION OF GEOGRAPHERS, INDIA

Published by

CONCEPT PUBLISHING COMPANY, NEW DELHI - 110059

ISBN 81-7022-980-4

First Published 2002

Published and Printed by
Ashok Kumar Mittal
Concept Publishing Company
A/15-16, Commercial Block, Mohan Garden
New Delhi-110059 (India)
Phones: 5648039, 5649024
Fax: 091–(11)–5648053
E-mail: publishing@conceptpub.com

Contents

Presidential Address

Tables

Figures

Foreword

A confluence of two successive millennia is an opportune time to reflect on the past, place the present in perspective, and set an agenda for the future. The dusk of 2000 and the dawn of 2001 for Indian Geography was celebrated at the Indian Geography Congress held at Nagpur. Here the National Association of Geographers, India took up the recommendation of its Task Force on Indian Geography to compile and publish all the Presidential Addresses in the form of a book. As the convener of the Task Force and President - Elect, I was entrusted with responsibility of pursuing the recommendation.

I, however, opted to devolve the assignment to the youngest member of the Task Force – Dr. Anu Kapur of Delhi University. She had authored a book on Indian Geography; her credentials as an erudite scholar were established; and she carried a felicity of literary expression. The freshness of her youthful perspective was deemed as no less critical for scrutinizing the academic world dominated by the age.

The choice proved to be providential. Endowed with a creative mind, Anu set out to accomplish much beyond the given mandate. Initially the book was conceived as a collection of Presidential Addresses delivered at the annual Indian Geography Congress; she cast the entire work into an extended mould. Beginning with a critique of the evolving scene of Indian Geography followed by an evaluation of the marching saga of the National Association of Geographers ,India she placed the Presidential Addresses in a wider perspective. The status of Indian Geography left so much to be desired vis-à-vis international standards and the state of the National Association emerged so worrisome that Anu decided on 'Voice of Concern' as an expressive title of the book. She views the Presidential Addresses as a kind of 'Concern for Voice', underlining at the same time that little had been done, in actual, to respond to the situation. The book does channelise a heartfelt concern for the discipline and the Association in India .

Writing a preface to such a profound document is both daunting as well as self-fulfilling. Daunting, because it is difficult to embellish what is already well done; fulfilling because it is a realization of a vision with the inception of which I have been associated. The obligation lends me a sense of rare privilege.

The book is organically woven in three telescopic components: Indian Geography, National Association and Presidential Addresses. The scenario of Indian Geography is captured through a survey of works pertaining to geographical knowledge that were piled over centuries. Tracing the emergence of geography departments, societies and journals for the purpose was equally imperative. The performance of National Association of Geographers, India, is assessed through an inquiry into its institutional functioning, financial management, journal quality, conference logistics, and spatial reach. Likewise, the Presidential Addresses were not to be just reprinted; each is proceeded by a condensed biographical note. In a way, the profile on the career trajectory of twenty-two presidents, along with their photographs, provide a special flavor to the book. Crafted through extended interviews and intensive study of curriculum vitae of each president, the write ups are not an eulogy but an effort to grasp the essence of the person. The viewpoint is essentially the author's and need not be universal; but one hopes that the spirit of presentation will be appreciated. Equally laudable is her ability to cull data from apparently innocuous sources and churn it for deriving inferences. This is clearly evident from the 46 self explanatory tables which punctuate the text. A score of maps have also been pressed into service to convey messages having a spatial bearing.

On the basis of the narrative and discourse of the book, three phases can be discerned in the evolution of Indian Geography: the colonial phase when the thrust was not so much on learning the basic concepts of the discipline but accumulating the gazetteer type knowledge on India for reasons of administration and resource exploitation ; the post-independence phase when some centers of specialization in select branches of geography did emerge and geographers had umpteen opportunities for promoting their discipline but failed to make the desired impact, and the post-National Association phase from 1978-2000 when some institutional changes in the sphere of higher education, such as rotation of chairpersons , implementation of career advancement scheme, and introduction of national eligibility test, changed the ecology of the higher education in India, including that of geography. Today the reputed citadels of specialization are seen as dwarfed in quality though more diversified in the complexion of research and teaching.

The birth of National Association of Geographers, India in 1978 marks a landmark in the history of Indian Geography. With an all India coverage, it had 1260 life members on its roll in 2000, a quantum jump from a tally of 244 in 1980. This membership approximates the aggregate life membership of the next three ranking geographical societies, namely Geographical Society of India, Kolkata; Institute of Indian Geographers, Pune; and Indian Geographical Society, Chennai. Spatial scatter of the life members of National Association of

Geographers, India is wide, with more than a half of them dispersed at places at a distance of more than one thousand kilometers from Delhi. Special care seems to have been taken to ensure and strengthen the national character of NAGI. This was worked out, among other things, through an equitable regional representation of its members on the executive committee, in election to the office of its president, and in selecting the venue for the Indian Geographical Congress.

Impressive as it may appear, the size of the Association's membership pales into insignificance when compared with that of some of the international geographical societies. It is just one-tenth of the membership of the Royal Geographical Society, London, or one-fifth of that of the Association of American Geographers. The Association must reorganise itself if it wants to motivate as many geographers to join its community, and thereby promote the cause of the discipline. This may call for activation of the regional wings, which obviously have a nearer-home access to all variety of educational institutions and research organizations.

The author rightly underlines some serous maladies in the voice of the National Association, one of which is the sorry state of affairs of its journal, the Annals. This mouthpiece of Indian Geography does not receive the best research material for publication, its printing lacks the desired quality and its circulation is irregular. Things call for an immediate attention and action.

During its life span of nearly twenty-three years (1978-2000), the Association had 23 presidents but in reality there were 22 luminaries for one of them had been nominated for two intermittent terms. Twenty-two Indian Geography Congress have been organized by the Association. Since two presidential addresses were delivered at the first Indian Geography Congress at Chandigarh, a total of 23 presidential addresses is expected. The present volume carries 22 in all. The presidential addresses at the Patna Indian Geography Congress was delivered extempore and therefore is a missing document in this series .The ensuing Indian Geography Congress at Sagar in December this year will also have to go without a presidential address. The tragic demise of the President - Elect, S.S. Dhabariya, of Jaipur, on 1st May this year has created this vacuum . His death is an irreparable loss to Indian Geography. No less unprovidential was the sudden demise of C.P. Singh, professor at the department of geography, Delhi School of Economics on 5th December, 2000, the Association lost its dynamic Joint Secretary; Indian Geography an eminent political geographer. His family has made a biggest ever donation of Rupees one hundred thousand for initiating an appropriate activity to perpetuate his memory. The National Association owes to the family a gratitude for this generous act of grace as also to the family of late N.P. Ayyar, professor of Sagar University.

They recently made a contribution of Rupees twenty-five thousand for a similar cause. Though these donations have been received in 2001 while the purview of this book is till 2000 yet like some pieces of art – this book is not going to lose its value for years to come .

A book of this nature would be of enduring relevance to a wide audience. Social scientists, in general, could use it as a model to make a critical inquiry of the state of the art of their disciplines. Ones who ambitiously start societies and associations would find many yardsticks for undertaking an assessment of their achievements. For geographers across the globe, the book is a treatise to be conversant with Indian Geography. Geography students, teachers and professionals can draw information, ideas and messages of great value. The book is aimed at all who are 'concerned with' and 'feel concerned' for the state of our discipline.

Accomplished within as short a span as six months, the book is a sensitized version of excellence. It brings out both the strengths and inadequacies of Indian Geography, identifies opportunities several of which have remained unrealized, and defines tasks that must be taken up urgently by National Association of Geographers ,India . In a convincing manner, Anu calls for construction of the next version of the book in the year 2020. After twenty years, with as many presidential addresses in hand, and additional lessons learnt, the second such book should be in a position to project a more exalted state of Indian Geography with the National Association of Geographers enjoying a great glory.

The future of Indian Geography is not certainly without hope. A discipline that produces such sparks of brilliance, as the present one, is surely headed towards vibrancy of incandescence rather than morbidity of embers.

Panjab University
Chandigarh (India)
28 December, 2001

Gopal Krishan
President NAGI

Preface

I am a chance author of this book.

The do's and don'ts for a president are not spelt in the constitution of the National Association of Geographers, India. Freed from a roster of work, a president can perform ceremonious to functional roles. Within this range of choice, he could enroll members, augment funds, layout an exhibition, encourage expeditions, introduce exciting competitions, announce awards and host a congress. A president could do all this and more. He could also be a silent signatory and a condescending chairperson over meetings that he presides . Within this freedom to be and what to be, 22nd in the line of presidents of the National Association of Geographers, India, Gopal Krishan struck upon the idea of the need to collate and publish the Presidential Addresses of this Association. Twin objectives guided his decision – as convener for the Task Force Report on Indian Geography, he had accessed 14 presidential addresses and found them to be documents of exceptional value. Barely seven out of the twenty three addresses had been published by this Association . This aroused in him a desire to make them available in a collective form to a larger audience. The Association is in the throes of a grave shortage of funds. As president, Gopal Krishan, was well aware of his constraints. He could not garner funds through commercial advertisements, personal appeals or raising the levy on members. Royalty receipts from the sale of the Presidential Addresses seemed a possible source of revenue for the Association.

How do I fit in the scheme of things? I was not 'selected' from a list of geographers drawn for this work. Neither am I a case of the 'fittest'; there are more seasoned and adept geographers. It is also not a fact that Gopal Krishan began this book and it came my way through evolution. Chance is all that testifies in the court of explanation.

Gopal Krishan's term as president of National Association of Geographers, India draws to an end by December 2001. In early May 2001, he had made little headway to translate his dream into a reality. Most professors, presidents, chairpersons one must concede are embroiled neck deep in many works. A one line email reached me with a request to take on his 'vision'. I flashed back a long list of conditionalities all of which gravitated around a single core – as president, as geographer, he would live 'my concern' for the book. I thought he would balk his decision. Gopal Krishan bounced back one condition – the book must be released in December 2001, the month of end of his tenure as president. On his suggestion the Executive Committee of NAGI at its meeting on 4 June, 2001 unanimously agreed to the decision to hand the work to over me - with a contracted royalty towards National Association of Geographers, India.

Thus began this time bound book Voice of Concern.

It is difficult for me to condense in words the multifaceted care Gopal Krishan extended towards the book. The hunt for the presidential addresses, fixing appointments with presidents, shouldering responsibility for preparing the maps, scanning the photographs, and access to infrastructure at his department of geography, Chandigarh was not all. A hydra headed list of monstrous queries and questions daily flooded the space of his 'Outlook Express'. He never ducked my emails to the recycling bin . Reading endless number of drafts I churned in these six months, Gopal Krishan's tough and tenacious criticism of many of my ideas and words led to moments of anguish and despair. Yet he never handled a conflict from a pedestal of power. After all he was a professor, president and senior person of established repute amidst the community of Indian Geographers and I a mere lecturer and only an ordinary life member in the National Association ! To cap it all he agreed to write a foreword and thus 'saved me' from commenting on the merits and demerits of this book. A common Concern kept this Voice alive and took it to its destination. He kept his promise, I kept mine too. In ways more than one I feel it has not been mine but 'our book'. Carrying this feeling of togetherness it would not be out of place to forward a joint acknowledgement.

<u>Acknowledgements from us:</u> All the presidents of National Association of Geographers, India receive our heartfelt gratitude for responding enthusiastically to our numerous requests. Of the 22 presidents the untimely demise of Moonis Raza and Prakasa Rao meant that these were the ones we sadly missed. We remain in debt to Mehdi Raza, younger brother of Moonis Raza and Raghavaswamy, son of Prakasa Rao for their help in providing clarifications and material. Through speed post, emails, fax or in person the curriculum vitae and photographs of all the presidents reached us well in time. Photographs in the book speak of all those presidents who made special efforts to trudge to studios for recent and better takes. One is touched by all such acts.

Most overwhelming has been the response to requests for personal interviews. It is difficult to forget that: G.B Singh drove from Patiala to Chandigarh for this purpose, Gosal extended the invitation to his residence and allowed questions to spill into sessions that spanned across two days. In Delhi despite a troublesome spondalitis Sundaram sat through hours in all patience, Misra was his unhurried self over a long discussion at his residence, Aijaz in Gurgaon postponed his appointment with the doctor when he realised one was not in a mood to wrap up, Satyesh Chakraborty extended his stay in Delhi and devoted two days to share his bit, Bhat drove all the way to the department of geography, Delhi School of Economics, with a promise of a meeting over lunch that lasted till dinner, Pathak's response to our telegram led him to cancel appointments scheduled for a day at Delhi , he was full of answers till he boarded the train back to Calcutta. A drive to Aligarh saw Shafi had taken care to reserve an undisturbed block of time at his chamber in the department of geography. Despite an unannounced arrival, Mehdi Raza's warmth of reception with a much wanted lunch followed by a discussion about Moonis made the trip to Aligarh most memorable. Patna is a city which houses two presidents. Interviews with Dayal and Ram at their bungalows proved most worthy. Ram's desperate search for his presidential address, did not meet success and remains a 'gap' in this book. Surrounded by a hospitable family and four dogs Dayal's formidable age did not thwart alert response on many an incidents into the past.

Mahadev resides in Chennai, Kayastha in Varanasi, Alam in Osmania, Vaidyanadhan in Cuddalore, Das in Guwahati, Arunachalam in Mumbai and K.N. Singh in Addis Ababa, Ethopia. Geographical distances were overcome by enrolling this group of presidents in conversation over the e-mail and the telephone. Impairments of health in case of Mahadev, Das and Kayastha meant that questions had to be asked over short sessions and at times members of their family were interpreters – but the willingness to answer was universal with all of them. The regret to personally meet all of them lingers, yet one remains in debt to the space of learning all offered by narrating in much honesty their joys and pains of life as a geographer in India. The write up on the presidents would loose flavor had presidents not granted the time and thought for these interviews.

Most of the presidents have long left the departments of geography or institutes where they served. A maze of relationships had to be worked to reach some of them. The importance of links cannot be overlooked. Sachi Devi at Vishakhapatnam played a critical role in establishing contact with Vaidyanathan, M.M Das and Bhagawati at Guwahati were indispensable in leading us to H.P.Das; Majid Husain at Jamia University was our clue to Shah Manzoor Alam while Narinder Kaur gave us lead to Arunachalam; Prithish Nag, Surveyor General, Survey of India helped track C.R. Pathak and Satyesh Chakraborty. Harjit Singh, of Jawaharlal Nehru University, Centre for Regional Development, made the photographs of Moonis available from the department archives. Deepankar, student at the department of geography, Delhi made a special trip to Guwahati to secure a photograph of H.P Das. Despite a pile of work as Dean, Jawahar Lal Nehru Univerisity, M.H. Qureshi at the Centre of Regional Development, spent time to shed light on Moonis Raza . It is true that a healthy web of interrelationships keeps a system functioning and alive. We are grateful to all who became a part of the intricate design of this book. The blue print of the book meant that many more were enrolled.

B.Thakur, the Secretary General of the Association provided unlimited cooperation and access to records and files on many an aspect. Despite the fact that he was amidst his career shift from professor of geography, at the Delhi School Economics to vice-chancellor of Mithila University, his support has been continuous . Gathering the souveniers and abstracts of the Congress was no small a feat . We remain in gratitude to all those who sent in their personal copies specially Sri Kumar Chattopadhaya at Thiruvanthapuram, N.C.Vijayaraj at Dharwad, Surya Kant at Chandigarh and S. Rani Senthamarai at Chennai.

One was keen to expand the horizons of this book to associations other than the National Association, Mumtaz Khan at the University of Jamia was kind enough to provide details on the Rajasthan Geographical Association, V.K. Srivastava at the Gorakhpur on the Association of Marketing Geographers, Anargha Wakhare at Pune on Institute of Indian Geographers, Sachidanand Sinha at Jawahar Lal Nehru University , shared memories about the Saturday Club. The cooperation of all is highly appreciated. While collating information of the departments of geography, Ali Mohamad Chairmen at department of geography, Aligarh, and V.N.P. Sinha deserve a special thanks . Their couriers reached well intact .

The search for details or confirmation about many a question on Indian Geography took one to the learned in close proximity. From the department of geography, Chandigarh, A.B.Mukherjee was often consulted. Swarnjit Mehta, Surya Kant, K.D. Sharma, Karanjyot, Krishna Mohan and Smita at the department of geography, Panjab University, were all willing to put down their pens, cursors or mouse when variety of help was sought in their busy space. Noor Mohommad, chairmen, department of geography, Delhi School of Economis provided an undisturbed environ of work, his support is acknowledged.

While presidents, professors, chairpersons, secretaries of various associations were the sources of information, tabulating , mapping and proof reading were back breaking chores where students and other staff pooled in to provide valuable assistance. Neat and unrelenting to achieve a zero error perfection was Mohan Singh the cartographer at the department of geography, Chandigarh. Though the maps went through several rounds of alterations Singh's brow never furrowed. The twenty figures in this book carry the countenance worthy of a smile. Rakesh keyed in corrections and stayed late when need arose. Ensuring that material shuttled between Chandigarh and Delhi with all efficiency Manjit Singh Behl made many a late hour visits to the general post office. Chowkidars served tea and kept vigilant guard when one worked late in the department . In all care, Kehar Singh rode us in innumerable trips to save time and energy. All help is deeply acknowledged.

Students at both the department of geography, Chandigarh, and Delhi School of Economics were a veritable pool of joy and gracious help. At Chandigarh, Narinder, Bhawna, Ritu, Navita, Ekta, Gagandeep, and Brar all did a round of proof reading. Meeta, Neeti, Deepankar, Debanjali, Roshani, Azka, Shabana and Neha, at the Delhi School of Economics had this uncanny urge to offer help at the right time. They pitched a lot of support. Ripudaman and Ranbir Singh Kang, students at Chandigarh put in long hours to check and recheck data for which they deserve a special word of thanks. Perhaps most heart rendering was the quantum quality of help provided by Deeptima Massey, a research student at the department of geography, Delhi School of Economics. She toiled through work and learned to shoulder decisions and experiment with ideas. Vishal, at Lincoln University, designed the cover with great care. We bless our students - as we do believe that in our lives as teachers students are our true blessing.

In the penultimate stage the editorial team at the Concept Publishing Company were an eager and much needed support. Concept gave the National Association of Geographers, India a block royalty of Rs 25,000 with a promise of a fifty per cent discount on sale of books to this Association. Though one feels they could have been a bit more generous yet their offer is gratefully acknowledged.

Lost in work, when the midnight lamp burns, the telephone and door bell remains unattended, nourishing food reaches the table of work one knows that the snug aura of a family has done a lot to make this work possible. Here I would like to depart from the joint acknowledgements to thank Kanti mam, Gopal Krishan's wife who extended generous hospitality on all my three visits to Chandigarh. My parents, family in London and friends endured 6 months of my virtual absentia – without giving me up !! That's what love is about and made possible this *Voice of Concern*.

I would like to add that the scholarly responsibility of the book and any snags are mine alone .

Delhi School of Economics,
University of Delhi, Delhi.
28th December, 2001

Anu Kapur
Lecturer
Department of Geography

Voice of Concern

Located on the outskirts of the older part of Delhi, Ritz theatre is no longer an attractive cultural hearth for the people of the city. Built in 1941, it is tarnished and worn down today. Modern plazas, which have mushroomed in the newer realms of the capital of India, have gained popularity and taken precedence. Yet, for all who want to register an association in Delhi, Ritz remains an important landmark. A narrow lane on its left, which one could easily miss, leads to the office of the Directorate of Industries. Its colonial - barrack structure has a hall, where under the Societies Registration Act 1860, an association acquires legal recognition. Not just the societies for education, but charitable to religious, political to social, sports to art, museums to libraries, are among a host of others consigned the official seal in this court.

The National Association of Geographers, India received this stamp on 11th April, 1978. Popular by the acronym NAGI, it was conceived as a society of no small a dream. NAGI was to be an exclusive and professional association of the community of geographers. All its 17 founder members were geographers, the majority held ranks of professors and most chaired the leading departments of geography in India. Representing a rich diversity of themes which typifies the discipline of geography, the specialization of the founder members ranged from population to agriculture, social to environment, quantitative to cartography, economic to urban and regional planning.

Boldly announcing its intention to be National, is the design of its logo (Fig. 1). The deftly colored map of India on the Delhi-centred azimuthal projection of the world carries the message of national on the emblem. Including National and India in its five word title confirms that it was not a local, state or regional venture. That it meant to span the breadth and length of country can be gauged from the official address of its group of founder members. Drawing upon a large circle from different corners of India, the team drew its participants from Udaipur in the west to Gauhati in the east, and Delhi in the north to Chennai in the south. In the northern plains it swept members from Aligarh, Kurukshetra, Chandigarh, Banaras, Calcutta and Kharagpur into its embrace, while Sagar and Hyderabad pitched in from central and south India respectively.

It is not a meritorious achievement to enlist an association in India. On the rolls of the registration ledger of Delhi, today there are about 40,000 associations. All that it requires is a minimum of seven members, a nominal fee of Rs 3,500, a ration card or any other proof of identity and the address of the place from where the association will steer along its objectives. The office of NAGI at the time of its registration was the Indian Council of Social Science Research. Prior to its relocation and the sprawling campus on Delhi's southern Aravali Ridge, the Indian Council of Social Science Research was lodged in the Indian Institute of Public Administration, a research limb of the echelons of administration, located on the Ring Road which circles the city. Acquiring a niche within the prime institution of scholarship in India bolstered the image of this young geographical Association, and protected its survival.

Scorching heat hits Delhi in April, the month of the birth of NAGI. In May and June the mercury flares to an intolerable ledge of 42 degrees centigrade, the burst of the monsoon soaks the city in torrential showers, a short respite does follow, but by November the cold heralds its arrival, and temperatures in Delhi plummet to less than 5 degrees centigrade in January and February. The climate of the city is an omen that only adaptive and sturdy species can endure survival. In the year 2000, NAGI has crossed 22 years of existence in tough environments. Flaring tempers, clashing egos, moderating advice, chilling comments, and thawing actions – all have spent their force on this Association. From 1978 to 2000, despite the close to a quarter century of formidable times, NAGI has survived. Poised for the new century, its trials and tribulations demand listening with concern. After all it took years to form NAGI. Why did NAGI come into existence in 1978 is not the question, but the more pertinent inquiry is – why did NAGI not make a debut before the end of the 1970s? A search for the answer pulls one squarely to the genesis and characteristics of Indian Geography. A professional association is after all yoked to its discipline. It draws its members, objectives, characteristics, and sustenance from its very own community.

No Geographers, *No Geographical Association,* pre 19th Century

Who was the first geographer in India? When was geography studied in India? Was geography studied when there were no geographers? Ambiguity obstructs the beginning of geographical studies in India. Some rush to claim that the first undergraduate department was started in Lahore, now in Pakistan in 1920. Others say that in divided India, the first department of geography was inaugurated in the university of Aligarh in 1924. Many would question why a 'department' is given a special status to decide the inception of a subject – after all the existence of the discipline in a school or an under-graduate college is of equal importance if not more. This, however, is not the bone of contention, for the difference between the dates of such an origin of geography in a department or a college or a school would at most be a couple of years – all three would aggregate around the early 20th century. The more important fact is to realize that geography in India was pursued without this institutional presence and also without the exclusive tag of a specialist called a geographer.

If we rightly define geography as the science, which describes the earth and its life, it would be ludicrous to suggest that no one studied geography before the 1920s. A vast corpus of traditional Indian texts did embrace its study. Reference to place names, descriptions of rivers and mountains, and elaborate treatment of the relationship between the physical and human elements are penned in the Vedas, Puranas, epics, and also recited in the folk lores. The precise calculation of the circumference of the earth and the treatise of Surya Sidhartha by the genius Aryabhat are testimony to the advanced state of geography and astronomy in the country. As an aid in governance each historical rule in India compiled a document of information, which also contained geographical details. The Arthashastra, the compendium by Kautaliya, contains a range of themes including valuable geographical and statistical account of India in the Maurya period (321-181 BC). The encyclopedic Vishnudharmottara Upapurana of the Gupta period (300 - 350 AD) contains subjects as far ranging as politics to poetry, astronomy to anatomy, lexicography to medicine. The locational attributes of people and places, scenery and seasons are elaborated in six of its chapters. Drawings, paintings, and carvings embodying the earliest attempts of making maps can also be assembled from various parts of India.

The Hindu ashrams, Jain and Buddhist viharas, all forerunners of modern universities, were vibrant seats of learning. Important no doubt, these traditional centers of learning imparted education only to a comparatively small group of India's population – mainly the intellectual and social elite, the brahmins and the bhikshus. The purpose of education was to inculcate a set of values of an essential religious character and prepare its students for the service of temples and monasteries and as counselors to the State. In these roles the study of geography helped chart pilgrim routes, plan movements of trade and transport, identify site and situations of new towns, and design political strategies to usurp territories for expanding the domains of the kingdoms. In fact, it was in its assistance in the fulfillment of aspirations of political control and trade that geography metamorphosed into a valuable subject of study.

India's contact with the Arab world around the 8th century systematized the study of her geography. The waters on the east of India are called the Arabian Sea perhaps because Arabs came as traders, their compulsion to plan navigation routes and identify the market nodes forced a geographical inquiry. While commerce was an attraction for many, the fantasy for adventure and travel enchanted some to pen geographical descriptions. Albureni's India of 11th century is one popular account. Knowledge as an entity of totality was still the dominant view. Albureni's account of the religion, philosophy, literature, customs, astrology and the geography of India is a proof to this methodology. Lucid geographical narratives in the Tuzuk-i-Jehangiri, Ain-i-Akbari, Dastur- ul-aml exemplify that the Mughal court too was busy in the observation and collection of geographical details. Forts, gardens, palaces, new townships all display a heightened application of geographical knowledge. Architectural monuments, including the famous Taj Mahal, built by the Mughal emperors would lose their scientific and magical appeal without the appreciation of choice of setting, aesthetics of landscapes, merit of different rocks and the play of water and vegetation. Woven deftly into the works of scholars, a storehouse of geographical information and its application prevailed in the pre-19th century in India. Geography as a separate branch of study did not exist and there was no community of geographers. But by academic definition, neither were their historians, anthropologists, sociologists or economists. The intellectual and organizational fragmentation of the domain of knowledge gained foothold in Europe only by the early 19th century.

Geography was accepted as a science of its own rather than as minions of philosophy only when it proved its exclusive and direct worth. As a discipline of its own might and right, geography in Europe attracted popularity, not in the quiet chambers of the university but among the buzz of the adventurous explorer, the pathfinder and traveler and the trading houses and later the rulers. Geography became a profitable subject as it unbolted doors for discovery, trade and imperialistic gains. The memoirs and merchandise from the newly discovered lands whet the interests of the social and ruling elite. As these discussions in drawing rooms and clubs wove together larger number of members, geographical associations mushroomed in the western world.

A World of Geographical Associations, *None in India*, 19th Century

The inception of the first formal association - Geographical Society of Paris in 1821 cajoled many countries to follow suit. The rate of response was high; whereas in 1865 there were only 16 geographical societies in the world with 5500 members, in 1881 there were 60 societies, with 30 branches and a total membership of 30,000. Such was the boom that by 1930 Europe alone had 92 societies and over the world there were 137, signifying an average annual addition of over one association during 1821 – 1930 (Table 1.)

Table 1 : Prominent Geographical Societies of the 19th Century

Name	Year of establishment
Geographical Society of Paris, France	1821
Royal Asiatic Society, Calcutta, British India	1823
Berlin Geographical Society, Germany	1828
Royal Geographical Society, London, Britain	1831
Bombay Geographical Society, Bombay	*1832*
Mexico Geographical Society, Mexico	1833
Geographical and Statistical Society, Mexico	1833
Frankfurt am Main, Germany	1836
Brazil Geographical Society, Brazil	1838
Institute Historicoe Geografico do Brazil, Brazil	1838
Imperial Russian Geographical Society, Russia	1845
American Geographical Society, U.S.A.	1851
National Geographic Society, Washington, U.S.A.	1888
Geographical Society of Finland, Finland	1888

Based on: Wright K John., 1960, and Mckay D.U. 1943.

While seemingly geographical, these earlier societies could well be addressed as 'geopolitical associations'. " The colonial agitation was the work of a rapidly growing pressure group, the French geographical Societies . . . . national honour , scientific interests , and commercial prosperity were combined by the Geographical Society to justify its program . . . . of colonial aspirations" (Mckay, D.U. 1943). Sponsored by shrewd nobility in collusion with trading houses, the banner of these geographical societies helped enthuse a spirit of territorial nationalism which allowed small nations of Europe to cut the large continent of Africa like slices of chocolate and spread their tentacles across the globe. Take Britain, a nation of 94,000 square miles, it grabbed 13.7 million square miles in its colonial ambit. Excluding the Antartica, it wielded power over 26 per cent of the total land area as well as population of the world.

Dated 1832, Bombay Geographical Society appears in the list of early associations. On a comparative yardstick it has an early existence, considering that the Paris Geographical Society is only 11 years older and the Royal Geographical Society, London is barely a year older. But in no way is this an association of geographers of India. Bombay Geographical Society is not indigenous either by birth or by its focus of interest. To comprehend its non - Indian character one needs to trace how the Europeans, and specially the British, came to the country.

To the Europeans the know-how about the oceanic route to India forged ahead with ardent fervor since Vasco da Gama discovered its shores in 1498. A chronological study of historical maps makes this evident. Drawn on parchment by an anonymous Portuguese traveler, the Cantino Planisphere, dated 1502, is the oldest extant European map which shows an approximation of India's true shape. An improved version of this map was printed in the Ptolemic Atlas in 1513. Sponsored by the Spanish Emperor in 1519, the research by Jorge and Pedro Reinel had given a reasonably correct view of the configuration of the northern shores of the Indian Ocean. Secretly guarded, it is the skill of drawing maps that gave Portuguese a virtual monopoly of trade in India. The Dutch too gained ground. The engraved map of a greater portion of India in Jan Huygen van Linshoten's Discourse of Voyages unto ye Easte and West Indies, 1598 testifies the growing competence and accuracy in cartography. Plotting direction and distance, these maps glued the eyes and fleet of European sailors towards India. One among the many ships was Captain Lancaster's. It was unique not because it was the first vessel to set sail by the East India Company in 1601, but it ushered a period of critical transformation in India and its geographical data base.

The East India Company had received from Queen Elizabeth the Charter giving it monopoly for trade in the East. Though it had no initial dream of empire building, ample opportunities in India were a lusty temptation. The disintegrating political circumstances in India gave them easy access. Short of a hundred years the Company ascended in status from a trading outpost to one of political control. It altered not just the destiny of India but also engraved a deep impress on the character and growth of geographical information about India. It is the naval officers of the East India Company who formed the Bombay Geographical Society .Why Bombay? This city was the leading port for commerce, and it was on the dockyards of Bombay that the trading Company had dropped its anchors. Confirming the umbilical connection of the Bombay Geographical Society with the country back home is the fact that for five years, 1832 to 1837, the Royal Geographical Society, London patronized it as its own branch. Thereafter, it merged with the another breed of British ancestry, the Royal Asiatic Society, which was founded in 1823 by a Sanskrit scholar, Henry Thomas Colebrooke. Calcutta was then the first imperial capital and the Asiatic Society found a permanent lodge in the city. The stock of manuscripts, maps, and sea charts in the Oriental and India Office of the British Museum Library certify the nature and quality of geographical work these societies had accomplished in India. Though geographical works peaked under British tutelage in the 19th to early 20th century, there still was no association of geographers by Indians. Why this paradox? For an answer one needs to revert attention to the emergence of geography and the nature of geographical work which was being pursued in India.

Geographical Works, *No Geographical Association*, 19th to Early 20th Century

The British were the official couriers of the seeds of a segregated and defined discipline of geography in India. For over a hundred years the British used the tools of this science to measure, collect, organize and document the geographical facts of India. But the study of geography in India did not find a habitat of teaching and research till the early 20th century. The success of the geographical survey on the coasts of Chittagong and Cameroon in 1761 in furtherance of their imperialistic aims following the Battle of Plassey in 1757 led the British to sanction an office of the Surveyor General in India. Seeking precision in locating and measuring the land, the surveyors imported from Britain the plane table in 1793, prismatic compass in 1815, and the theodolite in 1819. Clad in khakhi bermudas, gum boots, sporting barrette caps, and carrying the tripods, these surveyors penetrated remote corners to map India. James Rennell, the first Surveyor General, produced the first Map of Hindoostan on a scale of 1:3 million in 1788. Following this success, the Great Trigonometrical Survey resulted in geodetic investigations of marked importance. By producing an interrelated triangulation series and using a theodolite, the heights of 79 major Himalayan peaks were determined. The highest among them towering to 8848 meters, also the highest on the earth, was named Mount Everest in honor of the former Surveyor General of India. Requiring mathematical calculations and competence in observation of physiographic features and structure, it was the geologist and not the geographer which was more in demand. Geologists also helped discover the mineral resources especially the coal beds so vital as fuel for the British laid railways. As a consequence and support to this lead role, the Geological Survey of India was set up in 1851 with Calcutta as its headquarters. While geologists had greater recognition, they played an important role to popularize geography in the coming decades. The strong focus in physical geography, the department of which Calcutta, was to be proud of later, is rooted in its allegiance with the geologists. In fact, the Calcutta Geographical Society, owes its birth in 1933 to geologists who constituted a sizable group among its founder members.

Pivoted by political motives, the orders of the British directors to the Surveyor General was not just the compilation and maintenance of maps but their preservation in a high order of secrecy. There was a strict rule that copies of the maps were not to be passed on to local officers, military, or civil without the sanction of proper authority. Inheriting this need for secrecy till date, the Survey of India stores a large group of maps which are classified as restricted. Mapped with zeal by the end of 1830s, one could distinguish between topographical, civil, and cadastral land surveys. The geographer with the East

India Company, John Walker, shouldered the task of compiling the Atlas of India. Drawn on a scale where every four miles on the ground is represented by one inch on the map, the vast territory of India meant that such details were going to take a fair share of time. And it did. Begun in 1882, the Great Atlas of India was completed only by early 20th century.

Surveys and maps were not the only tools for storing geographical information but describing and compiling statistics were additional supports. A plethora of travel accounts published in the 19th and 20th century verify the avid interest with which the Europeans wrote their observations about the land and the people of India. Though rich as a repository of geographical details, travelogues consume enormous time when read. As a replacement, the gazetteer was designed to satisfy the utilitarian value for administration. The gazetteer, a geographical dictionary in which names and descriptions of places are given in alphabetical order, was an innovation of Johann G.H. Hassel a German geographer in 1817. Though tightly structured, and dry in narrative, its role as a document assisting in governance was seen as most urgent. "Nothing, nothing is more costly to the Government than ignorance" is what W.H. Hunter wrote to the Viceroy of India in 1869. Motivated by this urge, Hunter authored the nine volume set of the Imperial Gazetteer of India in 1881; this was expanded to 26 volumes in 1907. A retinue of provincial and district gazetteers followed soon. On the eve of their departure the British left a legacy of 500 gazetteers on India.

Monumental and multiple was the role of the British in collecting, organizing and classifying information of the geography on India. A string of institutes established by them bear testimony to their encyclopedic efforts and scientific temperament (Table 2).

Table 2 : Institutes Established by the British for Geographical Information

Institutes established	**Place**	**Year**	**Information**
Survey of India	Dehra Dun	1767	Maps
Royal Botanic Garden	Calcutta	1787	Vegetation
Geomagnetic Observatory	Bombay	1840	Tectonics
Geological Survey of India	Calcutta	1851	Rocks
Census of India	Calcutta	1861	Population
Archaeological Survey of India	Calcutta	1861	Past cultures
Indian Meteorological Department	Pune	1875	Climate
Forest Research Institute	Dehra Dun	1906	Flora

Based on World of Learning, 2001.

Geographical studies acquired applied value in the institutes set up by the British in the early 19th century, but the concern for the discipline of geography did not crystallize till the 20th century. Whereas the Survey of India was set up in 1767, the first known department of geography in India was established only in 1924. A gap of over 150 years. The British were not naïve about the value of departments of geography, afterall some countries in Europe like Germany had inaugurated one as early as in 1817, while Britain, their home land, had a department at Oxford in 1887 and Cambridge in 1888. Even when the British set up a university in Calcutta, Bombay and Madras in 1857 followed by one at Lahore in 1882 and Allahabad in 1877 – a department of geography did not figure on their roster for nearly 75 years. Though vast in volume and rich in content, the concern of the British for geographical details seasoned neither teaching nor research. Why did geography make late entrance despite its applied value, despite the presence of the subject in European universities, and despite the establishment of universities in India? Perhaps some answers are there in the requirements for which the colonists established universities in India.

Universities but *No Department of Geography,* early 20th Century

The expansion of the government machinery created a demand for the educated clerks as the colonists needed canon officers to man their works to support the authority and to shoulder orders in the increasingly sophisticated pattern of government administration. The pressing need came to limelight when Lord Macualay in 1835 recommended the use of English as the medium of instruction and promotion of western education among the 'natives'. In this philosophy were conceived the universities of the British Raj in 1857. These established universities were only affiliating and examining bodies, they carried out neither teaching nor research. This peculiarity was noted by the Shimla Education Conference of 1901: " How different is India? Here university has no corporate existence in the same sense of the term, it is not a collection of buildings, it is scarcely even a site, and it is a body that controls courses of study and sets examination papers to the pupil of affiliated colleges. They are not part of it. They are frequently not in the same city, sometimes not even in the same province". (Tickoo, C. 1980. Content with their role as examining bodies, the universities had to wait for good 70 years for the Indian Universities Act of 1904 to embark upon post-graduate teaching and research in both the Humanities and the Science. Colleges multiplied from 25 in 1885, to 65 in 1882, and 191 in 1901. Geography had no place on any campus.

Who ploughed to sow its place? Difficult to pinpoint, yet it is probable that the germination came from the Indian Science Congress. " Scientific research in India might be stimulated if an annual meeting of research workers could be arranged". Armed with this intention, two British chemists inaugurated the Indian Science Congress Association in 1914 under the umbrella of the Asiatic Society, Calcutta. Throwing open invitation, its first meet drew 105 scientists from 6 different fields of science, among these was geology but not geography. The Congress however was a model of the collective role an association can perform for the pursuit of academics. To promote the importance of the subject five geographical associations became active in different parts of India :

Curzon Geographical Society, Aligarh 1925
Madras Geographical Association, Madras 1926
Patna College Geographical Society, Patna 1929
Calcutta Geographical Society, Calcutta 1933
Bombay Geographical Association, Bombay 1935

Of the five only the Bombay Geographical Association was the joint effort of school teachers of geography. The other four were creations of an incipient number among the scholars who foresaw both the academic and applied role in the study of this discipline. These four were the brain child of the British. E. W. Dann, founded the society in Aligarh, Gilbert W.Slater energised the one in Madras, H.Lambert, was the first president of the Patna Society while it was a team of geologists including A.M.Heron, C.S.Fox, W. D. West along with D.N.Wadia who promoted the Calcutta based association. All the four societies were the efforts of non-geographers. E.W. Dann was a social scientist, H.Lambert was an educationist and principal of a college, Gilbert W.Slater was an economist, while geologists dominated the Calcutta based society. Advocating the cause for geography within the sphere of education, all the societies played a key role in their own region of influence. Using different channels, all furrowed a site for the discipline.

Madras Geographical Association held Summer Schools and undertook field excursions to stimulate interest in the discipline, the Curzon Society gave lead to the first exclusive journal called Geographer, while it was the resolution of the Council of Calcutta Geographical Society which pressed for a section of geology and geography in the Indian Science Congress from 1934-35 onwards. As a sequel, when the Indian Science Congress celebrated its silver jubilee in 1938, H.J. Fluere, C.B. Fawcett, L.D. Stamp, A.G. Ogilive and W.T. Gordon, the leading British geographers, were among the invitees.

The mid -1920s is a watershed in the institutionalization of the discipline of geography in India. It was in this time that India's first geographical associations were formed and under-graduate classes were first started in colleges affiliated to Lahore in 1920, Aligarh in 1924 and Patna in 1927. The maiden seeds for the discipline had been planted. To gain root in a sterile landscape, the pioneers face enormous hardships. The academic succession in geography evolved slowly :

Year 1925 : Number of Universities in India 20. Geography in none.
1947 : Number of Universities in India 37. Geography in 17.
Year 1925 : Number of Geographical Societies in India 1.
1947 : Number of Geographical Societies in India 6.
Year 1925 : Number of Geographical Journals in India 0.
1947 : Number of Geographical Journals in India 6.

A nebulous existence, practiced remotely and distanced from each other, was the state of the discipline of geography when the British left the soil of India in 1947. By mid- 1940s " the total strength of students pursuing studies in degree classes is approximately 1000, with a total teaching staff of 74". (Stamp, 1946). The small and isolated numbers could not adhere to form a leading geographical association. Moreover India was under the spell of colonial rule – without a nation where was the chance of creating a National Association.

A Nation, Good Time for Geographers, but *No National Association*: 1947-1978

National Association of Geographers, India, was registered as a society in 1978; India gained independence in 1947. It took over 30 years before a national level association of geographers came into existence. Good times rarely bond communities. From 1950s to the end of 1970s geographers in India saw good times; this in no way implies that geography too saw good times. Never in history did opportunities open so many doors to geographers as during these decades.The multiplication of departments, swelling number of doctorates, sojourns to pursue doctorates under renowned mastereos in leading universities of Britain and the United States of America, increasing geographical journals, research projects, and invitation from different wings of the government departments in India – this and much more flooded the space of geographers. Qualifying the good in these times is the data in Table 3.

The departments of geography grew in number from 17 in 1950s to 48 in the 1970. The addition of nearly two departments per year had no precedence in all decades past or future. The sequence for adopting the different levels of teaching varied. Some universities like Delhi, Magadh, and Karnatak started under-graduate teaching before post-graduation, while in others like Sagar and North Bengal post-graduation preceded under-graduation. In some universities like Agra and Amritsar post-graduate classes are conducted in colleges .Some like Madras, started intermediate classes in 1926, ran a one-year diploma course from 1932 and offered a post-graduation in 1948. The advantage of being able to straddle the physical and human sciences, the pure and the applied realms gave geography the flexibility to fasten in different types of institutions.

Table 3 : Evolution of Indian Geography till 1980

Feature	Numbers			
	Upto 1950	1951-60	1961-70	1971-80
Departments of geography	17*		48*	
Geographical journals (added in each decade)	5	12	19	19
Doctorates from India (in each decade)	8	29	151	395**
Doctorates from Britain* (in each decade)	6^	10^	5^	
Doctorates from United States of America ^	1^	6^	4^	
Lecturers			209*	
Readers / Professors			34*	

*Based on : *Indian Council of Social Science Research, 1973*
***Association of Indian Universities (1940-2000).*
^National Committee for Geography, Calcutta, 1968. The number of doctorates from Britian and USA upto 1968 may not be all encompassing but could be treated as indicative.
Despite best efforts, data about Indian Geography could still be carrying a lacuna. This applies equally to all such tables. My apologies.

Geography pushed its case at all possible locales in centers of Earth Sciences, Social Sciences, Environmental Sciences to Schools of Economics (Table 4). Tradition recognizes that area is a staple concern of geographers. Thus, when departments of area studies like the Asian Studies at the University of Aligarh, African Studies at University of Delhi, and Soviet Studies at University of Bombay were started, geographers had a relative edge.

Table 4 : Anchor of Department of Geography in Different Types of Institution

Institution	Place
Arts and Commerce College	Jalgaon, Maharashtra
Centre for Rural Studies	Vishwa Bharati, West Bengal
College of Science and Technology	University of Calcutta, West Bengal
Delhi School of Economics	University of Delhi, Delhi
Department of Earth Sciences	Imphal, Manipur
Faculty of Science	Sambalpur, Orissa
School of Biological and Earth Sciences	Tirupati, Andhra Pradesh
School of Human and Environmental Sciences	North-East Hill University, Meghalaya

Fascination for geography was widespread and people from the neighboring sciences specially geology and commerce were drawn to its study. Carrying a hybrid interest, many among these became leading scholars in the discipline (Table 5).

These were buoyant times on many other fronts. The bazaar of geography brimmed with a variety of journals. Whereas one had to choose from five journals in 1950, by the end of 1970s there was an offer from as many as 55 periodicals. Since most editorial boards of journals had a limited or at the most an in-house system of referees, there was comparative ease in adding to ones list of publications. Almost all journals were hatched and maintained by the individual departments of geography – limited circulation meant that most remained buffered even from reviews by critics (Table 6). Geographers could add glory to their curriculum vitae in an unlimited manner.

Table 5 : Attraction for Geography Among Scholars of Other Disciplines, Pre-1980s

Name	Discipline	Department
Gupta, D.	Commerce	Calcutta
Dubey, R.N.	Commerce	Allahabad
Prakasa Rao, V.L.S	Commerce	Delhi
Chatterjee, S.P.	Geology	Calcutta
Chibber, H.L.	Geology	Banaras
Vaidyanadhan, R.	Geology	Waltair
Bagchi, K.	Geology	Calcutta
Deshpande, C.D	History /Education	Bombay
Ali, S.M.	Mathematics	Sagar

This is an exemplary and in no way an exhaustive list .

A season of schools were also initiated in the early 1960s. The first Summer School of Geography was held in Simla in 1962, followed by an Autumn School at Aligarh in 1966, and a Summer School of Applied Geography at Banaras in 1966. These became focus of discussion and training to which geographers flocked from different parts of the country.

In varying flavor and frequency came the scope of personal exchange of views and news from the outside world to geographers in India. The first International Seminar on geography, held at Aligarh in 1956, attracted as many as 66 foreign and 103 Indian delegates. The International Geographic Union held its first meet in India in 1968. Touring across various departments, it organized 40 symposia and as many as 32 field study meetings. Never has the International Geographic Union set foot on Indian ground thereafter. The Indo-British Geography Seminar was held twice: once in 1972, followed by a quick repeat in 1979. The third one did not take place for the next 15 years. The first Indo-French Geography Seminar was also held in 1978, New Delhi. Till date it has seen no repeat. They were indeed favorable years.

Table 6 : A Bazaar Brimming with Geographical Journals* by 1980s

Year	Name	Place	Year	Name	Place
1926	Indian Geographical Journal	Madras	1926	Geographer	Aligarh
1936	Geographical Review of India	Calcutta	1953	Bombay Geographical Magazine	Bombay
1955	National Geographical Journal of India	Varanasi	1955	Geographical Outlook	Ranchi
1956	Indian Geographer	New Delhi	1956	Oriental Geographer	Gorakhpur
1956	University Geographical Journal	Nagpur	1958	National Geographer	Allahabad
1959	Journal of Geography	Jabalpur	1960	Aligarh Geographical Journal	Aligarh
1961	Ajmer Geographer	Ajmer	1962	Geographical Series	Baroda
1962	Deccan Geographer	Secunderabad	1964	Geographical Series	Allahabad
1965	Geography Teacher	Annamalai-puram	1965	Geographical Thought	Gorakhpur
1965	Geographical Observer	Meerut	1965	Uttar Bharat Bhoogol Patrika	Gorakhpur
1966	Indian Journal of Geography	Jodhpur	1966	North East Geographer	Gauhati
1967	Transactions	Bhubaneshwar	1967	Bhudarsan	Udaipur
1967	Indian Journal of Regional Science	Kharagpur	1968	Geographical Knowledge	Kanpur
1968	Studies in Geography	Jaipur	1968	Journal of North East India	Guwahati
1970	Geographical Viewpoint	Agra	1971	Analytical Geographer	Delhi
1971	Bhoogyan Darpan	Banaras	1973	Indian Geography	Raipur
1973	Indian Geographical Series	Patna	1975	Avadh Geographers	Lucknow
1975	Research Bulletin	Bhuba-neshwar	1977	Yuva Bhoogol	Gorakhpur Vidya Patrika
1977	Geographical Research	Saharanpur	1977	Geographical Bulletin of India	Patna
1979	Population Geography	Chandigarh	1979	Transactions, Institute of Indian Geographers	Pune
1980	Annals of the Association of Rajasthan Geographers	Bhilwara	1980	Hill Geographer	Shillong

**This is a representative and in no way an exhaustive list.*
The first issue of NAGI Annals was published in 1981.

A flood of students rushed to enroll in graduate, post-graduate, and research courses as colleges and departments opened doors to teach geography. Ushering widespread opportunities for placements, the demand for faculty in colleges and university departments outnumbered the availability of trained personnel. Students were quickly absorbed into teaching some by their own alma-mater. Take Chandigarh, its entire faculty that was inducted in 1970s and 1980s had completed their education from the same department and most joined without even a doctorate. Of a total of 18 lecturers appointed in Patna between 1960 to 1980 all did their graduation, post-graduation, and doctorates from the same university. Most had the chance to join the departments when they were young. The average age of lecturers who joined the department at Patna between 1960 to 1970 was 22 years, at Chandigarh they were between 22 to 25 years. Even in the colleges of the University of Delhi most appointment of lecturers in the pre-1980s fell below 24 years in age. Birthdays and appointments are not easy to gather yet a sample from three universities confirms that the comfort of being absorbed , and that too at a young age, was a surety. Such is not the fate of even the most brilliant doctorates of today.

In these years, the quest for a doctorate acquired rapid popularity. Whereas India had only 8 doctorates upto 1950s by 1980 the number shot up to 606, the major percentage were conferred in 1960 to 1980.Convinced that the indepth grasp of the subject requires supervision of eminent geographers in leading universities of the West, many flocked to pursue a doctorate abroad. Britain held special appeal. Tracking a list in the Directory of Indian Geographers (1968) revealed that 40 geographers carried a foreign doctorate. Of these 68 per cent chose Britain as a destination for higher studies. Filled with nostalgia and the urge to serve their newly independent country, majority returned home .The auspicious hour greeted most with the opportunity to start or atleast chair a department of geography (Table 7).

Some like the department of geography at the Delhi School of Economics from 1960 to 1970s had an entire faculty who had studied abroad. Aligarh had a lineage where the entire generation of chairmen preceding 1960 had acquired a degree outside India. Such a reception to foreign degrees would today be rare because the pre-1980s were indeed propitious years. With a clear edge over their counterparts in India, those who obtained their doctorate abroad became a leading and distinct group–the first elite in geography. Lesser competition and much acclaim allowed their selection at a young age to the ecclesiastical mark of attaining professorship.

The education policy in the universities of India was such that professors chaired departments continuously – unlike with crops in agriculture - there was no rotation. The longest serving chairmen in the history of departments of geography belong to the years preceding the mid - 1970s. Unchallenged, some governed for 15 to 25 years (Table 8).

Table 7 : Placement of Geographers in India with a Doctorate from a Foreign University, till 1968

Designation	Total	Per cent to total
Professor and Chairman	17	42
Reader and Chairman	5	13
Lecturer	5	13
Others*	13	32
Total	40	100

Based on : National Committee for Geography, Calcutta, 1968.
**Others include associate planners, project directors, map officers and college principals.*

Lengthy tenures meant that departments could acquire fame for specialization as courses of study were designed whose continuity was assured. It is under the extended umbrella of one-person rule that departments gained identity. Aligarh acquired popularity for agriculture, Chandigarh for population, Patna for economic geography, Banaras for urban land use, Sagar for applied geography and Delhi for urban and regional planning.

Table 8 : Long Tenure of Chairmen in Departments of Geography till 1980s

Department	Chairmen	Years
Patna	Dayal, P.	24
Aligarh	Shafi, M.	22
Chandigarh	Gosal, G.S.	20
Tirupati	Reddy, N.B.K.	15

Note: This sample is confined to some of the presidents of NAGI whose curriculum vitae carried this data.

Armed with foreign degrees, secure in their in-house estates, many chairmen ventured out to seek projects for their department. Government saw a promise in them and assigned research projects and grants. Difficult to piece together, yet the history of work by most departments does confirm that the University Grants Commission, among other agencies, actively sponsored numerous department level research up to the end of 1970s. The spirit of teamwork permeated the departments of geography and ingrained a culture of long hours of work. Stream lining projects was considered important not because it helped access funds, purchase equipment, and train and employ research scholars but importantly, departments derived a sense of prestige from them. Many projects like the Damodar Valley Diagnostic Survey, sanctioned by the Planning Commission in 1959, spanned across three departments: Patna, Calcutta and Kharagpur. Today projects to individual teachers are the rule - they do not and cannot include the entire faculty of a department !

Even in times of national adversity, fortune continued to smile on departments of geography. After Indo-China war of 1962, the Terrain Analysis Cell of the Ministry of Defence approached geography departments to undertake projects of terrain evaluation in areas of specific needs. The Terrain Evaluation study in Bikaner and Jaisalmer District (1967–1969) by the department of geography, University of Delhi, and Terrain Evaluation of Punjab Plains, Punjab Himalayas, and Shipki-tract, Rajasthan border, 1965 – 1968, by the department at Chandigarh exemplify efforts to fulfill defence needs of the country .

The departments of geography at Aligarh, Banaras and Osmania were able to attract the Special Assistance Program of the University Grants Commission in the early 1970s. Others like Patna and Punjab were granted the Center for Development Studies and Department Research Support Schemes respectively. Backed by additional finances, these sanctions allowed the departments to expand and experiment their activities of teaching and research.

Nurtured within the precincts of a university, the departments of geography in India operated much like little fiefdoms. Each with a stable ruler, funds to play, journal to publish, small though growing number of students and an expanding base for recruitment of new faculty. Majority of the leading departments started their own geographical association. By the mid 1970s geographers in India had about 40 associations. Members were drawn from a small hinterland restricted either geographically around the department or in the zone of influence of the chairperson. Membership was thus confined such that the posts of presidents and secretaries circulated within a limited territorial or intellectual domain.

The portals of the university were not the only avenues where geographers prospered. Additionally the departments of planning, specially urban and regional planning, the census departments, statistical institutes, and the like were all willing to consult and engage them. Carrying the visa of area and regional planning, land and land use surveys, spatial analysis of population, agriculture and industry, and equipped with skills of mapping and the region as a geographical unit for analysis, geographers gained entry into a number of leading government institutions. Geographers were offered participation in regional plans in both the Center and the State Planning Boards. South-East Resource Region, Dandakaranaya, Malkangiri, Goa Regional Plan, Western

Ghat Regional Plan, and the Cuttack-Bhubaneswar-Puri Regional Plan among a host of others drew geographers into their own fold. When the master plans for towns and cities were designed, the Town and Country Planning Organizations too had geographers on their panel. Similarly, though the Census of India came into existence in 1850s, it was only after the 1961 census that a map division, headed by a geographer, was set up in the Office of the Registrar General, India, New Delhi. At the state and union territory level also, geographers were consulted for preparation of census atlases. The Census Atlas of Punjab for example was made in close collaboration with the department of geography at Chandigarh. There is little doubt that a wide vista of opportunities were thrown open for geographers.

Despite the approximate of 50 departments, 40 journals, 40 associations and 606 doctorates, forays into government departments and sojourns to foreign lands, a whimper of discontent began to float that all was not well with Indian geography. Gathering momentum was the impression that despite the good times geographers in India had failed to deliver the desired 'goods' to either academics or national development. They were falling from grace .It was time of concern. A collective voice was needed to take charge. Before harnessing the various signals which confirm this thinking, one needs to capture what dawned this stupendous growth and demand – after all what had geographers in India done to deserve these good times?

Source of the Good Times 1960 – 1980

Much as one would want, it would be false to claim that the popularity of the discipline or that of the geographers had fuelled the multiplication of departments and invitation into the corridors of leading offices of the government. The fact of the matter is that the mood of the nation for a few decades after 1947, the year of independence, was charged with the desire to provide education to its citizens and deliver all kinds of socio-economic development. People's hunger for education invaded every court and the country spawned schools, colleges and universities. To service this need, among other efforts, a network of universities and institutes were created across the country. Nearly three universities were added to India's academic landscape each year from 1940 to 1980. One every four months. Specially progressive were the years between 1960 to 1970 when 45 universities were added . Geographers rode on this hurried tide of emergence of new universities. (Table 9). Departments of geography were one among the many other disciplines which found entry. There is no doubt that geographers would have had to do some leg work to insist for the value of a department but a sanction was a relatively easy chore.

Table 9 : Proliferation of Universities in India after Independence

Years	Number of new universities	Total universities
Before 1900	6	6
1900 – 1909	4	10
1910 – 1919	5	15
1920 – 1929	12	27
1930 – 1939	5	32
1940 – 1947	10	42
1948 – 1959	29	71
1960 – 1969	45	116
1970 – 1979	31	147
1980 – 1989	49	196
1990 – 1999	52	248

Based on Association of Indian Universities, 2001.

To come to grips with the dilemmas of delivering socio-economic development, the Government of India set up planning, research and policy institutions. Foremost was the Planning Commission which every 5 years spelt the direction of development for the country. The emphasis on regional development in the context of planning came almost from the beginning of the first five year plan, but it was the third plan, 1961-66, which devoted a chapter on balanced regional development, while the fourth spelt plans for hill areas, flood prone area, drought prone, industrially backward area and the like. Planning in India, initially was seen analogous to an extended exercise in budget making. But very soon thanks to the influence exercised by P.C.Mahalonobis and others, it became quite clear that no attempt at planning was going to succeed unless the spatial data base and its modalities were significantly enlarged. This created willingness to explore the role of geographical participation on regional respects of national planning. Mahalonobis invited O.H.K. Spate, the geographer at the University of Canberra and A.T.A. Learmonth, from University of Liverpool to spend a couple of months to report on the possibility of geographical contribution to national planning. Under the Technical Cooperation Program of the Colombo Plan, Learmonth put together a team of two economists, one statistician and four geographers to undertake a regional survey for planning purposes. It was efforts like these which served to redirect the attention of geographers in India to issues of problem solving by using the frame of regional development. This unlatched the flood gates for geographers in India to engage themselves in efforts of initiating urban and regional planning at various centers. A number of urban and regional planning organizations sprouted all over India between 1955 to 1975. Geographer-planners could cut a profession in their ambit. As nutrition to grasp the complexities and problems facing development, the Government of India launched several centers for social science and policy research. They too served as possible havens for geographical work. The blue print of planning and research institutions relied on a team of.social scientists and the scope for involvement by geographers was an inherent part of this design (Table 10).

Table 10 : Research and Scientific Institutions* Established in India

Years	Number	Illustrative institutions
Pre – 1940s	18	Indian Meteorological Dept., Indian Council of Agricultural Research, Census of India
1940 – 1949	5	Dept. of Architecture and Regional Planning, IIT Kharagpur
1950 – 1959	19	Planning Commission, Centre for Rural Studies, Indian Institute of Public Administration
1960 – 1969	15	Institute of Applied Manpower Research, Indian Council of Social Science Research
1970 – 1979	14	Institute of Development Studies, Institute of Social and Economic Change, National Institute of Urban Affairs
1980 – 1989	6	Institute of Himalayan Studies
1990 – 1999	1	National Institute of Wastelands and Rural Development
Total	110	

Compiled from numerous sources including World of Learning, 2001.

*Note: * Only those with any possibility of employing geographers have been considered. Many non-government institutions have mushroomed in the 1990's, but these have been excluded.*

Though swimming in the pool of opportunities, prolific growth of departments of geography in universities, urban and regional planning projects, social science institutes, yet geographers by the mid of 1970s were in troubled waters. Their discipline had an unsure identity and a low status. In the end of 1970s, within the realm of academics and in the eye of the public, their subject fetched a weak poll.

Low Status in Good Times

Indian geography was unable to chisel a sharp identity by the end of the 1970s. The call of cry came from many quarters. Established in 1969 as a body promoting social sciences, the Indian Council of Social Science Research accommodated geography in their revised list only after considerable debates. To glean the struggle which geography had to withstand, here is a record of decisions by the Council: The scope of social sciences covers the disciplines of Economics, Education, Management, Political Science, Psychology, Public

Administration, and Sociology. In addition to the aforementioned disciplines, the Council will also be 'concerned' with the social sciences aspects (not physical geography) of courses such as Anthropology, Demography, Geography, History, Law and Linguistics. In 1971 the Council broadened the definition to some extent and stated that grants-in-aid under the Research Grants Scheme will include Economic, Human, and Political Geography. It was only when the National Register of Social Scientists was to be drawn that the decision to include the discipline as a whole and not in part was made. It would for instance be neither practicable nor desirable to compile a National Register of Social Scientists for Economic, Human and Political Geography and not for Geography as a whole. While persuasion had granted geography a place, it failed to guarantee performance. From 1968 to 1980, the Council sponsored 1087 research projects, geographers could attract only 42. Under the program of developing the relatively less-developed fields, the Council had initiated several schemes like special promotion of publications and organizing workshops and seminars. Geography was identified as one such discipline in need. An inclusion in this (relatively less-developed) category further affirms the rank at which the discipline stood. Some could argue that such an assessment on the part of Indian Council of Social Science Research is a diluted test, yet it cannot be denied that it is an indicator of sorts.

The Indian Science Congress Association harbors and promotes the cause of physical sciences. Geographers could not make an impact even within this body. At Baroda, in 1942, the Congress abandoned its separate section on geography and amalgamated it with geology. What is woeful is that despite completing 38 years of joint existence in 1980, only 2 geographers could get the honour as its president, one in 1967 and the other in 1977. It took another 20 years for the third one to be elected to this august office.

It could be stated that the performances both at the Indian Council of Social Science Research and the Indian Science Congress Association are too small an arena to raise fingers on the discipline. After all research projects one knows are sometimes dependent on the members of the selection team, while elections to the post of a president often depend on the stronghold of number of members than their performance. Agreed, but does the lack of geographers in the selection panels and among the electorates not depict the state of affairs? Not the chicken and the egg story, but a viscous circle that needed to be broken! Geographers proved weak on this ground. Although boundary disputes tend to be unprofitable, and the study of geography can fit a number of moulds yet in the tripod division of knowledge into the physical, humanities, and social sciences, geographers in India were unable to create a lasting place for themselves in any domain.

Geographers proudly possess the region as their precious and somewhat genius baby, but losing ground in quarters of regional planning is also record of their plummeted status. In regional planning organizations, for instance, after an admission of one or at the most two geographers, neither did their team expand nor could the posts for coming generations be redeemed. Take the renowned Indian Institute of Technology; India has six such institutes. A masters program in regional planning was introduced in one at Indian Institute of Technology at Kharagpur in 1952. There were no takers in the other five centres. Despite 30 years of existence, uptill 1980, Planning Commission, the apex body that carved the need for regional planning, had recruited only two geographers on their officer's rank.

Nearly 400 Town and Country Planning Organizations were busy laying plans for different regions by the end of 1980. The question is not if their plans materialized or failed – the issue here is that only a handful of geographers were part of this group. According to a guestimate, a leading town planner in Delhi remarks, "In India geographer – planners are a modest 400 to 500." (Kapur, A 1998). This is the figure for 1996, but in 1980 the number may well have been half. A different kind of gauge for the low visibility can be made from the Directory of Who's Who of Geographers in India. A bold venture by a private publisher, it does not include all geographers, yet its 806 members could be taken as a fairly representative sample of the community. A check in it shows that only 14 per cent of the total geographers were in professions other than teaching. The bulk of 692 or 87 per cent were confined to the teaching profession. Published in 1982 it is a sort of summary of the stock of geographers for the pre-1980s.

There are other symptoms that confirm its weak score. Many disciplines within social science were able to set up institutes of national stature to further their cause. Economists had the Institutes of Economic Growth and Policy Research, while sociologists had their string of social work centers, besides a stronghold within the social science institutes themselves. Geographers could make little claim. The one and only National Atlas and Thematic Map Organization, established in 1956, that too by a geologist turned geographer, was also unable to add new branches to its headquarters at Calcutta. It confined itself to producing maps and atlases and did not envelop research in other geographical themes. The Institute of Development Studies, Mysore started in 1971 was another effort of geographers to work along with other social sciences. It too could not sustain. Attempts to salvage geography's faltering status and foster interdisciplinary blood were made when the Center for Regional Development was set up at Jawahar lal Nehru University in 1972. Its objectives were unique as it set forth a faculty where a core of geographers along with other social scientists would lecture and research on issues of social relevance in the paradigm of regional development. Piecemeal and an island within itself, the Center however, could not steer along the entire community of geographers. India could not even boast of a geographical museum or a national map library, let alone a geographical institute of national repute.

Gaining headway disciplines like geology started exclusive recruitment to train manpower under Geological Survey of India. In similar vein was the Indian Economic Service. These disciplines serviced a demand in society and could draw a national level test. Geographers failed on many fronts. Even amidst the best of times of the 1950s to mid-1970s, geographers were impotent to create centers which could endure or display their works.

Some could well argue that working in a team of social scientists, the language of geographers is difficult to understand. It could not avoid the use of technical terms, especially from physical geography. It could also be stated that sectoral rather than regional plans found convenient political popularity and geography was beyond the comprehension of the bureaucrat or one holding a public office, but even within the confines of the university, it was not a subject of repute. Comparative data is hard to come by, but here is an attempt. Theoretically, when the universities were established, they offered a world of equal opportunities for all disciplines. But in the 1970s with a faculty three times that of geographers, economics was being taught in 219 different centers of higher education. With only 88 centers to its credit the visibility of geographers was less than one third (Table 11).

Table 11 : Comparison of Geography with other Social Sciences - 1970

Institution and Faculty	Economics	Sociology	Geography
University departments	69	49	48
Affiliated colleges	150	34	40
Total	219	83	88
Professor	75	20	19
Reader	121	36	34
Lecturer	468	164	209
Total	664	220	262

Based on Indian Council of Social Science Research, 1973.

Agreeing that a crowd is not the only proof of strength, one could draw solace from the tribe of sociologists for their numbers matched with the geographers. In academics, after all, it is work rather than sheer numbers which adds weight to a discipline. Geographers did not add meat in this direction.

Extremely difficult to evaluate yet an acid test is the insignificant number of seminal texts or reference books by geographers in India till 1980s. With no research institutes, lack of repeat orders from planning organizations, lesser number of departments of geography, and few books to their credit, geography carried a dwarfed image.

It needed redemption. Who was to take on the challenge of pulling the subject out of its morass? The swamp was large, and geographers needed to weld a collective strength. By the mid 1970s India had geographical associations that had celebrated their silver and golden jubilees (Table 12). Despite years of existence, it was perhaps their isolated functioning and small strength of members, which deterred them to heed the larger issue at hand.

Table 12 : Age of Some Geographical Associations of India in 1978

Association	Year of inception	Age in 1978*
Aligarh Geographical Society (formerly Curzon Geographical Society), Aligarh	1925	53
Indian Geographical Society (formerly Madras Geographical Association), Madras	1926	52
Patna Geographical Society, Patna	1929	49
Geographical Society of India (formerly Calcutta Geographical Society) , Calcutta	1933	45
Bombay Geographical Association, Bombay	1935	43
National Geographical Society of India, Varanasi	1946	32
Indian Council of Geographers, Bhubaneshwar	1947	31
Rajasthan Geographical Association, Bhilwara	1965	13

*Note: * The year of inception of National Association of Geographers, India. The term association and society are used as synonyms.*

An attempt to coordinate and bring together the innumerable geographical associations was made when the Indian Science Congress met for its Silver Jubilee celebrations in 1938. But this failed. As an aftermath and a need to project a national body, or perhaps the fear of loosing identity, the Geographical Association of Madras and the Calcutta Geographical Society quickly added the prefix India in a rechristening ceremony in 1940. Names, however, do not change personalities.

Another attempt towards a national level association was made when the Indian Council of Geographers was created at the Delhi Session of the Indian

Science Congress in 1947. But this too was short lived. " All the existing geographical associations in India are university-centered, and for this reason their field of activity is limited." With these words was born the Association of Indian Geographers in 1955. "....... it tried from the very beginning to rid itself of the university, regional and provincial basis.......". However, an analysis of its 20 founder members shows 11 belonged to Delhi and 9 were employees in a college or department of a university. This Association attempted a national appeal, but by 1975 it ran out of steam.

The hunger for a national association lingered in these abortive attempts. Discussion with a cross section of professors also confirms 'the air was filled with the thought and intention' for a national association. Camouflaged in this expression was the more genuine need to arrest the sinking discipline and to give it direction and visibility. It is often proclaimed that there is no greater strength than in the self, and the realized self has power to lever great change. All members of the community of geographers, who were sensitive to the state of the discipline, lent energy to this common need. In the quantum pool of thought and intention, came into being in 1978,the National Association of Geographers, India. Echoing the need of the times, it was not created but was born: A Voice of Concern for Indian Geography.

National Association of Geographers, India

In a short 22 years the National Association of Geographers, India has swelled to become the largest society of geographers in India. Its 1260 life members, along with another 100 associate, annual and institutional members give it an unchallenged supremacy among all other geographical societies operating in the country. Comparing life members, NAGI has a lead of over 700 members from its next in the league, Calcutta Geographical Society of India, Calcutta and Indian Institute of Geographers, Pune. Outnumbering all the age-old associations, its youthful success in attracting members sees no parallel in the history of geographical organizations in the country.

To capture the voice of concern the architects of the National Association of Geographers, India wanted to reach across the country. With a natural verve for regions so that all areas are contained, NAGI carved five territorial divisions in India. Differing in size, area, population, and even the number of departments of geography, the homogeneous criteria for regionalisation seems to be 'common location' Hence the names North-Western, Northern, Western, Southern and Eastern Regions (Fig. 1).

Fig. 1 : Territorial Organisation of National Association of Geographers, India 2000

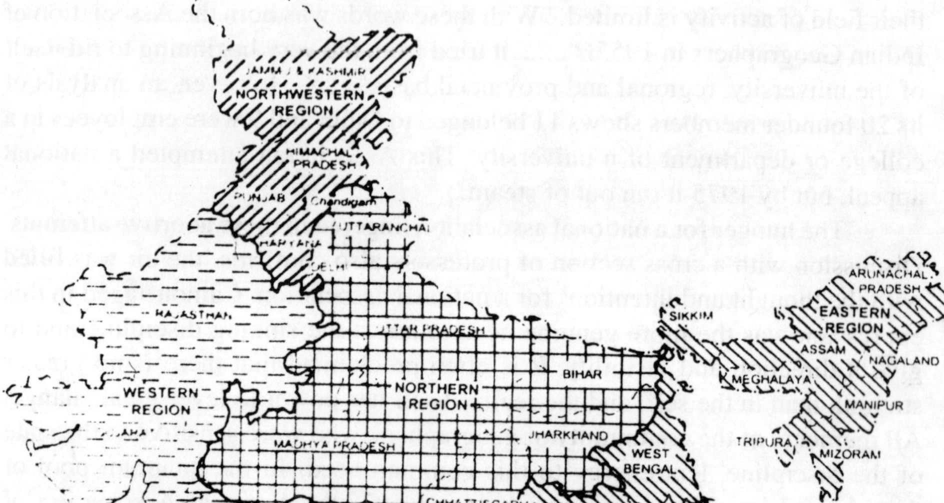

With a need to gain national coverage, it saw its logical base in Delhi. The country's capital offered advantages of site and situation. The headquarters of the Indian Council of Social Science Research is in Delhi, and moreover its chairman late J.P Naik provided genuine support to national level associations: the seed money to register the association, a venue to hold meetings, and lending even its address to NAGI are all its acts of deep care. Gathering financial support from the Ministry of Education and the Department of Science and Technology implies that in the formative stage Delhi was a profitable choice.

An organic functional system was designed with a main nucleus of the Executive Committee which contains a series of subnucleii of the President, Vice President and Secretary General and Editor. All the members constitute the General Body. The Executive Committee, represents the General Body to execute decisions. Sandwiched between and answerable to both is the trio team of Presidents: past, present and elect. Members can opt from a range of possible enrollments : life to annual, individual to institutional, honorary to benefactor. Integrated and interactive is structural organization of NAGI (Fig. 2).

Fig. 2 : Organisational Structure of National Association of Geographers, India (NAGI)

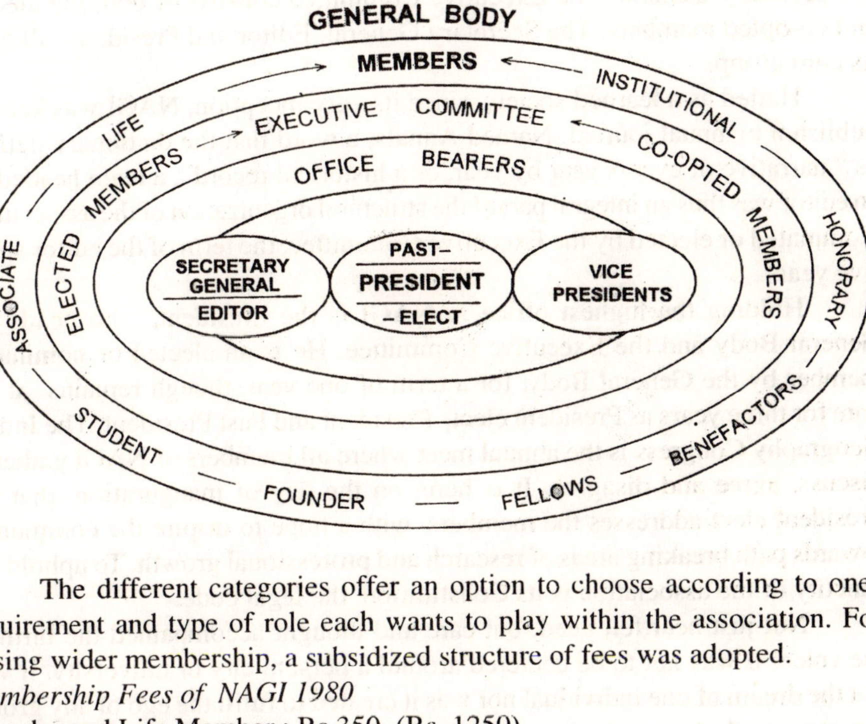

The different categories offer an option to choose according to ones requirement and type of role each wants to play within the association. For raising wider membership, a subsidized structure of fees was adopted.

Membership Fees of NAGI 1980

Founder and Life Member : Rs 350 (Rs. 1250)

Members : Rs 35 (Rs. 200)

Institutional Members : Rs 100 (Rs. 5000)

Associate Members : Rs 20 (Rs. 75)

Student Member : Rs 5 (Rs. 50)

(Figures in parenthesis are membership fees in 2000)

Any and all who have an interest in geography could be its members. Geographers from all walks of life: students, teachers, research fellows, scientists, planners, cartographers, publishers, authors, to travelers the association welcomes all. There was no discrimination of caste, class, or creed. In the organization the aggregate strength of the life members is the highest. Modeled on the lines of a parliament, its members elect or nominate the Executive Committee as well as the President, Secretary General, Editor. There are some co-opted members as well. The Executive Committee has to have a minimum of 17 members, not exceeding a maximum of 35. Organizing and recording minutes of the meetings, which at times run into hours, is the work of the Secretary General. The Executive Committee consists of both the elected and co-opted members. The Secretary General, Editor and Presidents all form its core group.

Hailed as a learned society, since its very inception, NAGI was keen to publish a biannual journal. Named Annals, a word that the dictionary defines as " narrative of events year by year, or a historical record", a team headed by an editor was thus an integral part of the structural organization of the association. Nominated or elected by the Executive Committee, the term of the editor spans five years.

Holding the highest office in NAGI is the President, who heads the General Body and the Executive Committee. He is an elected or nominated member by the General Body, for a term of one year, though remains at the core for three years as President elect, President and Past President. The Indian Geography Congress is the annual meet where all members of NAGI gather to discuss, agree and disagree. It is here, on the day of inauguration, that the President elect addresses the members, with a hope to inspire the community towards path breaking areas of research and professional growth. To uphold the sanctity of the association is its Constitution, the legal code.

Not just heartfelt need, but care and thought accompanied the birth of the voice. It was not to be centered around a person, city or university. It was not the dream of one individual nor was it created to fulfil the ego of any group. It represented a larger ideology, and its purpose was to serve the cause of Indian Geography. It was to be a discipline-centered body transcending the life of its founder members and presidents. Today nearly 40 of its life members, 5 founder members and 2 Presidents are no longer alive, yet NAGI lives on.

To begin with little NAGI had limited funds. Its kitty in 1980 was a meager Rs. 50,000. It had no permanent place of residence. Its crib, a make shift arrangement, shuttled between a cupboard at the Indian Council of Social Science Research and the generous home of some of its founder members. Till date its pool of money is a paltry Rs. 0.7 million and there is no roof over its head, yet NAGI has survived to cross an adult age to reach 22. Through its life journey how has NAGI fared? How national has it been? What participation has it evoked? Has it been a voice with concern?

An Enduring Voice

Each year the voice of NAGI attracts 50 life and 100 other members to its list. Each year, the NAGI, Annals have reached its life members and subscribers. Each year it has been holding its Congress. A yearly meet of the General Body and several meetings of the Executive Committee are a regular feature. Every financial year its accounts are audited and a balance sheet prepared. Its financial status though weak does not record losses. NAGI has endured. This may seem a meaningless claim yet the history of most associations is filled with infant or juvenile mortality.

The Association of Indian Geographers closed shop in two decades. The Saturday Club, run by a team of geographers from Jawahar lal Nehru University, could not cross its seventh birthday. The Curzon Geographical Society of Aligarh hibernated for long; formed in 1925, it resurfaced after a pause of 22 years. Some bifurcated and later sought mergers in order to survive – take the Patna College Geographical Society founded in 1929, it split into two in 1973 to form the Association of Geographers, Patna and the Geographical Research Center. In 1987 both joined hands to publish the Geographical Perspective. By 1999 it sought a new alliance and formed the Bihar Association of Geographers. In an attempt to survive some like the Indian Council of Geographers formed in 1947, changed identity to become the Indian Council of Geography Teachers in 1953, and again amended themselves to be called the Council of Geographers in 1961. NAGI till date has suffered no such aberations.

Journals in geography too suffer spasms of irregularity; some have been forced to close down. Of a sample of 51 journals floated between 1925 – 1985, 15 had been discontinued and 18 were irregular. Sustaining a journal is a challenging task and the rate of survival among geographical ones is less than 33 per cent (Kapur, 1998; Sinha, 1986).

There is little doubt that NAGI does have a long traverse ahead as on the other end of the spectrum there are geographical associations and journals in India like the Indian Geographical Journal, Geographical Review of India and Geographer which have crossed 50 years of publication. Yet, let us not forget that NAGI was a product of troubled times in the discipline, and it still persists. Each year 150 geographers gravitate to seek its membership. These include the annual, student, and associate members, many of which are ephemeral. The durable and permanent staple of NAGI are the life members. From 244 in 1980 the life members increased to 1260 in 2000. Though rate of growth has varied in the quinquineal period, yet not a single year has gone when NAGI has not seen the additions (Table 13).

Table 13 : Increase in NAGI Membership, 1980-2000

Phase of registration	Number of new life members
By 1980	244
1981-1985	390
1986-1991	131
1991-1995	277
1996-2000	219
Total	1260

Based on Membership Forms of the Life Members of NAGI.

In 20 years, 36 issues of 20 volumes, can be counted. Twenty-two Congress, one each year from 1980 to 2000, have been held under the banner of NAGI. The constitution categorically states, "the annual meeting of the General Body of the Association shall ordinarily be held in December – January every year". Eighty-five per cent of these annual meets have stuck to dates in the month of December to January, giving the schedule a stamp of traditional permanence. A gathering of the General Body and Presidential Address followed by the presentation of papers has also been a permanent feature of each event. Financially, NAGI has not been in debt nor has it milked its corpus fund to bankruptcy. The money it collects through registration of new members, donations, advertisements, memorial funds and grants from the Indian Council of Social Science Research and Government Ministries has kept it afloat.

In the year 2000, NAGI stands as an association of 1260 life members, 36 issues of the Annals, 22 Indian Geography Congresses,. 23 Presidential Addresses and a sum of Rs. 0.7 million in its coffers. In these 22 years of standing, on many fronts its national ethos is also intact.

A National Domain

For effective representation in 1978, NAGI made a territorial division of India into five regions.(Fig 1) An index to its national character is the fact that it has drawn its founder members, life members, presidents, and authors of the journal from all regions. Its annual Congress too has toured through diverse parts of the country (Table 14).

Table 14 : National Domain of NAGI

Region	Founder Members		President		Life Members		Venue of IGC		Authors in NAGI Annals	
	No.	**Per cent to total**	**No.**	**Per cent to total**	**No.**	**Per cent to total**	**No.**	**Per cent to total**	**No.**	**Per cent to total**
North Western	5	29	9	39	249	19	5	23	74	23
Northern	3	18	5	22	388	31	4	18	38	11
Western	2	12	1	4	252	20	5	23	68	20
Southern	4	23	5	22	160	13	5	23	90	27
Eastern	3	18	3	13	135	11	3	13	28	8
Outside India / Others**	0	0	0	0	76	6	0	0	35	11
Total	17	100	23	100	1260	100	22	100	333*	100

*Note : * This excludes the two issues of 2000.*
*** This includes ones who are foreign based and those that could not be identified.*

A handful of 17 founder members with a near equal distribution from all regions had rolled the tune of the national image of NAGI. Its life members too come from all the five regions. While the north does dominate yet its less than one third share means it is no where close to acquiring absolute majority. Today NAGI has a member from every State and Union Territory of India. A more fine grain analysis shows that 140 districts contribute at least one life member of NAGI, this is close to double of the districts containing a department of geography in India.

Hypothetically, if the 22 Indian Geography Congress are divided by the five regions, each region should have held a minimum of four Congresses .The data in the above table confirms that except for the Eastern Region, where there have been 3, the Indian Geography Congress has marched in an equitable manner to all its counterparts. Measuring venue to venue along the railway track, the Indian Geography Congress has covered, in 21 years, an aggregate distance of 41,884 kilometres, a length which almost equals the circumference of the earth (Fig. 3)

The catchment of the Indian Geography Congress confirms the sustenance of an all India attraction for NAGI. Drawing from the list of participants in the four Congress held in 1981, 1997, 1999 and 2000, it can be concluded that members from all the five regions do attend this meet. Though it is but natural that the majority belonged to the region in which the Congress was held, yet in all the four Congresses, all regions did make their presence felt.A breakup at the state level also revealed that in the four Congresses, members from 60 to 70 per cent of the states of India found representation (Table 15).

Fig. 3 : March of the Indian Geography Congress 1980-2000

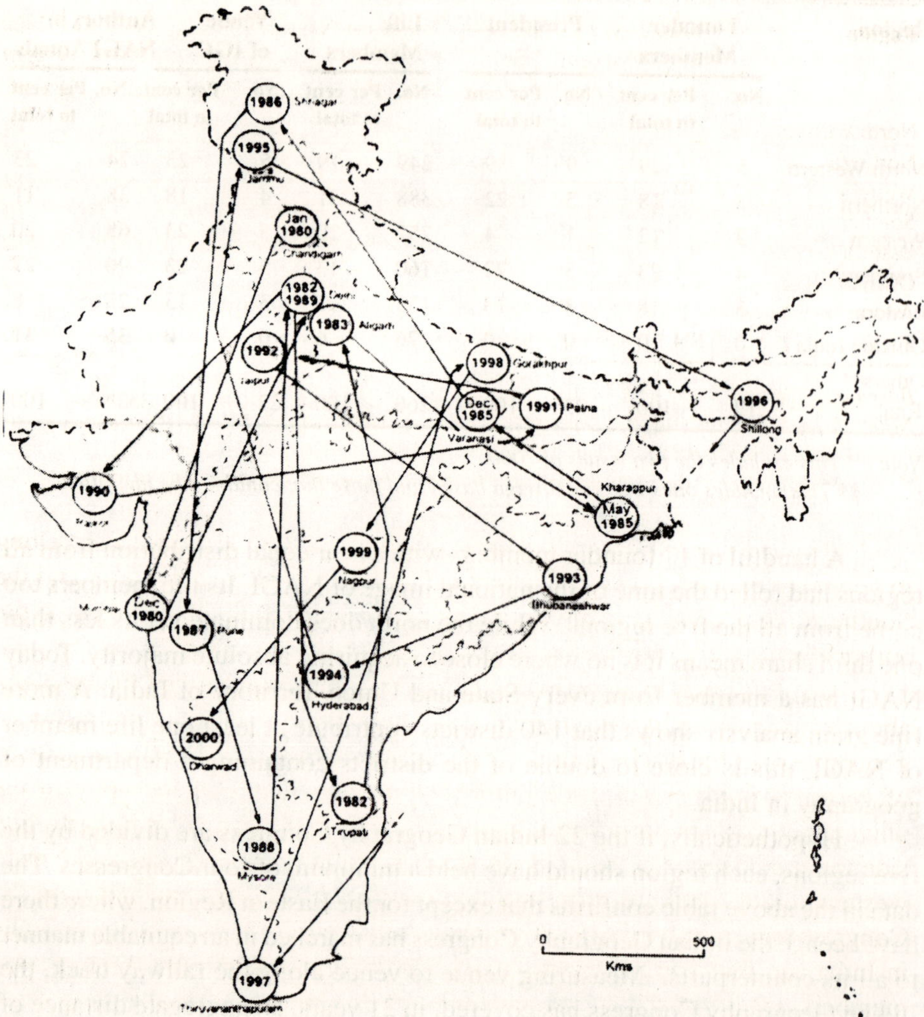

In the choice of presidents, their scholarship rather than place of residence merits greater attention. Yet presidents too have been chosen from across the nation as far as Tirupati, Guwahati, Chandigarh, Mumbai, Kolkata to Delhi. Delhi is the only city which has provided 4 presidents, but one needs to remember that it houses not just 3 universities but also institutes of national importance. The only exception is the Jawahar lal Nehru University, which has taken a share of 2 presidents and 3 presidential terms.

Table 15 : Catchment of the Indian Geography Congress

Region	Delhi 1981* No.	Per cent to total	Thiruvanthapuram No.	Per cent to total	Nagpur 1999 No.	Per cent to total	Dharwad 2000 No.	Percent to total
North Western	23	11	15	8	16	9	41	18
Northern	91	45	18	9	23	12	77	34
Western	40	20	10	5	35	18	55	24
Southern	29	14	91**	69	70**	39	22**	10
Eastern	18	8	17	9	39	21	26	12
Outside India	3	2	2					
Addresses not known		0	0	0	2	1	4	2
Total	204	100	190	100	185	100	225	100

Based on : Records from the host departments of the IGC.

*Note : * These are participants for whom accommodation was provided by the host: Jawahar lal Nehru University.*

*** Participants from the Region in which the IGC was hosted.*

The 265 contributors of research articles to the NAGI Annals also belong to geographers from across the regions. The North Western , Western and the Southern regions have a near equal presence with 20 to 27 per cent of the authors belonging to each of these realms .

To seek near equal distribution from each region would be a false claim about effective regional representation. In essence, it is the distribution of geographers in India which makes the inquiry meaningful. There is no census of geographers, therefore, the number of departments of geography in the universities is used as a surrogate (Table 16). When this number is placed along side the members of NAGI, the domination of both in the North and North-western regions emerges. Despite this overlap, NAGI has tried to hold the Congress and stretch its zone of influence outside this heartland of geography in India and thus bring the peripheries within its ambit. All the three planks: members, meet and the Annals champion the unimpaired national domain of NAGI.

One could argue that mere persistence or the numerical maintenance of a national character does not answer the more relevant question: how actively has NAGI attracted participation? Participation is an all encompassing word and its purview, for example, covers keeping and reading the NAGI Annals, writing and reviewing it; attending the Congress, presenting papers, debating, contesting elections, nominating, and voting all are forms that embody the spirit of involvement. Responding to appeals for donation, collecting advertisements, enrolling new members are essential ways of being a part of an organization.

Criticism and care each is a role in the orchestra of an association. If a well designed questionnaire is circulated to the members, a measure of participation can be gathered for all the above spelt out variables. An attitude and opinion survey have their advantages for capturing the perception of the members of the association, but time and resources curbed this exercise. The inability to undertake a questionnaire survey however led to a search for an objective criteria for measuring participation.

Table 16 : Regionwise Distribution of NAGI Life Members vis-a-vis Number of Departments of Geography, 2000

Region	**No. of departments**	**Per cent to total**	**Per cent to total NAGI members**	**Location Quotient**
North Western	11	14	21	1.5
Northern	30	38	33	0.9
Western	14	18	21	1.2
Southern	11	14	14	1.0
Eastern	12	16	11	0.7
Total	78	100	100	1.0

Index of Participation

At the outset one clear measure of the desire to participate with NAGI is the enrollment of members. It is only when the people from the geographical group want to associate do they seek its membership. There is no better, long term, and economical way of being involved in NAGI than by seeking its life membership. This gives access to a series of brochures announcing decisions and forthcoming programs, a free set of the biannual NAGI Annals, a license to become, nominate or elect members of its decision making executive committee and also nourish the secret hope of becoming its President ! The numerical strength of NAGI has grown eight fold over the last 22 years. Many have bonded a life long commitment.

From its list of seventeen founder members eight became presidents, four secretary-generals and one an editor. A sustained relationship can also be verified from the group photograph of the first Indian Geography Congress held at Chandigarh in 1980; amidst the 195 participants that can be counted, nine became the president of NAGI in the ensuing 20 years (Fig. 4).

Attendance in the Executive Committee meetings and the General Body is further proof of involvement. In a sample of 40 Executive Committee meetings held in the last 20 years , nearly 553 members participated , this is an average of 14 per meet. The General Body has always had members way

Fig. 4 : An Enduring Relationship - First Indian Geography Congress, Chandigarh, 1980

A joyful coincidence : interspersed in the second row from below are seated 7 life members who were to become the presidents of National Association of Georaphers, India : Gopal Krishan, R. Vaidyanadhan, Aijazuddhin Ahmad, C.R. Pathak, L.S. Bhatt, S.L. Kayastha and N.B.K Reddy.

above the minimum requirements of a quorum of 10 percent which testifies an involvement with NAGI. The Indian Geography Congress is hosted by different university level departments of geography and leading institutes of the country. It is in its departments, that geography thrives, and 18 Departments and 4 of the most prestigious institutes have shown their involvement with NAGI by holding the Congress in their precincts. The fact that there is usually a competition amongst various departments to host the meet, and sometimes the General Body has to vote the matter to reach a point of consensus, proves that NAGI is much in demand. Laid out with sessions of paper presentations, panel discussions, key note lectures, meetings of commissions, followed by local field excursions , in its three days, the Congress packs a variety of ways of being part of NAGI.

The announcement of the venue sets into motion a series of circulars seeking participation to the Congress. Response to the call takes the shape of abstracts of research papers. Response is conscious participation and the Congress has attracted nearly 3928 abstracts of papers over its 22 years. This total is based on an average drawn from a sample of 17 of the 22 Congress, for which the abstract volumes were available. Though numbers may vacillate, yet on an average each Congress initiates a response from 178 members to write an abstract of the paper they would like to present (Table 17).

The inability to arrange the funds to travel rather than other preoccupations deter authors of abstracts from reaching the venue. The number of persons, which present their papers at the Congress, is less than that of the ones who send in their abstracts. But other members join in to listen and discuss the papers, thus, swelling the attendance. A head count of the members who attend the Congress is difficult to gather. Of the 22 Congress, authentic lists of participation was available for only the 19th and the 21st meet. Estimating crowds is a science at which few are adept, and lack of records marred a satisfactory conclusion. To broaden the inquiry some tallies were attempted. In the group photograph of the Congress held at Chandigarh in 1980, one can count 195 participants, but 350 is the often quoted number for this meet. It was in the auditorium of the English Department , of the University of Panjab that the first Congress was inaugurated . A check confirmed that the auditorium has a seating capacity of 300. People who attended the Congress recall that many stood in the isles, while some blocked the doors. The 350 figure thus seems correct for the day of inauguration, though participation in the deliberations of the Congress could be closer to count in this group photograph. As a rule, numbers do peter out later in the sessions. The group photograph of the Indian Geography Congress held at Centre for Regional Development, Jawahar lal Nehru University, Delhi, embraces a gathering of 197, though it arranged accommodation for 204 participants: the organizers insist it was a for six Congress in the organizer reports or the secretary-generals. Pooling together this diverse variety of data one can conclude that on an average 259 members participate in a Congress. In aggregate, nearly 5700 geographers have thus shared time with the NAGI, some as repeaters and some first timers.

Table 17 : Abstracts submitted for the Indian Geography Congress, 1980 - 2000

Year (Month)	Venue of IGC	No. of abstracts
1980 (Jan)	Chandigarh	151
1980 (Dec)	Bombay	n.a
1981 (Dec)	Delhi	258
1982 (Dec)	Tirupati	261
1983 (Dec)	Aligarh	228
1985 (May)	Kharagpur	271
1985 (Dec)	Varanasi	305
1986 (Nov)	Srinagar	189
1987 (Dec)	Pune	58
1988 (Dec)	Mysore	120
1989 (Oct)	Delhi	78
1990 (Dec)	Rajkot	121
1991 (Dec)	Patna	n.a
1992 (Dec)	Jaipur	240
1993 (Nov)	Bhubaneswar	132
1994 (Dec)	Hyderabad	n.a
1995 (Dec)	Jammu	175
1996 (Oct)	Shillong	n.a
1997 (Dec)	Thiruvanthapuram	104
1998 (Dec)	Gorakhpur	221
1999 (Dec)	Nagpur	n.a.
2000 (Dec)	Dharwad	124

n.a. : Souvenirs and abstracts of the Indian Geography Congress not available.

Writing for the NAGI Annals is another index of participation. The combined stock of the Annals contains 468 pieces of writing which consist of: 219 research articles, 165 book reviews, 56 short communications and 28 obituaries.

The number of inclusions in the journal, however, is not a comprehensive list of participants as it takes more than one author to write a research article, similarly there are authors who have written more than one article. The advantage of the published document of the Annals allowed one to build an in-depth data base to settle on these details . It has taken 355 authors to produce 219 research papers. About a dozen authors have made 2 contributions while 5 have made three . There is an enthusiast who crosses all limits with 7 research articles to his credit .An entire issue of the Annals could well be devoted to his claim, so overwhelming has been his response to NAGI! While more authors have participated through the medium of research papers – an opposite picture emerges for the book reviews. Fifty-eight members have authored the total of 165 reviews; three reviews per author is the average.

Participation is not just confined to the published works, editors confirm that the ratio of 1: 5 is the general norm while screening and rejecting articles. The question is not whether the articles have been accepted or for reasons good or bad rejected. But, writing and mailing an article for considerations by the editors of Annals is an undeniable measure of participation with NAGI. Writing and publishing with NAGI is only a small though important scale of involvement with the Annals. Disseminating knowledge is the key function of a research journal, and the readers of NAGI are also active participants with the association. A count of all life, institutional and subscribers members would not suffice, as one knows that the zone of reading expands through borrowings from a library to lending out personal copies. In the Departmental library at Chandigarh the NAGI Annals in the last three years had been consulted 46 times. The boundaries of any journal can stretch to limits one is unable to draw. How can one judge the reach of NAGI?

Beyond Comparison: International Geographical Associations

An immediate temptation is to compare NAGI with the world class geographical associations. As pageants in a beauty contest set the benchmark about who is beautiful, comparing NAGI with the best geographical associations is a genuine hobby of the members of a professional community. Defining best is a value-loaded term vulnerable on numerous fronts. But there would be little difference of opinion if National Geographical Society (USA), American Geographical Society (USA) and the Royal Geographical Society (UK) were chosen. Among the world of geographical associations they do fall in the high quartile. Many parameters for comparison are not wanted – just one or two relevant ones usually suffice to bring the message across. Here are the parallels for perusal (Table 18):

Table 18 : Beyond Comparison : International Geographical Societies

Name	Year of establishment	Members, 2000
Royal Geographical Society, U.K.	1831	13000
National Geographical Society, U.S.A.	1888	11million
Association of American Geographers, U.S.A.	1904	7000
National Association of Geographers, India	1978	1260

Based on web sites of the international societies and the secretariat of NAGI.

One could read the data in the above table and freeze dumbstruck. Comparing the incomparable. Some could disagree with the attempt to contrast associations of India with those abroad and claim 'If an association has to be compared with those abroad, so should all indices of development'. To draw a parallel of NAGI with international associations is like holding a candle to the sun. But even a little lamp dispels the deepest of darkness, and though the class of international geographical societies are beyond comparison today, it would be worth comparing the position NAGI holds among the societies in India.

Worth Comparing: Geographical Societies in India

Like a nestled hierarchy of settlements, geographical societies in India range from the informal, the unregistered ones in colleges, to the ones in the university departments which hold together a larger group of affiliated colleges within their embrace. A number of informal associations are present in colleges. Run with voluntarily resources pooled as per requirements a lecture, field trip and an occasional newsletter are the limit of their activity. There are also the state level associations, the earliest Rajasthan Geographical Association made in 1965 and a recent effort, the Panjab Association of Geographers and the Bihar Geographical Associations. Spanning across states are the regional associations like the Calcutta, Madras, Pune and Varanasi. Within this mosaic how does NAGI claim its apex status? One simple criterion could be its numerical dominance (Table 19).

Whether young or old, state or regional, city or town based, college or department wise, specialized or general ones, on number of life members, NAGI outranks all other geographical societies in India. Its unchallenged supremacy can be seen by the fact that the society next in order trails at a numerical low of half. Another important character is the spatial distribution. For example, let us say if NAGI has 1000 members, but if over 500 belonged to Delhi, its comparative edge would loose glitter. Take the Calcutta Society; of the total of 558 life members, 279 belong to West Bengal within which Calcutta occupies the lion share of 50 per cent. (Table 20). The picture was near similar for the National Geographical Society of India, Varanasi. Even the recently formed Bihar Association of Geographers recruited about 90 per cent of its members from the city of Patnā alone. A smaller size and proximity could have a functional advantage, but these associations cannot claim a national status. NAGI stands apart from all other geographical societies in India by embracing a heterogeneous mix. A map of the spatial distribution of NAGI members shows distribution across India (Fig. 5).

Table 19 : Worth Comparing : NAGI vis-a- vis other Geographical Societies of India, 2000

Society / Association	Year of establishment	Life members in 2000
National / Regional Associations		
National Association of Geographers, India	1978	1260
Geographical Society of India, Calcutta	1933	558
Indian Institute of Geographers, Pune	1954	528
Indian Geographical Society, Chennai	1947	241
National Geographical Society of India, Varanasi	1946	121
State Level Associations		
Rajasthan Geographical Association, Bhilwara	1965	275
Bihar Association of Geographers, Patna	1999	114
Association of Punjab Geographers, Patiala	1998	151
Theme Based Associations		
Association of Population Geographers of India, Chandigarh	1979	211
Association of Marketing Geographers, Gorakhpur	1983	50
Cousin Associations		
Indian National Cartographic Association, Hyderabad	1979	1870
Indian Society of Soil Survey and Land use Planning, Nagpur	1986	360
Regional Science Association of India, Kharagpur	1967	346

Based on information from different associations.

A continuous belt of members occurs from Rajasthan, Haryana, Uttar Pradesh, Bihar. It begins to stall near West Bengal and scatters when it reaches the North-East amidst as a patchy occurrence in South India. Large parts of Maharashtra, Andhra Pradesh and Tamil Nadu stand out as uncovered spaces.

Table 20 : Spatial Concentration of Life Members of Some Geographical Associations in India, 2000

Name of Association	Total life members	State with largest number of life members	Per cent to total in the state
Geographical Society of India, Calcutta	558	391 (West Bengal)	70
Indian Institute of Geographers, Pune	528	216 (Maharashtra)	41
Regional Science Association of India, Kharagpur	346	85 (West Bengal)	25
Indian Geographical Society, Chennai	241	119 (Tamil Nadu)	49
Association of Population Geographers of India, Chandigarh	211	50 (Punjab)	24
Association of Panjab Geographers, Patiala	151	130 (Punjab)	86
National Geographical Society of India, Varanasi	121	68 (Uttar Pradesh)	56
Bihar Association of Geographers, Patna	114	101 (Bihar)	89

Calculated from the list of addresses of life members of different associations.

Fig 5 : Spatial Distribution of Life Members of the National Association of Geographers, India 2000

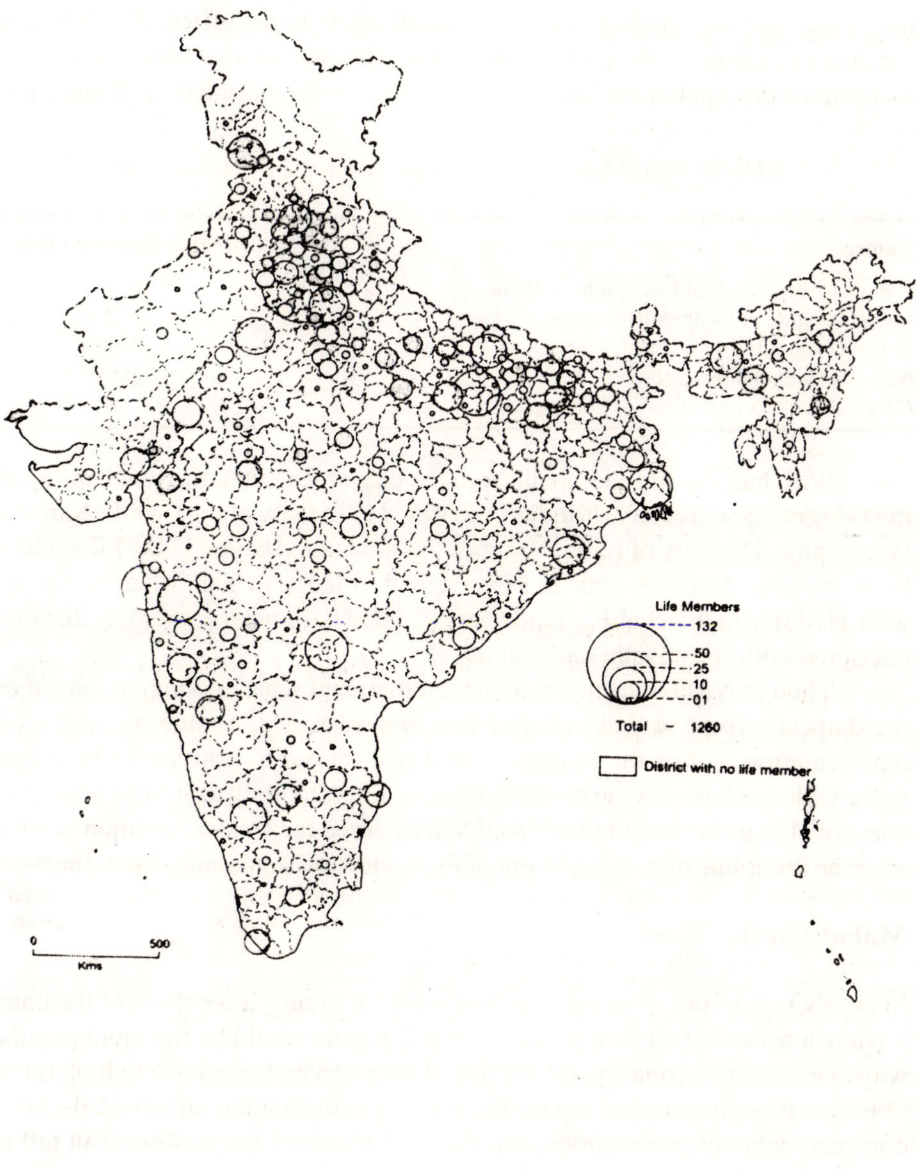

Another measure of the sphere of influence of a geographical association is the distance from which they net half their life members. A reference to median the value which relates to a middle point has been chosen as a measure for the comparative spatial reach of associations.With the office of registration for an association as the point of reference, the median distance is used as a measure of the spatial spread or concentration of the association.(Table 21)

Table 21: Spatial Reach of Geographical Associations in India: 2000

Name	**Median distance (Kms.)**
National Association of Geographers, India	1033
Indian Institute of Geographers, Pune	772
Indian Geographical Society, Chennai	591
National Geographical Society of India, Varanasi	300
Geographical Society of India, Calcutta	0

With half the life members from the city of Calcutta, the reachability of the Geographical Society of India is confined to the city alone, while National Geographical Society of India, Varanasi has not fanned beyond 300 kilometers. Even societies from Madras and Pune stand a ledge of half when compared with NAGI which stands giant apart at 1033 kilometers, median distance measured both from Delhi and Nagpur (Fig. 6).

Though NAGI cuts no ice at the international scale of comparison but on the domestic front, it can make claims of dominance, continuity, and wide representation. Is this the mileage NAGI had set out to achieve: to be a loud voice with reach across the country, or more importantly was it to be a voice of concern? Let us not forget that NAGI had emerged for greater common good to steer the discipline of geography out of the wallowing status and give it direction.

Malady in the Voice

Many aberations puncture the tune NAGI set out to sing. Take the NAGI Annals – while a review of each of its 219 research papers would be the more popular way of assessing its quality, yet the risk of subjectivity forced one to look for an objective though quantitative criteria. Poverty in the number of issues, depleted contents, delay in publications, and the need to enroll guest editors, all tell us that the house of the Annals is in dire straits.

The NAGI Annals was started with a promise to deliver an issue biannually. Both the constitution and the minutes of its executive meetings record with euphoria " the Annals shall be the official organ of the association, and the

Fig. 6 : Spatial Reach of the Geographical Assocaitions in India 2000

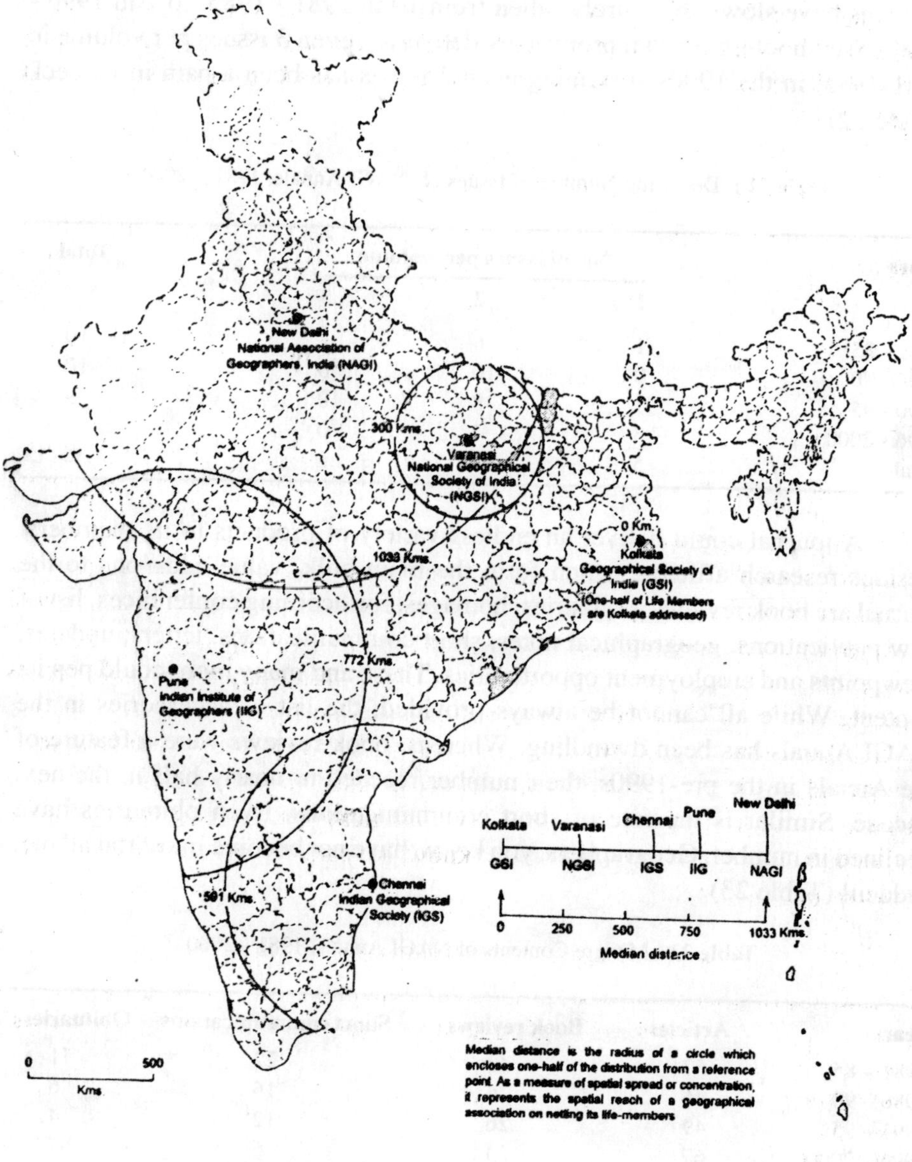

association will publish the Annals half yearly". From 1980 to 2000 the number of issues have slowly but surely fallen from 10 in 1981 - 1985, to 7 in 1996 - 2000. Overshooting its own promise by delivering even 3 issues per volume in 1981-1985, in the 1990s sustaining even 2 issues has been a pain in its neck (Table 22).

Table 22 : Declining Number of Issues of NAGI Annals, 1981 – 2000

Years	No. of issues per volume			Total
	1	2	3	
1981 - 85	1	6	3	10
1986 - 90	0	10	0	10
1990 - 95	1	8	0	9
1996 - 2000	3	4	0	7
Total	5	28	3	36

A journal could deliver an endless variety of products to its members. Besides research articles, which form the main bulk, value additions to the journal are book reviews, obituaries, homages, forthcoming conferences, list of new publications, geographical notes, short communications, letters, updates, viewpoints and employment opportunities. These and many more could pep its content. While all cannot be always provided, the list of accessories in the NAGI Annals has been dwindling. Whereas, book reviews were a feature of the Annals in the pre-1990s, their number receded to nearly half in the next decade. Similar is the fate of short communications. Even obituaries have declined in number. Geographers, you know, have not become immortal all of a sudden! (Table 23).

Table 23 : Meagre Contents of NAGI Annals, 1981 - 2000

Year	Articles	Book reviews	Short communications	Obituaries
1981 – 85	57	40	22	11
1986 – 90	46	76	16	6
1991 – 95	49	26	12	4
1996 – 2000	67	23	6	7
Total	219*	165	56	28

**By comparison, Annals of the Association of American Geographers carried – articles during 1981-2000*

Academic contents apart, NAGI Annals has been unable to provide an introduction to the journal and editor's note, or record its budget and list of members. The fact that of the 23 presidential addresses only seven have been published in the Annals speak of its depleted plight. The journal overlooked the fact that information classified as 'others' is the interactive space for members to share news and views. Variety does add spice; without it this publication as an organ for the Association is insipid and dull (Table 24).

Table 24 : Decline in the Features in NAGI Annals, 1981 – 2000

Year	No. of issues	Editor's note	Geographical record	List of members	News about members	Journal Introduction	Seminar report	Budget
1981 – 1985	10	9	4	5	9	9	1	0
1986 –19 90	10	10	0	1	7	1	9	3
1991 – 1995	9	1	0	0	0	0	4	0
1996 – 2000	6	0	0	0	2	2	4	0
Total	35	20	4	6	18	12	18	3

Plain to shaded, mono to twin, glossy or mat, carrying world maps on some –is the changing cover jacket of the NAGI Annals. In the last 20 years, 10 different types of toppings have arrived in the mail. The result, Annals has lost identity even in looks! While variety is the spice – a judicious understanding is required to know where uniformity is virtue. Each volume of the Encyclopaedia of Britannica is similar in size, color and layout. Besides making it easy to identify and use, its appearance lend aesthetics to libraries, public and personal. The NAGI Annals have no cover advantage.

Producing the faltering numbers of issues and malnutritioned contents of the Annals stitched between slices of varied hues of jackets has also been an uphill task. Delays are common. Today in August 2001, the 2000 volume languishes in a printing office. This is not the first time. The Editors desk confesses – the publication from 1997-1999 got delayed. To rescue the crisis of emergency a team of nearly 10 guest editors had to be rushed to provide assistance. Maladies have put the journal in the intensive care.

Interviews with a handful of leading geographers also confirm the poor health of the Annals. When asked to grade the top 5 geographical journals in India, the Annals ranked as low as the second, third and even rock bottom among the list. A user-based index is the number of times the NAGI Annals was issued compared to other geographical journals in India. NAGI Annals notched a share of only 29 out of a total of 230 geographical journals issued by faculty and students at the Department library at Chandigarh in the last three years. This is a low of 12 per cent of the total (Table 25).

Table 25 : Low Rank of NAGI Annals Among Users

Journal	1998	1999	2000	Total
Transactions of Institute of Indian Geographers (Pune)	19	39	8	66
Geographical Review of India (Calcutta)	14	29	21	64
National Geographical Journal of India (Varanasi)	5	10	31	46
NAGI Annals (New Delhi)	9	13	7	29
Indian Geographical Journal (Chennai)	12	11	2	25

Based on statement of journals issued at the Geography Department Library of Panjab University, Chandigarh.

While the print media lasts and is thus vulnerable to critical comparative scrutiny, the tune of the annual Indian Geography Congress has to be heard to be known. What one tends to hear could be questioned on grounds that this is what one wants to hear. A looking glass to discern the characteristics of the Indian Geography Congress is the graph of attendance to this annual meet. Over the years its curve shows a declivity. When the first Indian Geography Congress was held in 1980, the total number of life members was one-fifth the number in 2000. Considering that the number of life members have swelled logic suggests that attendance to the Indian Geography Congress should have at least remained the same if not gone up. This has not happened (Table 26).

Table 26 : Participants in the Indian Geography Congress *

Year	Venue	Number of participants
1980	Chandigarh	350
1981	Delhi	300
1983	Aligarh	300
1985	Kharagpur	350
1986	Srinagar	200
1989	Delhi	205
1991	Patna	120
1994	Hyderabad	343
1997	Thiruvanthampuram	196
1999	Nagpur	227
2000	Dharwad	259

*Note : * Data of participants was available for only 10 Indian Geography Congress.*
Data has been culled from different sources like the souvenirs, secretary reports to organizers statement, its total reliability therefore may be questioned but it can be used as an approximation.

The magnetism of the Congress over the years has waned. The lack of luster in the Congress would clearly spring forth if one had a count of the number of members who do not repeat their attendance to the gathering. It could be argued that the absentees have reasons other than the attraction of the meet. But another confirmation of the weak pulse of the Indian Geography Congress is the condition of its specialty groups called Commissions. Initiated as early as in 1985, to bring together like-minded interests of geographers, who could discuss and navigate their areas of specialization towards more fruitful gains, NAGI sets up Commissions of study. Professing diverse interests, the members of NAGI formed many such groups at different points of time (Table 27) :

Table 27 : Number of Commissions in Indian Geography Congress

Year*	IGC number	No. of Commissions
1985	6	10
1987	9	11
1993	15	22
1995	17	26
1996	18	26
1997	19	29
2000	22	11

Based on brochures, minutes of meetings and Indian Geography Congress circulars.
**Information was available only for the years listed above.*

Eliminating the ones which repeat themselves, 42 different commissions in a sample of 7 Indian Geography Congress can be counted. The capacity to devise commissions on the traditional to the most modern streams of geography seems to be a hallmark of the Congress. There are ones on geography of marketing, sustainable development, politics and environment, population and development, gender and geography, social justice and human rights, global warming and climate change, geography of peace to geography of health and many more. However, creating and sustaining require different quality of intellectual muscle. More than 38 per cent of the commissions died after their first to second meet, while 42 per cent fizzled in the third to fourth round. The Association of American Geographers with a membership strength of 7000, have 54 specialty groups; NAGI with its 1260 members, has sported 42 different commissions. The protagonists and enthusiasts at the Indian Geography Congress have clearly been out of touch with realities at their home (Table 28).

Table 28 : Dismal Survival of Commissions in Indian Geography Congress

No. of Commissions	Years of survival
16	1 to 2
18	3 to 4
0	4 to 5
8	5 to 6
42	2.6 (median value)

There is no document to prove the outcome and work of any of the commissions which survived. Thus, a group in name could be as good and bad as being redundant. In some Congress meets, the dismal performance of the commission forced its annihilation. But like stubborn weed, the commissions aggressively breed under the disguise of new names and members – choking the Congress of quality!

The ratio of research papers read vis-a-vis those submitted in the condensed shape of an abstract is another infirmity of the Indian Geography Congress. Less than half the number of abstracts turn up in the shape of papers which are to be presented. Barely a fraction of the papers docked for submission on the scheduled dates. Organizers lament that what of last minute, in many cases the full-length papers have not reached the destination till date! Those who finally present their papers complain that the audience was sparse and moreover seemed least interested. The audience flings back to say that the papers lacked methodological and conceptual clarity and offered limited scope to generate debates. An unmelodious cacophony is the result of this endless circle of accusations. Pungent gossip, unconstructive criticism, endless politicking and efforts to sabotage the functioning of meets further pollutes the air. Written in deep anguish, letters to the secretariat and incidents narrated confidentially in interviews held with some geographers shed light on the deplorable state of the Indian Geography Congress (Table 29).

Table 29 : Mismatch between Abstracts Published and Papers Presented

IGC Venue	Year	No. of abstracts published	No. of papers presented	Presentation/ publication ratio
Varanasi	1985	305	150	0.5:1
Pune	1987	228	58	0.3:1
Mysore	1988	186	120	0.6:1
Thiruvanthapuram	1997	179	104	0.6:1

Based on Abstracts and Souvenirs of different Indian Geography Congress

The decision takers in NAGI are the office bearers of the executive committee. A total of 22 Presidents, 5 Secretary Generals, and 4 Editors have reigned the helm of affairs of NAGI in the last 22 years. Many have occupied multiple positions. Thus:, three have been Presidents and Secretary Generals, two Presidents and Editors and one has held the office of President twice. Frequent control by some office bearers, have meant that for many years NAGI was cuffed within the grips of a handful members. Some office bearers dominated the executive committee for nearly a decade. One could claim that patronizing has virtues of parenting, but it also stifles the germination of innovative ideas and circulation of fresh actions. It is within the chambers of power that strong though less publicly known conflicts of dissent, fiery discussions, resignations, followed by condescending agreements have impeded the growth of NAGI. Young NAGI was dragged into the court from 1991 to 1993, is proof that at times arguments transgressed limits that required legal counsel. Carrying the complexion more of ego rather than wisdom, these judicial battles have resolved with time but the malice tattooed the image of the association.

Fiscal crunch and lack of even a small office to run a secretariat drags NAGI further down. Financially, NAGI in 2000 has assets of only Rs 0.7 million. Possessing just one cupboard it has no room, nor an office nor a promise of land to its credit. A blue print of an architects plan of a building for the association lies abandoned among the frayed file. It is a grim reminder of limited efforts and unfulfilled dreams.

Repeated appeals to members for raising funds falls on deaf ears. Even donations to start a memorial lecture to perpetuate the members of eminent of the geographical community fetch paltry sums. Here is one illustration. Moonis Raza died on 18th July in 1994. He was a founder member of NAGI and the only President with a 2 term nomination. He established the Centre for Regional Development at Jawahar lal Nehru University and was also the Vice Chancellor of University of Delhi. A three-member committee was constituted to raise money to start a memorial lecture to honor his name. The bank interest from the Rs. 10,000, which was collected, is not even enough to pay the third class railway fare to a deserving speaker from Bombay to Thane!

Even proposals requesting members to cover the postage cost for the NAGI Annals receives rejection, tinted at times with tones of extreme anger. All those who enrolled as life member in 1980 with a payment of Rs. 350 have received 36 issues of the NAGI Annals free of cost. Even if the number of issues were divided by this life membership fee, the Annals have reached the doorstep of members at Rs. 8.50, less than the price of a coke in the market today. One has to understand that the days of free lunch are over! The publication of the Journal is making the single largest dent on the exchequer of the association. It is unable to plough 10 per cent of its costs into the financial reserves. A worrying situation is that grants from the government exchequer have been small, even the Department of Science and Technology has contributed only Rs 25,000. It was way back in 1985 that the Indian Council of Social Science Research had given an endowment of Rs 1.50 lakhs towards the publication. The collection of funds other than from membership fee have dried to a trickle.The corpus fund has not augmented, and with the decline in the value of the currency, its worth is a shrunk morsel. Donations and appeals, one knows, are voluntary acts, and lack of response could be read as anything between indifference to resentment. Measured on any side of the scale, the Association has been the sufferer.

Waste abounds amidst poverty. The expenditure of holding the Indian Geography Congress is the responsibility of the organizers who hold the annual meet. While the decisions of the Executive Committee have prevented the corpus fund from being skimmed, what adds remorse is the manner in which hosts collect funds only to fritter it on stationery, souvenirs, dinners and lunches. The total expenditure of the nineteenth Indian Geography Congress, held at Thiruvanthumpuram, amounted to Rs 0.35 million. Each participant costed Rs 1800,. One and a half times the amount to become a life member of NAGI today, which is at Rs 1250. It was a decision made in an Executive Committee meeting held in 1997 that a fixed sum of Rs 50 per delegate would be saved for the corpus fund of the NAGI. Thiruvanthampuram honorably sent a cheque of Rs 10,450. One wonders why more could not have been saved and sent (Table 30).

Table 30 : Liberal Expenditure on the Indian Geography Congress*

Head	**Rupees**
Printing of Abstract, Souvenir, Stationery and Seminar Bag	85,751.00
Travel (including local) Expense	83,525.00
Food and Accommodation	1,29,730.00
Honorarium for Memorial Lecture	6,000.00
Indian Geography Congress Proceedings Publication	30,842.00
Auditor's Fee	4,000.00
Refund to NAGI	10,450.00
Contribution to Annals' Printing	13,800.00
Miscellaneous	5,060.00
Total	3,69,158.00

**Based on the Financial Statement of the 19th Indian Geography Congress, held at Thiruvanthampuram, 1997*

From super star to low star a line needs to be mutually drawn, which both the hosts and guests agree to respect as the minimum acceptable limits of service, something like a slab of basic needs. Austerity is afterall a time tested way to refuel the bank balance. In the 22 Indian Geography Congresses, even if Rs 20,000 had been saved at each occasion, NAGI today would have been richer by Rupees 0.5 million. While without doubt, the honest intentions of the hosts are warmth and hospitality but these bills could well have prevented NAGI from being hospitalized!

Why has NAGI suffered severe abuse? After all among its members are some of the most handpicked Indian geographers. Take the designation of its life members, authors of its research articles and the status of its founder members and presidents. All belong to the group of the highly educated wherein. professors, readers, lecturers constitute the lion's share (Table 31).

Table 31 : Academic Designation of Life Members of NAGI, 2000

Designation	Founder members	Per cent to total	No. of life members	Per cent to total	No. of authors	Per cent to total
Professor	17	100	101	13	68	28
Reader	—	—	127	16	42	18
Lecturer	—	—	507	64	26	11
Research Scholar	—	—	^	^	26	11
Scientists	—	—	14	2	51	22
Others**	—	—	40	5	24	10
Total	17	100	789	100	237	100

Note : ** *Life members and authors for whom the designation was not available have been excluded.*
^ *Category was not made.*

One knows more by fact than data that most life members and authors have acquired a doctorate, nearly all teach either at the under-graduate or post-graduate level in the university, many have chaired departments, most have supervised research, some have written research papers and authored books. A fist full of NAGI members have even been appointed to the position of vice-chancellor. India today has 248 Universities, each headed by a vice-chancellor. From the community of geographers, 14 are estimated to have held this office, in varying capacity for different lengths of time (Table 32).

Of this group of vice-chancellors, nearly half have been Presidents of NAGI. Yet, virtually penniless, landless, and loveless the plight of NAGI bonds with the millions of poor in India. While it is clamored that the poor in India are a victim to their illiteracy and ignorance, situated amidst an highly educated and affluent gentry of members, NAGI ekes an existence of poorest of the poor.

From where does the Casualness, Carelessness, Callousness come ? Why do a host of maladies afflict this only national level geographical association in India?

Table 32 : Geographers as Vice-Chancellors in Universities of India till 2000

Name	University	Office in NAGI
Ahmad, E.	Ranchi	—
Ahmad, F.	Hyderabad	—
Alam, M.	Srinagar	President
Das, H.P.	Gauhati	President
Dayal, P.	Magadh	President
Desai, A.B.	Gujarat	—
Gupte, S.C.	Pune	—
Misra. R.P	Allahabad	President
Mukherjee, S.	Kalyani	—
Ram, L.N	Patna	President
Raza, M.	Delhi	President Twice
Shafi, M.	Aligarh	President
Singh, R.L.	Meerut	—
Tewari, C.B.	Meerut	—

I have not reached an all-encompassing or perfect explanation. It is commonly agreed that individuals are products of both their genes and the environment – while a biological and genetic inquiry of each specie of this Association is well beyond my expertise, as a geographer I am tempted to explore the academic environment in the universities of India when NAGI was growing up. For let us not forget that NAGI was largely a product of the departments of geography in the universities of India. The majority of its members, 100 per cent of its presidents, 70 per cent of the authors of NAGI are men of the university. Of the 22 Indian Geography Congress, 77 per cent were held in a department of geography within different campuses of India. What was happening in universities of India in the last 20 years? Does NAGI mirror the ethos of the academic community at large? An insight into the milieu of the departments of geography between 1980 –2000 could be one possible frame of reference for understanding the plight of this national association. An association, afterall, is an assemblage of a species of community within a particular environment.

Ninteen Eighty is not a turning point in the history of geography in India. In this year no important geographical discovery, research or work was published by geographers in India. No exclusive center for geographical studies was inaugurated. Neither was any geographer in India awarded any glory or fame. No geographer of repute died this year. It could have been an ordinary year. Yet I choose to elect 1980 as a watershed because in this year NAGI created a hatrick– the first Indian Geography Congress, the first Presidential Address and the first manuscript of the NAGI Annals, all cluster in this one year alone.

When NAGI set to sail strong winds of change began to blow in the universities of India. Despite a pronged anchor of the meet, members, and journal the crew of NAGI rode rather than steer the tide. Where did these winds come from? Which direction did they blow? Has their intensity ebbed?

Again I have neither a perfect nor a complete answer. I do believe that when a similar set of questions are posed even with reference to the planetary winds blowing across the earth there is no satisfactory answer - only descriptions and some correlations are forthcoming. Hemmed within this 'universal limitation', I gather strength to describe some of the characteristics which gripped universities in India between 1980 –2000, the time when NAGI was gaining ground.

Environment for NAGI - 1980-2000

In every department of the university in India much has altered during the two decades from 1980 - 2000. Permanent and long chairmanships have yielded to short and temporary terms of service in chair; the limited scope for promotions has been converted into a mass scale agenda, remotely distanced examinations have replaced the personalized screening of admission to courses offering a research degree, student strength in departments have swollen from a handful to hundreds. Pressing demands on the exchequer have created mal-distribution of limited financial resources. Salaries have taken precedence over replacement and maintenance of infrastructure. Much of this was not achieved peacefully; strong unions backed strikes on the campus to make headway with demands. As tranquillity gave way to turmoil, quality both in teaching and research got sacrificed on the altar of quantity. I enrolled as a post-graduate student in department of geography, University of Delhi in the session of 1980. An eyewitness report is an anemometer of the milieu of events. Here is mine.

The University of Delhi was set up in 1857. It took 102 years time lag to create a department of geography under its tutelage. Established in 1959, the habitat of the department was the Delhi School of Economics. At birth it was signatured the Department of Human Geography. In 1976, the prefix 'human' was dropped, and since then it has been department of geography. Curiosity of why it had been named Human involved a search among the attic of historical records. "At the Delhi School of Economics we have named this department as the Department of Human Geography for a specific reason - - - when students of economics study problems to agricultural economics, they do not know anything about the natural conditions of the region , when we had to select certain clusters of regions for the purpose of our study, we found that we were right at the heart of the problem which was of a geographical character. We thought we needed a Department of Human Geography for the simple reason that we wanted to emphasize that a particular part of geography is closely allied to economics, political science and also agricultural economics." This was the explanation given by the then Director of the School, B.N. Ganguli in the inaugural year of the Department of Geography. (Ganguli B.N. 1959)

The department at Delhi School of Economics had gained repute as a center for urban and regional planning, by the 1970s, but in 1980s it had no tag of specialization, I think it little cared to boast about a single track agenda, more over this dilution was a corollary to the changes in the university where it became no longer possible to toe the entire faculty in a single cart. Monocultures are anyway known to be unsuccessful in the longrun. The university of Delhi introduced the principle of rotation of chairmen in its departments as early as the 1970s. Rotation freed the departments from the shackles of long rule of one person and his all-abiding area of research interest. In the university of Delhi, all appointments of chairmen were however, confined to teachers of the professors rank. In 1980 the department of geography had only one professor, three readers and four lecturers. Finances were tight but the dedication of teachers made learning a pleasure. There was no specialization nor was there any choice to opt for certain courses of study, but ecological and environmental studies formed a good quarter of the curriculum. In fact, in the 1980s these were courses unique to geography and in the School neither the discipline of Economics nor Sociology had ventured into this field. The pride of the School was the Ratan Tata Library, whose 96 national and international periodicals on geography and over 10,000 books were a treasure available for long hours. The library remained open from 8 in the morning to 10 at night and did not shut down even on public holidays.

The department of geography carried a welkin of sedate conservatism; where teaching was given precedence over research. In the air of apparent calm, however, there lurked an uncomfortable tension. Unable to curl upward on the career graph, majority of the faculty members felt stagnated. The pyramid of promotions in the university was narrow at the top and broad at the base, few professors and too many lecturers was the structure of things. This blocked the path to promotion. A sense of frustration ran rampant among the majority of teachers at the University of Delhi. The seething frustration fuelled its 5000 odd teachers to go on strike in 1983. Heralding a victory for the Delhi University Teachers Association, this 109 day long strike ushered in the Merit Promotion Scheme. It was a watershed in the life of the University of Delhi and for this matter universities across India. With this scheme lecturers were promoted to grades of readers and readers to that of professors on the length of their service. Some conditions of research work were applied, but these at best were chimerical. The success of collective action stirred the power of unions, and strikes by teachers, karamcharis and students was to thereafter become a way of life on the campus. Between 1997 - 2000 the Delhi University Teachers Association alone called a strike, for nearly 114 days. Ninety per cent were for pay revisions. While the tradition of taking classes was unique to the Delhi School of Economics, yet the politically charged atmosphere on the campus embroiled the best of brains and the most neutral among the faculty of members.

The Merit Promotion Scheme overnight inverted the structure of faculty at the Delhi School of Economics, from a single professor, the department of geography had 3 more on the rolls in in the course of a year. Whereas a report of the University Grants Commission Review Committee of Geography in India for 1968 categorically states "out of 20 Departments of Geography for which data has been collected, as many as 9 do not have a single Professor", by mid 1990s, professors dominate the scene. This summersault took place in departments of geography universally across India:

Table 33 : Inverted Structure of Faculty in Departments of Geography, 1965 – 2000

Year	Designation			Total
	Professor	Reader	Lecturer	
1965	7 (9)	17 (22)	53 (69)	77 (100)
1995	40 (36)	40 (36)	30 (28)	110 (100)

Based on Association of Indian Universities, 2001.
Data in parenthesis is per cent to the total faculty. Requisite information was available for only 10 departments.

How 'merit promotions' have impacted on the quality of teaching and research is difficult to correlate. Some claim that this 'mercy' rather than 'merit' scheme has murdered incentives for research and serious teaching, others say it was introduced simply because teachers had done little research, while some vehemently suggest that an inner fire fuels work which no external force can ignite or extinguish. In the debate, the teacher-friendly promotion packages have gained ground and these are baits unions commonly use to garner votes. One fact remains, the virtually assured security of promotions restricted the movement of faculty from one department to the other and dawdled the spirit of healthy competition which at times is an essential incentive for work.

The relationship between teaching and research or performance for promotion has not been exclusively altered by the Merit Promotion Scheme.

The University Grants Commission introduced a public examination to test the eligibility of candidates for academic appointments throughout the country in 1993. How a few multiple choice and essay type answers can judge the aptitude of teaching and research of students remains to date a mystery for me. I have seen many students, who failed the Test, have written better dissertations and made lucrative careers, while those who have qualified the Test have fatigued even to complete their thesis. Whatever the paradox, qualifying the Test gained a point of greater jubilance than acquiring a degree in research. It became the legitimized visa for appointments not only in teaching but also in government sponsored research projects. A degree in research got reduced to a weight less than that of its papers worth.

By 1982, I had completed the Master of Philosophy from the School. Interleaved between a post-graduation and a doctorate, a Master of Philosophy course had been introduced in the University in 1977. The motto behind its introduction was an urge to upgrade and strengthen training in research. The National Entrance Test wiped the Master of Philosophy and the Doctorate off their high pedestal. Though students continued to enroll for these programs, the grist to strive for excellence was dampened.

While departments in the university were still absorbing the rapid onset of these changes, a high tide of students seeking enrollment knocked at its shores. In 1980 I was one among a small batch of 23 students pursuing a post-graduate degree, by 1990 numbers swelled to 63. A three times growth in 10 years. News of similar additions comes from across India. Chandigarh, Patna and Utkal, all record an equivalent demographic surge (Table 34).

Table 34 : Demographic Surge of Post-Graduate Students in Departments of Geography, 1960 –2000

University	Year of establishment of the department	No. of students				
		1960	1970	1980	1990	2000
Chandigarh	1959	17	46	40	32	40
Delhi	1959	5	n.a.	23	63	50
Patna	1949	17	25	32	50	55
Utkal	1970	0	8	16	32	48

Based on information published in department souvenirs, handbooks and journals or office records.

The rise in enrollment is not to be read as a sign of growing popularity of geography as a discipline of study. Nearer truth would be the fact that India's growing population hungered for a degree in higher education as a passport to secure better jobs or gain access into the Indian Administrative Services. In the case of the latter, the competitive examination for the services includes geography as one of the optional papers. This bloated the strenght of classrooms in departments of geography. I suspect that the comparative ease to gain admission in geography vis-a-vis other social sciences, like economics and sociology where competition was stiff, also contributed to the swelling number in geography. From 1980-2000, the addition of new departments in geography also nose-dived to less than 10. A distinct slackening compared with the earlier decades (Table 35).

Table 35 : Fewer Births of Departments of Geography, 1980 - 2000

Decade	No. of new post – graduate departments*
1931 – 1940	1
1941 – 1947	3
1948 – 1950	2
1951 – 1960	9
1961 – 1970	12
1971 – 1980	5
1981 – 1990	6
1991 – 2000	0

*Note : * The total number of departments is 78, but the precise year of establishment could be ascertained for only 38 departments, while for 40 departments the decade of establishment could be known.*

The lack of emergence of new centers also funneled students into the existing departments of geography. The process of demographic expansion was unplanned. Seats were created to satisfy misplaced demands and had little in common with an allurement for geography. Unfortunately, the process took an enviable toll as far as quality was concerned.

Growth in numbers was not assisted by a supplement in financial grants, expanded class room space, or additional faculty. Numerical pressure claimed its toll through overcrowded classrooms and declining teacher-student ratios. In the department of geography at the Delhi School of Economics, the cartographic lab was converted into a classroom, while classrooms gave way to additional space for the office. Finances too were meager. The University Grants Commission provides an annual grant of Rs. 1,784,530 to the department of geography at the School. (Kapur A. 1998). Of this, only a lump sum of Rs. 20,144 is given to meet the stationery and other equipment needs of 100 post-graduate, 40 research and half dozen faculty members. It is a paltry Rs. 135 per head, not enough to even purchase a notebook, pen and pencil! Stingy grants left little in their wake to undertake fieldwork, shop for surveying instruments or to modernise the laboratories. While in the 1980s, one managed domestic house keeping by reorganising curriculum and dropping field trips, in the 1990s squeeze on funds began to pinch severly. Demands to purchase machines like computers, scanners and software packages were costly and could just not be fulfilled.

The lax and near defiant attitude of the staff which man laboratories and libraries were a spoke which also slowed the grind of work. Cartographic laboratories became near redundant and outmoded equipment rusted in corridors and junk rooms. The installation of private xerox machines added to mass duplication of notes and reading material and thus kicked the culture of referencing in the library. With very few students occupying the 110 seating capacity in the main reading hall the shutters of the Ratan Tata Library today are pulled down by six in the evening.

In the decades of 1980 to 2000 much in the departments of geography changed – the Merit Promotion Scheme, National Entrance Test, unions, and strikes, demographic growth, financial crunch, and lax karamcharis and students, this however was not the end. Universities lost shine but they still remained a haven for those seeking employment – the security of time bound promotions, limited hours of teaching and practically no strings attached to performance converted vacancies into golden pastures that means fair and foul all were deployed to gain a position. The result, as universities in India today are blighted by shortsighted meanness so typical of second rate academics and municipal politicians, one began to notice that teaching was reduced from a profession to a job. Few cared to even understand the distinction. I secured a post as a lecturer in my own alma - mater in 1998. The School where I came to learn and the one where I began to teach was a very different place.

Two decades drew to an end. Departments of Geography in India failed to make a durable mark. Lukewarm in their commitment, split into hostile factions, they exist inflicted with maladies which the National Association of Geographers, India strongly mirrors. Given its maligned performance should NAGI shut shop? Should a replacement for NAGI be created?

Surprisingly, its most hard core critics are not in favor of either the annihilation of this association or starting a new venture. NAGI continues to find empathetic response. After all despite the climate of turmoil, NAGI had the metal to survive. No other association today has come to threaten its national image. To continue a postmortem of search for its maladies would be like living stuck to the past. But there is little reason for complacency. An adult at 22, NAGI needs to abandon its acts of fun and frolic, unkept promises as well as egoistic conflicts and forge ahead. The crying needs of the discipline summon it to set to work. What could NAGI do?

To scrub off its tarnished image and redeem its position, NAGI needs to heed the basic necessities of the discipline of geography. After all, NAGI's desire to do something meaningful would depend largely on the breadline of the discipline. The needs of any discipline could range from funds to faculty, workspace to machines, writing books to establishing libraries, and training and finding placements for students. The list is ever evolving and endless. Like tributaries to a river system, all the needs could be poured into an association, there can be many roles, many ways of selection, many ways of prioritization, many types of blue prints – here is mine.

Needs of Indian Geography and Role for NAGI

Uncounted and disintegrated within itself, riddled with disparities, torn with issues of standards, tepid and out of tune with research and unable to bolster its status are the hallmarks of the discipline of geography in India in 2000. Within this rests the role for NAGI.

Census for Integration : Teaching is the main occupation of geographers in India. Schools, colleges, and departments in the university are their main domiciles for work. A count among a small sample of geographers forms the basis for this news. The Directory of Indian Geographers, The National Committee for Geographers, 1968 lists 798 geographers. Of this 87 per cent are teaching in the departments of geography. A decade later, a directory of Who's Who of Geographers in India, published in 1978 lists 803 geographers, and of this 14 per cent are not directly involved in teaching. A glimpse of the life members of the National Association of Geographers, India reveals that of a total of 789 for which designations were available, ninety three per cent were in university and only one per cent in schools. These samples are too small, and updation is the need of the hour. In a sense they are misleading for the number of geographers in schools exceeds far more than the ones in the university. The reason is that geography along with history is a staple ingredient of social science studies taught at all levels in the 0.7 million schools of India. Not all schools have a geography teacher. Even among the 98000 higher secondary schools, where an in-depth knowledge of the discipline is a pre-requisite, geographers are missing. In a random sample among the schools in Delhi, only 1 in 3 had a geographer. If the capital which houses three departments of geography, one at University of Delhi, second at Jawahar lal Nehru University and third at Jamia Millia University, faces this famine it would be fair to estimate that less than a quarter of the higher secondary schools in India have a geographer on their rolls. This is about 20,000 geographers. The school teachers evoke the seeds of interest in the discipline, and thus ensure the crop which later comes to flower in colleges and departments. A strength of the community of geographers in schools across India needs to be known.

Though seemingly easy to grasp, when compared to schools, a count of the presence of geographers in colleges and departments is also fraught with problems. Here is an attempt. India today has a total of 248 universities (including 40 with the status of deemed). Among these, only 78 have departments of geography, as listed by the Association of Indian Universities, 2000. The matter is not that simple. For instance, Bihar has 8 universities but 20 centers for post - graduate teaching, 8 at the level of the department and 12 run through the principals of colleges. Of the 10,555 colleges in universities across India in 2000, how many offer under–graduate and others post– graduate teaching is still not known. Take the University of Delhi, it today has 68 colleges under its wings. Out of these, only 12 colleges offer courses in geography, and that too at the under-graduate level. On the other extreme is the Jawahar lal Nehru University which has no college under its jurisdiction and therefore offers no under-graduate teaching. How many geographers are there in the departments of geography in the universities of India? A sample from 45 universities across India gave a total of 384 members in the faculty. Taking an average of 9 members puts the total at 702 in the 78 departments of geography. Adding triple the number in colleges means an addition of 1900 to 2500 geographers. The dilemma of the number of geographers in the university needs to be solved beyond conjectures and estimates.

Cartography is one known skill of geographers that gives placements in different type of institutions . Take the Census of India which alone engages 90 to 100 geographers. With 419 geographer-cartographers on their pay rolls, the National Atlas and Thematic Mapping Organization is another body of recruitment. Besides the concentration in these two institutes, a more fragmented occurrence of geographer-cartographers is found in a host of other centers such as the National Institute of Urban Affairs, Geological Survey of India, Wadia Institute of Himalayan Geology along with some private business houses. The ones trained on the electronic format and skilled at digitizing and using softwares of Geographical Information System are new entrants. What is their exact pool?

Serving as urban and regional planners, land use and environmental planners in the capacity of research assistants or members of teams are a handful of geographers in India. Employed within the Town and Country Planning Organizations and Regional and State Planning Boards, these are geographers who have taken the subject beyond the walls of academia into its applied role. How many and where are they? A scrutiny of the membership of the Institute of Town Planners in Delhi, and discussions with a renowned town planner leads to the conclusion, " geographer-planners are a modest 400 to 500". One needs to go beyond harnessing guesses. India has a number of social science and development centers, and other research institutes. What is the strength and status of geographers within these centers?

Unaccounted and fragmented is the existence of the community of geographers in India, though the discipline is common to all, yet nothing and no one welds them together. Isolated and out of reach with each other, the evolving theoretical and conceptual underpinnings of the discipline does not cross travel. The result is that each interprets the discipline in their own myopic way. Is it not time to assess the problems and potentials of different practitioners of geography? Is it not time to raise a platform to integrate all of them? India's largest association of geographers needs to heed this lack. After all, it pays rich dividends to conduct a census.

A headcount of geographers, the first of its kind in the history of geography in India, would take NAGI to the heart of every geographer and expand its base for membership and subscription to its Annals. These are peripheral profits, an assessment of the resource of geographers in terms of number and type will help enroll new talent, discover latent roles and open scope for wider interaction, exchange of ideas and experiences with the community. The labor to conduct a census is, of course, unavoidable, but as the discipline benefits, NAGI will reap the fruits. Not a single but a bonanza is what NAGI needs to bag. Stretching to rank and then bridge the disparities is another role for the Association.

Ranking to Bridge Disparities : The centers for in-depth learning of geography are supposed to be the departments of geography. There is, however, considerable variation between the intellectual environs of the 78 departments across the country. A fertile mix of faculty, facilities, and students create the intellectual ground for learning and research in a department. Unfortunately today no department of geography in India can claim even a near perfect combination on all the three fronts. Many are bankrupt on all three grounds. Bitter but true. Should departments in India not be ranked in intellectual competence? Ranking does trigger debates about the means and modes of exercise, but the fear of ruffling feathers should not halt this inquiry. After all, it is only by assessing disparity can bridges be built. To date geographers in India have addressed the discipline as if there is a uniform group of faculty, students, and facilities in all its departments. In terms of the rigours of teaching, research, and imparting skills, a wide chasm separates departments across the country. It could well be argued that disparity exists even within a batch of a single class of students, true but I have seen that a 2 to 4 year exposure in one department grinds the sharp discrepancies and brings most students to what one can call a "minimum common level". Across India, departments of geography are dissimilar in age, size, faculty, and infrastructure. (Fig. 7)

On one side we have departments as old as Aligarh where post-graduation began in 1933 and on the other hand are ones in North East Hill University which saw an inception in 1973. A sample of 38 out of the 78 post graduate departments shows that nearly 39 per cent have a standing as old as 40 years, some having crossed the quarter-century mark , while 16 per cent are yet to reach the adulthood figure of 21 years. One half of the departments in India are younger than 35 years. How does age bear upon the character? Perhaps accumulated resources and a stable faculty is a hallmark of the older and long established ones, while the younger still grope to collect funds and fix the strength of its members. The halo of a past glory is one tag which age has definitely added to the prestige of the older established departments (Table 36).

Table 36 : Age of Departments of Geography in India, 2000

Year of establishment	Age as in 2000	No. of departments	Per cent to total
Before 1960	39 and More	15	39
1960 - 1979	19 – 39	17	45
1980-2000	19 and less	6	16
Total		38	100

Based on data for 38 departments of geography for which year of establishment could be precisely ascertained.

The governance of universities also lays impact upon a department. It is claimed that in terms of autonomy, functioning and finance Central Universities are overall better than the ones under the control of the State, while lesser benefits gravitate to the ones deemed to be university (Table 37).

Table 37 : Departments of Geography According to University Governance, 2000

Type of University	No. of departments	Per cent to total
Central	8	11
Regional*	1	1
State	68	87
Deemed	1	1

Note: Regional University is one which is funded by both Centre and State.*

Out of the 18 Central Universities in India, geography is in 8; no less than 68 are in State Universities. What divides the departments of geography most sharply is the financial support. Here the Special Assistance Programme, under the auspices of the University Grants Commission, creates a sea of disparity.

Fig. 7 : Department of Geography in Universities of India : 2000
(Named by Place of Location)

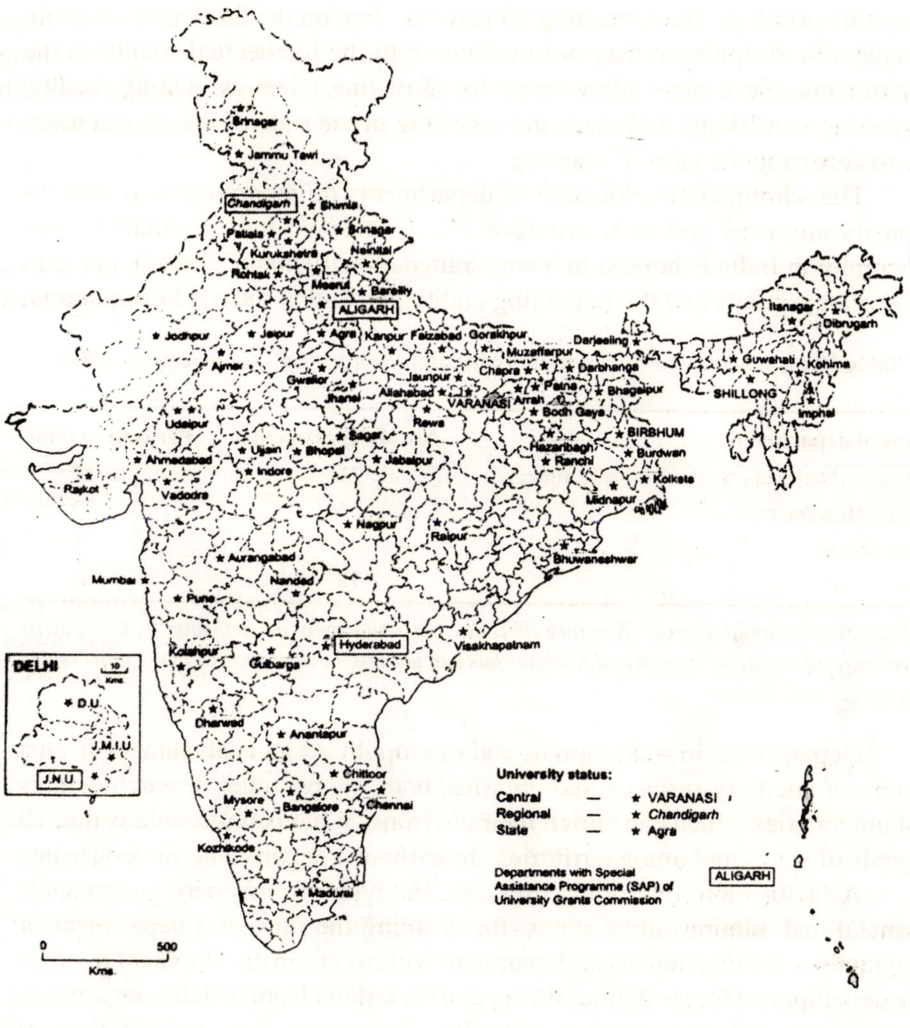

Departments with this programme are flushed with funds touching Rs 50 to 60 lakhs for a term of five years; while ones without this benefit, exist on crumbs less than Rs. 2 to Rs. 5 lakhs. Today, of the 78 departments, only 4 (Aligarh, Osmania (Hyderabad), Jawahar lal Nehru University, (Delhi) and Chandigarh) enjoy this privilege, the remaining 95 per cent live on the brink of starvation. The payoffs of opulence may not measure upto the intellectual wealth in the departments, but it does allow scope for attracting talent as visiting faculty, organizing workshops, seminars and investing in the state of the art machines for modernizing the labs of mapping.

The administrative location of departments of geography also impacts upon its environs and infrastructure. From metropolitan to small towns, geography in India is housed in a wide range of settlements. Twenty per cent are in state capitals and the remaining eighty per cent at district headquarters.

Table 38 : Administrative Status of the Venue of the Departments of Geography -2000

Venue of department	**No. of departments**	**Per cent to total**
Capitals* (National / State / Union Territory)	21	27
District Headquarters	56	72
Other places	1	1
Total	78	100

*Note : *The National Capital Territory of Delhi has geography departments at three of its universities; the state of Jammu and Kashmir has two geography departments at the universities of Srinagar and Jammu.*

Departments in state capitals and metropolitans gain advantages from a variety of ancillary services like libraries, book shops, other research centres and universities which can enrich their environs. What is noticeable is that 10 capitals of states and union territories are without a department of geography.

A factor more overriding than age, the type of university governance, financial and administrative status, for deciding the rank of a department of geography is the location of the department within certain development regions. The development locale defines the type of hinterland from which a department draws its strength of students and faculty. One cannot disagree with the fact that the department of geography, lets say at Patiala in Punjab vis-à-vis Muzaffarpur in Bihar, enjoys advantages which are governed largely by its administrative merits and development index of the area in which it is placed. After all, departments cannot escape or isolate themselves from the socio-economic disparities which grip India. A classification of the departments along the lines of development indicators sets an overwhelming number amidst regions of low and moderate index (Table 39).

Table 39 : Development Index of Districts in which Departments of Geography are Located

Development index*	Number of departments	Per cent to Total
High (>125)	34	44
Medium (75–125)	24	31
Low (<75)	20	25

*Note : *National Average 100.*
For details on development index, refer Figure 1., Presidential Address, G.Krishan, p. no. 425

As islands of prosperity do exist amidst the sea of impoverishment, so also a brilliant teacher and student does root in any variety of setting. This, however, is the exception rather than the rule.

Disparity along the above list of indicators inpacts strongly upon the level of geographic literacy which is imparted and acquired in a department. The interpretation and absorption of a curriculum , the vigor of research and the availability of sources of literature, in some manner or other, are a product of the habitat of the department of geography. Many could refute and reject the relationship between all the above-mentioned indexes in influencing the intellectual rank of a department. Some would be tempted to suggest that the correlation to establish an intellectual rank needs to be worked out, others could lament that these are proxy indicators, while some could say that they are spurious–all such reactions confirm the need to evolve measures to rank departments. A list of the faculty, their publications, number of national and international scholarships bagged by a department, number of projects completed, the distance from which a department draws its students, and the placement record of the alumni of a department and many more could help create a meaningful rank of the 78 departments of geography in India. Only by identifying the disparities can one hope to create measures to merge the gulf. Who else but the National Association of Geographers, India is adept to take on this task? Its list of life members draws multiple representation from all departments of geography, the venue of the Indian Geography Congress could well serve as the melting pot sensitizing geographers to the strengths and weaknesses of their departments, and initiating a search for modalities to overcome the gaps. By promoting quality through managing quantity, NAGI could fill another pressing but latent need of the discipline .

Managing Numbers : Each year the departments of geography have a turn-out of about 4000 to 5000 post-graduate students and doctoral candidates. A simple calculation forms the basis of this estimate. On an average around fifty students pass the post-graduate examinations every year from a single department. Taking 78 departments puts the annual collective turnover to 3650 geographers. An annual addition of hundred doctorates is data derived from the total doctorates conferred in geography in the last 20 years by universities in India. The Master of Philosophy program is not a universal course of study in all the departments; but data from three universities Delhi, Panjab and Bihar, puts the average ratio of Doctorates of Philosophy vis-à-vis Masters of Philosophy at 1:4. The addition of another 400 geographers, takes the tally to over 4000. A margin of around 1000 has been added to give leverage to the geographers which gain a post- graduation through colleges, though they could well be more or less. Only a census can bring accuracy to these estimates. The question is not simply how many geographers does India produce each year but it is more vital to know how many does she need ? What type of geographers are in demand? Are we managing numbers?

With a rolled degree in hand, 5000 geographers head for the streets to earn a livelihood. Does the discipline of geography equip them for tasks ahead? In the years preceding 1980s expanding number of schools, colleges and some research institutions did absorb a majority of geographers. Teaching soaked the supply, in fact if one recalls, the 1960s and 1970s were times when many joined the faculty at ages as young as 22 to 23 , some were also accommodated from even other streams such as geology, commerce and mathematics. (Table 5). Such rosy times are certainly not on the cards today. The long queues of even first class students at the doorstep of the university are proof to the despairing situation. Has geography in India reached saturation in terms of the scope for inaugurating new departments? There are two ways in which the question can be answered. One by comparing the number of departments in geography vis-a-vis numbers in other social sciences and the other by taking a count of the potential universities in which there is an absence of a department of geography. A comparison with economics and sociology shows that geography trails to half when compared with economics and short of nearly 20 when compared with sociology . A flash back to the situation in the mid 1970s points to the fact that gaps have widened (Table 40).

Table 40 : Lesser Number of Departments of Geography vis-à-vis other Social Sciences

Discipline	No. of departments	
	1970*	2000**
Economics	69	148
Sociology	49	92
Geography	48	78

*Based on : *Indian Council of Social Science Research, 1973, and **Association of Indian Universities, 2001.*

Another view to the potentials for expansion of geography is the universities without a department of geography. Today there are 57 universities where geography could be started. These are universities apart from ones of engineering, medicine, management, agriculture or language. Nearly half of the universities where there is scope for department of geography have been in existence for over twenty years. The prospects of adding the numerical count of department of geography are thus most promising.

Table 41 : Universities with a Scope for Starting a Department of Geography.

Year	No. of potential universities*
Before 1900	1
1900 - 1910	1
1910 - 1920	0
1920 - 1930	3
1930 - 1940	1
1940 - 1950	1
1950 - 1960	4
1960 - 1970	4
1970 - 1980	6
1980 - 1990	19
1990 - 2000	17
Total	57

*Based on : Association of Indian Universities, 2001. *For explanation, see the text.*

However demanding like a piece of cake just because another discipline has it or a university is without a department is hardly a valid argument to push one's case. One has to work to deserve a slice of goods. The flip side of managing numbers is fulfilling needs of society. In the 1960s paying heed to the call of urban and regional planning, geographers framed their curriculums and research in this direction, while some marked attendance in leading planning organizations. Though ephemeral and weak, yet their efforts to contribute towards the development needs of India did bring a booty of rewards to the discipline and allowed scope for placements to expand.

When environmental issues trumpeted loud on the streets of India in the mid-1980s, geographers turned a deaf ear. Despite defining and defending their discipline for years as a study of interrelationships between man and environment, it was the social activists and not the geographers who drew the attention of the country to its burgeoning environmental problems. Leaving aside being leaders, even as sequel, geographers did not champion policies, or take front rank positions in the Ministry of Environment and other public offices.

Neither have they produced vibrant literature on this theme. Disciplines like economics, sociology and even the pure sciences like botany and chemistry clawed away the recognition. A fertile ground of contributing to the needs of India and managing numbers by advancing in this direction was thus lost .

Two powerful forces in early 1990s evoked universities to respond to new demands of the society. Firstly, the information technology, and secondly the wave of privatization and globalization. Both have created new avenues of employment among the private sector. While the latter gave birth to a fresh set of disciplines like Management, Finance, Business Studies, Human Resource Development and Computer Sciences in universities, it is the information technology which hit squarely questioning the adequacy of the departments of geography in India. Cartography, the science of information processing through graphicacy got a new lease of life with information technology both from computer automation and imageries. The latter created a virtual deluge through quickly relayed remote sensed imageries of all parts of the earth, and the former made it possible to quickly assemble, correlate and convert information into digestible knowledge for making decisions. Availability of computer software specifically called the Geographic Information Systems means that the discipline of geography was to be its most ardent and fervent applicant. Though this software lies firmly within the ambit of geography yet departments in India failed to deliver a timely response to the demand. Geographic Information Systems had been in use in geography in the United States of America since 1970s. Till 2000, of the 78 departments offering post-graduation only five offered this in their curriculam of courses. Of these, barely three had labs fitted with adequate machines and minds to train and conduct research. More than just being crippled by finances and lack of trained faculty, it is the slumbered posture of geographers which blocked them from preempting and responding to the prime time need of the hour.

The departments of geography have to assume an obligation to equip their future generations to met the demands placed by the society. Students of the subject have a right to master technologies which can be useful and are going to be increasingly used, and without which they can sometimes feel second class citizens in the sphere of opportunities in industry. In no way does this imply that the quality of a geographer should be measured only by the elegance and sophistication of his geographic information system wardrobe. The immediate problem is one of balance and proportion in adopting the new yet not throwing out the relevant. Redoing curriculums in a fetish mood of 'modern fashion' is not the answer. In the long run managing numbers is about producing geographers who have both an in-depth and updated understanding of their discipline and can plug in to fulfill the requirements of society.

Managing numbers is not simply a game of inaugurating new departments, initiating a placement cell or advertising job opportunities for geographers in the NAGI Annals. While these can be done alongside, it is the fine tuning of supply to demand which is the kingpin to its success. Geographers can ill-afford to loose opportunities one after the other. To avoid gross mismanagement , NAGI has to take a lead role. A critical landmark can be achieved by initiating an embargo on trade.

Trade Embargo : Two thousand one hundred and thirty two geographers have been conferred the degree of a doctorate in India from 1940 to 2000. The first was given in 1940. The rate of addition of doctorates has seen an unrelenting upward curve since 1982 with a slight dip in 1995 –1996 that quickly picked itself thereafter (Fig. 8).

Half of the doctorates awarded belong to the two decades of 1980's and 1990's. Over the years the number of universities granting a doctorate have shot up from 2 to 84. Not only has the addition of more departments caused this voluminous growth but the average number of doctorates by a single department have more than doubled from 5 in the 1960s to 13 in the 1980s.

The productivity of departments has not been uniform. On one end of the spectrum are a handful of large producers like the department of geography at Banaras which alone has produced 192 thesis, Calcutta and Agra are close competitors for the second position with 123 and 119 doctorates each. On the other end, there are 38 centres which are small producers with less than 10 doctorates in the last six decades.

Age of departments, size of faculty, student strength are factors which influence numbers, but the attitude of mass production of doctorates cannot be overlooked. It is here that the issue of quantity verses quality needs to be brought into daylight.

Table 42 : Increasing Number of Doctorates in Geography in India, 1940 – 2000

Decade	No. of univ. that conferred a doctorate	No. of doctorates	Average no. of doctorates per univ. per decade
1940 – 1949	2	6	3
1950 – 1959	9	24	3
1960 – 1969	24	133	6
1970 – 1979	46	351	8
1980 – 1989	64	804	13
1990 - 2000	98	814	8
1940 – 2000	84*	2132	7

Note: Some universities, which do not have a department of geography, could also grant doctorates which are supervised by faculty in colleges.*

Fig. 8 : Annual Number of Doctorates in Geography : 1940-2000

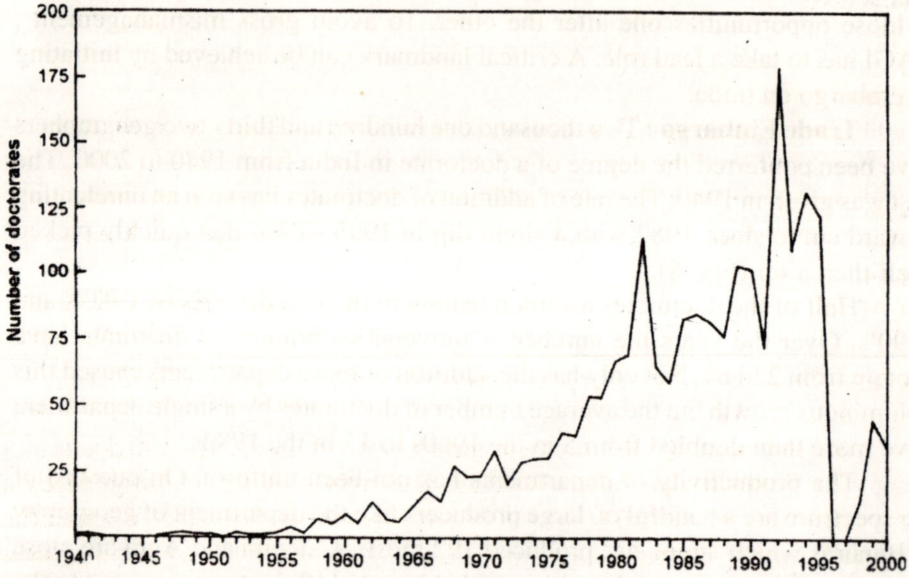

More alarming than the proliferation is the quality of doctorates being submitted in the discipline of geography. All the 2132 doctorates hold the prestigious degree, but examiners admit that only a small percentage are worthy of the prefix Dr. to their name. Passing a verdict is not easy, but interviews with a group of geographers each of whom had supervised and examined above 25 to 50 thesis, did confirm that not more than 15 to 20 per cent of the thesis belonged to A-Grade category. Revisions were rarely sought and most examiners admitted that refusal rather than rejection governed the behavior towards a thesis, poor in content and clarity. Having never supervised or examined a doctorate, yet keen to gain insight into the state of affairs, I read the examiners reports of over 40 dissertations. It seemed rather clear that more students were passed in a mood of compromise rather than competence. The menace gets stronger when one detetecs that a collusive, though subtle, trade operates where supervisors are in league to mutually pass their 'own' candidates.

Table 43 : Frequency Distribution of Doctorates at Departments of Geography in India,1940-2000

No. of doctorates	No. of departments
1-10	37
11- 20	16
21-30	9
31-40	7
41-50	5
51-60	0
61-70	1
71-80	1
81-90	2
91-100	1
> 100	3

Based on : Association of Indian Universities (1940–2000).

Departments of Geography in India today award about a 100 doctorates each year. Who will prevent dilution in the highest of degree awarded by a university? Let us not forget that in the final it is these doctorates who run the engine of the departments. Are we not derailing our discipline by handing over the wheels to the less competent ? Should the National Association of Geographers, India not pledge ways to prohibit such trade and augment high quality research.

Augment and Direct Research : The research output of the discipline stands little match to the total number of departments, geographers and doctorates. Feeble research publication augurs poorly for the intellectual interest and stamina of geographers in India. Whatever be the basis for sizing: the number of books or research papers, score remains poor.

A word limit of 3000 to 5000 is the average requirements for a research publication in a journal in India. This is less than 12 to 15, double spaced sheaves of the standard A-4 size paper. To write even this seems a daunting task for the majority. Less than 0.3 research articles are written annually by geographers in the university departments of India. If the faculty in colleges were added to this, the number would fall to a dismal decimal. The basis of arriving at this odious conclusion: In India there are 15 journals in geography which publish with some regularity. In the 309 overlapping years of their publication they have produced 4070 articles. This gives a number of 13 articles per journal per year. Articles published each year by the journals varies from 16 by the NAGI Annals, 12 by the Geographer of Aligarh and about 20 by the Geographical Review of India from Calcutta. Taking the average at 13 in the 15 journals the total annual production is of 195 articles. The total faculty strength of the 78 departments of geography averages to around 702. The division of 195 articles by 702 members staff members gives a per capita output of 0.3.

The possibility of geographers in India giving preference to publish in a foreign journal was not ruled out. A check spanning 20 years of three international geographical journals, the Annals of the Association of American Geographers, Transactions of the Institute of Geographers and Geographical Review (United Kingdom) proves that publication by geographers in India were conspicuous by their absence. Only 3 out of nearly 2000 articles had been authored by geographers in India (Table 44).

Table 44 : Negligible Number of Research Articles by Indian Geographers in Foreign Joùrnals, 1970 to 2000

Journal	Research articles	
	Total No.	**By Indian geographers**
Annals of the Association of American Geographers	1007 (1970 to1999)	2
Transactions of the Institute of British Geographers	503* (1992 to 1998)	0
Geographical Review	461 (1981 to 1998)	1
Total	1971	3

*Note : * Excluding data for 1990, 1991 and 1999, which could not be accessed.*

Revealing was the anemic state of journals in India which managed to publish only 13 articles per year while the foreign journals are two to three times better fed, containing 30 to 40 articles in one volume.

Not only are geographers in India publishing less but in many cases it is taking more than one geographer to summon an article. It took 355 authors to write 219 articles published by the NAGI Annals. Nearly 100 of the total articles were written by more than one author. While the passion for research is apparently less, the inclination to review seems even lesser. The 36 issues of the NAGI Annals carry only 165 book reviews – this is less than 5 reviews per issue. Even of this small a number, thirty five per cent were written by nine geographers.

Writing books has also not been their forte. A bit more difficult to sum, yet a clue to the forlon state can be deduced from the recommended readings in the curriculums prescribed by departments. Under the umbrella of the University Grants Commission a 12 member team of geographers drawn from leading universities of India designed a model curriculum for geography in 1989. This labored and exhaustive report lists a range of 44 compulsory and optional courses of study for the post-graduate level geography in India. Of its 638 painstakingly drawn list of recommended readings, Indians were author of only 132. In semblance with this low 20 per cent of the total, are the ones in the curricula of the departments at the University of Delhi , Chandigarh and Patna. All these three list over 25 courses of study, in none does the count of books by authors from India cross the one-third mark. A visible drop in this percentage would surely occur if duplicate titles, publications by the Government of India, and non-geographers were to be added.

Table 45 : Indian Authors Listed among Recommended Readings in Curricula of Departments of Geography.

	Curriculum Details			
	Number of courses	**Total readings**	**Readings by Indian authors**	**Per cent to total by Indian author's**
Curriculum Report*1989	44	638	132	20
Delhi, 2000	30	380	104	27
Patna, 2000	27	181	69	38
Panjab, 2000	26	323	73	23

*Note : * G.S. Gosal (1989).*

Concept Publishing Company is one of India's leading publishers of geography books. Engaged for over a quarter century in the business of publishing, they have 185 books by geographers. Edited and co-authored works form an overwhelming 42 per cent of the total geography books published. Editing a book is no blemish, but one would agree that such books, if not carefully crafted, are disintegrative in substance and message. Rarely do they serve as good texts. In India, absence of text books on even the most elementary courses like Environmental Geography, Biogeography and Resource Geography cripple -support material for students to read and learn. Augmenting the needs of writing text books has for long been an agenda of the National Association of Geographers, India. But the spadework to motivate geographers with support and material is a role that NAGI needs to own.

Why do most geographers in India not research and write? The slate of work and hours on the time-tables punctuated by summer, autumn, and winter breaks do give scope to pursue these goals. Freedom from the worry about promotions, assured by the merit promotion career advancement schemes, and with it the need to constantly watch over the shoulder of competing colleagues, more publications from geographers should have been tabled. But this has not been its happy outcome. Like any creative work of art, a book requires a bit of inspiration and lot of perspiration. To enjoy the nectar of belonging to a discipline of repute and status, publications is a dire necessity. Sheer numbers is however not the passport for climbing the rung of high status. The worth of a discipline is not necessarily measured on the scale of number of publications. Geographers even with their small number could have seen an exalted status if, quality out weights pages had been their motto. Unfortunately, this has not been the case.

Quality, an experiential process, is difficult to partition into components such as the structure of a sentence, grammar, accuracy in citing references, originality of ideas, methodology, and the like. Judging the flavor of substance, and style in publications, and sorting them into good, bad and the ugly are highly subjective issues. In the interview with geographers the question of listing 10 best books by Indian geographers drew a heterogeneous response. What was more critical was that nearly all, took a fairly long time to elicit authors, and crossing the mark of 10 best books was difficult. Comments, that most works were pedantic and not simulating, much writing even by senior geographers was bogged by philistine statements and was tepid in character were openly forthcoming. When questioned about the quality of their own works most of them were honest to admit that only a few from their long list were 'gems'. One must admit that evaluating one's own work with detachment is an art which few possess! Acidic comments may provoke strong criticism but just a few can deny that stock lot and barrel geography publications have gained very little in terms of status. Augmenting qualitative production is the need of the discipline. The role of NAGI is to find the ways.

Research is a personal insight into critical problems requiring intellectual attention. No association of geographers can dare to or should dictate the topics for research. However, spelling the broad direction and preempting lucrative areas does add manure for better selection of themes. The purpose of research is, no doubt, a personal gratification, but when integrated with the issues of mainstream concern, it draws greater rewards both at the level of personal satisfaction and the status of the discipline. What have been the themes of research by geographers till 2000? It is difficult to gather and comment on all the research done by geographers in India, therefore, this analysis is restricted to the doctorates and the publications in the NAGI Annals.

I confess, I have not and could not have read the 2132 doctorates undertaken by geographers. I have also not read all the 219 articles published by the NAGI Annals. Instead, by following a careful study of the titles and banking on hindsight too, a rudimentary classification of the themes of research pursued by geographers in India has been worked. Reading all of them no doubt would have perfected the categories. Following a less perfect route added ordeal to the chore. Like a rag picker sorting the wide variety was the first round of experience. The themes were diverse- from slope analysis to health analysis, from study of a historical text on geography to the changes in land use over historical times of a region. Many titles carried overlapping themes, thus deciding whether a study of urban land use is to be part of urban or the land use category, or a study on resources and development belongs to which group became a vexing decision. Adding to the subjectivity were also the general and casual nature of titles. Many titles promised too much, and one wonders if they delivered all that which they pledged. Braving many such haunts, to discern the trends and themes, doctorates were grouped into three phases: pre-1960, 1960 to 1979 and 1980 to 2000. In total terms research on urban, agriculture, and population took a near equal slice followed close on heals by land use. Together these four themes constitute 46 per cent of the total doctorates; a sizeable 974 thesis belong to this cluster (Fig. 9).

The popularity of these core themes have vacillated over the years. Urban has risen to an all time high of 20 per cent in 1960s but crashed down to 10 per cent in 1990 – 2000. Land use has gone the way of the urban. Interest in both population and agriculture has stayed more stable, though agriculture lost some ground in the 1960 to 1979 period. Physical geography has had low attraction. U-shaped valley is the trend of works on environment as a clear sag occurs in the 1960s and 1979. When the world was taking on the agenda of environmental problems, geographers fell into a pit. They did not head the call of the siren. They lost an opportune moment in history to partake and address environmental issues. Gathering speed, as if to make up lost ground, research on environment saw a steep rise to 6 per cent in the 1980 to 2000 when nearly 55 doctorates were submitted. Research articles published in the NAGI Annals follow a near similar trend to doctorates, except that articles on regional planning and development take precedence.

It is seen that geographers research interests in India have fixed to a few themes– does this spell commitment or confinement ? Perhaps more of the latter. Geographers in India are ridden by operating within a comfort zone, choosing topics of research which have precedence in terms of methodology and data sources. A check of the titles in doctorates reads like carbon copies: where the area of study differs but the theme remains virtually the same. To cite an example–take the study of land use in a city, it is followed by hundred similar works where the name of city is changed all else remains the same! Not only is the need to exercise originality missing but geographers have also been immobile where their area of study is concerned.

Fig. 9 : Persistent Themes of Doctoral Research in Geography : 1940-2000

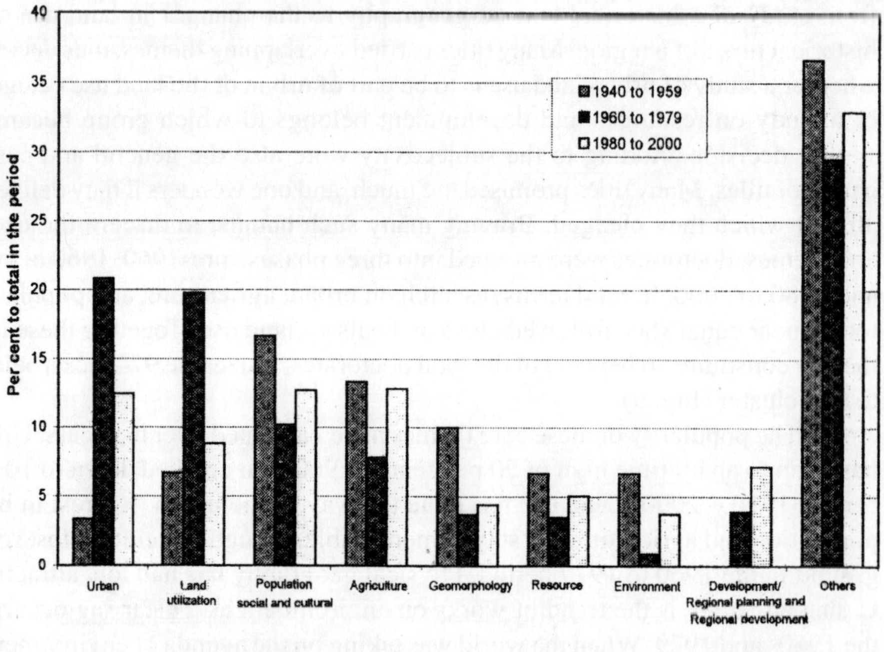

Table 46 : Area Focus of Doctorates vis-à-vis Location of Department of Geography*, 1940-2000

Decade	The same State		Other State/India		Other Countries	
	No.	Per cent to total	No.	Per cent to total	No.	Per cent to total
1940 – 1949	3	50	0	0	1	17
1950 – 1959	11	46	7	29	2	8
1960 – 1969	77	58	33	25	2	2
1970 – 1979	220	63	68	19	12	3
1980 – 1989	578	72	123	15	16	2
1990 – 2000	577	71	140	17	12	1.5

*Note: Association of Indian Universities (1940–2001). *For explanation, see the text.*

A common feature of almost all the doctorates is to confine their geographical area of study to the state or union territory in which the department is located. Nearly 1466 thesis out of the 2132 met this description. Such a tendency has not only persisted , but has been steadily increasing over the decades. (Fig. 10)

Fig. 10 : Spatial Bias in Doctoral Research in Geography 1940-2000

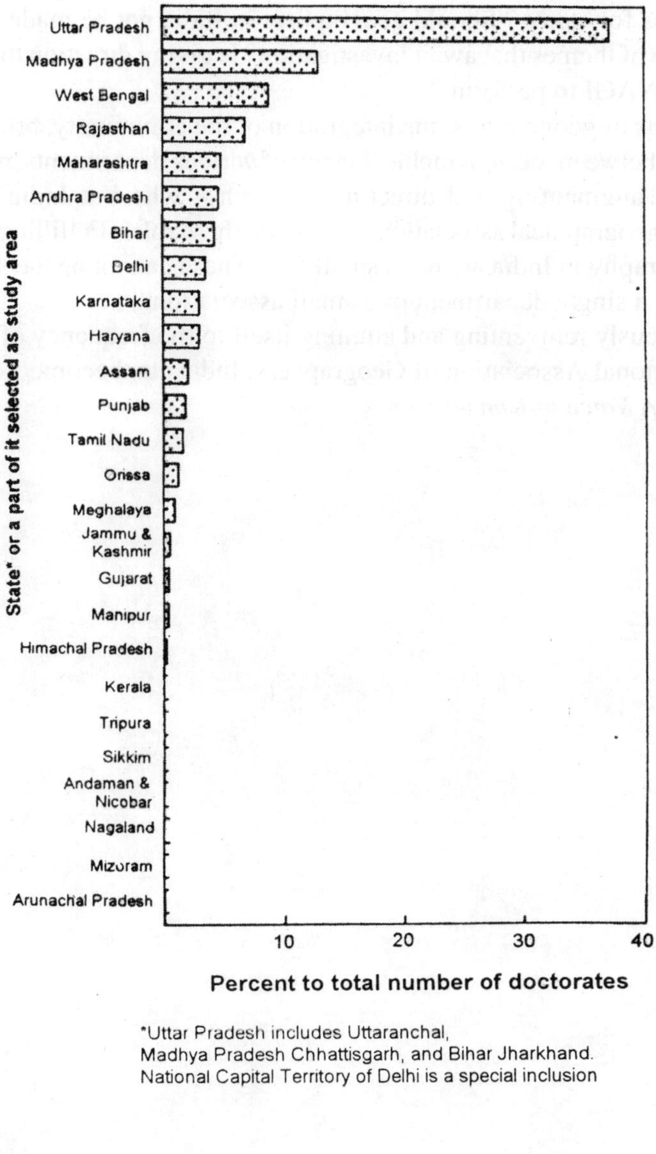

*Uttar Pradesh includes Uttaranchal,
Madhya Pradesh Chhattisgarh, and Bihar Jharkhand.
National Capital Territory of Delhi is a special inclusion

Despite growing accessibility and scope for widening ones comparative understanding of India, the inertia of geographers to stay within their own backyards has increased from 58 per cent in 1960s to 71 per cent in the 1980s. Less than 2 per cent geographers have ventured outside the territorial limits of India. The result is that 65 per cent of the total doctorates relate to Uttar Pradesh, Rajasthan, West Bengal or Bihar, while studies on Kerala, Himachal Pradesh, the North Eastern states and the islands in the Bay of Bengal and the Arabian Sea or macro level works on India have received a low focus of inquiry. Should geographers not be periodically made aware of the need for dispersal in their choice of areas for study ? Should geographers in India not be made aware of the wide range of themes that await investigation? Is giving direction to research not a role for NAGI to perform ?

A census of geographers, the integration of the community, bridging the yawning gaps between the geographic literacy of various departments, managing numbers, and augmenting and directing research – who but India's largest national level geographical association can take on these roles. Fulfilling pressing needs of geography in India are not a small feat. These cannot be the work of a single person, a single department or a small association.

Consciously reinventing and attuning itself to the frequency of an inner voice, the National Association of Geographers, India can become for Indian Geography - *A Voice of Concern.*

Concern for the Voice

What can you say about an Association
That has no land, no hearth,
Low funds, no research project,
No publication, apart from a journal,
Which was has seen a crisis of leadership,
And sees cracks in its foundation ,
what you can say,
about this Association is that ,
Before the end of each year, or
In the beginning of the new,
it spells a
Concern for Indian Geography

Around the time of the year when the shortest day transits to days of longer sunshine, the National Association of Geographers, India is unfurling the flag of the Indian Geography Congress . Ten out of the twenty two Indian Geography Congress have taken place around the 25th to the 28th of December while the remaining half have spilled over into the month of January. A cool climate takes over most parts of India, ensuring that whatever be the venue, the inaugural day of the Congress would be most pleasant in this tropical part of the world. Amidst the traditional ceremony of lighting the lamp, presenting the bouquets and wishing the occasion all success rises the President of the Association to deliver his much awaited address . An august company of distinguished guests and a hall packed with around three hundred geographers all lend an eager ear to the speaker .The president after all is about to spell his perceptions of the state of Indian Geography , rake questions which could lead to path breaking avenues of research and suggest ways to activate the Association he presides.

It would be erroneous to conclude that the 22 presidents of NAGI are the only Indian Geographers who have raised the above inquiry. A select bibliography appended in this book proves that other geographers have also reflected and written about the status of the discipline. Since India has a number of other geographical associations it is well possible that their presidents too have tendered such thoughts. After all, when one writes a key note or a presidential address, it is a momentous time to pause, reflect and condense ones thoughts on critical aspects of the discipline . The position and the platform of a president can cajole even the most reticent to announce the state of the art of their discipline. Whose concerns should one make a note about? Logic demands that opinions of all the reputed geographers should have been included but limited access to resources and time made such an inquiry difficult . Some could suggest that the words of relevant geographers should be weighed. How to sift the relevant from the important is a task riddled by its own set of problems ? The scope of this book is thus confined to the words of the presidents of NAGI. They may seem small in number, yet on different fronts most are among the best in Indian geography. The reason for this qualifying conclusion is not far to seek. A glimpse at the profile of NAGI presidents would set to rest many in doubt.

Profile of NAGI President

All the presidents of NAGI were born in the pre-independence phase of India. Majority share birth years in the 1920s and early 1930s. The average age of the NAGI president is 60 year. Before attaining the honorable position of a president, each has spent a good 20 to 30 years, if not more, in the service of the discipline. The result most of the presidents of NAGI that fall within the bracket of 1980 to 2000, have in a way grown with the discipline. Their assessment and critique of the discipline are thus distilled precipitates of a reservoir of experiences and first hand observations. This does give the presidents of NAGI a place amidst the pioneers in the subject (Table 46).

More than sheer congruence with time is the fact that most of the presidents of NAGI have personally been responsible for inaugurating a department of geography or at least building one from infancy. The role of Dayal, Das, Gosal, Arunachalam, Reddy, Vaidyanadhan cannot be overlooked in building the department at Patna,Gauhati, Chandigarh, Bombay, Tirupati and Waltair respectively. Unique inter disciplinary institutes like the Centre for Regional Development , Jawahar Lal Nehru University, Delhi, the Institute of Development Studies at Mysore and the Centre for Area Studies, at Osmania were the creation of Moonis, Mishra and Alam. One who did not have the opportunity to inaugurate a department or institute played a key role in attracting repute and fame to their respective departments: Shafi and Aligarh, Bhat and Indian Institute of Statistics, Reddy and Tirupati, Gopal and the Panjab University run almost synonymous.

Pursuing a doctorate at a foreign university and returning to India with a fervor to enrich the discipline is a feature common to many of these 'old guards' of Indian Geography. This is evident in the careers of more than half the presidents of NAGI. Dayal, Shafi, Das, Chakraborty, Bhat, Singh, Alam possess a doctorate degree from United Kingdom. Incidentally, Dayal, Shafi, Das and Chakraborty all share the common alma-mater of the Univeristy of London. To the United States of America belong Gosal, Pathak, Misra and Mahadev. Presidents like Gopal who took a doctorate in India, obtained an honours of a

Doctorate of Science in Hungary, while Sundaram also furthered his education from a foreign land . Infact both Gopal and Sundaram were associated with the University of Cambridge in United Kingdom. Indian Geography has attracted scholars from different disciplines – among the presidents is Vaidyanadhan from the stream of geology while Prakasa Rao hails from commerce. Some geographers in India have cut a profession outside the mainstream of academia. Among the presidents of NAGI Sundaram hails from the Planning Commision, Bhat from Indian Institute of Statistics, Chakraborty from Indian Insititute of Management, Calcutta and Pathak from the Indian Institute of Technology, Kharagpur.

A hallmark which lends the presidents of NAGI a place of eminence among geographers is the fact that many among them have propagated and popularized new fields of study in the discipline in India. The role of Gosal with population, Vaidyanadhan with geomorphology, Kayastha with environment, Arunachalam with cartography, Pathak with regional science, Shafi with agriculture, Ahmad with social theory, Moonis with regional disparity, Prakasa Rao with regional planning and Gopal with administrative geography is difficult to overlook. A fascination for maps is common to most geographers, among the presidents of NAGI, Singh G.B. and Gopal have created innovative atlases, while Arunachalam has been a connoisseur of the study of historical maps of India.

Geogaphy in India in the 1950's and 1960's proliferated under the leadership of first generation geographers 1950s. By the mid 1980s a second rung begun to take over. The presidents of NAGI mirror this dimension. Gosal was the first president of NAGI and his doctorate student Gopal is the 22nd President. Similar is the relationship between Moonis and Ahmad, Dayal and Ram.

If the best among Indian Geography have authored books, research papers, undertaken projects, floated journals , organized seminars and taken front ranking positions in a variety of academic decisions – the presidents of NAGI have been no less prolific . A passion for the discipline and a zeal for professional success is a trait the presidents of NAGI share with other eminent Indian geographers.

Displaying common traits , yet the presidents of NAGI in no way are a similar or homogenous group. Differing in style, posture and intellectual vigor even their diversity has parallels with Indian Geography. Within their diversity lurks a unity. The platform of NAGI is a single feature which sets them apart. Here what, strings them together is the fact that all have taken time out to present a presidential address and raise some Concern for Indian Geography.Written across a sweep of 21 years, by 22 different geographers do the presidential addresses share a common concern? Can the dynamic or static complexion of Indian Geography be read through them ?

Table 46 : Profile of NAGI Presidents

President	Age*	Place**	Specializations
Gosal, G.S.	53	Panjab University Chandigarh	Population Geography, Geographical Thought
Das, H.P.	58	Gauhati University	Economic Geography, Urban Geography
Arunachalam, B.	47	Bombay University	Geomorphology, Cartography
Raza, M.	56	Jawahar Lal Nehru University, Delhi	Regional Development Education
Reddy, N.B.K.	53	Sri Venkateswara University, Tirupati	Urban Geography, Agriculture Geography
Shafi, M.	59	Aligarh Muslim University	Agriculture Geography, Applied Geography
Pathak, C.R.	50	Indian Institute of Technology Kharagpur	Regional Science, Urban Geography
Singh, K.N.	68	Banaras Hindu University	Cultural and Social Geography
Alam, S.M.	72	Osmania University	Urban Geography
Vaidyanadhan, R.	56	Andhra University, Waltair	Geomorphology, Photo Interpretation
Chakraborty, S.C.	57	Indian Institute of Management, Calcutta	Environment Management, Urban Policy
Raza, M.	64	Jawahar Lal Nehru University, Delhi	Regional Development, Education
Prakasa Rao, V.L.S.	73	Institute of Social and Economic Change, Bangalore	Regional Planning, Urban Geography
Ram, L.N.	54	Patna University	Urban Geography
Mahadev, P.D.	59	Institute of Development Studies, University of Mysore	Regional Planning, Urban Geography
Kayastha, S.L.	69	Banares Hindu University	Regional Geography, Environmental Geography
Dayal, P.	74	Patna University	Agricultural Geography, Economic Geography
Bhat, L.S.	65	Indian Statistical Unit, Delhi	Regional Planning, Regional Development
Misra, R.P.	66	University of Delhi	Regional Planning, Regional Development
Ahmad, A.	65	Jawahar Lal Nehru University, Delhi	Social Geography, Geographical Thought
Sundaram, K.V.	69	Planning Commision , Delhi	Regional Planning, Regional Development
Singh, G.B.	63	Panjabi University, Patiala	Agriculture Geography, Cartography
Krishan,G.	60	Panjab University, Chandigarh	Population, Development, Administrative Geography

** Age at time of becoming NAGI President. **Place of Longest Services.*

Common Concerns

Most of the presidents of NAGI assess the state of Indian Geography as being far from healthy. Over two decades of speeches, the opinion hardly seems to improve, infact at times it acquires a tone of anger and despair. Gosal in couched hesitancy states " . . . the performance of geography as a discipline in India brings one to an encouraging conclusion that it has come a long way in establishing a place among the sciences . . . there are some weak links in geographic training in Indian university ." Arunachalam takes a more assertive stand " . . . university geography has come of age in India , but it shows all symptoms of adolescence in its waywardness and rash zeal for concepts and techniques anew". Moonis uses an interesting analogy " . . . the discipline of geography in India tends to acquire the dimensions and characteristics of a dinosaur : a huge body , a long tail, and a tiny little head". Dayal assesses " . . . geographic studies suffer from certain obvious deficiencies and imbalances" – An apparently frustrated Ahmad adds " . . . the further you explore the question the more disgusting the exercise becomes". Shafi disagrees "one comes across very intensive and useful work of applied nature being done in the Indian universities". Picking words with apparent care, Gopal states, "the evolved scene of Indian Geography resembles a polycyclic landscape….. the best and the rest go together."

To support their verdict, the presidents provide concrete evidence. Ahmad laments " over the years we have lost ground in many areas that were dear to us and were due to us" while Dayal confirms " unfortunately the involvement of geographers in planning till today has been only marginal" Vaidyanadhan draws strength from a critical observation "...sometimes perusing through the papers in Indian geography journals one is apt to wonder if some of them are geographical at all." For Moonis " quite a bit of spurious research" seems to be evidence of the state of affairs. Arunachalam notes "...the callously and indifferently written text books in geography that almost verge on scandal." In the same vein Alam states "...the undergraduate syllabi in economics, political science, sociology compared to geography are far advanced." With a sigh filled with whisper, Vaidyanadhan asks "who will come to a geographer? "

The presidents pick on a variety of reasons to explain the deplorable state of the discipline Arunachalam detests "the jargons of modernity and respectability that have been learnt and often indiscriminately employed ... there are significant gaps in geographical research," while Moonis identifies the "Achilles heel of geographical research in India to be its incapacity to move from the study of the particular, to transcend the concrete, to genaralise." The grouse of Bhat is that "traditional methods of teaching and research lacked logic and objective methods of explanation." For Vaidyanadhan "most geographic research is a post mortem analysis and bane of geographic research in India seems to have been the waywardness of a majority of the researchers." With a touch of sarcasm Ahmad asks " will we continue to teach the alphabet at all levels of education from primary to the graduation ?" Alams contention is that "geographers in India are preoccupied with discussions of dichotomies in geography, . . . syllabii have not kept pace with the changing geography of mankind." Dayal and Moonis attack the influence of quantification. For Dayal the fetish of quantitative techniques by no means is a qualitative revolution and at its worst it has been used as "mere embellishment to conceal lack of thought and judgement." Moonis describes the quantification mania in India as a "tendency to hide the paucity of thought, confusion between statistical and causal relationships." Even the emphasis on " GIS and remote sensing equipment appears crazy" to Ahmad. But on flip side Misra quips, "apparently we are very far behind others even though GIS has geographic trade mark." Gosal too maintains that "we cannot do advanced farming with primitive implements and technology." Pathak toes a similar line by saying "geographers must employ latest technology for public welfare." Ahmad attacks the edifice of the system as the cause for the deplorable state of affairs His unsparing words echo an anguish "individual initiative and freedom are curbed under the domineering authority of a department leader." Misra adds "teachers who know nothing of geography teach geography."

Though each presidential address is filled with crisp comments on the deplorable state of the Indian geography a remarkable fact is that not a single president loses hope about the future of the discipline. On the contrary dismissing, as if, the ground realities of the condition, an ambitious list of themes for research which require attention is drawn by them.

Themes and Questions for Research

Nearly all the presidents pick the importance of development studies for geographical research , but the emphasis differs, resonating perhaps the tune of the times. Bhat speaks of regional development, Moonis of ecodevelopment, Kayastha of quality of life, Sundaram delves into backward area development while Gopal on sustainable development.

There is little in common among presidents over the thrust areas of research that need to be given importance. Gosal urges the great significance of population, Das states the need to draw attention to burning social issues like illegal inmigration and conflicts of the country. Land should be considered as the ultimate asset of the nation and land development should proceed in a systematic manner is the omnipresent concern of Shafi. Reddy states we should evince greater interest in studies on geopolitical aspect of our country. For Singh, G.B., a critical inquiry into the pros and cons of the green revolution is the compelling need of the hour, while Singh, K.N. underlines the study of the voluntary agencies in rural development as most urgent. Alam stresses the need to focus on key urban issues for in depth analysis, while preserving the heritage is the all out motive of Mahadev. Reddy states "no task is more urgent than the identification of pockets of poverty both spatially and socially" further he adds " it is necessary to understand the complex geopolitical problems of India with reference to the international setting." In an apparent air of doubt Mahadev asks " can we save nature of all its glory."

Broadcasting a fresh wave of ideas are the pointed questions strewn across some of the presidential addresses. Their purpose is to generate innovation into the otherwise stagnant themes of research. Prakasa Rao and Gopal share a special penchant in terms of the total number of research questions raised . Prakasa Rao's sweep of inquiries range from the unexplored potential of the toposheet to natural regionalisation and its utility in planning of ecosystems and conservation of natural resources. Also asked is how to integrate urban with rural administration ? What are the patterns of rural settlements and commuting patterns? The searching questions in Gopal's long list include: are backwardness and development two different commodities or do they lie on two ends of the same continuum? How does the performance of various state compare in respect of decentralized planning? Is intra- state disparity in India a function of their physical size, or development level, or social structure or ideological orientation ? How far has the degree of homogeneity or heterogeneity of population composition affected the development process in parts of India? Which are the most appropriate indicators for assessing the ecological health of any area ? What are the quantitative measures of sustainable development ? What is the optimal spatial unit for decentralized planning – a district or a block or a village or town? To what extent has the Backward Area Development Program been a success?

Demanding a more in-depth understanding of the state of Indian Geography, the research agenda of some geographers is tipped towards the status of the discipline . Sundaram wonders "what kind of geographers do we forsee in the next millennium? What attributes and qualities do we expect in them?" Gopal poses another set of fundamental questions "What form should Indian Geography acquire to be more authentic in our context? What paradigm or methodology or content are involved? How does one convince the lay person that geographical knowledge, cartographic techniques and spatial perspective are central to day to day life of anyone?

In their address, the presidents are in a mood of obligation and debt to the esteemed position they hold in NAGI and thus speak about the Association. Arunachalam feels an organisation, like NAGI must give a "dynamic and sympathetic lead to School Geography." Dayal spells a specific desire "One would very much wish for a report on Indian Geography to cover the entire period after 1950 to present a connected picture and detailed scholarly critique of the achievements and tasks, the strength and weaknesses and the trends and prospects of geographical studies and research in the country." Vaidyanadhan adopts a buffered approach while making a critical comment on the state of the National Association of Geographers, India. " .... It is very easy to find lacuna in the conduct of many of these associations. It is now our duty, for each one of us, to realize our responsibility, as members of this association." His words though familiar do tug at our inner voice .

Boldly, subtly, with humor or with a current of anger the presidents raise numerous issues. A careful study of their addresses is an exercise worth labor and time. It is in the medley of sombre thoughts and fresh ideas that one hopes to find ones own.

Have the Presidents lived the concerns they voice ? To catch a glimpse of the personality behind the president, the soul behind the speech, the life behind the works a profile about each president precedes their address. While assessments are often tinted with subjectivity a fact remains : one after the other, from 1980 to 2000, 22 Presidents of the National Association of Geographers, India till date have said their bit and left. The nearly one lakh words which collectively form the presidential address record the care. Their concern stays.

This wide and universal theatre,
wherein we play in,
And all the men and women merely players,
they all have their exits and entrances.

As You like it –Shakespeare.

Presidential Address

Gurdev Singh Gosal
1927-

In the class of learned men Gosal can be bracketed as a university man. Born on 1st April 1927, he began teaching at Government College, Ludhiana, Punjab in 1950, and joined Panjab University in 1959. With a good 70 per cent of his life spent in teaching and research, the lure for the environ of education beckons him, even at the age of 74, to vigorously get down to complete his much awaited book titled 'History of Geographical Thought'.

Gosal enjoyed the university and the university too gave him quick accolades. Standing as if on a high speed elevator - he was awarded a doctorate in two years, appointed lecturer at the age of 23, became chairperson of the department at 34, professor at 38, elected member of the university senate at 39, dean student welfare at 40, dean university instruction at 53, dean college development council at 59, and thereby rose many other ranks of university. Gosal, however, was not driven by the automatic levers dispensed by position and power. That he thrice refused the position of a vice-chancellor proves that he could exercise conscious choice to switch off the temptation to land at this highest rung in the hierarchy of a university.

Privileges of family, social contacts, and burning ambitions are often quoted as crucial elements which lend force to the gradient of a career graph. In the case of Gosal none of these factors operated. Belonging to a cheerful family of farmers, in the village of Goslan, in district Ropar, Punjab, the settlement gave him his surname and his father the spirit to 'always be first'. His family was neither literate nor affluent. A self made man, Gosal abhorred the snares of socio- political networking. Instilled more with determination than ambition it is Gosal's grand clarity of thought that cut quickly his professional journey.

Young he decided that teaching and not farming was to be his vocation. Backed by a first class first he was appointed reader straight after his post - graduation in 1959. Quick to filter the fact that a sound bedrock of learning is an essential pre-requisite to impart knowledge, he set out in search for an institution of repute. By the mid - 1950s the United States of America was a more promising destination for geography and had begun to supersede United Kingdom. Weighing options, it is Gosal's ability for alert appraisal which won him the Whitbeck Fellowship in 1953 and took him to the University of Wisconsin at Madison. In the 1950s, Hartshorne, Robinson, Trewartha, Olmstead were among the galaxy of renowned faculty of geography at Madison. Gosal obviously knew how to make a near perfect choice for himself. An unclouded hindsight signaled him towards the study of population geography under the grand master Trewartha. "wrench it till it is all meat" was Trewartha's steel like philosophy towards research. All of Gosal's fifty maps in the dissertation had to meet the grueling scrutiny of Robinson, the author of the famous book Elements of Cartography. Armed with a strong intellectual muscle, mincing without wincing, the meat of Gosal's dissertation titled 'Population Geography of India', found approval in a short 24 months. If Wisconsin was a golden period of Gosal's apprenticeship, building a department of excellence in geography at Panjab University with a thrust on population geography was his undeterred dream.

Gosal's commitment to his specialization took multiple ramifications. Motivating a handful of students to work on different aspects of population and recruiting them at an early stage in the department, may seem like inbreeding but it ensured the perpetuation of his objective. Founding an Association of Population Geographers of India and launching its journal of Population Geography in 1979 were landmarks not only in the country but even in the international circuit.

When the newly established mapping division in the Census of India in 1962 was in search of expertise to prepare its Census Atlas of Punjab, Gosal was an obvious choice. He not only became the chief architect and executor for the project, but the work carries the stamp of his careful supervision. Thirty out of his 37 research papers and 11 out of the 12 doctorates he supervised revolved around the axis of population is further proof to Gosal's devotion to the study of population geography. To stay abreast with research Gosal participated in the International Geography Union Commission on Population Geography and International Symposiums at Pennsylvania State University 1967, London 1969, Canada 1972, Australia 1988, and Germany 1989. The faculty, association, journal, research papers, seminars, symposia and works with the Census were strands Gosal braided to strengthen the department of geography at Panjab University, Chandigarh.

Those were the days when chairmen of departments were not rotated like the game of musical chairs. Gosal's unchallenged chairmanship for two decades from 1961-1981, could and did pipe the music closest to his heart: population geography. It is, however, the quality rather than the sheer volume that put the department of geography, Chandigarh into renowned limelight. Research assistance, grants, and projects flowed to the department from diverse quarters like the Ministry of Defence, Indian Council of Social Science Research and in the later years, the prestigious status of Special Assistance Program from the University Grants Commission too was to accrue from these years of work. It is no surprise that the first Indian Geography Congress of the National Association of Geographers, India 1980 was held at department of geography, Chandigarh, and its first President was none other than Gosal.

Population geography was not his exclusive domain of interest. Even without personal contact, Hartshorne's influence on geographers is omnipresent. Gosal had the good fortune to be his student. Stimulating lectures by Hartshorne on the study of geographical ideas and thoughts cast an indelible impress on the young Gosal. When the load of administration bit into his time, Gosal dropped teaching population geography, but continued to lecture on philosophical aspects of the discipline. His legacy of six generation of students at the department certify that his lucid grasp over the subject caught their unblinking attention.

Scholarship, poise and dignity are fragrances which can be collected in the quiet chambers of reading, research and writing. Unfortunately they cannot always be confined. The erudite Gosal was drawn into the echelons of the University of Panjab. Elected successively as member of the senate and syndicate while he tried to balance academics with administration, his witty self claims "his black beard quickly turned white." The responsibilities did steal, perhaps a bit too early, the solitude for reflective thinking in furthering geography. Universities, however, it must be remembered are kept alive not merely on the shoulders of researchers and teachers, and it is only when the structure of the entire system is healthy can scholarship be upheld. Further it is not mere books and research, but the faceted experiences of life that channels wisdom. Gosal enjoyed the university in a wide spectrum of ways. He epitomizes the best in a university man.

Frontiers of Geographic Research and Teaching in India

G.S. GOSAL

May I, first of all, say how grateful I am to the General Body of the National Association of Geographers, India for doing me such a great honour by electing me to the presidency for its first annual conference. I take it as a measure of the regard and affection which my colleagues in the Association have for me personally, and also for the humble work which we in the Geography Department of the Panjab University have been doing in the field of Population Geography for the last two decades. For me personally, the choice of this field as an area of specialization was not an accident, rather it was a compulsion from within. As born and brought up at a farm in a small village in Punjab, I had wanted to specialize in Agricultural Geography and had nearly completed my plans for it. However, while working on a research seminar on population change in India with Professor Glenn T. Trewartha at the University of Wisconsin in the early fifties, I discovered that my genuine interest lay in Population Geography and I felt forced to change over to this new but over-ridingly important field of specialisation, especially in the Indian context. Even after completing my doctoral programme at Wisconsin in 1956, as I worked on the various facets of the population problem in India, my conviction about the great significance of this sub-field within the whole orbit of India's geography has been increasingly strengthened.

It is over 30 years when we got independence. Remarkable progress has been registered ever since in various spheres of socio-economic activity in absolute terms. But when measured against the massive, fast growing numbers, much of the progress seems neutralised, or at the most only a marginal gain is felt. When this progress is examined in the regional perspective, further complexities of the problem arising from the staggering increases in population

---

1st Indian Geography Congress
Chandigarh, 1980 January

come to light. In the Indian context, therefore, studies of development and population have to go hand in hand to enable to know where we stand in our efforts to move forward in social and material terms. It also follows that while speeding up the pace of developmental activities, it is desirable that population numbers everywhere in the country are simultaneously checked. With a passive demographic base at the very initial stages of development, India cannot afford to allow itself to follow the economic history of developed countries. Since accelerating population growth and its multi-dimensional implications are the crucial problems in the total Indian scene, it is only incumbent on perspective. In other sectors of population studies also, Indian Census, which has reputation of providing data even upto the village level since 1951 (upto district level for a century), facilitates studies at local, regional and national levels, especially for the post-independence era. The generalisations drawn from much different scale studies, for different periods during this era, when compared and inter-related, can lead to formulations of ideas of wide application and validity in multi-level welfare planning. These are only indications of what population geographers in the country should do to make their own contribution towards solving problems which apparently have been defying a solution.

Geography is a spatial science par excellence. It tries to examine how all that constitutes the content of the human sphere is integrated and organised in the perspective of space. With a focus on synthesis, it is a science which gives a better overview of the totality of human life on the earth. It can serve the cause of human welfare better if its research activities are oriented to societal problems at different levels of the spatial scale. A comparison of the problems, their genesis and implications at different locations can provide an insight of its own kind for developing theories which can facilitate a clear understanding of not only the processes which affect the quality of life in different parts of the earth but also the solutions for the problems associated with it.

The regional disparities in the totality of life constitute a crucial dimension of social injustice in the present world comprising developed, developing and backward areas. Within regions there are serious inequalities among areas and between villages and towns. Within a settlement, rural or urban, there are contrasts between one section of the inhabitants and the another. Even in a genuinely socialistic pattern of society, these disparities are only at a low level, but never absent. This is so because different parts of the space are endowed with different resources, people with differing backgrounds and varying levels of efficiency. While it may be futile, therefore, to strive for a social order of spatial and structural uniformity, the disparities must be narrowed down to the extent it is humanly possible. This should be the goal while working under any political system.

One of the basic prerequisites of planning social and economic amelioration of mankind throughout the world and among different sections of the populace everywhere is a comprehensive knowledge of the spatial disparities at local, regional and national levels in all their dimensions. This task is essentially the craft of the geographer. It is a very challenging task which geographers in the country must accept and carry out effectively if they want that geography should find a place that is due to it among the major disciplines dealing with reality. Their findings with regard to spatial inequalities in individual spheres of socio-economic activity or total development and the causal factors associated therewith will surely lead them to make prescriptive suggestions for future planning. For a person who has successfully helped in diagnosing a problem must also be a party to finding its solution. It is thus on the basis of the rigour of their own discipline that the geographers can play their rightful role in a team of planners.

It is understandable when one hears people saying that they need not define their discipline. The inter-disciplinary approach to knowledge which we hear and talk of so often does not mean a diluted knowledge of all disciplines but collaboration with other disciplines on the strength of comprehensively acquired ideas of our own field. Only well-developed disciplines prosper in mixed seed-beds. They wither when shielded from the light. In this context it may be emphasized that without being rigid about the peripheries, we must master the core of our discipline knowing it to its depths and in all its complexities. The necessity of precisely knowing one's craft is clear even to a layman.

A country of sub-continental size, massive population, long and varied history and complex problems of all kinds, India provides a big laboratory for geographic research, especially in the context of its immense diversity. Geographers must apply all their tools of analysis to understand the synthesis that India is, and comprehend the regional inequalities that characterise it. Only such an understanding can help in formulating a strategy of development for the country.

There can be no uniform strategy of regional development for each and every country. The strategy has to be evolved in the context of physical, cultural, economic, demographic, political and historical background in each case. It is just not possible to transplant a model of development, howsoever logically and ably evolved, in an area without taking into account its background. Same problem can occur in different areas for different reasons. In each case the remedy has to be according to the causes of the problem. Using their skill in uncovering the vertical as well as horizontal integration of phenomena over the earth, the geographers have, therefore, their own share to contribute both in discovering problems of areas and in solving them.

As a part of the development strategy in such a diffusedly densely populated country like India, there can be no escape from a pattern of decentralisation or dispersal of developmental activities if the benefits of socio-economic progress are sought to be brought to all parts of the country and to all sections of the society. Centralisation of development may fit in well in highly urbanised-industrialised countries with a lot of vacant land interspersing between the settlements. Decentralisation which is commended for areas thickly covered with population, however, does not exclude the growth of nodes of centralised development. A combination of aggregational and dispersal patterns of socio-economic development, therefore, will find favour in all closely settled developing lands. The two strategies are inter-related and inter-dependent. Centralisation alone will widen the disparities which must be avoided. Even in developed societies concentration is being supplemented with dispersal on ecological, social, economic and strategic grounds.

Our experience with the major centres of development has not been very satisfactory. While they have grown as focus of development, their role as centres of diffusion of traits of modernization has not been so effective. Within a few miles of every important centre or metropolitan area, one finds backwardness still persisting, giving the centres an appearance of islands of development in an ocean of poverty. In such a situation the regional disparities in socio-economic development have got accentuated and have led to aggravation of social injustices.

It does not, however, mean that there should be no centralisation of any developmental activity. In fact, wherever dictated by economic rationale and viability, it will have to be there. On the other hand, whichever activities can stand the cost of dispersal and decentralisation should be brought to the small towns and villages. What is actually required is that the processes of diffusion of new ideas, innovations and technology from the major centres of growth should act simultaneously with the development of small dispersed nodes to achieve complete spatial coverage of the country in terms of all welfare activities. In other words, concentration and dispersal have to be integrated in functional terms. There is no dualism between the two.

In this connection it may further be stated that with the growth rate the rural population in India is experiencing, there is bound to be abundant surplus labour in villages. Agriculture has a very limited capacity to absorb the future growth of labour force and industry has to come in major way to meet the emerging unemployment problem in the countryside. If this surplus labour were to be moved to towns for employment, the costs of doing this will be colossal, apart from creating unmanageable environmental problems. Consequently India will have to think in terms of a rather diversified, intensive agriculture and decentralised pattern of industrial development articulated through an efficient system of growth centres. There must be an integration and co-ordination of agricultural and industrial development so that each sector is complementary to the other.

The centralisation-cum-dispersal pattern of development which has been suggested above in the Indian context, if worked out thoughtfully and imaginatively, has the potentialities of strengthening the ideals of democracy and socialism in the country. While large-scale heavy industry has to be centralised, agro-based industries labour-intensive manufacturing works, electronics industry, engineering goods industries, and the like should find place in small towns and selected villages dispersed all over the country. The small nodes of industrial development should be functionally connected with industries in major towns and cities.

A comprehensive and meaningfully hierarchical network of nodes of industrial and productive activities presumes the existence of the necessary infrastructure. In particular, the construction of a close network of metalled roads and railways and the extension of electric power to every settlement, rural or urban, are necessary. With a view to generating skilled and technical labour in small towns and villages, which may be locally available for the proposed decentralised pattern of industrialisation, industrial training institutes should be opened at selected rural sites and small towns.

The main highways and the rail routes should become major "corridors of development", while the link roads, which will encourage spot and string development along their routes, may connect the small nodes with the main corridors of development which may in turn be linked up with metropolitan or territorial industrial complexes. What is essentially required is an appropriate system of nodes and links suited to India so that the benefits of modern socio-economic progress should reach the entire society.

Another basic principle underlying the proposed decentralisation of developmental activity is that planning should start from both ends (i) from local areas (or even individual settlements) so that specific needs and native problems of individual settlements are taken care of, and that these local area plans build up into regional and national plans, and (ii) from the national level so that an overview of national requirements is the guideline for formulating ultimate targets, which are and these targets are proportionately allocated down to the local area units. There should be a proper reconciliation of the targets arrived at from the two approaches. The strategy of regional development outlined above, if implemented effectively , can go a long way in reducing the spatial inequalities in economic and social terms. By way of recapitulation it, if may be stated that while the task of uncovering the spatial disparities in socio-economic development in all their aspects is that of the geographer, that of formulating a comprehensive strategy of development in all its dimensions is the collaborative function of economists, geographers, sociologists, etc.

An examination of the overall performance of geography as a major discipline in India brings one to the encouraging conclusion that it has come a long way in establishing its place among the sciences dealing with reality and that it is making steady progress in various directions. Geographers have been showing concern for problems of development and regional planning. They have also responded well to collaborative work with colleagues in allied disciplines and inter-disciplinary projects on the strength of their own knowledge and ideas. What discipline is better fitted for such an integrative role than the one concerned with spatial arrangement and organisation as changing through time? Consistent with the requirements of the times and the nature of problems facing the society, they have increasingly taken to quantitative methods of analysis and synthesis, although a lot remains to be learnt and applied appropriately. Thus far they have been preoccupied with studies of specific problems in specific areas or places. It is already overdue now that they should subject these studies of the specifics to comparative analysis and drawn generalisations of wide validity. It is their distinctive function to develop theories regarding spatial relations on the face of the earth. The theories must grow out of the facts that make India.

In the sphere of the Geography of Development, there is a need to develop the theme: People, Resources and the Government. Whereas state plans for socio-economic development are the same within administrative units, there are wide spatial inequalities in achievements within the units. The political patronage in areas and differing receptivity of the people to plans within the region, even having a similar resource base are potent factors in this regard. Geographers should come in a bold way in studying these problems of spatial organisation within their local areas and make prescriptive recommendations.

Both in methodological discussions and actual works, geographers have, of recent, been heard raising an argument between the theoretical - deductive approach and the empirical-inductive approach which was set forth by Plato and Aristotle some 2500 years back. Unfortunately, some devoted followers of the theoretical-deductive approach are less than patient with these who insist on the empirical observation of things on the face of the earth. The latter emphasize the tradition of field study in geography, the former maintain a long continuing interest in theory building. Both are essential. The progress of geography, like the progress of any field of learning, requires close and receptive communication between the theorists and the direct observers. The two approaches are mutually inter-dependent and there is no dichotomy between them. Sound theory does not ignore reality ; it attempts to explain it. It seeks to discover the system into which particular pieces of reality fit. On the other hand, a theory which is not based on a thorough understanding of many particular pieces of reality is likely to be neither sound nor significant. Neither the theory nor representative pieces of reality can be studied profitably independent of each other. Why then should we sometimes slip into the futile exercise of seeming to promote one by degrading the other ? The two need to be encouraged simultaneously.

There are some weak links in geographic training in Indian university. The need of a good grounding in the philosophy of geography cannot be over-emphasized. We must clearly know what precise contribution we as geographers are to make which no other subject specialists can make as well. Once we are able to answer this question satisfactorily, only then are we ready to join an interdisciplinary team or to represent our subject at all. Secondly, physical geography is suffering from unjustifiable neglect both in teaching and research . The curriculum in physical geography needs to be broad-based and sharpened so that it may provide a comprehensive understanding of the physical resource base. An understanding of the totality of nature is necessary for developing good analysis and synthesis in geography. Thirdly, we must master our methodology and tools of analysis consistent with the time in which we are placed. We cannot do advanced farming with primitive implements and technology.

Lastly, while we must make use of all the secondary data available to us on the various problems under study, we must not shirk the need of supplementing it with primary information collected in the field. Howsoever efficient and quick the modern tools of analysis may be, there is no substitute for fieldwork. Of course, the methods of fieldwork have to be evolved in line with the nature and objectives of our discipline so that we are able to clearly understand the dynamic organisation of phenomena in space. What a perceptive and insightful mind can observe in the field is not obtainable even with the most sophisticated tools of analysis. Both approaches are integral parts of the geographic methodology and must go hand in hand.

Hari Prasanna Das
1922

In 1952 when Das boarded Majola, a warship converted to a passengership, at Bombay, and set out for the London School of Economics to acquire a doctorate he had two clear missions: to study the geography of Assam and spread geography in Assam. Completing his doctorate under the supervision of Dudley Stamp in a short twenty-one months, Das returned home with a dissertation titled 'Forest Resources of Assam'. On the foundations of his first mission he quickly laid the blocks of other publications: Problem of Forestry in Assam, 1958, Land Use in Assam,1959 and Geography of Assam 1970. The additional dozen publications and seven doctorates he supervised all confirm that Assam was the nerve center of his research interest. Even with limited publications, Das made an unparalleled contribution to the meticulous understanding of the geography of Assam. He also had a second resolution to fulfill – the dissemination of geography as a discipline of study in the state of Assam. Serving as the chairmen at the department of geography, University of Gauhati, till his retirement in 1984, he not only inaugurated the North-East Hill Geographical Society in 1968 and floated the Journal of North-East India in 1970, but also unfurled the cause of geography outside the confines of the department. His persistence opened way for geography in schools and colleges of Assam and provided opportunities which teachers were quick

to seize. To propagate the discipline, Das published a four volume set of Adarsh Bhugol or Ideal Geography, which became a popular Assamese text for seventh to tenth standard class in schools .

Das was aware that to safeguard the study of the discipline a smooth functioning of the university administration was a critical necessity. He worked with vigour not only in a number of committees but also took on various administrative posts in the university. He served as dean of the Science Department, rector of university and was also acting vice-chancellor for a term. Responsibilities like director of the sports board and warden of hostels also fell on his shoulders. As Secretary Instructor of Colleges for over a decade, Das was associated with the administration of a dozen colleges in Gauhati. With growing involvement in these multifarious activities, Das neglected his personal research but not his pupils. Though conventional in approach, yet the assiduously prepared lectures made Das an esteemed teacher. He firmly held the belief that geographers had to first serve and understand their 'immediate' environment . Assam was a state which strongly captured the interest of Das. Nostalgically he reiterates that even a short journey outside Assam makes him 'home sick' . More than a provincial zeal, Das was keen to work for the region through the medium of education in the realm of geography.

Das's bonding with the land and people of Assam runs long and deep. It is his family that kindled this patriotic sentiment. Das was born on 1st March, 1924 in the village of Kaithal Kuchi, about 80 kilometers to the west of Gauhati. Nalbari was the closest town and it was here at the Gordon High School that Das pursued his basic studies. He graduated from Cotton College and then enrolled at the department of geography in the University of Calcutta for his post-graduation in 1946. His father, a famous headmaster in the Gordon High School, had studied geography for his Bachelor of Teaching degree. While Das inherited a passion for geography and teaching from his father, the attachment for the study of Assam was sown when he journeyed through inaccessible tracts of this mountainous state for an appraisal of forest wealth. He recalls that, as a research fellow in the aftermath of a post-graduate degree, the inclination to study forest resources of Assam found rewarding outlet when the Chief Conservator of Forest, M.C.Jacob, rendered all help and guidance. Extensive fieldwork into the remote interiors of Assam aroused in Das an ardent desire to serve this less developed state of India. Today, despite a faltering health, many seek his wise counsel about geographical issues pertaining to the region. And why not? After all, throughout his four decades as a professional geographer Das remained undeterred towards his goal to study the geography of Assam and spread geography in Assam.

The Problem of Immigration in Assam : A Geographical Review and Interpretation

H.P. DAS

At the very outset let me express my sincere gratitude to the office bearers and members of the National Association of Geographers, India, for electing me President for 1979-80 and giving me this privilege to address the first annual gathering at Chandigarh in an atmosphere of unique beauty and grandeur. This association was started only last year and therefore this conference with the attendance of a huge number of geographers from the length and breadth of the country is a historic and significant one. And it has been very appropriate to hold the first annual conference of the Association in this flourishing planned city in as much as the Association with its established beginning here is expected to flourish like the city towards the purpose for which it is being established. On this occasion I would like to dwell on a problem of North-Eastern Region- Immigration in Assam – which has been a cause of great concern during the last few months not only for the region but for the country as a whole. As a geographer of the region I have felt it to be proper to present a picture of the problem before this geographical audience for the problem remains without being properly understood outside the region for a variety of reasons including its remote location. In view of these circumstances my address will be somewhat a departure from the conventional presidential addresses which in most cases deal with the conceptual and methodological problems of the discipline.

The Problem

The process of immigration to Assam is not a new phenomenon but it dates back to the historic past. It has at present immigrants from all parts of India and the neighbouring countries. The number of immigrant population as per the 1971 census records was estimated to be 6 million, or 41 per cent of the state's

---

2nd Indian Geography Congress
Chandigarh, 1980 January

Fig. 1 : Immigration to Assam, 1971

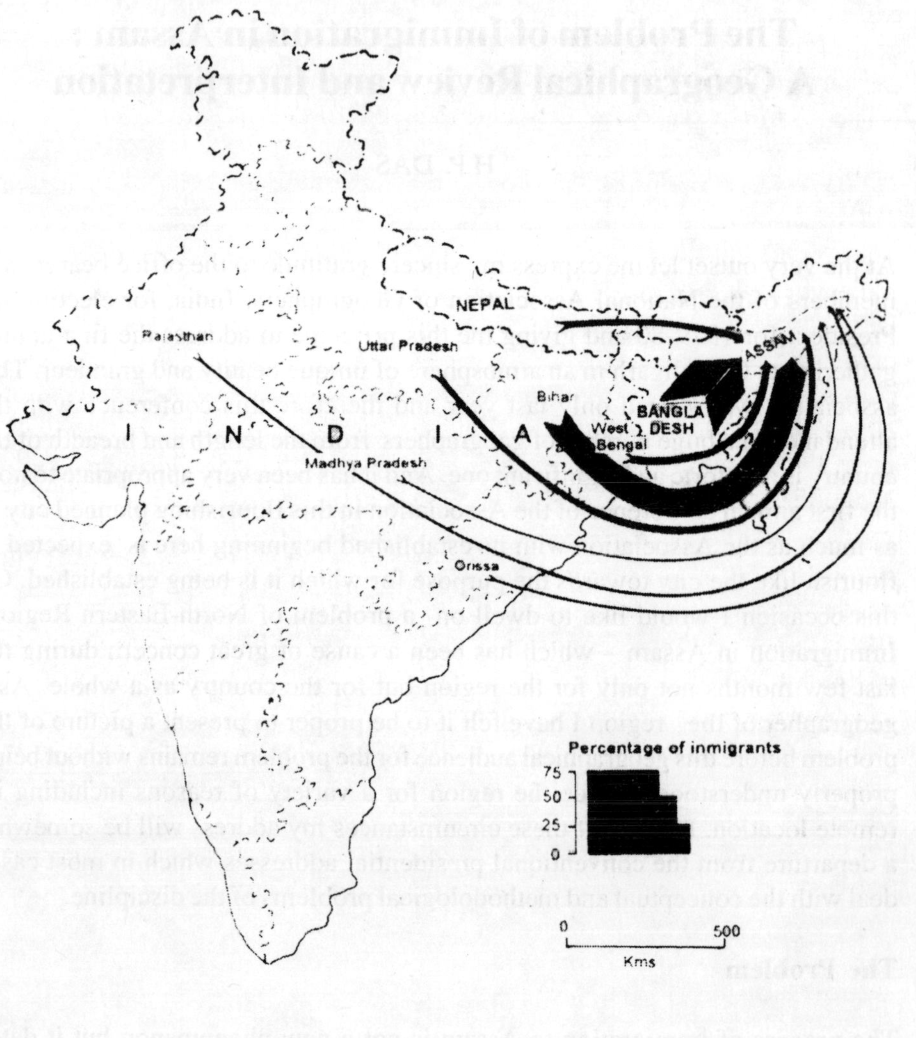

population of which 1.5 million or 10 per cent were recorded to be borne outside the state. Constituting thus two-fifths of the total population, the immigrants in the state are now a demographic, economic and socio-cultural reality and their existence is of great significance. What is attempted in this paper is to present an overview of the problem dealing with the types and causes of immigration, its impact and the resulting effects in the region. The treatment of these vital aspects, is hoped, will help to understand the problem in proper perspective.

Historical Background

The process of immigration dates back to the days of early Aryan settlement in India when streams of Aryan people came to this part after crossing the North-Bengal plain. It is said that *Narakasura*, the earliest mythological Kirat king of Kamrup (Ancient Kamrup with its capital at Pragjyotishpur included many parts of North-Bengal and Bangladesh) brought a large number of Aryans from Northern India for promotion of Aryan culture in this region. Neverthless, the most notable stream of immigration took place in 1228 A. D. when a group of Mongoloid people from Hukong valley entered Assam through the north-eastern gateway. Having defeated the local tribes these people not only settled but ruled the area till the British occupation of their kingdom in 1826 in the wake of Burmese invasion. The Burmese invasion was so great that it not only led to the loss of their kingdom but caused depopulation of the area at that time. The descendants of these immigrants, who are known as *Ahoms,* now constitute one of the major population groups of Assam. Even during the *Ahom* rule, immigration to the region took place both from its west and east. The area was subjected to invasion by the Muslim rulers of Delhi and Bengal many of them stayed back as prisoners or captives and later they became an integral part of the state's indigenous population. On the other hand, the Buddhist people from upper Burma belonging to present *Khamti, Phakial* and other communities came down to upper Assam and settled there.

Modern Immigration

The new type of immigration or what may be called the modern immigration, however, took place with the annexation of Assam to the British Raj. A large number of people from the adjacent states and beyond moved into the region for a variety of purposes. They were the labourers from Bihar, Orissa, Andhra Pradesh and Madhya Pradesh, office clerks and professionals from Bengal, traders from Rajasthan, artisans, porters and wage laborers from Bihar, Madhya Pradesh and Uttar Pradesh, soldiers and office attendants from Nepal, followed by East Bengal. Muslim peasants and Nepali livestock ranchers came to the region in search of agricultural pursuits. The immigrants thus may broadly be divided into six major groups : (1) Tea labourers, (2) East Bengal Muslims, (3) Bengali Hindus, (4) Nepale, (5) Marwaris and (6) Hindustanis, and their number is estimated to be 10 per cent, 15 per cent, 9 per cent, 1.7 per cent, 0.5 per cent and 4.5 per cent respectively in 1971 (Figure 1). Besides these groups there are small groups of Punjabis, Manipuris and others in the state. Since the above five groups constitute the bulk of the immigrants a somewhat detailed treatment of them would be necessary.

Tea Labourers

The tea labourers from Bihar, Orissa, Andhra Pradesh and Madhya Pradesh were brought by the British tea planters when they started tea plantation in Assam and for this labourers were not locally available. With the growth of tea industry their number increased by leaps and bounds and it became 14,00,000 in 1931, from a mere 400 in 1858. After 1931 the immigration of tea them slowed down and many of the labourers who were brought under a contract system left the tea gardens with the expiry of their contract, but majority of them stayed back in the gardens. A section of them, called ex-tea garden labourers after coming out of gardens have settled permanently as agricultural labourers, small farmers and wage earners. At present tea garden labourers constitute about 10 per cent of the total population of the state and most of them are Assam born *genoese*. At the district level their percentage is highest in Dibrugarh (34 per cent) followed by Sibsagar, Darrang and Cachar with 22, 16 and 15 per cent respectively. Lakhimpur and Nowgong have only 6 per cent and 2.5 per cent respectively for the concentration of tea gardens is less in these two districts. The tea gardens labourers are a distinct group of people and they form an inseparable part of the Assamese community.

East Bengal Muslims

The immigration of East Bengal Muslim peasants (mostly from Mymensingh district) to Assam began towards the end of the last century. Gradually their movement grew so large that it became a type of undeclared invasion of the state. Goalpara, the adjoining district of East Bengal, was the first place of their landing in which their movement was facilitated by the then *'zamindars'* who extended tacit approval to their coming as cultivators to cultivate lands under easy terms of tenancy. Because of this the population of the district increased by 30 per cent in 1901-1911 as against 2 per cent in 1891-1901. As the years passed by the movement was further intensified and the immigrants began to spread to all other districts, specially to the '*Charlands*' (riverine lands formed by the alluvial deposits of the river Brahmputra) of Kamrup, Darrang, Nowgong and as far east as Lakhimpur. This incessant movement grew vigorous when they were granted periodic settlement of land by the then provincial government. The government is said to have encouraged their immigration on political consideration and appointed a Special Muslim Land Revenue Officer to look after their land settlement. However, the government could foresee the consequence of this movement and, therefore, it introduced a Line System as early as 1920 and imposed certain restrictions on settlements in some areas. In 1931, the total number of immigrants was estimated at 5,75,000, and the impact of their inflow was very well realised. Mullan in the census report of 1931 commented : "it is sad but by no means improbable that in another thirty years Sibsagar district will be the only part of Assam in which the *Assamese* will find himself at home. Wherever there is wasteland, thither flock the Mymensinghis. In fact, the way in which they have seized upon the vacant areas in Assam valley seems almost uncanny. Without fuss, without tumult, without undue trouble to the district revenue staff, a population which must amount to over half a million has transplanted itself from Bengal to the Assam valley during the last twenty five years". This mass immigration continued unabated till 1941 and their number increased from 3000 in 1901 to 9,00,000 in 1941. After 1941, their immigration slowed down, but even then till partition about 1,00,000 immigrants were reported to have entered Assam.

The stream of migration did not restrict itself to the pre-partition and partition days only. The flow continued to the rich plains and forest areas of the region through both the western and southern gateways. So long East Bengal formed a part of Pakistan, due to hostile relationship with India, the border was guarded by military and para-military organization and it restricted considerably the rate of illegal immigration or infiltration. But during the uprising against the Pakistan regime and the army crackdown on the Bangla Liberation Movement in March, 1971, the border was virtually thrown open and massive Bangladeshi infiltration took place to Assam and other north-eastern states.

The East Bengal Muslim immigrants and their Assam born generation constituted about 15 per cent of the state's population in 1971 and their percentage of distribution at the district level was 34, 25, 37.5, 11.5 and 1.5 in Goalpara, Kamrup, Nowgong, Darrang and Lakhimpur respectively. By and large, they are concentrated in the rural areas and are cultivators by occupation. As a matter of fact, they have revolutionized the agricultural landscape by introducing many new crops including jute and vegetables on a commercial scale.

Bengali Hindus

The immigration of Bengali Hindus was initiated by the Britishers when they brought them for their office and other professional works. The stream of movement was intensified along with the opening of new railway lines, post and telegraph offices, development of tea and petroleum industries. But the most conspicuous mass migration took place at the time of partition and immediately thereafter. Owing to insecurity of life and property, the Hindus left East Pakistan (Bangladesh) for India, and Assam being the adjacent state to it had to receive a large number of Hindu displaced persons. The 1951 census gives the total number of refugees in Assam (including present Meghalaya) as 274,455 of which 272,075 came from East Pakistan. Cachar being the nearest district received the highest number (93, 177), followed by Goalpara with 44967 and Kamrup with 42871. Sibsagar district received the lowest number (75140, while Darrang and Lakhimpur received 18,833 and 13,965 persons respectively. The process of refugee immigration was further intensified when the refugee rehabilitation schemes were implemented by the government and when they were given physical and social shelter by their relatives and acquaintances. The movement of East Bengal Hindus virtually stopped during the Pakistan rule. In 1958 their number was estimated at 4,87,000 and it rose to 6,28,249 in 1961. Their number was estimated to be 1.3 million in 1971 or 9 per cent of the State's population and the districtwise percentages were put at 17.5, 18.2, 10.7, 19.1, 10.6 and 15.2 in Goalpara, Kamrup, Darrang, Nowgong, Dibrugarh and Cachar respectively. The immigrants belonging to this category are mostly engaged in service and commercial activities in the urban area.

With the emergence of Bangladesh in 1971 a new situation, however, arose and lakhs of Bengali Hindus crossed over to their Hindu counterparts. Assam being the nearest and most secured place for this stay naturally had to face the onslaught of this development.

Nepalese

The *Nepali* immigration began when the British administrators brought some *Gorkhas* as soldiers and others as gatemen, *chowkidars*, etc. for their personal service. They were also brought to clear jungles and to work as menials in the oil fields. But their movement grew stronger when they came in large number during the last few decades to take up cultivation and livestock ranching in the hilly and riverine areas. The period 1911-31 was the most important for Nepali immigration and their number was estimated at 83,306 in 1931. The total number of *Nepali* speaking population was estimated to be 215,213 in 1961 and 250,000 or 1.7 per cent of the state's population in 1971. The Darrang district was reported to have the highest percentage (40), followed by Dibrugarh with 24 per cent. In other districts it would vary from 1 to 8 per cent. The Nepali immigration has been still continuing in the form of chain migration.

The majority of the *Nepali* settlers are graziers by profession and, therefore, they have occupied the *charlands*' or foot-hill regions. Many of them live in the outskirts of urban areas supplying milk and fuel to the urban dwellers. The reason of their stay in such areas is the availability of fodder for their cows and buffaloes. At present a major part of the business of milk and milk products is in the hands of the graziers. Besides, a large number of Nepalese are employed as porters, *chowkidars* and office peons throughout the region.

Marwaris and Hindustanis

Although the *Marwaris*, as they are called primarily because of their coming from *Marwar* of Rajasthan, began to come in the pre-British days, their movement became significant along with the establishment of British rule and subsequent development of tea industry and other commercial and industrial establishments. With a small beginning of 1891 persons in 1901, their number at present is estimated to be 70,000 or 0.5 per cent of the state's population (1971). The *Marwaris* are concentrated mostly in the urban and industrial centres and virtually the entire business and commercial transactions of the state can be said to be in their control.

The immigration of *Hindustanis* (Hind's or distorted Hindi speaking people) to Assam started with the beginning of British rule when their services as washerman, barbers, sweepers, cobblers, load carriers, etc. were required. Then the Second World War gave another boost to their coming because their services as wage labourers were increasingly required at that time. Later, the extension of railway lines and steamer services opened up new avenues of employment to *Hindustani* labourers. Their movement was further intensified after independence when their services were in great demand as a result of industrialization and urbanization and subsequent growth of inter and intra-urban transport system. Their number was estimated to be 650,000 or 4.5 per cent in 1971. The *Hindustani* immigrants are also mostly concentrated in the urban and industrial areas, although their number is not insignificant in the rural areas.

The influx of other migrants such as *Punjabis* and persons from other states is primarily a post-independence development. Of these, the number of *Punjabis* is somewhat significant and they are mostly engaged in commercial and industrial establishments of the region. The number of immigrants from other states is not high, and in whatever professions they are, they are settled in the urban areas.

Causes of Immigration

The factors which have led to the large scale immigration to Assam since the beginning of the last century are many. The ground plan for this was, however, laid by the Britishers in their efforts to consolidate administration, exploit natural resources and develop tea plantation by the lines of transport and communication. Although the beginning of immigration was an induced one, later it turned to be a self–motivated one leading to a kind of invasion of the region . As already mentioned, the cause of tea labour immigration was the unwillingness of the indigenous population towards wage labour. Secondly, the absence of English educated persons in Assam at the time of annexation led the Britishers to bring in the officers, clerks and specialist from Bengal to run the administration as well as the railways and postal services. Thirdly, the low density of population, and the existence of innumerable tracts of vacant lands and abundance of culturable wastes along the river Brahmaputra attracted the land-hungry and oppressed East -Bengal peasants, who, in their turn, did not fail to take advantage of such a situation. Fourthly, the tendency of local people to remain confined with agriculture or at best some other limited services and, therefore, the absence of occupational diversification led to the coming of skilled and unskilled labourers as well as traders and business men who found the region to be a virgin land with immense prospects for their purposes. The absence of regulatory laws of the government towards immigration also facilitated large scale immigration from East-Bengal.

It is worth noting in this context that certain political forces are also reported to have worked for large scale immigration (from East-Bengal) to Assam towards fulfilment of their political interests. During the pre-partition days there was a concerted move of a section of political leaders to make Assam a Muslim majority state and consequently there was also demand for inclusion of Assam into East Pakistan, both in the press and on the platform. But for the timely intervention of local political leaders the demand did not materialise and Assam, excluding the Sylhet district, was kept in the territory of Indian Union. The intensity of the above problem can be gauged from the fact that the Muslim population in Nowgong district was only 4 per cent of the total population in 1901, and the percentage increased to 35 in 1941 and 40 in1951.

The latest phase of immigration, or what is called the infiltration, has taken place following the emergence of Bangladesh in1971. Since its inception political instability persisted in the country and therefore insecurity of life and property led many Bangladeshis to move into the neighbouring states of India and many other taking advantage of the situation crossed over to the region in search of good fortune and living. The legacy of political interests continued and certain political parties encouraged and helped their coming for they could with elections on their strength and support. The physical and social shelter provided by the earlier migrants to their brethern also paved the way for their mass movement to the region.

Impact of Immigration on Population Growth

The impact of immigration has been clearly reflected in the population growth of the state. Today Assam experiences the highest growth in the country. Between 1901 and 1971 it recorded a rise of 11.4 million persons and its growth had been 343.57 per cent as against 132 in India and the highest among all the states in the country. This growth rate may appear to be magnified because of the low base population, but that the growth is very high is evident in the higher growth rate in every census decade (Table 1).

Table 1 : Population Growth in Assam, 1901-1971

Year	Population	Decadal Per cent Variation, Assam	Decadal Per cent Variation, India
1901	3,289,680	—	—
1911	3,848,617	+16.84	+5.75
1921	4,636,980	+20.19	+0.32
1931	5,560,371	+20.05	+11.02
1941	6,694,790	+20.45	+13.51
1951	8,0208,856	+20.12	+14.02
1961	10,837,329	+34.99	+21.63
1971	14,625,152	+24.71	+24.57

Source – Census of India, 1971, Series – 3, Assam Pt. II A.

The abnormal growth of population in the state over the last decades not just due to natural cause but it is primarily the result of large scale immigration to Assam from different parts of India and from the adjoining countries since the days of British rule. Had the population growth in Assam since 1901 taken place at all India rate the total population would not have been more than 8.5 million. There is thus an excess of 6 million persons in the present population of Assam which is constituted by the immigrants and their descendants.

The post independence period has been specially significant when, in addition to migration from the various states, massive immigration from East Pakistan now Bangladesh, and Nepal has taken place to the region. The magnitude of foreign immigration can be realised if population growth rate for this period is studied carefully. It can be seen that the population growth rate of

Assam during 1951-1971 was 34.72 per cent as against the all India average of 23.15 per cent and Assam's own increase of 20.2 percent before 1951 (Table 1 and Figure 2). Assuming 23.15 per cent as the normal growth rate which allows for normal inter-state movement of people, we may conclude that the extra growth rate of nearly 10 percent is primarily due to the presence of foreign immigrants. On this basis, out of 14.6 million persons of Assam in 1971 about 1.5 million persons can be put as foreign immigrants. As already mentioned, the number has greatly increased after 1971 with the emergence of Bangladesh, and against Assam's present projected population of 18.8 million, different sources give the number as high as 3 million. This figure may appear too high, but by all considerations it can be safely concluded that the number will be not below 2 million.

Fig. 2 : India and Assam : Decennial Population Growth Rates, 1901-1971

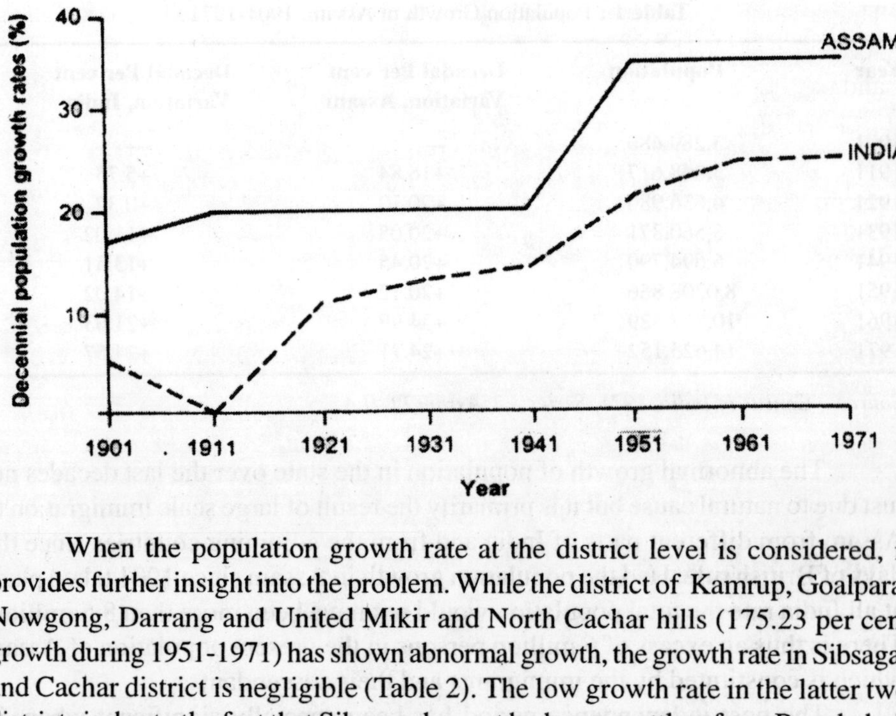

When the population growth rate at the district level is considered, it provides further insight into the problem. While the district of Kamrup, Goalpara, Nowgong, Darrang and United Mikir and North Cachar hills (175.23 per cent growth during 1951-1971) has shown abnormal growth, the growth rate in Sibsagar and Cachar district is negligible (Table 2). The low growth rate in the latter two districts is due to the fact that Sibsagar has not had many settlers from Bangladesh and Cachar has been used as a gateway for the rest of Assam.

The abnormal rise of the Muslim population in some of the districts further proves that the growth rate was unnatural and it is the result of large scale migration from Bangladesh. Of course, the migrants from Bangladesh are not only Muslims but a large section of them are Hindus. It is worth noting that the abnormal growth of Muslim population is considered by some to be the result of high fertility ratio among them and shunning of all family planning programmes. The point arises here is that had this been true, the population of Cachar (34.48 per cent Muslims in 1951 and 39.13 per cent in 1961) should have shown an abnormal rise in 1971. But the decennial population increase in Cachar for this period was only 24.29 per cent, the second lowest among all the districts of Assam.

Another indication of the abnormal growth of population due to foreign immigration is the sex-ratio of the state as well as the districts specially selected for settlement by illegal alien immigrants. The sex-ratio of the state declined steadily from 1901 to 1961 and thence it showed an upward trend. The conclusion that can be drawn is that initially the illegal immigrants were different exploring settlers, and later when they felt secured, brought their wives to settle permanently. Thus, all these prove beyond doubt is that the abnormal growth of population in Assam is primarily due to the rapid increase of immigrant population, both national and foreign.

Table 2 : Population Growth in the Districts of Assam, 1951-1971

State/ District	Population 1951	Population 1961	Per cent Increase 1951-61	Population 1971	Per cent Increase 1961-71
Assam		10,837,329	34.97	14,625,152	34.71
Kamrup	1,490,329	2,062,572	38.39	2,854,183	38.38
Goalpara	1,108,124	1,543,892	39.32	2,225,103	44.12
Nowgong	886,955	1,210,761	36.51	1,680,895	38.83
Darrang	923,562	1,289,670	39.64	1,736,188	34.62
Sibsagar	1,212,224	1,508,390	24.43	1,837,389	21.81
Lakhimpur	1,126,294	1,563,842	38.85	2,122,719	35.74
Mikir Hills	165,440	279,726	79.21	379,310	68.28
North Cachar					
Cachar	1,115,865	1,378,476	24.29	1,713,318	24.29

Source : Census of India, 1971, General Population Tables Series, J – Assam, Part II-A.

Immigration and Associated Effects

The impact of immigration, besides population growth, has become apparent in a number of ways. Specially, the ever increasing number of immigrants has led to many socio-economic problems. It is to be recognised, however, that the immigrants have contributed substantially to the socio-economic development of the state. The development of tea plantation industry, ever increasing jute production, productive livestock farming and the growth of trade and commerce have been possible with their help and support. Their services in the facilitative, vocational, utilitarian and constructional enterprises have been of immense value towards the economic growth of the state. Besides, they have contributed significantly to the development of *Assamese* society. But the immigrants, especially the ones who came in recent times, have created more socio-economic and cultural problems than their contribution. The number of such immigrants is becoming increasingly high and if their influx continues at the present rate, the identity of the state as the homeland of *Assamese* people may be at stake in the near future. Because of their presence, the indigenous people feel uncertain of their future for they feel that their language, culture and economic opportunities are being enroached upon. Such an attitude on the part of the indigenous people appears to be not without any basis. There are records of attempts made by the Bengali Hindu elite to impose Bengali language and culture on the native people, and the controversy was raised by them regarding *Assamese* as the language of administration and education in the state. There is, therefore, reason to be doubtful over the probable strategies they might take against the indigenous interests. The demands of the tea labour community, East Bengal Muslim immigrants and *Nepalese*, for more representation to the legislature and other policy making bodies of the state on the basis of their population strength have generated reactions among the indigenous people. They feel that more representation by the member of the immigrant community would result in shifting of legislative power from the indigenous to the non-indigenous section of the population. In addition, the growth of exclusive immigrant settlements in the form of 'cultural islands' and 'outposts' throughout the state is being a cause of great concern to the indigenous people as these are supposed to have far reaching consequences on the socio-economic, cultural and political life of the region.

In any case, the socio-cultural and economic interaction between the immigrants and the indigenous population has been so far cordial. Except for minor conflicts with the *Bengali Hindu* immigrants, no socio-economic or cultural tension has taken place. But the entry of thousands of illegal *Bangladeshi* immigrants in the recent years is now adding a new dimension to the problem. The earlier immigrants of Bangladesh origin, who have created extensive pockets, are harbouring illegal immigrants by providing physical and social shelter to them. Once inside the state these illegal immigrants get settled and mingle with the early comers from the same origin, making it difficult to detect them as illegal ones. These are the places where conflicts are reported to have taken place frequently resulting in communal disturbance and imbalance.

From all these it now appears that the prediction of Mullan that "Sibsagar district will be the only part of Assam in which Assamese will find himself at home" is coming to be true, and there is every reason to be apprehensive of the future of the state in so far as its identity and integrity are concerned.

It is worth mentioning in this context that the problem of illegal foreign immigrants has been so tremendous that it has led to the mass movement in the region during the last few months. The movement was launched for the deletion of foreigners names from the voters lists, postponement of mid-term election (which has been over in the country a few days back) in the region till the names of foreigners were deleted and deported from the region. The movement including the *Gana Satyagraha* was an unprecedented one in which lakhs of people from every corner of the region irrespective of their age, sex, caste, creed, religion and language took part. And it was so much peaceful that Inder Jit on his visit to Assam commented on performance of the *Gana Satyagraha* as the one which was not only in the finest "Gandhian tradition but would have gladdened Mahatma Gandhi". But unfortunately, vested interests are trying to ignore the problem or minimize its magnitude and are also painting the picture of the movement as uprising against Indian citizens from other states. A religious and communal bias is also being imparted to the problem . That these are blatant lies will be borne out by the fact that thousands of *non-Assamese* population belonging to all sections courted arrest and actively participated in the movement in support of the demands.

The problem of foreign immigrants is, in fact, like cancerous growth, which is striking at the very core of the integrity of the country and, therefore, it is not just a regional problem, but a problem of the entire nation. But it appears that due attention is not being paid to the problem by the centre and, therefore, the people of the region feel insecure and uncertain about their existence. The leading journalist M.V. Kamath rightly puts that the people of the region feel unloved, uncared for and neglected by the centre in all respects and that had such a cultural invasion taken place in Punjab or somewhere near Delhi, it would have taken a different turn. The utter neglect shown by the centre is further evidenced in the fact that the people have to make a movement for the construction of a bridge over the Brahmaputra, extension of broad gauge railway line and establishment of a refinery in spite of its own oil reserves, etc. These social and economic problems of the region call for serious attention of the centre, otherwise the very integrity of the region with the country will be jeopardised.

Concluding Remarks

The problem of immigration to Assam is now a demographic, socio-economic and cultural reality and the existence of immigrant population as high as two thirds of the state's population is of great significance. The problem, however, needs to be looked from two perspectives : one regarding the "immigrants" (immigrants from different states of India and the neighbouring countries) and the other regarding the illegal foreign immigrants.

The immigrants irrespective of their caste and creed, religion and language or the reasons for which they came or had to come to Assam today from an indispensable part of the composite *Assamese* society. They have, therefore, a great responsibility not only for the economic growth of the region but for the socio-cultural development and integration of the region. Like the earlier immigrants who have integrated with the host society and is now an integral part of it, all other immigrants instead of creating "cultural islands" and "outposts" should strive for socio-cultural assimilation and integration with the rest of the society. They should leave their soujourner's attitude and make Assam their motherland and identify themselves as an integrate part of it. The *Assamese* society has a long tradition of flexibility in the matters of their own socio-cultural values and has been maintaining an attitude that has facilitated the process of integration. The process would definitely be quickened once the immigrants appreciate the need of identifying themselves with the mainstream of the society. At the same time the indigenous people should do their best to bring the immigrants into their folds, if the immigrants are to mean for them "more constructive gains and less destructive conflicts". With only cordial and harmonious relation between the two, the state will remain as a place of peaceful living as has ever been.

The problem of illegal foreign immigrants needs more attention and it should be treated as a national problem. All effective steps should be taken by the centre and the state for detection and deportation of foreigners soon and for sealing the borders to prevent further influx of foreigners. Among other measures, the maintenance of a National Register of the citizens of the region will go a long way for preventing further influx.

Last but not the least, I would like to draw more attention of the geographers to such burning social issues of the country. I feel that they as social scientists have special responsibility of studying such problems and offering suggestions for their . solution. I am sure that the geographers by adding a spatial dimension to such problems can put them in proper perspective. This is how they can enrich the cause of geography and enhance their contribution to the society.

REFERENCE

Bhuyan, M.C. (1977), *Immigrant Population of Assam*, An unpublished Ph.D.Thesis, Guwahati University.

Bhuyan, P.K. (1979), *Assam's problem of foreign infiltration, The Assam Tribune*, November 25.

Census of India *(1961), Assam*, Vol III, Part II – A.

Census of India *(1961), Assam*, Vol III, Part II – C.

Census of India *(1971), Assam, Series 3,* Part II – A.

Das, H.P. (1970), *Geography of Assam*, National Book Trust, New Delhi.

Deenabandhu (1979), *Assam in the coils of a foreign python, The Assam Tribune,* November 26.

Goswami, P.C. (1963), *Economic Development of Assam,* Asia Publishing House, Bombay.

Jit, I. (1997), *Assam is not burning, The Assam Tribune,* December 9.

Mullan, (1931), *Census of India,* 1931, Vol. III, Part I.

Robinson, W. (1975), *A Descriptive Account of Assam,* Reprinted, Sanskaran Prakashak, Delhi.

Balasubramanium Arunachalam 1933 -

If a picture is worth a thousand words, then a map is a picture worth a lot of condensed spatial information. All geographers use maps for research , some design and compile maps to build an atlas, while some teach the science of map making. Arunachalam's relationship with maps goes beyond these mundane uses. He searches for the indigenous maps of India, probes the mathematical principles upon which the foundations of these maps were raised and then infers the historical geography of regions. Arunachalam taught geography in colleges and department of the University of Bombay for forty long years. He used the strategic location of the city of his professional placement to further the study of maps. Bombay, India's leading port for maritime trade and naval movement, has a stock of nautical charts. Arunachalam thus chose to specialize on maps of maritime navigation.

The fishermen, boatmen to the officers and chief hydrographers of the Government of India were all a repository which Arunachalam tapped to solicit knowledge about maps. Akin to an adventurous school boy, he traversed from Kutch to the Sunderbans, scouting the seven thousand kilometers long coast of India. Sailing on weather ships, cargo vessels, rowing boats or with coast guards, Arunachalam ventured out into the sea to reach off-beat islands in the Bay of Bengal and the Arabian Sea. One question that troubled Arunachalam as he made these field trips was that without formal education, without latitude and longitude and use of sextants and compass, how did the native boatmen design maps? Pointing towards the stars the natives unfolded the mystery of drawing near perfect maps to Arunachalam. To exhibit their skills the boatmen often used the sand beach as a slate to illustrate the maps. Discussions in the chambers of officers of naval and shipping companies furthered Arunachalam's comparative understanding of map making. Traditional texts, archives and antiquė shops selling rare books were additional haunts from where Arunachalam retrieved maps of the past. Such being the passion, it is no surprise that the department of geography at the University of Bombay can boast of a collection of about eight to nine thousand maps. The rich variety of cadastral, topographic, naval and historical maps along with fascinating editions of atlases earned the department of geography at Bombay the reputation of a national reference library for maps in India .

Arunachalam is not just a traveler and collector, he is also a researcher. Forty of the sixty papers authored by him orbit around the theme of maps. Three of the four research projects he investigated had the study of maps as their core concern. Both in historical perspective and content, Arunachalam picks a variety of topics for research. Caligraphy in cartography, indigenous traditions of navigation in South India, Jain pilgrim maps and cartography of Chola administration, all exemplify this vast sweep. Arunachalam's research is not static. His inquiry of medieval traditions of Indian cartography was quickly followed by that on the indigenous traditions of Indian cartography. The skills of coding local maps to interpretation of aerial photographs, imageries and application of geographic information systems are proof to his evolving research. Papers on digital terrain models and on isopleth mapping through computers and geographic information systems are essential ingredients in his list publications. Prolific in number are his works, yet on a yardstick of time, Arunachalam's professional interest in maps was aroused late. He had spent twenty years in teaching and research, had passed his 40th birthday when his inquisition moored towards a study of maps.

Born on 1st July 1933 in Calicut, Arunachalam went to school in Cudalore, a small town twenty-two kilometeres to the south of Pondicherry. With physics, mathematics and geography at his intermediate level, geography was not a subject of his first preference. Arunachalam wanted to study statistics. Though a second preference his performance in the study of geography was outstanding. Scoring a first class he won the meritorious Senior Thompson Prize of Presidency College in 1953. Despite academic distinctions Arunachalam's formal education terminated with a masters degree. Family obligations thwarted an opportunity to study further. Arunachalam never took a doctorate, he never went abroad to study and he never took a teaching assignment in a foreign university. In this sense Arunachalam is a self learner. A genetic loading from a father, who was a middle school teacher, could partly explain his scholastic aptitude but Arunachalam had no intellectual mentor or supervisor. At the young age of twenty-one he was appointed lecturer at the Ruparal College in 1953 and shifted to the Parle College in 1960. When the department of geography was started at University of Bombay in 1969, Arunachalam soon found a placement in it a year after.

In the first twenty years of teaching, Arunachalam's research interests hovered around the regional geography of Maharashtra and geomorphology. A keen desire to disseminate the importance of geography motivated him to write a series of school text books and regional texts on Maharasthra. His interest in geomorphology is displayed in his publications on Coastal Features in the Vicinity of Ratnagiri, Shifting Water Divide in the Gatpuri – Trambak Ghats, and the Coastal Changes in the Kochi Embayment. How then did Arunachalam shift to the study of maps?

A historian working on an assignment brought a sheave of 300 year old maps to Arunachalam to decode in the mid 1970's. The task ignited his imagination and captured his interest. To crystallize his research Arunachalam displayed remarkable dexterity. He was one of the founder members of the Indian National Cartographic Association, and became its President in 1990. An active interest in the Society for Indian Ocean Studies and Maritime History Society were additional forums that Arunachalam used to forge ahead his study of maps. Today at the age of 68, despite a coronary problem he pursues two ambitious projects – firstly to establish a Maritime Museum in Bombay and secondly to compile his life times work in a book titled 'Native Indian Cartographic Traditions'.

While most researchers were engaged in conventional themes of land use, urban studies and regional planning, Arunachalam carved a unique picture . This is why among Indian Geographers, Arunachalam's name with maps is inseparable. Whereas geographers use maps as tool for research, Arunachalam researches on maps.

Neglected Frontiers of Indian Geography

B. ARUNACHALAM

The National Association of Geographers, India and the Elders of geographical wisdom in the country have done me the signal honour by inviting me to deliver the Presidential address to this august gathering convened at the behest of the 4th Indian Geography Congress being held in this Urbs Prima in India. I deem it not as an honour done to an individual but as a recognition of the lead given in recent years to professional geography by Maharashtra as a whole, and Bombay in particular. On this august occasion, I cannot but recall the pioneering efforts of that dynamic Cambridge-trained geographer, late Principal C.B. Joshi, who left no stone unturned to place geography formally in the saddle of the University of Bombay, and steer it through against all opposition in an almost single man's crusade; it is as a tribute to this pioneer that this relatively young Department of Geography of the University of Bombay has been shouldered with the responsibility of giving momentum to the good that is intended in the cause of geography. With the willing co-operation of all of you gathered here, and the vibrant team of geographers in Western India and Greater Bombay, I feel confident of carrying out the tasks set to us in the years to come.

It will not be out of place to mention that it was in Bombay, the first Indian professional society of geographers, namely, the Bombay Geographical Society, was organised as early as 1832 A.D. at the instance of Honourable Mountstuart Elphinstone, the Governor of Bombay Presidency, as a limb of the Royal Geographical Society, London to encourage geographic researches. The Proceedings and Transactions of the Society in 19 volumes carry significant contributions to Indian geography. This Society was amalgamated with the Asiatic Society of Bombay in 1873; the valuable collection of books, maps, geological specimen, globes etc. is a treasure-house given to us as a legacy and preserved in the Asiatic Society of Bombay. A successor Society, the Bombay Geographical Association was set up in 1935 by a group of enthusiastic geography teachers of the city, doing yeomen service in the interest of school geography, apart from bringing out a research annual, the Bombay Geographical Magazine. In spite of

---

3rd Indian Geography Congress
Bombay, 1980 December

this early lead and a fervent plea to the University of Bombay made by Sir Patrick Geddes as early as the twenties of this century, geography came to be taught at the graduate and post-graduate levels only by the late fifties. The Ruparel College and the Parle College were the fore-runners to the university department set up in the end of 1969 under the Chairmanship of Dr. C.D. Deshpande, who is also the founder member of the National Association of Geographers. The discipline has grown in strength and vitality over the years.

University geography has come of age in India, but it shows all symptoms of adolescence in its waywardness and rash zeal for concepts and techniques anew. Over 70 universities today offer courses in geography at the undergraduate and post-graduate levels. A large number of doctoral theses are being turned out year after year, even a casual scrutiny of the Indian Council of Sciences and Research Review of Research in Geography will bear testimony to the fact that the production rate of research papers is not only high for the relatively young discipline but also highly diversified ranging from studies in traditional and conventional sub-fields to themes on emerging frontiers like geography of crime and justice; hunger, poverty and nutrition, perception and behavioural studies and the like. The range of techniques of geographical analysis has also widened to encompass not only the traditional cartographic tools and case studies but also sophisticated tools of quantification and rapid processing techniques like the use of computers. The jargons of modernity and respectability have been learnt, and often indiscriminately employed. Yet, a careful, perceptive eye cannot but observe that there are significant gaps in geographical research carried out in India. There are many vital areas of inadequate knowledge , if not absolute ignorance. It is perhaps equally true that there is something wanting in geographical training and education in the Indian scene. Our goals are still blurred, lacking in direction and practical pragmatism, some may even venture to say that the soul is missing! It is to some of these neglected frontiers of Indian geography that I intend rivetting your attention, so that meaningful guidelines may emerge at the end of the professional deliberations of this Congress.

Geography Education in School

In the decades since Independence, a perceptible vigour of growth, both in numerical strength and in diversification of specialisations, has been witnessed in university geography in India. School geography, at the same time, is in hopeless shambles. The reasons are not far to seek; the reduction in the status of geography in schools as a lesser partner of the agglomerate social studies, the fact that geography teaching is the last unwanted fringe of work-load to a group of teachers who are uninitiated in the discipline and equally uninterested in teaching the subject; the callously and indifferently written text-books in geography that almost verge on scandal; and the imposition of a systematic, scientific outlook to a hitherto regionally oriented syllabus structure in the garb of updating. The mechanical teaching of the subject in a sterile, unimaginative and uninteresting manner has brought to geography the unique distinction of the most hated subject in the school curriculum. This attitude, imbibed while young and impressionable, persists long after the student has entered the portals of a college. Even the public image of geography is not one worthy of preservation. Why is university geography so hopelessly divorced from school geography in our country? Is it not a sound principle to catch the children young and train them in 'good' geography? Is it not the duty and responsibility of the university and college community of geographers to render a helping hand to our less fortunate brethren and sisters in the school faculty? The real pillars of strength for university geography have to firmly rest on the plinth of school geography. Looking to the very large number of school teachers who teach geography but do not have even the rudimentary knowledge, skills and training in the subject, the task of bringing them into the fold of professional geographers through training and guidance is stupendous. My own limited experience in Bombay convinces me that these teachers are eager to learn and practise geography but just do not know where to go and whom to approach for guidance. Surely, short term crash and sandwich courses for the school teachers are not beyond the capacity and competence of the university system. It is also high time that the National Association contemplates a school wing.

Text-books in School Geography

This brings me to yet another related aspect: school text-books in geography. The way they are written, whether they help in teaching geography or not, they have made history. The books are written by professional authors with little insight into the subject and its special needs for explanation or its relevance to the specific levels of education. As far as my experience in school text-books in Maharashtra goes, they are indifferently written in an uninteresting manner. The public criticism in the press of the bad quality of geography books is now-a-days bringing to the market a new crop of books written by experts, but with the critic in view. Either way, the poor child becomes a victim. Writing good school text-books in an absorbing and educative manner, taking into consideration the age and earlier training as well as vocabulary of the child, should not be treated as beneath the dignity of academic geographers in Colleges and University; on the other hand , writing a really good text-book for primary and secondary levels is a challenging exercise in mental discipline, much more difficult to achieve than writing a couple of professional research papers to the enlightened. We owe it to the promotion of Geography to train the younger minds in the right geographical perspectives: geography must be actively practiced rather than passively learnt. This cannot be achieved unless an ambitious School Text-books Programme is taken as a national task, and an organisation, like our National Association of Geographers, India must give a dynamic and sympathetic lead to school geography.

University Level Books in Geography

Let me now turn to the teaching of geography at the under-graduate and post-graduate levels in our colleges and universities. Perhaps no other university discipline is so directly concerned and related to its local and regional environments and landscapes as geography is. Yet, all our courses are heavily biased in favour of western concepts, western models and what is worse western environment examples. The reliance on foreign books is heavy; though of late, Indian authorship is on a steady increase still the orientation is western. The plight of students carrying out the studies through regional language media is still worse and is detrimental to scholarship. Look at any book on physical geography, or urban geography, written and published, may be , in India; poverty of Indian examples is striking, and an indigenous character and vision are altogether missing. Spate, though three decades old, is still our bible on India. Even the efforts of National Book Trust have not been able to give a complete regional coverage of India from an Indian point of view. The need for good Indian text-books both in English and regional media is urgent. Can the National Association of Geographers, India help in commissioning groups of experienced teachers and researchers to carry out this task, especially as a high priority to produce compendiums on physical geography of Indian and regional landscapes of the Indian states? The immense variety of Indian landscapes ranging from the perhumid to the arid, glacial to the selva, lend themselves for rich explanatory descriptions, that can set a model for most of the third world countries, and yet, physical geography is the least developed and the most ignored aspect of Indian geography.

Gaps in Indian Geographical Research

Geographical education in India has been fortunate to absorb and assimilate the rapid strides of progress that the western world has been witnessing since the forties. The Quantitative Revolution as well as the Conceptual Revolution that, have rocked the western world have placed at our disposal a range of sophisticated analytical tools and concepts nurtured in the western environs. The initial impetus to Indian geography has come through the testing of the western models in the Indian context, though this exercise at times has been carried too far: it has however not logically led to the innovation of Indian models. The deductive Central Place theory of Christaller, the ecological models of urban structure, studies to examine stages in the growth of a primate city growth pole theory and the like have all found their echoes in the Indian realm. Many of the achievements of geography in India over the last three decades have resulted from its ability to address itself to range of Indian problems, especially those of urban development and problems concerned with population, transportation, resource development and industrialization. Many of these problems are common to the developed countries of the West- the only difference is that India is passing through a phase of development that they have already gone through – and Indian studies have positively helped in building a bridge in the international forums through such comparative studies.

While good in themselves, these studies are just not adequately and directly addressed to the basic concerns of the development process and experience that India is undergoing as the world's largest, densely peopled democracy. The 'urban' bias in Indian geography is being overdone, every university, whether located in an urban metropolis or a rural interior, deems it necessary to specialize in urban geography. Is this really necessary? Is Indian urban geography becoming hackneyed and is it a specialisation of convenience rather than utility? In a country, predominantly rural and agricultural, why has Indian geography developed intellectual indifference to the problems of rural development? Environmental hazards like floods and droughts, and the permanent threat of food shortages also pose compelling interests to Indian geography. If the western world has no parallels to such Indian situations, the field is rich enough to provide ample ground for indigenous virgin research through primary field investigations. Problems of persistence of subsistence economy in spite of a Green Revolution, the nebulous concept of `integrated' rural development of the Indian country-side, the apparently insoluble problems of land ownership and land tenures, traditional, custom-bound routeways of Indian socio-economic circulation like the periodic markets and fairs all deserve a better deal from Indian geographers to work out strategies for planning rural development. Surely, lack of professionalism and career-orientation in geographical training, in spite of the possession of invaluable assets in the innate spatial logic and visual and coherent point of view is indeed distressing and is positively detrimental to the building of public credibility and an image of productive utility of the discipline.

Commitment to Nation Building

The Sixth Plan of Development strategy of the nation envisages the active participation of universities in national development. The Plan intends to involve universities not only in the need for conservation, but also in the utilisation of this knowledge to solve the problems of the community. Towards this end, the Plan suggests a three-pronged strategy: (a) to create an awareness in the extension of frontiers of knowledge preservation and enrichment of environmental assets of the nation, such as soil, water, flora and fauna; (b) to commit university research to studies on problems having a bearing on the improvement of the quality of life of the people of their region through transformation of natural resource of the area into meaningful wealth for the people, and (c) to promote co-ordinate programmes of action-research through co-operative team efforts of an interdisciplinary and multidisciplinary nature, rather than through individual, uncoordinated, often duplicating pieces of research.

The world of Indian geography in the university systems has here a God given golden opportunity to prove their mettle and demonstrate their vitality and purposefulness in the cause of the national good. The Thrust Area Programme Committee of the Department of Science and Technology , the Department of Environment and the Planning Commission are engaged in the vital task of building national and regional inventories and data banks of earth-resource and useful man-power. The geographers with their innate ability to synthesise on an areal frame co-existent physical and human phenomena to generate an organic whole and to develop a synoptic point of view are indeed ideally suited to plunge into this nation-building activity in collaboration with other social, natural and earth scientists. The ecological principle used in geography to recognise links between co-existing areal phenomena and the regional principle used in identifying concrete regional (spatial) unities should come to the aid of the geographer in complex territorial regionalisation of production complexes. The blending of the map-making skills with techniques of primary data collection concerned with landscape indicators in the field and use of quantification for rapid processing, not to speak of the ability to use remote sensed data makes geographical cartography at once an analytical and synthesising tool in the preparation of blue-prints for planning at the area level. Given the necessary professional edge through intensive training, the geographer in India can become an important and useful member of any planning cell. Look at the immense prospects for the professional utility of the geographer in a set-up where planning units are being visualised at the grass-root level in every district of the country and the market for his cartographic skills when every planning cell contemplates a local/ regional/ national atlas. The million dollar question is: can and will Indian geographers build themselves into national, regional and local grids of co-operating and interacting teams committed to these specific goals of national priority? Can geographical training in the schools, colleges and universities be restructured so as to give the right orientation and consciousness of local, regional and national environmental problems of conservation and wise use of resources? In this year of productivity, can we pledge our research interests to the priorities of the National Data Bank and Resource Inventory so that the geographers too can contribute their mite in pulling the 'Juggernaut' of Developing India? Can the National Association of Geographers be raised to the status of a national pool of talents and expertise, eagerly sought for its advice by the administrators, planners and builders of India?

Last but not the least, before I close my address, may I pose a question for contemplation by the peers of Indian geography? Most of our universities offer a course on development of geographical thoughts, we wax eloquently on the achievements of different schools of thought like the German, the French, the British, the American, the Russian and the like. Are there no Oriental Schools of thought nurtured in some of the oldest civilisations of the world? Do we have Indian schools of thought in one or more aspects of our discipline, evolved under the impact of cumulative experiences and observations over centuries? With a long history of sciences, and a hoary tradition of astronomy, navigation and maritime travels for commerce, apart form colonisation, the Indians in the past did possess traditions of physical geographical concepts, cosmogony, topographic details, cartography and the like. In the current century itself, at least four universities have Department of Geography half a century old and their research achievements are accessible. The history and evolution of Indian geographical thought is an unexplored frontier inviting challenges. Shall we accept?

My rambles through the realms of Indian geography in schools and colleges, in educational training and research, may perhaps appear to be too severely critical. My observations are not intended to be mere petty fault-finding, nor are they a result of despair. It was mainly to highlight the large number of gaps in our knowledge frontier and the inadequacies in our utilisation of our professional talents and skills. Unfinished and uninitiated tasks are many ; let us check-list them, establish priorities and tackle them in an united effort. Let us deploy geography more purposefully in the cause of the development efforts of the nation. Let us commit ourselves and pledge to generate 'good' and 'useful' geography in education, training and research in the interests of healthy citizenry and professional expertise.

Voice of Concern

Moonis Raza
1925 - 1994

On a summer evening of 18th July 1994, in the city of Boston, United States of America, a cardiac arrest bundled Moonis Raza to the carpeted floor. He died at 5:00 p.m. with no one at his side. Moonis was buried at the city graveyard, where a small group of family members attended his funeral. There was no geographer to lay the wreath. Moonis was not a non-entity. Perhaps he was one of the most charismatic geographers India has ever produced. His flair for language, captivating extempore speeches, powers to organize and generate brilliant ideas see few parallels in the academic landscape of Indian geography. Had Moonis died on native Indian soil, dignitaries, politicians, heads of leading institutes, colleagues, friends and students from diverse disciplines like geography, history, economics, sociology, demography, and education would have thronged in stampede numbers. Such was the personality of Moonis that few could resist him. He had his way with most people in most situations.

Cutting a career across a varied terrain , Moonis notched landmarks which few geographers in India have been able to surpass. No geographer in India has taken the prestigious Shiromani Award, nor has anyone been the principal of an engineering college, or the chairperson of the Indian Council of Social Science Research. No one has enjoyed a second nomination as the president of the National Association of Geographers, India. Till date few geographers in India have supervised a dozen doctorates without a doctorate degree to their own credit. He was one of the few geographers in India who grasped the patterns of disparity at a pan–India scale. No other geographer in India has enjoyed such a loyal comrade of followers – who labored and worked in accordance with his ideas. Much geographical research in India till date ripples like concentric circles around the creative ideas set in motion by Moonis. Many geographers in India have attained recognition but none the Moonis way .

Moonis was not the only gifted child of his parents. Rahi Masoom Raza, the man famous for the script of Mahabharat, a popular television serial in India, was his elder brother. Born on 2nd February, 1925 in Ghazipur, a district headquarter in eastern Uttar Pradesh, Moonis lost his mother at a young age. With a father who was a prosperous advocate in the district court meant that Moonis along with his eight brothers and sisters were left to fend for themselves. A common bond among the siblings was a stock of some of the finest English and Urdu classics which their father had collected over the years. Few can deny that prolific reading in our young days fills our reservoir of words that spring to life when we speak and write in years to come.

Hailing from a culturally proficient family, Moonis set out to do his graduation from the Christian College, Allahabad. For a post-graduation it was the department of geography at Aligarh Muslim University which became a carefully considered decision. From 1945 to 1947 Aligarh played a critical role in the life of Moonis. The raging student politics on the campus, rather than the department of geography, shaped and sharpened the analytical abilities of the twenty year old Moonis. At the heal to India's independence, those were times when political organizations and rallies ran rampant. Moonis became the student leader of the Communist Party of India at Aligarh. His commitment ran deep and severing ties with the family, the labour camps at Kanpur became his refuge. After five long years when Moonis returned home to Aligarh in 1950, his alma-mater offered him position as lecturer in 1950. A malignant tuberculosis and threat of a police arrest forced Moonis to seek a haven in academics.

Home is where the care is and the sick lad needed nursing . Nothing would cure, Moonis had to be rushed to Czechoslovakia for a lectimoy. Besides half-a-lung, the politically active years had left a deep intellectual and emotional impress on Moonis .The killer instinct to survive, the intense ability for analytical thinking, the adept power to assign work and a heart felt care for the down trodden were characteristics which gave Moonis an immediate edge to fascinate one and all. He used his charm to hold office and bewilder officers. But he was no superficial charmer – a burning passion to throw light and give attention to problems of social and spatial disparities were his academic objectives. He was alert to recognize that the shortest path to reach this goal was not through geography alone. Moonis was drawn to the field of education at large. Though his interest in regional development sustained, yet education as a field of study and work came to distinctly dominate .Here is the audit: of the fifteen research projects that Moonis undertook, forty per cent were on education and fourteen per cent on regional development; in the slice of the nineteen papers presented at international seminars an almost equal share of sixteen per cent belong to education and regional development; of the thirty-one academic addresses delivered as lectures on special invitations thirteen were on education and only two on regional development . Forty-six pieces of writing can be counted by Moonis as author, co- author and editor of books. Among these though twenty per cent belong to regional development and thirteen per cent to education the largest, an eleven volume set is on the theme of higher education. In the domain of his thirty-six research papers published in various journals, thirteen are on education and only six on regional development. Of the eight different administrative positions enjoyed by Moonis half have been within a government institute of education. But these were not his only pursuits – urbanisation, medieval and colonial history, ecological issues and resource geography embraced his interest. A theme running common to most of his works was the search of unity in diversity. In fact it is in synthesis that lay Moonis's greatest talent: Artfully knitting past with future, tradition with modern, micro with macro, spatial with social parameters, scientific with poetic language, he wove an intricate web of words.

Moonis above all was a people's person. Granting favours, discussing ideas and debating issues, in all hospitality and at great ease Moonis was perpetually surrounded by students or colleagues. He had a renewable spring of ideas to share and air. Enrolling many into his fold of thinking, he initiated numerous joint works and accomplished many a mission. More than heading offices and pushing papers it is the spontaniety of Moonis's words and ideas that set him in a class apart .

It indeed is a twist of irony that a person so full of life should suffer the pains of stone silence for twenty-two months in the intensive care unit of the All India Institute of Medical Sciences, New Delhi. A medical decision for treatment in the United States of America distanced him from his people. The misery of half-a-lung, uncared for in the zest to lead a full life, had taken its toll. Though the body gives way, a charismatic soul lives on forever.

Untitled

M. RAZA

I am beholden to my peers and colleagues in Indian geography who have done me the signal honour of electing me to the august position of the presidentship of the National Association of Geographers, India. I am greatly touched by this magnanimous gesture; and I do not have the words to express my sincere gratitude to them. I take this opportunity of rededicating myself to the objectives of the National Association of Geographers, India – the symbol of the united endeavours of Indian geographers and of promising to work, as its president, to coordinate the significant role of geography in providing the much needed spatial dimension to the development process and to sharpen its focus. Development, like freedom, is indivisible. The integrity of the planet earth as a human settlement is seriously endangered, on the one hand, by the encapsulation of development in a few enclaves of affluence and, on the other, by the chronic persistence of under-development over a major part of the globe. What is true of the world as a whole is also true within the developing nations wherein small pockets of the green or the white revolution will not be able to co-exist with vast hinterlands of marginalised humanity continuing to struggle for survival in abject poverty, hunger and degradation.

Development is operationalized through the mechanism of interaction between social man and non-human nature and proceeds through a triangle of forces. Nature indicates the directions of its optimal appropriation and lays down the expanding limits of human freedom. Technology aids natural processes, bends them to human (or shall we say, humane) purposes and thus extends the range of freedom. Institutions are either conducive to or restrictive of man-nature interactions. It is through this system of interdependencies that the development process unfolds itself.

Viewed in the historical context, development has led simultaneously to integration of and differentiation within the space economy, and in this process national space as a relatively semiclosed economic field emerged on the world scene quite late in history in response to the consolidation of the home market

---

4th Indian Geography Congress
Jawaharlal Nehru University, New Delhi, 1981 December

through socio-economic and political instrumentalities. But this process of integration was at the same time a process of spatial differentiation operationlized through the territorial division of labour. The model is neither of a number of fields operating at the basal level as closed systems nor of a homogenised and undifferentiated monolith, but rather of a multi-level and hierarchical system of fields within fields, of a system of interdependencies nesting into a larger system of interdependencies. Viewed thus, national development is *national* only to the extent that it subsumes regional development, sustains it and is sustained by it. Lack of adequate concern for this principle of spatial justice has led to the generation of serious strains and stresses in the polities of many developing societies in contemporary times.

The current tensions and strains in the northeastern region of India, for example, are essentially a function of the unfinished tasks of nation building and reflect the inadequacy of the strategies evolved since independence to correct the inequities and distortions embedded in Indian space during the period of colonial rule. Since these stresses have now acquired alarming proportions and are threatening to strike at the very roots of the unity and integrity of the nation, a united national response is called for to meet the challenge posed by them. Such a response, if it has to escape the quicksands of chauvinism and separatism, must be based on a scientific analysis of the geographical factors generating these stresses.

The base on which the edifice of the northeast rests rather precariously is provided by the tribal people of the region. Having lived in isolation from the rest of the country for centuries, they have developed a strong sense of ethnic identity. Inhabiting areas generally unsuitable for settled agriculture in their micro worlds at a low level of technology, they have fallen an easy prey to the moneylender, the land-grabber or the forest contractor, and they tend to see the 'outsiders' in the image of their exploiters, who alienate their lands or destroy their forest. This feeling of relative deprivation and of being at the receiving end becomes further accentuated in situations wherein the scale of immigration of non-tribal people transforms the demographic profile basically, reducing the tribals to a minority in their original homelands. It is these social realities which, in composite states like Tripura, Assam, West Bengal and Manipur in India and Chittagong hill tracts of Bangladesh wherein the tribal and non-tribal people live together in differing mixes, provide fertile ground for chauvinism among non-tribal and separatism among the tribal peoples. In predominantly tribal states and centrally administered territories like Nagaland, Arunachal Pradesh, Meghalaya and Mizoram, these strains get reflected in state-to-state or state-union relationships.

Among the non-tribal people of the north-east the *Meiteis* of Manipur and *Assamiyas* of the Brahmaputra Valley have a cultural tradition of great chronological depth and of considerable give and take with the mainstream of cultures developing with Ganga Valley. This has, on the one hand, tended to strengthen their regional identities and, on the other, to strengthen their role as sub-nodes of cultural diffusion in the north-east. They have to establish equitable relations with the tribal formations, which have coexisted with them for centuries and at the same time to come to terms with the waves after waves of immigrants who have settled in the pioneer fringes of their territories. There are five major components of such immigrations.

First, *Santhal* labour who provided the basic inputs for the tea industry from its very inception and continues to do so up-to-date.

Second, Bengali *bhadralok*, who rode the waves of modernization-diffusion, generated by the requirements of imperialist expansion and consolidation in eastern and north-eastern India, whose essential role remained dysfunctional as it was rooted in the basically spurious character of the westernization-modernization process itself, and who continued to be a cultural enclave floating in the hinterland of north-eastern polities.

Third, Bengal peasantry or the *Mymensinghis*, who were being squeezed out from areas of high agricultural density and skewed land distribution and who crept into the adjacent open lands in the vicinity with uniform ecological conditions – bringing with them the technology of water management in water logged areas, increased intensity of cropping and cash-crop cultivation; and who got assimilated in the rural polity of Assam so much so that the share of the *Assamiya* speakers in the total population of the districts of present Assam rose sharply from about one-third in 1931 to more than 60 per cent in 1961.

Fourth, *Nepali* transhumance herdsmen, who provided the animal husbandry component in the traditional economy of primary production of the region which was concerned, by and large, with crop agriculture alone, and who were encouraged, particularly in the colonial period, to settle down in clusters within the north-east and provide bulwarks for the empire.

Fifth, *Marwari* businessmen, who though numerically insignificant, have tended to occupy the commanding heights of Assam economy and have filled in the vacuum created by the migration of British capital, particularly in the tea industry.

The strains and stresses generated by the large-scale influx of culturally diverse elements have provided fertile ground for separatist tendencies to emerge and get accentuated among the *Assamiyas* in Assam and *Meiṭeis* in Manipur.

The immigration of Bengali peasantry from across the provincial borders before 1947 and from across the international borders since independence has created a further complication in the situation as the bulk of these immigrants happen to be Muslims. The cultural and linguistic tensions have, therefore, tended to get intertwined with communal strains. This provides fertile ground for forces of majority and minority communalisms to raise their heads and flourish in the surcharged ethos of the contemporary northeast.

The multi-layered and multi-faceted system of stresses and strains that provide the ballast in the explosive situation of the northeast essentially rests on the regional structure of disparities in the levels and rates of growth in the development processes in independent India wherein not only rich have become richer and poor poorer but rich regions have also become richer and poor regions poorer. This has been operationalized firstly through disparate doses of inputs being ploughed in the agricultural sector of different regions producing the wide spectrum ranging from *Jhum* to four crops a year, and secondly, through the beheading of production cycles so that the comparative advantages of resource rich regions are eliminated, and while petroleum is produced in a backward region, the petro-chemical industry comes up in an advanced region.

The complexity of the current problems of the northeast lies in the fact that the five generators of tensions and strains mentioned above, which generally operate singly in other parts of the country, have in the case of the northeast intertwined with one another. *The linguistic-cultural, the ethnic-tribal, the religious-communal tensions are sprouting in the ground fertilized by regional inequities in the development process and are posing a serious threat to the unity and the integrity of the nation.*

The solution of the political problems arising out of these strains and stresses are intrinsically linked with the processes of economic development and they cannot be tackled without a strategy based on the integration of a national home market through a territorial division of labour and the development of territorial production complexes, through the multi-layered nesting of local, sub-regional and regional markets; through the interlacing of the sectoral and the regional approaches; and through combining growth with justice so as to minimise interregional disparities.

We are paying a heavy price for ignoring the spatial dimension of the development process. It is the task of geographical research in the country to focus attention on this and similar other inadequacies and limitations of the Indian planning experience. With the identification of this crucial task, let us look critically at the emerging research landscape of Indian geography as a response to the development imperatives of recent years. Considerable evidence indicates that there is now a stronger concern for the study of the problems of development and planning in Indian geography. This trend, which emerged in the work of geographers working in governmental or quasi-governmental organisations and was characterized by some of the constraints of directed research, steeped into universities and academic institutions, wherein it flowered under conditions more conducive to innovative ideas. There has been a growing realization, both in the ivory towers of the academia and in the corridors of power that in a vast country like India with geographical diversities of a high order, there has to be an intertwining of the sectoral and the regional approaches to planning in order to optimize rates of growth and simultaneously minimize regional disparities. The geographers have responded, in a restricted manner though, to the challenge of providing the regional component of the planning effort at different levels. To the extent that they have done so, they have not only enriched their discipline by the findings of their applied research but have also established the utility of geographical research for planned development.

In order to shoulder their specific responsibilities in developmental research, Indian geographers are increasingly coming to terms with other disciplines within the framework of multidisciplinary research designs and strategies. Geographical research, with its holistic concerns, thrives best in such an academic ethos and contributes to the correction of the distorted visions of fragmented disciplines. De Castro in his classic The Geography of Hunger drew our attention pointedly to the basic inadequacy and infirmity of such distortions in the following words :

> "Since the middle of the nineteenth century a kind of university instruction has developed which is no longer interested in transmitting a unified image of the world, but rather in isolating, and mutilating facets of reality in the supposed interest of science. The tremendous impact of scientific progress produced a fragmentation of culture and pulverized it into little grains of learning. Each scientific specialist seized his granule and turned it over and over beneath the powerful lens of his microscope striving to penetrate its microcosm with a marvellous indifference to and towering ignorance of everything around him. Recently in Europe and the United States an extreme development of this type of university education has created within the culture a sort of civilization, directed by men whose scientific outlook is rigorous but who suffer from a deplorable cultural and political myopia."

The geographical approach provides the necessary correction to such narrowness, whereby one goes on knowing more and more about less and less till one ends by knowing everything about nothing. It is the essentially holistic concerns of geography which enable it to interface with other disciplines – the principle of spatial variation being provided by the former and the specific aspect or facet of reality being identified in terms of the latter. This interaction of geography (as also of history) with other disciplines is deeply rooted in its very nature. In this context the identification of the exact boundaries of the subject matter of geography loses its relevance. Geography does not operate within constraints which are alien to its system and which have been improvised by some other disciplines to meet the requirements of their own development. Though geography has an autonomous realm of its own, it is organically linked with other disciplines with every fibre of its being.

With such a perspective on geographical research within an interdisciplinary frame, geographers – particularly in the spheres of Economic Geography and Regional Planning – have shown commendable initiative in entering areas of work which were hitherto considered alien preserves. This has not only enriched geography but has brought a new dimension into the analytical frame of the complementary disciplines as well. It may, however, be noted that quite a bit of spurious research has surfaced under the umbrella of multidisciplinary work, where some tend, for example, to be good geographers among economists and good economists among geographers – in reality they being neither. Geography can interact with neighbouring disciplines not at the cost but on the basis of sound geography; not on the basis of a nodding acquaintance with the jargon of the complementary disciplines but of a deep understanding of its concepts and methods.

It may be realized without much difficulty that the ideographic tools of traditional geography would have been found to be totally inadequate in handling nomothetic questions of the new phase. Thus, the curtain was raised for what has been called by some as the quantitative revolution in geography. It was ushered in the sub-continent rather belatedly when scholars of the developed world had already begun to realize not only the potentialities but also the limitations of these methods. However, there is greater evidence now among Indian geographers of both confidence and competence in the use of quantitative methods of analysis and synthesis. This has led to the posing of some pertinent questions which could not be posed before the availability of these tools; to the findings becoming more and more exact; to the substitution of rule-of-the-thumb by replicable methods; to increasing capability to transform non-mappable into mappable data ; and most importantly to the embryonic development of explanatory systems. This is a most welcome phenomenon, but it has unfortunately brought with it some inherent dangers. A critical assessment of the impact of the quantitative revolution in Indian geography is, therefore, called for.

The essential tool of analysis and synthesis in geography, as in all scientific disciplines, is logic. Logic may be either qualitative or quantitative/

symbolic. As has been noted earlier, the use of the latter on a significant scale is a late arrival on the academic landscape of geography. Its emergence should, however, not be mistaken for the institutionalisation of a new sub-discipline, sometimes mistakenly designated as Quantitative Geography – with a capital Q and a capital G. This caution is necessary for one comes across not quite often though academic snobs with turned up noses calling themselves "quantitative geographers" looking down from the rarified atmosphere of the elusian heights of their social irrelevance upon ordinary mortals smelling of the earth. There is not and cannot be a quantitative geography, for this would lead to the acceptance of a taxonomy wherein the categories of the first order would be quantitative geography and qualitative geography. Who in this right senses would accept the position that there is a geography, which has no use for quantification, or a geography which shuns all qualitative assessments?

Both quality and quantity are aspects of objective reality. Quality refers to that which makes a particular object what it is; it reflects its identity. It cannot, therefore, be broken up into homogeneous parts; the moment that is done, the identity is lost. Consequently, in itself it cannot be measured. Since quantity, however, is capable of being increased or reduced without changing its character, one has to select quantitative indicators of quality in order to make qualitative assessments. Let us take the example of health, which is an integrated quality, cannot be broken up into homogeneous parts, and, therefore, cannot be measured directly. What does the physician do to get over this difficulty? He selects quantitative indicators of health which can be measured, for example, for a tubercular patient: body temperature, blood pressure, body weight, Erythrocyte Sedimentation Rate, Red Blood Cells and White Blood Cells. The values and magnitude of these quantitative indicators help him firstly to diagnose, that is, to make an assessment about the quality of health, and secondly to prescribe that is to move towards changing the quality. Let us now take an analogous situation from the field of geography of regional development. To start with, the geographer has to diagnose-to identify the nature of the health of the region, which is a quality and cannot be measured directly. Depending on his analytical system, he may select the following quantitative indicators that can be measured: for example, (i) land capability index, (ii) aridity index, (iii) per capita income, (iv) percentage share of the secondary sector in the working force, (v) index of urbanization, (vi) literacy rate, (vii) index of income inequality, (viii) share of the deprived communities in the total population and (ix) share of working women in the total female population. The values of these indicators, either singly or after composition, help him to arrive at a qualitative assessment about the "health" of the region. Having completed the diagnostic part of his work, he takes up the next task-that of prescription. Once again he goes to the quantitative indicators within the framework of his theory of development and picks out the crucial constraints – environmental, technological and institutional. Having done this, he works out the elements of the proposed operational strategy to remove the constraints and generate the desired rate of growth. It is clear from the above that the geographer moves back and forth from qualitative assessments to quantitative measurements. They are both necessary components of research strategy. Qualitative evaluation provides purpose and direction to quantification and gets back from it accuracy, precision and depth.

The more geography moves from the descriptive to the analytical, from the ideographic to the nomothetic, the more would be the need for the use of quantitative tools. However, recent experience has shown that there are some serious dangers inherent in their use against which a clear warning needs to be given.

It has quite often been inadequately realized that quantitative methods are not a substitute for thinking. Tools in social science research are not autonomous, cannot be used for the sake of using them; in fact, they flow out of the conceptual frame evolved by the researcher through intellection. The more sophisticated a tool is, the greater rigour it requires in the thinking process. Even a slight error at the conceptual level gets exaggerated manifold through the unfolding of the research design, distorting the results beyond recognition. The questions that need to be asked of the data, which are inherently inert and passive, emerge from theory, which statistical methods, by themselves, are incapable of generating. Due to an inadequate realization of this basic limitation of quantitative tools, one comes across, quite often unfortunately, spurious correlations, where statistical relationships are confused with causal relationships; or, composite indices with variables which cannot be logically composited; or, factor analysis which fails to distinguish the trivial from the significant; or, principal component analysis where the choice of variables is determined by the column headings of official reports rather than by a rational effort to identify the components of the phenomenon being analysed; or regionalization schemes evolved without taking into account the distinctly different roles played by environmental, technological and institutional factors. With the increasing use of computer, there is a possibility of this kind of quantification mania acquiring alarming proportions. While the increasing use of new tools and techniques of analysis is an indicator of growing competence in the field of geographical research, the real challenge lies in developing theories and concepts which will enable the discipline to assimilate and "digest" the use of sophisticated tools. If this challenge is not successfully met, quantification would be reduced to a ritual, where terms such as regression coefficients and D^2 statistics would be used more to make the research paper " respectable" and publishable in "reputable" journals abroad, rather than to understand the complex social reality that is India. Attention needs to be particularly drawn to four virulent forms of the quantification phobia.

First, there is an increasing tendency to hide the paucity of thought by weaving a cobweb of mathematical signs and formulae. Not long ago, a doctoral thesis proved, on the basis of a computer intensive exercise, that urban centres in India and the US have a common feature-their populations are larger than those of their rural counterparts. If such a statement were to have been made without the use of terms and phrases like "matrix of correlation" or "orthogonalisation" of a whole set of variables into mutually independent components: even the kid of Anderson's tale would have cried out in embarrassment: "But , Mummy, the emperor hasn't got anything on!" Spate, in his inimitable style, has quoted a "most sublime" example from our sister discipline – Sociology:

> "... such epoch-making generalizations (and this is not a parody!) as that perhaps, people have more frequent, cordial and intimate contacts with their personal friends than with those who are not their personal friends; or that while one usually marries some one of one's own creed and class, quite often he or she is of somewhat opposite temperament. Although this last conclusion on mate-selection was arrived at by impeccably quantitative methods- - with 15 variables (variably dichotomized and double-dichotomized) into 44 subvariables, the complete inter-spousal correlation consists of 15 times 15 (=225) submatrices containing 44 times 44 (1936) elements...' – it is perhaps not fair to quote it against respectable quantifiers, since the generalisation is based on 25 university couples, a restricted sample not likely to be of practical use to colleagues with adolescent daughters."

Second, statistical relationships are, not rarely, confused with causal relationships. From the given data, wherein every time X undertakes a railway journey the train is late, one cannot conclude that the travel of X is the cause of the train being late or the lateness of the train is the cause of the journeys of X, whatever be the value of the coefficient at whatever level of significance. Causal relationships should be rooted in logic, in the conceptual frame of the scholar which is evolved through the rigours of intellection and not through statistical exercises. Quantitative methods validate theory, they do not generate or replace it.

Third, it is something inadequately realized that while statistical methods are positivistic and value neutral, the premises underlying them are not. Let us take the example of the valuable monograph of the 1961 census entitled Levels of Regional Development in India, wherein the indicators of distributive trade, manufacturing and infra-structure – which constitute Block V in the study – are assumed to move together in the same direction. How do we interpret this result? It is well known that the Colin Clark hypothesis of the share of the territory sector as an indicator of economic development is just not tenable in most of the developing economies, wherein it is an indicator of disguised unemployment rather than of economic development. The preponderance of tertiary activities in the Indian urbanization process is more an indicator of the dysfunctional character of urbanization, as the growth of centres of consumption rather than of production. It is clear that an essentially erroneous assumption cannot be validated by being stamped under the seal of Kendell's Method of Ranking Coefficient.

Fourth, there is a serious danger of falling a prey to what C. Wright Mills calls the "perversity of abstracted empiricism," i.e. to minimize the initiating role of a hypothesis and an analytical frame in the strategy of research and ultimately to end up by denying their role altogether. To begin with, the cart is put before the horse and then the horse is dispensed with altogether with the fond (but naive) hope that the cart would ultimately "generate" its own horse! Experience has, time and again, demonstrated the sterility of such an approach, and has shown that, in the field of social science research, tools and methods are subservient to and flow from the analytical frame and cannot be developed autonomously of and for themselves. As Guelke has pointed out "theories define data, not vice versa". States has drawn our attention to the erroneous tendency whereby "relative sophistication in the measurement and description of a set of abstracted relationships has tended to become the major gauge of scientific truth, and in this unsatisfactory way, methodology of research has been inverted." The indicators chosen and the sophisticated multivariate techniques used by Soja, for example, to analyse economic development in Kenya are rooted in his theory which states that imperialism has been the major instrument of modernization in that country. If one is able to show that Soja's basic theoretical assumption itself is erroneous, the entire house of (computer!) cards collapses! Theory is of the essence. "Abstracted empiricism" is based on the rejection of this essential element; and leads to the blind alley wherein the task of the research is reduced to the punching of cards or getting them purchased at the rate of one paisa a card; and lo and behold! the computer provides the answer. Let us take the example of a fairly sophisticated exercise based on the data provided by the census monograph cited above but using the computer-intensive principal component analysis instead of the comparatively simpler method of Kendell's ranking coefficient. To start with, the twenty-four variables, used in the earlier study, were reduced to fifteen more efficient ones on the basis of a study of the correlation matrix. It would be reasonable to expect that in measuring the levels of development, the choice of indicators or their abridgement would have been given far greater attention since it constitutes the crux of the methodology; it is through this that the pertinent questions tha need to be asked of the data are identified. In this case, the questions were no formulated through an understanding of the social situation – at least, there is no indication that they were. The indicators selected for an earlier study were accepted lock, stock and barrel and the "inefficient" ones were discarded on the basis of their internal statistical properties, without a critical examinatio of their relevance to the analytical frame; in fact, the whole exercise ha proceeded without any analytical frame, without any initial hypothesis. Th results obtained in the study under consideration through the "intellection" o the computer suffer from two basic lacunae:

First, the components are not "identifiable"-in the sense that no economi interpretation in terms of real variables is possible; and this perforce the schola has to do himself.

Second, there is an underlying assumption that it is sufficient for a subse of variables simply to move together to be represented by a component. It is for instance, stated therein:

"It is clear that the following variables - income, literacy, minoritie (sic), immigration, retail manufacturing and registered factory workers, numbe of establishments run on electricity, roads per mile, irrigated area, tenancy an the rate of increase in population are positively associated with developmen on the other hand, scheduled castes and tribes, hired workers, agricultur labourers, proportion of labourers, and cultivators and rural population a negatively associated with development."

It is obvious that we have a paradoxical situation on hand :

First, the incidence of tenancy moves in the same direction as the gener index of economic development, and

Second, indices of development of capitalism in agriculture- such incidence of hired workers and agriculture labourers move in a directi opposite to the level of economic development. The method obviously assum that there is nothing fundamentally counter–developmental about the dynami indicated by the above; and that the logic of the development process obtaini in any given situation is, in some way, optimal also. It amounts to assumi that the logic of the underdevelopment is, in some way, also rational a legitimate. And, that is swallowing hook, line and sinker – the neo-imperial bait of the "modernization" ideology.

The dangers inherent in the use of quantitative tools of analysis – some of which have been discussed above – do not indicate that they should be left like hot potatoes or touched , if at all, by a long pair of tongs. Such a conservative attitude would seriously restrict the development of geography and inhibit its interactions with other disciplines. It should, however, be clearly realized that quantification is not a convenient substitute for thinking; and that the more sophisticated the statistical tool, the more sophisticated analytical frame it requires. It is only through the intertwined process of the development of theory and sophistication of analytical tools that the discipline is destined to develop.

It follows from the above that the Achilles' heel of geographical research in India continues to be its incapacity to move from the study of the particular, to transcend the concrete, to generalize. It is symptom of its theoretical anaemia that the overwhelming concern with specific minutiae has inhibited the development of theory – the discipline tending to acquire the dimensions and characteristics of "a dinosaur: a huge body, a long tail, and a tiny little head". Geographical science having failed, like *Hanuman*, to identify the *Sanjivani* of theory, carries the whole mountain of infinitesimal facts on its hefty shoulders. The hunger for more and more undigested data is a symptom of the same disease. Theory provides a tool to separate the grain from the chaff, the relevant from the irrelevant, the significant from the insignificant, the trivial from the important. Under such circumstances, explanations would not become available; and the researcher can, at best, come to terms with the surface of phenomena under examination. It may, however, be noted with some satisfaction that most geographers did not, unlike some of their more revered counterparts in some other disciplines, lose touch with the earth while soaring into the ethereal heights of airy nothings, so as to end in vacuous quibbling, semantic jugglery and meta-theoretical acrobatics. In contrast, fortunately, Indian geography still smells of the earth. The source of its major strength lies in its tradition of down-to-earth empirical work; of its major weakness in its " spongy organism without theoretical spine". While it has escaped the sterility of theory-mongering, it is sunken deep in the mire of blind and directionless empiricism. This has led, first, to its incapacity to move rapidly from description to analysis, from identification to explanation, and second, to its inability to abstract macro-generalizations from micro studies.

In the absence of theory-building on the basis of indigenous experience, there is a continual tendency to fill the conceptual vacuum by importing ready-made goods from the glittering departmental stores of the developed world, particularly of its English-speaking segment. This had led to a situation where new developments quite often do not occur inside the organism of Indian geography as the inevitable consequence of an evolutionary process within its realm of ideas. They are just mechanically aggregated to the amorphous mass in response to the latest intellectual fashion in the west. This has given to Indian geography a highly fragmented character. Thus, layers after layers of academic work, related not only to different decades but different centuries of geographical thought , co-exist in the largely invertebrate system of Indian geography. Not rarely, some Indian scholars still tend to acquire the character of research assistants validating a hypothesis evolved in one another of the developed countries of the West. This is generally due not to the paucity of financial but of intellectual resources. Though there have been some pioneering endeavours to build conceptual frames on the basis of indigenous experience, they have been too few and still embryonic to be able to compete with goods from abroad. Import substitution, therefore, continues to be a major national task not only in the sphere of the economy but also, and perhaps more so, in the realm of the intellect. There is, fortunately, definite evidence of theoretical initiatives of significance in the recent past, which leads one to hope that intellectual dependence would soon be a thing of the past and Indian geographers would no longer be content to be only " hewers of wood and drawers of water" in the field of research, but would be generating knowledge in the true sense of the word and on an adequate scale.

On the occasion of the Third Indian Geography Congress, dear colleagues, let us rededicate ourselves to this noble objective so that we may serve the cause of our discipline and enable it to play its rightful role in national development.

Nalagatla Bala Krishna Reddy
1929 -

A port on the Andhra coast of India called Allur is the place where Reddy was born on 1st July, 1929. At the age of five when Reddy's father admitted him into the Ramakrishna High School, little was he aware that one day his son would be the chairman of the Andhra Pradesh State Council of Higher Education. After all no one in Reddy's father or forefathers generation had been to school. Belonging to a family of semi-landlords, Reddy recalls his parents may not have been literate but a liberal intellectual environment prevailed at home. Heated debates and lively discussions on the Indian National Movement for example were a topic of common conversation. The milieu charged Reddy towards active politics.

In his days of youth Reddy was not an arm chair communist; for him organizing and participating in meets and demonstrations was a common practice. He was the General Secretary of the City Students Union at Karnatak University in 1948-49, Government Training College Teachers Association in Nellore in 1956-57 and the Andhra Association at Banaras Hindu University in 1958-59. It is the attention Reddy devoted to spearhead his political commitment which drafted him to study geography. Not that active politics and geography have much in common but in the case of Reddy there is a relationship. Reddy wanted to pursue medicine. He had zoology, physics and chemistry as his courses of study at the under-graduate level. But the hours spent in political meets were a distraction which took precious time away from preparing for medicine and thus forced him to take up geography. Politics perhaps had come his way only to veer him towards academics. As soon as he completed a post-graduation in geography, his interest in politics waned and he set his mind to books.

Reddy's intellectual ability is apparent on many fronts. Abstaining from bandwagon of politics his grades jumped from the second to a first class first in his post-graduation degree. Marxian ideology had influenced his youth but did not colour his research. An analytical temperament reinforced by a training in the science subjects instilled a marked objectivity in his research. Reddy had a greater interest in physical geography. But he was aware of his limitations and opted for a doctorate on 'Urbanisation in the Krishna and Godavari Deltas.' Though his initial research stayed away from physical geography, his techniques of analysis even with the human parameters were not lay descriptions. With publications on Refinement of Nearest Neighbour and Reflexive Neighbour Analysis, Delimitation of Polynuclei Urban Zones and Moment Analysis he contributed to the methodological facet of urban geography. Set on a hard rock of quantitative analysis, quality is also an hallmark of Reddy's publications.

The attraction for physical geography made him undertake a certificate course in geomorphology and photogeology in 1978, a decade after his doctorate. Thereafter his research spanned both the physical and human aspects of the discipline. Nearly one third of Reddy's sixty research papers, four out of his eight research projects and seven of seventeen students he supervised for a doctorate worked on physical geography. Reddy was not just a researcher, his ability to impart knowledge was duly acknowledged by the Government of Andhra Pradesh as they confered on him the honour of the Best Teacher Award in 1984. Here, Reddy's bachelors and masters degree in education were additional assets. Endowed with pre-requisite skills, after some hiccups of unsettlement, with a year at the Government Arts College at Srikakulam, twelve years at the Karnatak Science College and a year at the department of geography at Dharwad he finally settled to a devoted tenure as founder and chairman of the department of geography at the Sri Venkateswara University, Tirupati, from 1972 to 1989.

To live life as a recluse around research and teaching was not the way of Reddy. Seeking a wider interaction he not only took frequented a dozen conferences in India and half a dozen abroad, but also sought an active participation in the various geographical associations in India. He was the president not only of National Association of Geographers, India but also of Indian Geographical Society, Madras; Institute of Indian Geographers, Pune and Indian Council of Geographers, Bhubaneshwar. Reddy's wise counsel and friendly cheer to dissolve vexing situations won him a place in numerous administrative posts of the university. He was a member of the senate and academic council and a trustee in the Board of Management of Sri Venketeswara University, Tirupati. Despite his prowess, Reddy could not become the vice-chancellor of a university. But he says a better proposition came his way. On his retirement in 1984 he was appointed as chairman of the Andhra Pradesh State Council of Higher Education, a position where he liaisoned and coordinated the activities of vice-chancellors of 10 universities of Andhra Pradesh.

Today at the age of 72 as Reddy sits on the portico of his house and compiles his book 'Patterns of Political and Cultural Antecedents of India: A Geopolitical Analysis' and looks out at the road which leads to the famous temple of Sri Venketeswara on the Thirumala hillock of Tirupati , one fact is clear that from his village Allur, Reddy has indeed come a long way.

Perspectives on Indian Geography

N.B.K. REDDY

At the very outset, I express my profound gratitude to the distinguished members of the National Association of Geographers, India for the great honour they have done to me by electing me as the President of the Second Annual Conference. It is with immense humility that I have accepted this great responsibility. Although I am fully aware of the fact that I am quite unequal to the task, yet I have to accomplish it as I have to perform it as my duty. In fact, it is the affection in abundance, the warmth in lavishness and the support in profusion that I have received from the distinguished senior geographers and the ebullient young geographers of the country that has prompted me to be cheeky and accept this challenging task of delivering the presidential address at this conference of the premier organisation of geographers in the country.

It is indeed paradoxical that although geography is a subject of great antiquity, as a modern academic discipline and applied science, it is only 150 years old. Indian geography, being hardly 50 years old, is much younger than modern geography itself.

In 1947, at the dawn of the Indian independence, there were just three universities teaching geography. Presently, the subject has grown, and has been carried into about 70 universities and a large number of post- graduate colleges. The adolescent spurt of a phenomenal growth which took place in the 1960's and 1970's is marked by a hesitancy and tentativeness of approach and a 'crush' modelling after the West. This adolcscent phenomena, I trust, would soon pass into a stable phase of maturity and adulthood characterised by confidence and competence commensurate with the demands of a growing nation. It is imperative on the part of Indian geographers to provide the necessary perspective that would stand the stresses and strains of an over-populated country with a developing economy.

The report of the Indian Council of Social Sciences and Research Review Committee rightly indicates the present status of geography in India. It observes "geography, despite the late start it had in the Indian universities, has manifested

---

5th Indian Geography Congress
Tirupati, 1982, December

considerable potential for growth in recent times. Geographers have produced a sizeable volume of research literature over a wide range. Geographical research is still dominated by the traditional methods of cartographic compilation of history, archaeology and of qualitative description. A noteworthy trend in geographical research today is the increasing use of quantitative methods to study spatial structure, spatial organisation and spatial process".

The comments made by Professor Moonis Raza on Indian geography cannot be more true when he says "Indian geographers have , by and large, shown little interest in theoretical discussions on the nature of geography. The reasons are partly historical. When the controversy between the exponents of environmental determinism and possibilism was raging in the West, modern Indian geography had not been born. It did not get involved in the ideological turmoil through which modern geography acquired its philosophical foundations and its intellectual rigour. By the time geography emerged on India campuses, the storm had already passed. Having 'improved' and uncritically accepted a complete system of ideas without participating in the making of it, Indian geography tended to develop at best, as a dinosaur. The tradition continues. Concern for theory is still considered futile pedantry and search for logical systems is equated with esoteric cause. This has led to a situation where new developments do not grow inside the organism as the inevitable consequence of an evolutionary process in the realm of ideas. They are just mechanically aggregated to the amorphous mass in response to the latest intellectual fashion in the West. This has given to Indian geography a highly fragmented character".

Professor C.D. Deshpande's comments are significant in this context. According to him, "It is not surprising that those who have been trained in the United Kingdom, the United States of America and more recently in the Union of Soviet Socialist Republic and the East European countries have influenced our research activity. Lamentably, the influence of France and Germany, which significantly continues more rigorously in the natural aspects of geographical science, is lacking. But, apart from these exposures, it is time that we review our problems through our own perspective. Amazingly enough, while we are open to accepting the themes and the techniques of Western geographers, often very uncritically, we are not sensitive to the rigorous application of logical thinking, precise expression of our thoughts in writing and meticulous documentation which almost every research paper reveals".

The historical development of geography has had its share of controversies. Controversies of a philosophical and methodological character are dialectical in nature and may lead to progress. But too much of controversy might shake the very foundations of the subject and results in waste of talent in a futile diatribe, creating more heat than light in the process. It is in this context that the great controversies that raged in geography, these are: determinism versus possibilism, nomothetic versus idiographic, physical versus human, theoretical versus empirical, micro versus macro, disaggregation versus aggregation, regional versus systematic, etc. need to be examined in the Indian context.

It is, no doubt, true that the quantitative and conceptual revolutions as well as the problem oriented and applied approaches have elevated the status of Indian research. Equally, there has been an increase in the technological sophistication, modelling and communicative jargon.

But despite these developments and the large volume of output, Indian geography is yet to make a significant impact on the international scene. It is still weak in its conceptual, empirical, analytical and inferential aspects. There is a lack of 'in-depth' studies of a quantitative nature. While qualitative assessment has its own place, it is important to lay greater stress on quantitative methodology. Quantitative methodology fixes the seal of exactness on the data. Use of quantitative techniques would make assessment, scientific prediction, enumeration and communication more accurate, manipulable and meaningful . It is, therefore, necessary to strengthen the classical tradition retaining the gains of the quantitative revolution.

There is immense need for initiating certain major thrusts for the development of the subject, and for applying knowledge of geography to solve some of the problems of the country. In a country where more than half of its population is living below the poverty line, a great deal of research work needs to be done by geographers with the object of ameliorating the distressing conditions of poverty. The magnitude of the population problem in India is accelerated by poverty, illiteracy and regional and social disparities. It was estimated that about 360 million people in the country were classified as poor. It is indeed a staggering figure. Poverty is the biggest pollutant in India and the most effective device to control the rapid population growth is economic development. The country cannot make worthwhile progress unless this stupendous population growth is arrested. The main pockets of poverty have to be identified and located both spatially and socially. No task is more urgent, more imperative and more categorical than solving this problem. The crux of the population problem of India lies in the rural densities and chronic rural poverty. The problem in its all aspects needs to be studied in detail so as to find proper solutions.

It is necessary to understand the complex geopolitical problems of India with reference to the international setting. Panikkar, in his pioneering geopolitical study of India and the Indian ocean, brilliantly summed up the situation, as follows: "Geography has been at all times one of the great and most regrettable gaps in Indian knowledge. Worse than our lack of interest in things historical has been our utter neglect of geography. Geography constitutes the permanent basis of every nation's history. It is one of the major factors that determines the historical evolution of a people. Today, free India has to realise her position in the world where geography has placed her in relation to other countries. She has also to understand the strength and weaknesses arising from her geography. A nation can neglect geography only at its peril."

In this context it may be said that had the geography of the country been different, the history of India too would have been very different from what it is. In the early days both the land and sea frontiers of India were impregnable. All the early invasions came from the northwest through the Khybar and Balan passes. Had these two passes been guarded by Indian rulers, Indian history would have been totally different. Later, when the maritime powers were emerging and growing strong, Indian rulers failed to take note of this development. The pressure came from over the sea and eventually the country came under maritime British power. As such it needs hardly be stressed that we should evince greater interest in studies on the geopolitical aspects of our country.

There has been a growing tendency to apply foreign models to the Indian setting. If foreign models are uncritically accepted and applied they become blind imitations. Such applications stifle incentives for indigeneous approaches towards original and creative thinking . It is needless to state that the Indian context is unique and as such the methodology and constructs havę to be validated in an Indian frame of reference so that the interpretation would carry a sense of realism.

Social, cultural and historical geography are some of the neglected fields in geographical research. These are almost untouched by geographers. India with its hoary antiquity, rich and diversified cultural traditions provides a fertile ground for research in these fields. Such studies go a long way in understanding the complete socio-cultural problems of the country.

The teaching of geography in schools and colleges needs a fresh look. The introduction of social studies in schools in the late forties greatly affected the scope of geography. There is an urgent need for strengthening geography at the high school level, since it is here that a strong foundation could be laid. The school syllabi and the teaching of the subject needs to be redrafted and reoriented so as to provide greater awareness of man's environment and interaction between man and environment. College geography too has not kept stride with the development of the subject. Particular emphasis may be laid on awareness of man's immediate environment and regional geography. The subject has to be made more relevant to provide a broad base for an inter-disciplinary super structure at higher academic levels. Also, studies with greater empirical bias relevant to a region and studies that are more problem-oriented need to be introduced without neglect of theoretical issues.

The modern era of scientific and technological developments has thrown a great challenge to the geographical science in India. The need for wider application of geographical approach to various practical problems in India is increasingly felt especially in the field of Regional Planning, Resource Development and Management, and Environmental Planning. Geographer's task is to know and tell others about the environment. With the rapid growth of population and urbanization, besides increasing regional disparities, the need for regional planning and scientific landuse planning acquired greater urgency.

The technological aids for a well planned research effort have to be three fold, these are: the utilization of (a) simple technology, (b) intermediate technology, and (c) sophisticated technology. Besides the choice of appropriate technology which is of crucial importance, it is necessary to blend the three levels of technologies into a proper mix to suit the highly diversified physical, socio-economic and cultural setting of India. It will also provide the basic infrastructure for concerted research effort and lay solid foundation for future research. Technological developments such as remote sensing, aerial photography and computer technology have opened up new vistas for speedy data collection, data storage, data retrieval and data analysis. The implications of these technologies in geography are far reaching and their utility in geographical research is immense.

More than 50 per cent of the country's land surface is yet to be mapped geologically on one inch scale. Only a very small part of the country is surveyed for ground water. For purposes of block level planning, large scale maps have to be prepared and this can be accomplished by employing a large contingent of cartographers. Resource planning is possible only if the surveys are conducted at micro level and mapping too is done at that level. All these require a large number of cartographers, geographers and surveyors. Suitable training programmes have to be initiated accordingly.

Regional planning, resource planning and eco-system planning are other areas which demand the attention of Indian geographers. An integrated approach involving these three areas of research is required to achieve development without upsetting the ecological balance. In this we can derive benefit from the experience of the developed countries and avoid the pitfalls they had. We need development without environmental degradation. The country has to achieve a dynamic equilibrium and not a static equilibrium of the system.

India has a large scientific and technological man-power which itself is a resource and a major force for social and economic development. Yet the real potential and capability of the large community of scientists have to be fully harnessed for national development. We are close to the limits of non-renewable resources. Yet we have to improve productivity and ensure the minimum basic needs of our vast population. It requires the use of more energy, but it has to be tapped from renewable power resources. The world is already facing an acute energy crisis. Most of the non-renewable resources are finite and may last for half a century or atmost for a century. Hence, scrupulous conservation and management of resources is imperative, lest there be a scarcity which will ultimately lead to a crisis. For optimum and all-round utilisation of resources and to eliminate regional disparities, regional planning would provide the necessary strategy.

For many more decades to come, India will remain essentially agricultural. Agriculture will continue to provide necessary finance for investments and raw materials to sustain the economy. The success of our planning mainly depends upon the development of agriculture and its stability. To achieve this end, research has to be carried out on various aspects of agriculture , cropping pattern, optimization of land use, development of irrigation and the supply of necessary inputs. Therefore , agricultural geography will have to play a prominent role in the economic development of the country.

In these days of hyper specialisation, the need for inter-disciplinary studies cannot be overstressed. For the purpose of integrating the knowledge and to counteract centrifugal tendencies, an interdisciplinary approach is imperative. Geography itself is an inter-disciplinary subject. Its inter-disciplinary nature is its strong point as well as its weak point. The geographer will remain as a generalist unless he deliberately chooses to strengthen his technical base in a specialisation. He should be in a position to enter into dialogue and discussion on interdisciplinary basis with confidence and competence only if he equips himself with sound technical knowledge in his field of specialisation. For instance, geographers have been talking about environment and eco-system ever since the inception of geography. But the field has been taken over by the engineers and the scientists while geographers remained as silent and helpless spectators. This is probably because they do not have the necessary technical base to tackle the problem of pollution and other problems of ecological degradation.

To conclude, it may be said that geography can play a crucial role in nation building. In fact, a geographer has the necessary intergrated perspective. However, he will be able to accomplish the task only if he can strengthen his technical base. The very fact that geography has witnessed a tremendous growth in a short span of time itself shows that the people have realised the importance of the subject as an academic discipline and as an applied science. There is virtually no sphere where the geographer cannot play a significant role. He has to exploit to advantage his generalist equipment and systematic approach and make a new thrust so that he will be able to play an important role in nation building. It is necessary that Indian geography should strive to discover and rediscover India. He has to work towards creating prosperous society where every individual can lead a happy life without the fear of exploitation and without the risk of scarcity. It is my fond hope that this conference should help in enthusing the geographers of the country to achieve this goal. May this conference provide a new perspective to the subject so as to make it more dynamic and useful to the society.

Mohammad Shafi
1924 -

'Mecca of Indian Geography', is what the famous British professor of the land use survey, Stamp, called the department of geography at Aligarh. A considerable share of sustaining this complement accrues to Shafi. Shafi is not the founder of the department of geography at Aligarh, established in 1924, he joined the department as a faculty twenty-four years later. Shafi belongs to the eighth batch of post-graduate students who passed out of the department. The Curzon Geographical Society and the journal Geographer existed 22 years before Shafi contributed his first paper to it in 1948. The long standing department, name of the society and its journal existed many years before Shafi made his presence felt.

Carrying the hallow of glory and excellence of the department forward, it is the recognition of Shafi's research as a doctoral student under the tutelage of Stamp in 1956 which makes him a critical partner in the complement. Acknowledgement by scholars of repute, specially those belonging to universities of the developed world, does put one in immediate limelight. In the conservative environ of the British universities, Shafi met his supervisor half-a-dozen times. Yet the inclusion of a sizeable reference from Shafi's doctoral work in the presidential address of Stamp at the International Geographical Union, at Rio-de–Janeiro in 1956 and its publication in the Geographical Review in 1957 affirms the perception the supervisor carried of his student. Despite the frugal meetings, Shafi worked tenaciously and submitted his doctorate in a brief span of twenty-one months.

A vortex of head spinning success gravitated towards Shafi when, in 1956, he returned from United Kingdom to Aligarh, the city which was to remain his permanent place of work and stay. He was promoted as a reader in 1959 .He had still to cross his fortieth birthday when he was appointed professor and chairperson of the department. His tenure of twenty-two years as chairperson was the longest that the department ever had. Honoured as Professor Emeritus on his retirement, his record of outstretched services at the department is unbeatable. In terms of the frequency of attendance at the International Geographical Congress, Shafi hardly has any parallel. He has the rare distinction of being elected as vice-president of International Geographical Union for two terms. With nearly ten per cent of all the articles in the in-house journal, Geographer, and a number of books published at the Aligarh University, he has a sizeable preserve through publications. Success is not confined within the department of geography. Though Shafi was vice-chancellor for only a year, he remained the pro-vice chancellor for eleven long years. He was awarded with the Padma Shri by the Government of India on the occasion of Republic Day, 2001. The same year Bhoovigyan Vikas Foundation, Delhi, conferred its first Bhoogol Ratna to him.

"A teacher should never rest on his oars" is what Shafi professes. Plodding from eight in the morning till five in the evening, and the ability to meticulously sift pages for facts built Shafi's reservoir of strength to participate in the discipline of geography in India in a variety of ways. From practical examinations to appointments, class lectures to presidential and keynote addresses, seminars to workshops, occasional writings in newspapers to scholarly books, Shafi performs multiplicity of roles incumbent upon a committed academician.

In Shafi's five decades of professional life, the 1980s and 1990s stands out as a block of maximum activities. It is during these two decades that he attended fifty per cent of the sixteen international conferences, and participated in sixty-six per cent of the six national seminars. Forty-one per cent of his forty-eight research papers were published in this decade. No less than seventy per cent of the twenty honours bestowed upon him fall in this time. While his chairmanship of the department had reached its tail end in 1984, pro-vice-chancellorship of the Aligarh Muslim University and a brief vice-chancellorship also fall within this bracket of time. It is not a coincidence that he was also elected as the President of National Association of Geographers, India in 1993.

Academic work, however, cannot be mechanically contained within a defined span of time. Shafi's exalted endurance of perseverance towards research transcends time. While the stamp of land use has its origin at the London School of Economics way back in 1954, a life time of devotion to issues on agricultural geography can be ascertained from his works which initially include themes like land use, agricultural efficiency, agricultural productivity and later proceed to regional imbalances and cost benefit analysis in Indian agriculture. Shafi's perceptive ability to compare and contrast the characteristics of agriculture in India vis-à-vis the West allowed him to challenge not just the feasibility of Stamp's method of land use survey in the Indian context but also question some premise of the von Thunen model. While the latter had asserted that it is the factor of market which dictated changing land use around an urban area, Shafi's conclusion for the situation in India was that it is the intensity of irrigation which has a more dominating control on land use.

Even at the age of seventy-seven he is engrossed in a chain of works. Barely has his book on South Asia hit the bookshelves in 2000, that he submitted his manuscript on Central Asia in 2001. In pipeline stands the draft of his book, 'Agricultural Geography - Concepts, Principles and Processes'. With an inexhaustible source of energy, from a primary and secondary schooling in the small town of Jaunpur, Shafi proceeded to undertake his undergraduate degree from the University of Allahabad in 1943 and a post- graduation from Aligarh in 1947. Setting sail from Bombay, on Balova, a Polish shipliner to earn a doctorate at the University of London, Shafi returned home with dreams of hardwork and success .

From Jaunpur to London, from a lecturer to a vice-chancellor, from medals in school to the Padma Shri Shafi has indeed come a long way. He claims 'he does not chase offices but offices chase him'. The pursuit continues, for pilgrims never cease.

Geographer and the Society with Special Reference to India

M. SHAFI

I am grateful to the general body of the National Association of the Geographers of India in holding their Fifth Annual Session at Aligarh and electing me its President. I am also thankful to you, Mr. Chairman for finding time from your busy schedule and gracing this occasion by your presence. I should also express my gratitude to our chief guest, Prof. Rais Ahmad, Vice-Chairman, University Grants Commission for inaugurating this Congress. Professor Ahmad is an eminent educationist and a physicist by profession. Had he not chosen Physics as his subject of specialization perhaps he would have been a geographer, like his elder brother, Late Professor Nafis Ahmad, a geographer of international reputation.

It was in February last that the University in collaboration with the Indian National Science Academy and the University Grants Commission hosted an International Conference of Food Systems with special reference to India, and after about ten months we are having the National Forum of geographers.

One of the objectives of the annual meeting of the geographers is to take stock of the developments that have taken place in the various fields of the subject, the new trends that are emerging and the thrust areas that need to be developed. If one makes a survey of the research work being done in the different fields of geography, one would come across very intensive and useful work of applied nature being done in the Indian universities, but by and large these works decorate the shelves of the respective departments and do not see the light of the day. The Planning Organizations in the country also do not seem to be aware of the work which the geographers are doing in the realm of agriculture and land use, regional development, rural development and urban transport, geomorphology and terrain evaluation , tourism and recreation, location

---

6th Indian Geography Congress
Aligarh, 1983, December

analysis in respect of industries, health and nutrition, population and tribal studies, and still the subject does not find the prime of position in the list of subjects attracting employment.

There was a time when the subject used to be descriptive but soon it passed from the realm of description to analysis. Still the analysis was empirical and largely based on the interpretation of maps. Indian geographers soon realized this shortcoming and statistical techniques began to be applied in geographical studies so much so that there was deluge of these methods and in some cases after the application of long, tedious, complicated statistical methods, the conclusion made the researcher none the wiser. To aim precision by the application of these methods is most welcome, but to apply them for embellishment of a work is hardly justified. Even with the introduction of these techniques in geography, the position of the subject in the "employed list" has improved only marginally. However, the quest for new philosophies around which to organize the content and approach of academic geography continues and in reviewing these trends, several important themes have emerged. The interest in more applied and socially relevant objectives has increased and there is an increasing emphasis on processes and the dynamics of change and the formulation of baseline reviews from which further investigation may proceed. There is a change in the scale of inquiry and a search for improved methods for disseminating the results of geographical research.

There is a great need of creating an awareness and consciousness among the people in general and the planners and administrators in particular about the scope and subject matter of geography and what the geographers are doing in universities and colleges. It is high time that the National Association of Geographers, India may constitute a liaison body which may interface with the planning agencies, administrators, Public Service and Public Corporations, industry and commerce to apprise them of the utility of geographers and the research work they are doing in the diverse fields.

What is hardly realised is that geography is not exclusively involved with a single view of the world and of society, but is concerned with the problems involved in complex interrelations and with the human consequences as well as the physical facts involved in practical and the real world problems. The breadth of geography is a source of strength in two major ways : first, in training students to identify the elements involved in complex problems and to analyse them rationally in both empirical and conceptual terms; secondly, it stresses competence in a number of skills not only appropriate to aspects of geographical problems, but of practical relevance to many jobs and problems in the contemporary world and which involved literacy, graphicacy and numeracy. It has to be emphasised that geography is neither an abstract academic study, nor a largely applied subject : it has elements of both. The ways in which we tackle the rapidly widening range of geographical information and the skills needed to handle geographical problems are both of critical importance for academics as well as for professions.

Geography as a discipline is in a flourishing state· in the United Kingdom, the Union of Soviet Socialist Republic, Canada, Australia, France, Germany and Japan, but it appears that in the U.S.A. the discipline is in a low key. Its recent history in the United States of America is as depressing as any English winter drizzle. In view of the unique nature of the subject there should not only be career opportunities for geographers, but the usefulness of the subject should be widely disseminated, both academic and practical and its stability in India should be reinforced. I have mentioned the crisis in American geography to point out that there is no scope for complacency. American geography is suffering serious contraction for a lack of academic viability. Geography's foothold in several of America's leading universities has been lost. The closure of the front ranked department at the prestigious University of Michigan is seen as a major setback. Perhaps, the main reason of the contraction and crisis is that geographical education is still regarded as a marginal activity by American schools and colleges. Something called geography is included in the social studies programme along with history and civics. The amalgam of social studies, where geography is taught by persons not trained in the discipline, has spelt disaster. The tragic consequences of elimination of geography as a discipline should be manifest as time passes and perhaps these universities, which have cast off geography, may reestablish it when significant damage to the human stuff has already been done.

It should be remembered that whatever else is achieved in a child's formal education, that child should emerge from twelve years of compulsory schooling competent in the general knowledge and understanding of the world in which we live. If this objective is to be achieved, it must surely not only be through viewing the world in historical terms. Geography, more than any other subject in the curriculum, prepares people for life in a rapidly changing environment in which their responsibilities will be not only at the local level but also at the national and international levels.

Again, the need for improvement in the ability to answer question is expressed in the research objectives of the application to techniques and methodology of geography commonly referred to as 'Applied Geography'

. In so far as most of the practical problems presented to geography are related in some way to the planning process, past or present, it is important that the process, whereby geographical distributions of human activities, structures and land uses come into being and change, be so well understood that they can be projected into the future, and as a result, both the immediate effects and the peripheral effects of changes in the assumptions can be assessed. To a large degree, the usefulness of geography to society will be measured by its ability to predict. As David Smith has pointed out that if geography does not broaden its domain of concern to include the full range of contemporary social problems with a significant spatial dimension, its contribution to policy research will be limited.

Today the problem facing the developing world are rather different from the developed industrialized world. The developed world is marked by nutritional affluence : affluences in food grains, milk, butter, meat and cheese, while the vast sections of the developing world suffer from under-nutrition and malnutrition. In India, the population has almost doubled during the last thirty years and may reach in the neighborhood of one billion by the turn of the century, and although the total production of foodgrains increased from 50 million tonnes in 1950-51 to 135 million tonnes in 1981-82, the problem of feeding the millions remains grim and by 2,000 A.D. the production may have to be raised to 235 million tonnes and at the current level of nutrition with consequential increase in housing, industrial and urban development, transport system, educational facilities and medical care, the production should be much greater. This at once brings the geographer interface with futurology.

Jean Gottmann identified the first megalopolis as the coalescing system of the metropolitan area along the eastern seaboard of the United States between Boston and Washington. Although the region is not a single city, it is rapidly becoming a megalopolitan area, as the separate metropolitan areas expand and extend towards each other. Constantine Doxiadis and his associates at the Athens Centre for Ekistics have predicted the evolution of Ecumenopolis, which means a universal city consisting of the entire inhabitable area of the earth. In the next fifty to seventy-five years, there may come into existence a world city, interconnected, functionally continuous though not spatially contiguous so much so that all people will be accessible to each other as are contemporary residents of a metropolitan area with the help of electronic intercommunication system, but perhaps man-resource imbalance may persist and food production in water may be more efficient than production on land. Similarly, many minerals are present in sea water and at the bottom in concentrations, which may soon be exploitable and the question of the ownership of the sea and its resources will soon arise.

If the population doubles in the next thirty years and the production and consumption capacities are proportionally enhanced, will the ecumenopolis be physically habitable in view of enormous problems of pollution? One could echo with Ronald Abler that man as a species has acquired the power to destroy himself. Simultaneously, he has acquired the potential to enrich the existence of his species to unparalleled degree. The next two decades may be filled with hazards but they are also filled with opportunities. If we fail to build successful economic systems in the future, we will fail abysmally. If we build on the present wisely and soundly, we can expect future benefits far out of proportion to present cost. We shall be successful if we are guided by the knowledge that the present is the beginning of the future, not the end of the past.

The delegates might be aware that the Ministry of Education, Government of India and the University Grants Commission have agreed to consider specific proposals from the universities which might wish to initiate academic programmes in futurology/futures research. In fact, many short and long term studies have been commissioned and eighteen such studies have already been completed and printed. The professional geographer does not feature in any of these studies. These topics relate to (a) an out-look of India's future for housing (b) prediction of food productions including rainfall uncertainties (c) urbanization with new growth centres (d) future transportation in India. Future research, in fact, has to be tackled not only on the macro level, but also at the micro level and what is more important is its consideration spatially : at the block and at the village levels. It must take into account the elimination and minimization of regional disparities and the existing as well as the future growth must be accompanied by social justice. The inventory of existing facilities should be prepared and planned at the micro level and the projected requirements should be analysed and planned, and the accomplishments of these task would require the services of the geographers in a big way. Currently a special emphasis is being given to hold workshops in specialized sectors : ocean futures, mineral futures, energy futures, steel, paper and glass futures, sugar, drug and textile futures, but there are certain important items which brook no delay in futures research : spatial availability of the futures of clean drinking water, food, roads, village commons, apart from the futures of the individual cities.

So far as the conservation of existing resources is concerned, the Government of India has taken the right step in appointing two commissions

: National Land Board and National Land Resources Conservation and Development Commission. The purpose of these commissions is threefold : (a) to co-ordinate the work of state board connected with the use of land, (b) make an overall review of the progress of the implementation of schemes and programmes connected with conservation and development of soils, and (c) formulating a national policy and perspective plan for the conservation, management and development of land resource of the country. When onc looks at the structure of these commissions, one wonders why academicians from universities have been left out. It is needless to point out how British geographers by conducting a land use survey of Britain , mapping out the then existing use of land, classifying the lands of Britain and applying the principals of land use planning, helped the country in augmenting its food resources and planning judiciously the allocation of land for various essential requirements during the second world war. The presence of geographers on these boards will substantially help in land use planning as well as the conservation, management and development of land resources.

The conservation of land resources will help in the judicious planning of the use of land, identify the lands of special qualities for special purposes, plan to prevent irrational encroachment on good agriculture lands, suggest after careful survey a better use of village commons for pasture and social forestry and an overall development of the rural landscape and the preservation of the environment.

Land should be considered as the ultimate asset of the nation and land development should proceed in a systematic manner. Layout plans and design have to be prepared on suitable maps marking out land for water courses, field channels, field drains and farm roads. Scheme of land development can be undertaken only if suitable maps for the purpose are available. Such maps should be on large scale. For most parts of the country villages on a scale 1 : 4000 are available, but these are accurate enough for purposes of sound land planning, and fresh maps in most cases need to be prepared. Besides, soil and land classification maps of these areas are also required. The cropping pattern, the modes of irrigation, the slope to which land need to be graded, the size and spacing of drains need soil and land use and land classification maps. The role of geographer in land development is thus self evident.

Again there are large areas in the country which are affected by saline and alkaline soils. These soils should be delineated properly because the reclamation methods are different for these two broad classes genetically : the saline soils are the parent materials from which alkali originate. In the process of alkalization, an intermediate class of soil has been identified, namely, saline-sodic. The alkali soils are the normal end products of saline soils. On the basis of detailed mapping the reclamation measure become more specific and easy to apply. The geographers with training in soil science can play a vital role in detailed mapping where reclamation projects are launched. In the matter of reclamation and utilization of wasteland, again, survey, mapping and analysis become important. Some of the causes of the origin of the wastelands are overgrazing and indiscriminate cutting of forest trees which upset the ecological balance. The wastelands, if properly treated and managed, can supply valuable fodder, feed, fuel to the village. In order to evolve the right strategy for the reclamation, the geographers would be of immense help in this regard. There has to be a systematic survey of the different categories of wastelands and the reclamation has to be done on scientific basis. If reclamation is not done scientifically, wastelands may deteriorate further leading to loss of productive area. Similarly, shifting cultivation has been practised from time immemorial in the tribal areas of Assam, Manipur, Tripura, Orissa, Madhya Pradesh and Andhra Pradesh. Such system of cultivation may have its use when population pressure was low and the *jhum* area could be left fallow for a number of years. With the increase in the pressure of population, the *jhum* rotation is becoming shorter and shorter and has led to rapid soil erosion. The programmes of reclamation, while preserving the soil should improve the economic condition of the people and owing to the diversity of the condition prevailing in areas which are subject to *jhum* cultivation in the country, the correct strategy can be adopted after careful study and survey. The marginal farmers and landless labourers can be inducted on these reclaimed land and the capital cost can be subsidized for them in accordance with the principles of growth with social justice.

Conservation of land resource, while on the one hand, would help in increasing the food production, it should also aim in eliminating or minimizing the food losses. It will be worthwhile to mention that several experts have estimated the minimum post-harvest loss in terms of percentage figures of grains and other cereals at 10 during 1976 in the developing countries. In terms of 1976 production, the figure for losses in developing countries alone amounted to 42 million tonnes of food grains. The reported loss of rice in the post-harvest system in India is about 6 per cent as per 1977 figures. Similarly, the reported loss of maize is 6 to 8 per cent and for wheat, barley and millets, the rate ranges from 8 to 25 per cent. A ten per cent loss of last year's production of 135 million tonnes in India would amount to over 13.5 million tonnes incurring a loss of about 14 billion rupees. The prevention of losses during the storage, transport , marketing, distribution and consumption constitute one of the most important tasks of the food system to improve the food situation of the developing countries in general and India in particular. In case of fruits and vegetables, the problem is not only of increased production, but also of low cost handling , packing, transport and processing. It is estimated that on an average in India in the states of Himachal Pradesh and Jammu and Kashmir, the consumption of wooden boxes for packing apples is about 40 million, which use about a million cubic meter of wood. The large scale consumption of wood for packing boxes leads to denudation in the Himalayas which in turn create the problem of soil erosion and floods. Field work at the village level should be conducted in India and more data should be generated so that geographers interface with planning agencies, particularly with the Indian Planning Commission, in order to submit concrete suggestions for the creation and promotion of a sound food system. Further, the attention of official agencies should be drawn to such researches as may be helpful at the levels of policy making, decision taking and implementation.

Ladies and gentlemen, these and many other problems need constant and necessary attention of the geographers of India. Perhaps the Executive Committee of the National Association of the Geographers of India may consider for constitution of study groups, apart from commissions which it has established. These study groups on subjects may keep on changing with the pressing requirements of the society, for example agricultural geography study group, study group on food system, developing areas study group, population geography study group, urban geography .study group, environment study group, group on futurology, and a few other can be added to the list. Each study group may pick up important problems facing the country and the society. The problem may be studied in-depth and discussed in a two day annual meeting of the group and the results communicated to a central committee appointed by the National Association of Geographers of India. The Central Committee may discuss the results of the study groups with the Planning Commission officials, administrators and with all those concerned with the problem.

Ladies and gentlemen, during the tenure of my Presidentship of the National Association of Geographers, India I shall try to serve the cause of geography as much as I can. I once again thank you for giving me a patient hearing.

REFERENCES

Abler, R. *et al.* (1971), *Spatial Organization*, New Jersey.

Beazley, C.R. (1897-1906), *The Dawn of Modern Geography*, 3 Vol., Oxford.

Boulding, K.E. (1967), *The Meaning of the Twentieth Century*, New York.

Dickinson, R.E. (1969), *The Makers of Modern Geography*, London.

Freeman, T.W. (1961), *A Hundred Years of Geography*, London.

Gottmann, J. (1964), *Meglalapolis: The Urbanized NorthEastern Sea Board of the United States*, Cambridge, Massachussettes.

Hartshorne, R. (1989), *The Nature of Geography: A Critical Survey of Current Thought in the Light of the Past*, Lancaster.

Kahn, H. and Wiener, A.J. (1967), *The Year 2000: A Framework for Speculation on the Next Thirty Years*, New York.

Paterson, J.H. (?), *Some dimension of Geography, Geography*, Vol. 64, pp. 268-78.

Stoddart, D.R. (1981), *Geography, education and research, Geographical Journal*, pp. 287-297.

Chita Ranjan Pathak
1935 -

In the drought prone habitat of the Bankura district of West Bengal is a small village called Sonardonga – which literally means dip of gold. To a family of landlords was born on 13th July, 1930 their child whom they named Chita Ranjan Pathak. The village was remote and even within a radius of 15 kilometers there was no school. Pathak's mother had never been to school and his father had reached barely upto class fourth. Not only was the level of literacy low, but an extravagant life style had pauperized the wealth of this family of landlords. Yet Pathak's life has been a dip into gold in more than one way.

With a graduation from the prestigious Presidency College, Calcutta, a doctorate from the University of North Carolina, United States of America, summer courses at the University of California, Berkeley and a post-doctorate at the School of Design, University of Harvard, Cambridge, Massachusetts, Pathak's education was a melange within a crucible of the most superior metal. Purity was added to the lustre not just with a hallmark of repute of the institutes, but from the distinguished teachers who tutored Pathak.

N.K. Bose, the eminent social scientist, lectured on cultural anthropology and the art of field observation at Presidency College. To launch his book – 'India and Pakistan: A General and Regional Geography', Spate visited the department of geography at the University of Calcutta; Pathak recalls that his lectures and discussions on regional aspects were most stimulating. Bunge and Haggerstrand took courses at North Carolina while Marbout and Isaard led the summer course at Berkeley. At Harvard, Berry was at the helm of affairs.

Dazzling intellectual energy thus reached Pathak. Reputed institutes and the best of teachers do not have to produce the best of students. The magnet to learn afterall lies within the field of the learner. Pathak yellowed his rivals with an outstanding academic record at every step of his learning.

Securing the first prize for the post-graduate examination, he wrote his doctorate in less than a year and was granted a waver of 90 credits at the course work in the University of Carolina. His more than working knowledge of French and German earned him not just high scores in languages but the fact that he translated Christallers' Central Place Theory from German to English with the help of a friend, denotes that texts in original language provided him deeper insight for study and review. Pathak perhaps is one among the few geographers in India who has a track of ten years of scholarships and fellowships. The Fullbright Scholarship, Smith Fund Scholarship, National Science Foundation Scholarship, Fullbright Alumuni Research Grant to the Senior Fullbright, British Council Visitorship, Pathak's treasury received remittances from sources so creditable they could be weighed in gold.

Sterling in nature is the specialization in geography which he set out to seek. For Pathak simplistic and descriptive studies of geographical phenomena were not a challenge . With mathematics ,economics and geography as courses of study at the intermediate level and mathematics, sanskrit and geography at the graduate level followed by a specialization in cartography at the post-graduate level, Pathak's aptitude clearly nestled within a quantitative field of inquiry. He wanted to 'apply' geographical concepts to solve problems of the real world . Even in his doctorate on 'Urban Pattern in the Piedmont Region of Raleigh in North Carolina', correlation and pattern analysis formed the core tools for analysis. Skills with the nearest neighbor analysis, simulation studies, gravity models and network analysis drew Pathak towards the newly emerging hybrid discipline of regional science .

Isaard, an economist at Harvard, considered neoclassical economics as a " wonderland of no spatial dimensions". It was in the mid 1950s that Isaard founded the discipline of Regional Science. Pathak was on the rolls of the universities of the United States of America as a doctorate and post-doctorate student for an extended period from 1961 to 1971. The quantitative and the regional science movement captured the attention of the 26 year old Pathak and became his fixation for a life time. In 1967 he founded the Regional Science Association and launched the Journal of Regional Science in India. The survival and renown of this journal owes allegiance to Pathak's life time devotion. Nearly sixty per cent of his books, half of his research articles, thirty of the total of forty-five papers presented by Pathak rotate around the theme of regional science. A special emphasis is on urban studies, industrial geography and regional planning. He laments that the demise of the quantitative school was brought not so much from the radicalists and humanistic school but from the fact that most geographers in India have limited ability to handle the advanced techniques of spatial analysis. Pathak's intellectual acumene and specialization had currency value in India.

When the Indian Institute of Technology, built in an old British prison at Kharagpur, started a course in Regional Planning, Pathak was recruited as its first lecturer in 1964. When the Center for Regional Development was inaugurated at Jawahar lal Nehru University, Delhi in 1971, Pathak was the first lecturer to be appointed. The sharp intellect of Pathak quickly perceived that the Indian Insitute of Technology, an institute of national repute, would be a better option for creative work. After a short stay of five years at the Center for Regional Development he went back to Kharagpur never to uproot himself again. Invitations to a score of teaching assignments from foreign universities and a dozen seminars did take him away for six years. But these were intermittent visits, and for Pathak, Kharagpur was the permanent 'base'. In his twenty-nine years at Indian Institute of Technology he not only supervised ten doctorates but also attracted numerous projects on district planning, rural industrialization, environmental impact assessment and locational analysis of ports like Haldia and Digha. Today private consultancies for remote sensing and geographic information systems engage Pathak in numerous ways.

In his life time Pathak may not have been crowned by political or administrative posts, or earned pots of wealth, but he holds the golden key of knowledge. In a way he personifies Sonardonga, the village he hails from.

Geography, Regional Science and Regional Planning : Their Interpretation

C.R.PATHAK

It is my proud privilege to welcome all the delegates to the 6th Indian Geography Congress and the 18th Regional Science Seminar to be held here during May 8-11, 1985. As you are kindly aware that this Congress has been postponed until today because of General Election held in December, 1984. We took also this opportunity to organise the 18th Regional Science Seminar along with the Geography Congress as large number of members of Regional Science Association are also members of the National Association of Geographers, India. Besides, it has given an opportunity to interact with the regional scientists who have actively engaged in developing methods and techniques of Regional Science relevant to Indian Regional Planning Problems. At the same time, the geographers who have been engaged themselves in fundamental research in geography should orient themselves towards application of their knowledge to the identification of planning problems for which they require expertise of regional planners and regional scientists, particularly for analysis and strategy formulation for solving those problems. Hence, this fortuitous gathering of geographers, regional scientists and regional planners would provide a comprehensive platform for discussion of the regional planning problems faced by the developing economy like that of India.

Role of Geographers, Regional Scientists and Regional Planners

At the meeting of geographers, regional scientists and regional planners, probably, there is a need to define the respective role of these experts in study and research relevant to their own field and also how they cross the boundaries of other experts as situations demand. Geographers from the very beginning have been keen observers of the phenomena and their interactions that characterise the landscape. Such characterisation of landscape varies from place

---

7th Indian Geography Congress
Kharagpur, 1985 May

to place and geographers throw light on the characteristics of such places and give a clear description of the phenomena and their interactions. The situation has arisen now that no problem could effectively be tackled unless they are analysed properly and develop and employ relevant tools of analysis not only to ascertain the relative role of different factors but also to bring out relevant facts which need proper attention. Those who develop such tools and techniques of analysis are identified as regional scientists. Based on their analysis, regional planners formulate strategies and find solution for tackling such problems. Hence, the geographers, regional scientists and regional planners have demarcated their own domain of study and research in most cases overlapping and cutting across each other's domain and they try to be a comprehensive regional planner with the basic understanding of geographic tools, that of regional scientists and then approaches of policy formulation of regional planning. Hence, such regional planners have been found to be very indispensable in this society. Hence geographic study and analytical techniques and policy formulation are nothing but serial stages of understanding region's problems leading towards rational solutions. While it is very difficult to distinguish geographers, regional scientists and regional planners, they themselves when work in the field and contribute their might to the problem solution may maintain their identity for academic purposes.

Objectives of these Disciplines

Now let me analyse the foundation of each of the above fields of study and define their domain of activities and see how they could interact with each other leading towards planning for national and regional development.

Garnsay claims that regional science is essentially synthesis of many of the older social sciences. It is necessarily inter-disciplinary and the theoretical frontier of regional geography. According to Isard, father of regional sciences, it differs from all existing social science because space is its central focus, and it differs from geography because of its emphasis on theory, static or dynamic, which untill recently geographers have eschewed. 'Geography', Isard implies, 'would probably become regional science, if its, emphasis shifted from purely descriptive.' Social sciences do not emphasize space, as much as they should, and geographers aren't sufficiently analytical, hence is regional science. 'Regional science will assume more generic name if social sciences do interdisciplinary regional studies and geographers become more analytical' (Isard).

Walter Isard writes "regional science is primarily a social science field. It focuses upon spaces and system of spaces, regions and system of regions, locations and system of locations; it is a new field of investigation and very much interdisciplinary. It draws concepts, methods and techniques of existing social science disciplines. It primarily concerns with the study of man and the spatial forms which his continuous interaction with and adaptation to physical environment take. It concentrates on the study of human behaviour and institutions as they vary over space".

Second, in treating spaces, regions and related areal and distance concepts both geography and regional science have an orientation different from that of other disciplines. If, for example, we view economics, sociology, political science, anthropology, geology, oceanography, meteorology, botany, etc. each is having a vertical orientation and alignment, then geography and regional science can be said to have a horizontal orientation and alignment, cutting across many of those fields with vertical alignments. In my view, this second fact explains why geography and regional science have much in common with so many disciplines. At the same time, however, geography and regional science are more than interdisciplinary, for reasons already cited.

If the combined scope of geography and regional science and their total ramifications and numerous procedures and methods are beyond the absorptive capacity and keen of one person, it seems appropriate that the overall body of subjects and techniques should subdivide, much as the human cell. Subdivision, along methodological channels, is a logical, and, at this point of time, a most rational procedure. I propose that (a) the social science segments which are theoretical and involve model buildings, advanced statistical techniques and comprehensive statistical frameworks oriented to general theory be viewed as one distinct field, a cell in itself, which we have already designated regional science, (b) the rest of the field, traditionally designated geography, either continues as it largely has in the past, or subdivide into two or more parts (example social geography (including political, cultural, historical and economic) and physical geography) including biogeography and related areas; and (c) one of the chief meeting grounds (zones) of regional science and social science geography be at the intermediate statistics level where the geographer with his feet well rooted in the facts of reality scrutinizes and appraises the abstract concepts, operational models and theories of the regional scientist and where the regional scientist with his logical schemata and broad framework suggests to the geographers new types of data which may be usefully collected and new and more efficient ways of processing and utilizing existing data and where together utilizing both the system and vectors approaches, they make possible a greater understanding of society in its diverse spatial and related forms.

It is to be observed that these views are consistent with those of T.R. Smith who maintains that important progress in the broad subject matter area of geography and regional science can be scored when 'cultivated by various proprietors using different implements.' They are not inconsistent with the view of Mass who would in line with the above discussion designate regional science as 'theoretical social science geography', but who does not object to the term regional science which term incidentally geographers have also suggested as a substitute for geography. They follow the thread of Kavesh's remarks except that I would proceed further. In a sense, I view the regional scientist and geographer as general spatial partitioners over the several social sciences, one at the abstract theoretical level, the other at the more empirical, grass roots level. Each attempts a partial (horizontal–type) integration of the social sciences an integration involving the synthesis of spatial knowledge and techniques but only at his own appropriate level of knowledge.

Regions change overtime. Such change is not simply the projection of the trend but is deliberately brought about of conscious social and economic interventions in pursuits of goals outside as well as inside the traditional economic framework. Such public interventions must seek their rationale in the synthesis of various goals. Many of the goal objectives because of inadequate social science theory rely heavily on intuition for their origin and criteria. Regional science theory tries to overcome such intuitive judgment by formulating guidelines for planning in dynamic setting of reality which requires publicaction.

The regional scientists' kit of tools such as input-output benefit cost, industrial complex, programming or factor analysis will be handy first to employ criteria to determine the finite number of alternatives to be considered and second to ascertain criteria for choosing from among the alternatives. The planners need to optimise within the system of objective functions and constraints which are intimately related to values and goals. The regional scientists have to resolve the conflicting values and goals, policies; the regional scientists should be able to make a more positive contribution to social analysts and policy formulation.

The role of regional scientists is further strengthened by their ability to develop superior tools and methods to identify the loci of decision making in the society within which he operates. His approaches should incorporate method of assessing the social as well as economic costs of public decisions whether or not there is decision to act. His competency lies in improving techniques of rational decision making and their application to the socio-economic variables whose behaviour he purports to analyse for planning valued social-goal achievements. Such social goals to be pursued through planning activity are not self-evident or emerge from empirical studies alone in crystal clear form but depends very much on the governmental policy for social welfare. Such planning exercise calls for constructing mutually consistent hierarchy, principle, programmes and projects of public action. Hence, planning is not divorced from the political process and brings the planners and regional scientists into directly with conflicting elements within the bureaucratic machinery and the rest of government structure, and indirectly with the society as a whole.

It must be cautioned here, that the geographers, administrators, regional scientists, regional planners all contribute to the decision making process of the government for public action – but may be used to serve vested political interests in a democratic setup. Whether such technocrats could directly work with and for the society above board bypassing the political vested interests are most controversial issues. Are such technocrats free from vested interests?

Conclusion

While on the one hand, geographers, regional scientists, regional and national planners develop finer tools of analysis and projections of societal goals and perfect the decision making process to project better the social behaviour, they must cut deeply into the body of values and goals of a society, identify the ways in which they enter into planning, administration and decision making in general, develop better procedures to incorporate the implications of a changing value and goal structure into our operational techniques (Isard). They must serve the societal cause and guide the decision makers to take correct stand and when situation demands should reach the society for direct social action through people's planning. The geographers, regional scientists, regional planners and other social scientists must employ latest technology in union for public welfare.

REFERENCES

Rodwin, L. (1985), *Regional science: quo vadis?*, Papers and Proceedings, *Regional Science Association*, Vol. V, pp. 3 - 4.

Isard, W. (1960), *The scope and nature of regional science*, (Presidential Address), Papers and Proceedings, *Regional Science Association*, Vol. VI, pp. 9 - 34.

Isard, W. (1966), *Regional science: retrospect and prospect*, Vol. XVI, pp. 1-16.

Hoower, E.M. (1963), *Where regional scientists?*, Papers and Proceedings, *Regional Science Association*, Vol. XI, pp. 7 -16.

Isard, W. and T.A. Reiner (1962), *Regional science and planning*, Papers and Proceedings, *Regional Science Association*, Vol. VIII, pp. 1 - 26.

Kashi Nath Singh
1932

If the postman had delivered the admission ticket for the under-graduate course in journalism at the Banaras Hindu University on the stipulated date, Singh today would have been a free lance writer. Teaching was second in his career options. If in his graduate days his teachers of geography had not evoked interest in the subject, today Singh would have been an economist. Geography was second in the list of his favorite disciplines. Despite a teaching career, the urge to write, with works hinged on economics have been an inherent feature of Singh's life. His voracious urge to write is reflected in the stock of twenty one books and ninety research papers and over a dozen articles in newspapers. Arthik Bhoogol ke Mool Tattva, in Hindi, which translates as – Fundamentals of Resource Bases, Resource Utilization and Economic Development was the text book co-authored by him. Not only does Singh have a volume of publications to his credit but many among them attracted raving reviews from international and national audiences. Here are some randomly picked samples : Spate and Learmonth in their book India and Pakistan – A General and Regional Geography write 'for an unusually vigorous commentary on urban land use refer to Singh 'Morphology of the twin township of Dehri – Dalmianagar' This was a paper Singh wrote the year after his post graduation in 1957. Another landmark was the research on the 'Territorial Basis of Town and Village Settlement in Eastern Uttar Pradesh.' The judgement of Spencer the editor of the prestigious journal of Annals of the Association of American Geographers was 'the paper is so good that I would like to make it the lead article in the June 1968 issue'. Farmer, the director of the Center of South Asian Studies, 1975, Cambridge affirms 'the referees appointed by the Institute of British Geographers for the paper titled 'India's Rural Development Strategy and

Emerging Patterns of Rural and Urban Relations' have reported most favorably', back home a review of the Survey of Research in Geography –1969-1972 , in the Sunday Magazine of the Indian Express ,1979, notes 'the book is like a curate's egg — however the best piece is the article on Caste by Singh'.

How did Singh acquire the prowess to innovative ideas and translate them into scientific writing ? Born to a family of small zamindars on 1st January, 1932, in Murharia a village located at the foot of the Kaimur range in Jharkhand, Singh's mother never went to school while his father studied only upto the fifth class. Amidst a family of semi-illiterates the essentials for education in the young Singh was instilled by two paternal uncles, one a headmaster of a school and the other a journalist. Singh's consistent devotion towards studies is seen in his mark sheets – a first division and a second position is the standard score in his intermediate, graduation and post-graduation. His alma-mater was the Banaras Hindu University. In the 1950s and 1960s, the department of geography at Banaras Hindu University was popular for studies on urban and rural settlements. As soon as Singh was appointed lecturer in 1957 at his own alma-mater, his aim was to strike a departure from the traditional research and cut into new directions. In his environ where learning was stereotyped, Singh says his drive for innovative thinking came from not just private study of foreign journals and sociological texts, but from the opportunities he got to interact with scholars of repute. He submitted his doctorate at the Banaras Hindu University in 1963, on 'Rural Markets and Ruruban Centers in Eastern Uttar Pradesh.' A Fullbright Scholarship in 1964 took Singh for a year to the Rutgers State University in New Jersey; followed by a teaching assignment at the East Stroudsberg College, Philadelphia State. The spin off from these visits was a close interaction with J.E. Brush. During his professional life, Singh traveled abroad 10 times and visited 23 countries in all the 6 continents, but 1975, he says is a memorable watershed for his road to creative thinking. This year, Sopher, the geographer from Cornelle University attended the international seminar organised by the Banaras Hindu University. Discussions with Sopher helped Singh to deepen his inquiry from description of settlements to an appreciation of the processes underlying these patterns. Perceiving every theme of research from an unconventional as well as conventional point of view lent Singh's publications an outstanding degree of intellectual vigor. Not only was Singh a researcher but also a versatile teacher. Taking on his class with humor, digressive anecdotes and a wide canvass of theoretical discussions, Singh's students never suffered a moment of boredom .

On the pillars of research and teaching Singh added to the reputation of the department of geography at Banaras. It was during his term as chairperson from 1978 to 1993 that the department captured the Special Assistance

Programme of the University Grants Commission. The fact that after his retirement the department lost this prestigious program , never to regain it, is proof to Singh's abilities and personality. Tall and imposing, beneath the veneer of a forthright and at times candid tone lurks a person interested in the finer understanding of social process and problems . It is no wonder that he calls himself a social and cultural geographer with additional interest in economic geography.

Today, as Singh enjoys his post retirement years in active teaching at the College of Social Sciences at Addis Ababa, Ethopia and completes his book 'Dynamics of Economic Geography and World Economy at the Cross Roads' he attributes his success to the people he met in this world of chance,. . . if the post man had not lost the admission ticket, if educated paternal uncles were not available, if he had not met Brush and Sopher, if he had not published in Annals, if he had not read sociology, if he had not got the assignment to teach at Ethopia —— life for Singh would have been different. Afterall, if, is the middle word of Life.

Voluntary Agencies : Their Role in Rural Development in India

K.N. SINGH

"Civilization exists precisely so that there may be no masses but rather men alert enough never to constitute masses". Georges Bernanos

I feel privileged to accord you all a very warm welcome to the best of our *Varanaseya* cultural tradition in the holy city of Varanasi and within the precincts of Banaras Hindu University, at the celebrated annual meet of the National Association of Geographers, India this morning. I am deeply thankful to the National Association of Geographers, India and to you all for the position as President, and to stand before you to deliver the Presidential Address.

You may soon realize that I have not picked up this occasion to give a very researched and conceptually or methodologically vigoured delivery. I have digressed a little from this tradition and I owe an apology to you all for this deviation. But I am conscious of your intellectual appetite: as such, I have picked up an issue which concerns rather deeply. This is the issue of poverty. Again, I have not tried to go into defining or measuring poverty. I am just offering a rambling, wildly straying piece of talk, of a discursive nature. My inquiry is: why is poverty so deeply embedded, layer after layer, amidst us all over? Wherever as geographers or academics or social activists we look around, in crooks and crannies, the 'wretched' of the Indian earth are there, in our hamlets and villages, cities and metropolises, areas and regions, north, south, east and west, cutting across religions, traditions and social strata. Although more entrenched in some than others. Why is this element geographically and societal so pervasive and universal, historically as ancient as our deep and heavy tradition, culturally, ethically and spiritually so much taken for easy status? Why don't we hate it so much that we do as a nation something to eliminate it or at last bring it above the hunger level? Do we really lack the resources or the will to do it? How far is it socially created and perpetuated, or maintained? Why do we even rationalize it as karmaphal or our past sins?

8th Indian Geography Congress
Varanasi, 1985 December

I have taken the topic of rural development and the role of voluntary agencies overarching the issue of poverty. How far can the issue of poverty be addressed and addressed by the activation of these voluntary agencies? Can they animate the governments and sensitize the public mind in general on one hand, and bring the activism necessary among the rural poor populace itself to do something vital and real about it? The talk contains an overview of the issue, and taken at some length the case of development – generated poverty, disparity and inequalities, creating and deepening dependency structure, and raising false expectations among the mass minds through the political pseudo-slogans. The paper highlights the concepts, and workings of the voluntary agencies in general, and their relevance in development at grass root micro-level. An issue has been taken up of organization of the poor at this level of community and locality with the active participation of the poor themselves, trying to challenge the traditional local elitist power structures. Two empirical success cases have been taken in final pages.

I have initiated my talk with the revolutionary remark of Georges Bernanos which animates us all to what kind of men and women we are making in our academics through our social development process and other structures. This prelude sets the tone for taking up the challenge.

While the Government of India with all its ramifications and tentacles of development planning is making a massive effort to develop and modernize the Indian society and economy, it's capability is understandably limited; probably it is the destined role of the people's organizations like the myriad of voluntary organizations and non-governmental organizations working in India in diverse fields of human activity at grass-root levels to transform the destiny of the masses. The purpose of this address is to highlight their role and significance in boosting up in tandom India's massive effort of uplifting the poor and the destitute with particular reference to rural situation. The voluntary organisations, alongside the government's committed and sincere developmental efforts, may make attempt to stem the tide of forces that have been creating and perpetuating the conditions under which 'masses' are created and poverty persists as a way of life.

An Overview

India has achieved much in economic, social and politico-democratic fields of human activity in the last thirty eight years after her independence : it is the eighth or ninth industrial giant in the world; it holds third position in the scientific and technologic size of personnel; it has a food-stock of 30 million tonnes; it is the political leader of the non-aligned, a comity of the largest number of sovereign states; and yet it is itself a divided and fragile nation within its dichotomic character, as if two nations live cheek by jowl, as Verghese puts it, India and *Bharat*; the former of the elite class, the educated, the rulers, the urban and urbane, the modern, sitting on top of the *Bharatis*, the latter, the residents of *Bharat*, the masses, the illiterate, the backward, the tribals and the scheduled castes, the resourceless, the dependents, the drawers of water and the hewers of wood, the rural and the rustic.

Professor Dietmar Rothermund of Heidelberg University rates modern India consisting of a modern nation of about 60 million people living in the midst of a vast agrarian nation of 600 million people.

Evidentally, there is a dichotomous character of these two societies, interacting with each other on a thin and fragile edge of interface, the dysfunctional consequences of which erupt increasingly in malignant forms of social discontent, group violence, massive political turmoil and other volatile symptomatic forms of restlessness. India will not be a nation state of self-reliant community of manifold social strata and ethnic groups which it has unless the state of dependency structure and social and economic dichotomies based on exploitation are obliterated. There is a whole lot of empirical information confirming "the fall-out of an unbalanced model of development which is unsuited to the needs of the majority of Indians" (Bakshi, 1985).

India's 'traditional feudalistic socio-economic structure has perpetuated on anti-people religious-ritual and moral order for economic benefit of the rulers and their hangers-on; this order has even eulogised the philosophy and cult of earning *punya* by feeding the hungry, the poor masses, the pious epithet being given to them of *daridranarayanas*; it has inculcated rather a wrong type of spirit in its social psyche and ethos and created a socio-economic outfit to create and perpetuate the masses and the poor and the ignorant among its people. The British colonial policy, overtly and covertly, strengthened this hierarchical and inequality-ridden socio-economic structure "and widened the disparities and inequalities, both among the people and the different areas, between villages and towns and cities and between classes and masses."

Indian political leadership had to wipe off all these immoral, exploitative multi-faceted mechanisms, but most of its 'planning in this area has been a large-sized paper tiger, even though 'the democracy has rooted well in Indian soil.' For millions, the life has stopped to flow in spite of planning. In fact, the prevailing situation presents the picture of the decadent ambience of the country's socio-economic scenario.

Development-Generated Poverty

What has turned out to be most dangerous and malignant is the new development-generated poverty and helplessness, alongside growing awareness that little could be achieved in this genre of democratic set-up and through the prevailing development planning. This new civilization of creating hungry and diseased resourceless masses is more dangerous and uglier in the backdrop of the fact that this nation is, on its own, capable of obliterating the mass poverty by creating social, economic and cultural conditions only if its rulers operate on their commitments. What is disturbing is that in spite of the knowledge that the prevailing type of growth-oriented development planning exercised through present bureaucratic structure, which has just become a turn-coat in the form of development administration only in name, and not in real form, content and functional commitment, under the aegis of a non-committal political leadership, is bound to create and widen disparities and inequalities, both among the socio-economic strata and the region. Nothing vital has come out to correct and stem the rot. Why do our plans and projects and several special acronymic programmes like Integrated Rural Development Programme, etc. for the target areas and groups, with all their interventionistic, corrective, monitored and evaluative checks and measures, fail to serve their goals? Why have poverty, illiteracy, unemployment, inadequacy in health and other basic facilities not been edging out from the face of India and are rather getting entrenched? Why after a sustained planned period have the number of the absolute poor increased from 200 million people in 1951, the first year of our Plan period, to 305 million in 1973-79, the end of the Fifth Five Year Plan ? Majority of Indians, over 300 millions, born after independence stay poor! Absolute poverty has as if stabilized at about 50 per cent or according to government's claims now at about 40 per cent of the total population. It appears as if "the more the Plans, the more the Poor' (Singh, S.P., 1981). Nirmal Mukerji rightly states that a large part of mass poverty increasingly witnessed in the villages is the "direct outcome of development" because the early production and growth-oriented policies, essentially required by the nation, allowed the technological, financial and input advantages to be cornered by the large landed and other resource owners like capitalists and industrialists, while small and marginal land-owners, the illiterates and other resourceless or skill-less persons could not take any substantial advantage. Professor C.T. Curian has succinctly put it : "Affluence and poverty are both products of development." Poverty, indeed, is the carcass left from wealth-owners who have developed an octopus-like capacity and tentacles to corner most of what is budgetwise designed for the poor, the backward and the ruralites, with the result that trickle-down process has failed, and growth has not induced social justice and benefit for the poor who would have taken care of themselves, had the minimum needs facilities been allowed to reach them; had the skill-formation technologies and requisite educational opportunities been given them; had the adequate prices of their produce and wages of their labour been paid them.

"Evidently this new variety of rural poverty which springs from development rather than under-development raises the question of the type of development to be adopted. If it continues to be poverty-generating, no amount of poverty alleviation will be able to cope, for the growth of poverty will keep outpacing its alleviation. If on the other hand, a model can be found which is poverty-reducing, alleviation programmes as such may be rendered largely unnecessary, at least in the long run, for the new development process would itself look after the problem" (Mukerji, 1985).

There is now a growing talk of "growth with social justice", instead of the formerly espoused 'growth for social justice", which was supposed to generate "trickle down process" and its social dividends to flow to the masses. However, the present development pattern can hardly ensure social justice as it "continuously spews injustice". As such, there is a strong case for adopting and executing such policies and launching such development strategies as poverty is steadily eradicated, rather than alleviated. Such strategies "will have to be something like poverty-eradicating growth and not poverty-creating growth which is what growth with social justice has unfortunately turned out to be" (Mukarji, 1985).

Although India's perspective of rural development with social justice may be stated to be "deeply rooted in the sense of history, in the finest values of the Indian tradition as expressed in *bahu jan hitay, babu jan sukhay* and in the Gandhian concern for the uplift of the 'dumb half-starving millions' or the *Daridranarayana*" (Joshi p. 18), the same values have hardly percolated in practice in the real world situation. One wonders if it holds in the field evidence what Joshi states that " — The values of social justice and the institutions of political democracy had struck deep roots in Indian consciousness, much before India has achieved modern economic growth" (Joshi, p. 18).

The Directive Principles of the Indian Constitution or the Gandhi-Nehru vision of a dynamic and buoyant, self-reliant and egalitarian, and forward-looking democratic India hardly" provide legitimacy to a development path which benefits the few but neglects the masses" (Joshi, p. 18).

Dependency Structure

Mr. Peter McPherson, administrator of the Agency for International

Development, blasted the power structures which themselves had replaced the old feudal oligarchies and colonial structures which themselves 'did not help the process of development, though they probably would like to' because of these strangleholds and their own vested interests. He noted that the universities, the bureaucracy, the public and private sector and even the military form the power structure, and have all become employers of last resort partaking most of the budget: "Every one of these groups say they are for poor people, and they believe, they want change. But the fact is there is not enough money left for doctors in the villages. There is not enough money left over for a better extension system". Then they go for foreign aid, when the policies and budget allocations of these countries do not help the poor people (Report in the Indian Express, Nov. 26, 1981). Quite naturally, this addictive dependency mentality makes one blind to one's country's social reality; it permeates the educational, scientific, technological, extension and all other relevant fields of activities which help self-reliant developmental planning and policy structures. "A vicious circle is generated. The interaction of the elite with its own people begins to diminish The people too are increasingly disoriented misunderstanding and tensions increase and the process of development gets stalled. Conspicuous consumption and waste abound (Suri, 1982).

Fellow delegates, we all are sharing evidently in these elitist gains. Could we make efforts in our own small way to really do something about the situation? In what ways?

Unhealthy Urbanization

Disparity and inequality have been rising all over India and its settlements throughout the hierarchical spectrum of settlements and classes and strata of people. While majority of the people are poor ruralites and tribals, even most of the urban poor are also recent or one-generation migrants of rural India, living in urban slums and squatter settlements. For instance, in our twelve largest metropolitan areas in 1971, over 26 per cent (Calcutta) to about 58 per cent (Greater Bombay) people were migrants, and of these the rural migrants constituted about 57 per cent and 67 per cent respectively. In fact, researches by Professor Ashish Bose and others have clearly shown that majority of these rural migrants are 'push' migrants because of increasing poverty and unemployment, but also due to intolerable and oppressive and disabling social conditions still prevailing and rather aggravating in the rural areas. So has been the unhealthy trend of 'push' migration on the one hand and concentration of economic power in the large cities and metropolitan centres on the other, that Indian urbanization has become top-heavy, growing at the cost of other smaller cities and towns, with an unabated and accelerated rate. And yet, the larger the city, the greater the squalor, crime, deprivation and poverty and larger the pockets of slums and squatter settlements. Thus, while the metropolitan-urban system is growing under intolerable weight and pressure of population additions and their civic facilities and employment-generating capacities are deteriorating, the villages are pushing out their healthiest youths into the cobwebs at an increasing rate. With less than one-fourth of her population being urban, India is said to be an 'over-urbanized' country. In spite of our bold refutation of the 'over-urbanization' theory, our system is verily having the overtones of over-urbanization and its fall-out. As such, there is need for real development to take place in the rural areas in order to help them as well as the cities and metropolises as well. Kathleen Newland holds the truth:

"If the usual vicious circle of urban development depleting rural areas is to be broken, rates of progress in cities and countryside must stay in balance. If cities are constantly favoured in national economic policies, people will quite sensibly flock to them. The cities will be placed in double jeopardy by the very attempts to favour them; their problems will grow with their swelling populations and the debilitated rural areas with which they interact will be less and less able to provide them with food, energy or markets" (Newland, 1981).

Crisis of Rising Ambitions

Why has the prevailing social and economic inequalities and tension disabilities, traditionally entrenched in India, created social and political restlessness now? This is because the suffering masses have the rising but as yet unfulfilled ambitions together with the growing awareness that the state of their destiny, deprivations and disabilities is not God-or Nature-given, but is master-minded and tailored by men, not of a superior genre though, by cheating and exploiting them in the garb of being do-gooders, leaders, Godmen and priests and protectors, and holding their *'Ma-baap Sarkar'* to ransom. They realize that the religio-philosophical moral order exhorting them for their *karmphal* in the 'other world' after death while tolerating the sufferings perpetrated by the exploiters, themselves living a luxurious and stylistic 'this worldly' life, is immoral and unreasonable. Centuries of denial of opportunities, of the fruits of their toil and conditioning to poverty that had stunned them into silence, resign, fatalism, helplessness and quiet suffering and atrophy have now become weapon in their hands to fight with for their rightful dispositions in the democratic body politic of India'. With every plan and project and every speech of the politician or the intellectual, their expectations for fuller life have been rising, and yet they are not seeing any fulfilment of even committed targets'. Frustrations are naturally skyrocketing.

"The other half, in *Bharat,* has gradually gained in political and social consciousness and becoming aware, is no longer willing to accept its lot. As it mobilises and gets organised, a culture of silence is yielding to a culture of protest. To some, like Mrs. Indira Gandhi, this is largely a law and order problem. But whose law to maintain what order ? Those seeking-stability have yet to recognise that India's problem is that there has been far too much stability and far too little change" (Verghese).

Voluntary Agencies : Relevance of Localism

Since voluntary agencies have to work at the grassroots levels, their territorial-geographical coverage has to be essentially small and localistic. The very size of India with over half a million discrete villages and over three-fourths of her 750 million people contained in them has produced thousands of localistic structures, widely differing from each other. Their variations range over physiography, climate, ecology, resource endowments, man's cultural responses, social and economic activity patterns, population, caste and religious structures, power structure, land tenures and settlement types and patterns. For all these, "all India planning from the top alone is not enough, if it is not supported by grassroots mobilization. It involves people speaking a bewildering variety of languages and dialects, creating complicated problems for understanding the rural mind and communicating with the rural masses" (Joshi, 1985, p. 18).

Moreover "——— working with the poor, especially organizing them to struggle for rights, requires persistent work. Changing caste, class and gender relations requires time, whatever the method, violent or non-violent, and it is only locally located voluntary agencies that have this type of persistence". Government officials, howsoever committed they could be, "are vulnerable to transfer and thus continuous contact and negotiation is not possible for them" (Jain, p. 7).

Communicating with the masses, inculcating faith in them about the genuine interest in benefiting them and chalking out strategies suiting them is not possible unless there is a deep study and appreciation of their culture, ways of life and their responsiveness and levels of resistances to the various innovations. As these masses live "at the same time in several centuries and at several levels of civilization". It "means imaginatively leading them, step by step, towards entry in the twenty-first century. Indian planner has to be one capable of combining a bird's eye grand view with the earthworm's nearness to grassroot realities" (Joshi, 1985, p. 19). The rural localities, however differing in scale, are symbols of inter-related cohesiveness and pervasive networks. This element must be capitalized upon fully to organize them into forming economically-socially viable units for self-reliant growth and modernization with minimal technical resource help from outside.

The voluntary agencies, in collaboration with the government-induced institutional and technological framework can help adequately for the motivational requirements of the masses. The achievement of these objectives makes it imperative to make area-specific plans, technologies, strategies and projects to take care of the varying situations in different localities of India. Area planning, in fact, is an essential feature if it also refurbishes itself keeping the people first.

Voluntary Agencies : Approaches and Strategies

Voluntary organizations can be classified on the basis of various criteria, such as their philosophy, concept and ideological basis of inception or foundation, policy, legal status, territorial level of their operational coverage such as local, regional, national or international scale, aims and objectives, work programmes, funding sources, style, methods and types of liaison or collaboration and partnership with government or the level of governmental control, diversity of approaches and strategies they adopt, and a host of other factors such as their performance and success levels, their capability, and acceptance, etc. (Singh, 1984, p. 46; Jain, 1985. P. 6).

These organizations vary widely in their approaches to various kinds of problems, affecting the people and areas. J. Singh has classified them into seven categories according to approaches they follow:

1. Charity: giving food, clothing, medicine, alms in cash and kind, land, buildings, etc.
2. Welfare: providing facilities for education, health, drinking water, roads, communication, etc.
3. Relief: responding to call of duties during natural calamities like floods, droughts, earthquakes, and man-made calamities like refugee influx, ravages of wars, etc.
4. Rehabilitation: continuing the follow-up of the work in areas struck by calamities and starting activities durable in nature.
5. Services: building up infrastructure in depressed and backward areas. Tractor hiring services, providing or facilitating credit, supply of seeds, fertilizers, technical know-how, etc.
6. Development of socio-economic environment around human beings socio-economic transformation on the area basis, covering all the people in a given

area target or concentrating only on a particular group normally neglected or marginalized, and in need of help.

7. Development of human beings: conscience raising, awakening, sensitizing, organising, recording of priorities to suit social justice, redeeming the past and opening doors to opportunities to the oppressed and exploited.

The success or failure, desirability, effectiveness, impact, etc. of the voluntary organizations depend on a host of factors, such as the geographical and ecological nature of the area of their operation, size of the territory under coverage, the social, cultural and political outlook and status of the people under operation, their general awareness, and level of resistance to the exploiting forces of the government, bureaucracy or the social elites, their capability of absorption of innovations and inputs, tolerance and acceptance, etc. as also on 'the corporate policy of the (voluntary) organization, workers' motivation and enlightenment and technical know-how, etc. Singh maintains that "the curve of acceptability of various approaches in official circles moves in descending order (1 to 7) - charity, welfare, relief, rehabilitation, services, development of socio-economic environment around human beings and development of human beings. Approaches 1 to 6 are related to delivery system, whereas approach 7 basically refers to the 'receiving' mechanism" (Singh, op. cit., p. 46). Obviously, the last field is the most vital area of action of the voluntary organizations, which are engaged in human resource development.

Singh identifies four well articulated strategies of voluntary agencies in the focus of the above approaches and the phases through which voluntary action programmes have progressed (Singh, op. cit. p 46). These are :

I. Simple charity, supplementing welfarism of the state.
II. Encouraging people's participation in implementing programmes launched by the government for larger benefit of the community or village.
III. Involving people in programme planning, raising resources, implementing activities and sharing fruits of development.
IV. Conscientising and organising people enabling them to demand and undertake planning and implementation of developmental programmes.

Need and Relevance of Voluntary Organizations

The voluntary agencies reflect the felt needs as well as the aspirations of the people who are poor and exploited, and they are destined to play a myriad role in the reconstruction and transformation of India, more particularly in the rural areas where they are needed most. The rural backwardness is aptly said to be in the rural minds. As such, rural masses have to be trained and educated to improve their skills, technologies and resourcefulness, and cultivate consciousness and fight for their rightful opportunities. As such, Indian countryside requires millions of trainers and technicians, social engineers and leaders, with their rural base and concern with the rural people and their cause, with technical expertise and wherewithal to improve and modernize the techniques of rural production, diversify the resource bases, and activity structures, forge social organization befitting the modern way of life and give back the human dignity, self-respect and prupose of life to the millions, who have been denied these basic human rights as well as the opportunities fulfilling the basic needs of life. The quality of the daily lives of the masses has to be improved, and that means improvement in all the things and situations which touch their daily lives.

No government, howsoever benevolent and expansive in its coverage in governance, welfare and development it could be, could cope with the myriad of hydra-headed problems faced by rural Indian masses under a hardened, hierarchical, archaic and basically exploitative socio-economic structure. As Adiseshiah has aptly remarked, the voluntary organizations can ill-afford to take the governmental jobs in development, yet they can do the job of "stimulating, organizing, involving and delivering action types of performance" which aim at eradicating poverty which is the priority programme for the Seventh Plan" (Adiseshiah, 1954, p. 15). In fact, the government and its agencies themselves realize their own limitations, as also the relevance and significance of voluntary organizations at various junctures of the delivery system of the programmes and projects of the government and their agencies. For instance, the Union Ministry of Education and State governments mobilized over 1000 voluntary agencies in adult education and other programmes. governments are needed to set right the public serving governance structures and macro and meso-block level infrastructures and preparing enabling environments for micro-level Non governmental organisations and other agencies to raise development on this basis.

Thousands of voluntary organizations, non-governmental organizations and other action groups of numerous political, non-political, non-party, social, religious and other organizations have been working in modern India. Most of them are small and weak and no more than to "shed light in a small area (each) without overcoming the darkness", yet they are now realizing their relevance and potential and the fact that their individual, isolated, discrete efforts "have no more than symbolic relevance" unless they make joint efforts. The inherent weaknesses in the government-operated development system, especially at the execution level, more particularly at the village or family level, being well known, it is no use dilating upon these weaknesses; rather, the voluntary agencies could contribute massively at these lower tail-end levels of the delivery system and energization of the people's efforts. The voluntary organizations have to focus specially on the underprivileged and improve their resource-creating skills and their opportunities of gaining access to the government-sponsored programmes and assets like land, house sites, etc. Provision of technical and other services in ways that build up people's initiative and enhance their resources are their essential tasks. Prof. Kabra rightly observes that "voluntary efforts have to be at best catalytic agents to energise the backward sections' articulation and mobilization potential for development" (Kabra, 1985, p. 10). He also rightly warns that "voluntary action does not have to move totally along lines parallel to plan programmes; but it must not merge with them or become dependent on them. As a watchdog and corrective, it has to build alternative force of power so that politics of planning changes in favour of the poor." (Kabra, 1985, p. 11).

Structural Changes Possible now on Technological Grounds

Technology has provided for ages a myriad of emancipative measures for mankind from millions of resource constraints, inadequacies and sources of drudgery, and for that matter, no society can afford to quarrel with it or resist from its benefits. India's limited Green Revolution was possible with the new technology of assured irrigation water, fertilizers, the miracle high yielding Varieties of seeds, pesticides-insecticides, tractorization, credit, services and a host of other attendant measures, inputs and factors. Agricultural research has brought out great possibilities for dryland farming also, which India has to adopt as simply there is no water for ever-increasing water needs of irrigation farming. Resources have to be credited out of the time-tested indigenous knowledge systems and technologies by modernizing them.

The success of the front has brought out many dividends in economic, political and social fields, but has also generated a myriad of problems exactly in the same areas with the added pressure on moral grounds that even with the appreciably enlarged size of the national cake, there are tens of millions who are debarred from sharing in these incremental additions. Population is growing unabated to climb up a billion mark by the year 2001 with over 100 million job seekers sitting on top of it. This swelling number of the unemployed, according to research findings, is attributed, among a host of factors, to the lack of right education, awareness and poverty and material resourcelessness of the masses. Industrialization and government services and even normal professions could hardly be expanded to absorb except a small proportion, leaving majority of them to depend on agriculture and allied jobs, and mostly to private initiatives of their own. As such, agriculture has to diversify not only to keep itself prosperous, but also to absorb increasing number of job-seekers, together with its allied rural activities like agro-industries and agro-services, etc.

However, agriculture cannot diversify to that extent unless the possible and practicable technology is adopted as a tool to bring out agrarian reforms by adopting stringent measures for structural change in the ownership of land, water and other assets and resources, and providing the resourceless access to these resources…….. it is now technologically possible to move away from a production system which is poverty-generating to one which is poverty-eradicating. There was a time when technology favoured large holdings and resourceful farmers. This is no longer the case and, in fact, ceased to be the case a decade ago. Technological breakthroughs have made it possible for fairly small landholders to produce enough to rise above the poverty line. Even those with tiny holdings can, if they use these as a base for developing subsidiary scale and land-size neutral and it is now activities, earn enough for a minimum level of consumption. What has stood in the way of converting the technologically possible into the practically achievable is, of course, political reluctance to touch structural reform of any kind …….. Unless political pressure is brought out, as was done by Teleṇgana movement or Naxalite movement, nothing seems to stir the political levers. Even recently, a conference of State Revenue Ministers called for lowering the land ceiling limits and considering inclusion of major sons in the definition of a family only under political pressure.

Structural reform covers reform in other systems and areas also such as credit, marketing and most important of all, in the social power structure, which has created the age-old stranglehold of the rural elites on the majority backward, poor and resourceless. Basic structural changes will hit the elite, and will hit their cohorts in the political, bureaucratic and industrial circles. In fact, such strategy will hit all the vested interests as no other rural development programme has even hurt so far. What is popular among and beneficial to the poor is naturally unpopular among the elite and their support systems.

"Rural development, starting from community development and coming down to Integrated Rural Development Programme, National Rural Employment Programme and the rest, does not pose any such challenge and remains within cosy limits. Nor it is surprising that the Indian ruling elites have used rural development to put structural reform on the back burner" (Mukerji, op. cit).

Scale and size-neutral feature of modern agriculture is in the offing. Since smaller land-holdings are technologically capable of being rendered viable units, land-holdings should be scrutinized afresh and ceiling should be lowered, although the whole programme should be simultaneously backed up with the 'linkage' and 'support systems' including tying up of the prices of the agricultural inputs and cost of living indices of the rural people with the prices of their produce and earnings of their labour. It is only under such overall coordinated price and cost of production as well as living systems that one can talk of minimum labour payments, release of bonded labour and the indebted, child and women welfare and other welfare measures for the exploited and down-trodden classes in the rural areas. It is unfeasible, even immoral and bad politics and pseudo-intellectualism when one talks of striking a balance between agricultural and raw material prices of the developing countries and those of the industrial goods and services of the developed countries in the international forums and of bringing out a new World Economic Order and not doing the same exercise between the exploited agricultural and rural sectors on the one hand and the industrial-urban sectors on the other, in the country itself. Prices of agricultural goods and wages of rural labour are kept much lower down artificially and there is a strong case for their parity with the prices of the industrial goods and payments to urban and organized industrial labour. It is again here that government fights shy of such measures and voluntary organisations must come forward to organise the ruralites to fight against such conditions. They must be constantly vigilant to see that benefits are not cornered by the rural elites but flow to the rural poor and the marginalised. Furthermore, one important element is to enable vast opportunities to open up by provision of training for micro-level as well as higher level for private entrepreneurship, cushioned by credit, land, other resources as a follow-up measure for youths to credit their own private jobs. This is a must for such a vast country like India. Informal sector jobs are vastly needed to be helped and strengthened.

Minimum Needs Programme

Obtaining the conditions in India in terms of resources and productivity on one hand and the population and its needs on the other, it is imperative to strive for a need-based rather than want-based economy. As such , the Minimum Needs Programme is naturally most relevant and dear to the heart and mind of the poor and the disavantaged of all the acronymic development programmes and projects, as it could, rendered successfully, strike at the very root of poverty and ignorance and set the country to real development paths. The nine facets under the programme are officially said to cover all minimum needs which a modern civilized society must ensure to all its citizens - elementary education, adult education, rural health, rural electrification slum improvement, nutrition programme, housing for the rural poor, drinking water to villages and village roads. The programme with all these is really laudable and vital, and yet it is not so vital, as it leaves the most basic need, i.e. food. There are still millions of the poor, whose earnings are limited and are not sufficient to procure even square meal a day, even though there is a 30 million tonnes surplus food stock in the country. What is required is food security for the hungry and the poor, not just the occasional doses and aids. Doses only produce lethargy and dependency - structures, and in itself is a poor and bad, development-defeating strategy. What the poor need is entitlements to opportunities to earn their food by employment and sweating in bread-earning opportunities. They need help and resources through skill, education and opportunities to help themselves earn their respectful living.

What could the fulfilment of the minimum needs do to the social good could be exemplified through one committed government-sponsored programme. The subsidised rice scheme by Andhra Pradesh although not a foolproof measure, has given several social benefits. "The poor no longer go hungry, as they used to even in the agriculturally prosperous coastal districts". They save about Rs. 25 a month to spend at times of unemployment. They are also less indebted than before. They can procure some more rice, vegetables, hair oil, clothes, etc. Open market prices of rice are held in check because green-card holders are no longer as dependent on it as before. The Paleru or farm-servant system, with some elements of bondage in it, is weakening; agricultural workers have better bargaining power, and as a fall-out, wages are rising. And agricultural productivity has not suffered with all this development.

What is the lesson then? What the voluntary organizations have to do is to pick up such vital needs and organise the poor to fight to get them fulfilled in the various states by propagating the advantages of such struggles. How many of the poor are even aware of these programmes ?

The Minimum Wages Act was passed in 1948. However, according to the Rural Labour Enquiry statistics, of the 20.7 million agricultural labour households (25.2 per cent of all rural households) in 1974-75, only about two per cent workers were aware of the Act and the wages fixed in their regions. And only one per cent of them were members of any organization or union of agricultural workers (Dogra 1984).

These instances make it imperative on the part of the voluntary agencies and other non-governmental and activist groups to work amidst masses and generate awareness among them about their rights and opportunities and strive for benefitting from them.

Organising the poor

Rural power-structure of both the traditional genre as well as that of modern development-generated brand can be reformed only through the organisation of the poor, down-trodden, resourceless, uneducated masses through the conjoin hands of an enlightened rural leadership and concerted and committed social policy. This is because even if the voluntary agencies help the poor organise, and if government's social policy is against it, overtly or covertly, it is rendered futile and leads to frustration. If increasing development leads to the sharpening of inequalities and greater restlessness, it implies failure of the government, the people and the voluntary organizations. The poor have neither the knowledge nor the means to act in their own best interest. Both these things can be brought about through their organization and sensitization.

"The point is precisely that there is no distributive mechanism working in the favour of this group : being unskilled and unfit of industrialization; being without landed property the group does not share in the upward thrust of agrarian and urban lands' capital gains; being without a fixed and regular employment, they cannot benefit from the wage gains of organised labour" (Development with Peace, Second U.P. Report, mimeo, p. 3). Having only raw labour of poor quality to offer, the only thing that can help him is a very large increase in the demand for 'raw labour'. This is exactly the only thing which does not happen in a process of economic growth and modernization.

A recent study by a Japanese team of geographers working in rural areas of Karnataka and reporting on weaker sections has concluded that "such government support (as being extended) has not yet realized economic base nor to uplift their living standard by themselves ...... It seems that the weaker sections in rural areas in order to increase per capita productivity are in need of more detailed and effective guidance from the government, as for example, the utilization of government assisted loans" (Fujiwara et al, 1984, p. 13). In fact, at tail end of the supply line and the delivery system, the corruption, greed and leakages flourish unabashedly, and it is at this level where watchdogs of voluntary organisations are needed to stop such pilferages of money and resources being cornered by the non-poor. It is these voluntary organisations which can pressurise for "greater decentralisation of authority with greater devolution of functions to village panchayats (which) can serve as a check on the leakages of funds by providing mass vigilance" (Rao, 1979, p. 13).

The Approach Paper of the Seventh Five Year Plan rightly observes in connection with anti-poverty programme : "In the ultimate analysis, the objective of removal of poverty can be fulfilled in the measure in which the poor themselves become conscious, improve their education and capabilities and become organised and assert themselves."

Who will do this job? A democratic government, alright, but with its mind bogged in votes could ill afford to undertake such programmes which undermine a part of its support base, which is the well to do exploiting minority (Adiseshiah. p. 16).

However, a committed government of India, as it envisages in the Approach Paper of the Seventh Plan, could legislate or pass an executive order for the organization of the poor. Once this is done, "the activity which the voluntary agencies, and only the voluntary agencies can handle is the organization of the poor to fight for their rights ..... to break the unjust status quo..... (Adiseshiah, pp. 15-16).

Voluntary Agencies : Examples of Field Performance

Two examples of field performance are being given in the sequel with a view to monitoring and assessing the effectiveness and capability of the voluntary organizations - one is the case of Maharashtra and the other of eastern Uttar Pradesh.

Pani Panchayat : Water for All

V.B. Salunke, who was involved in relief work in 1971-72 famine period, set up the *Gram Gaurav Pratisthan* Trust at Naigaon, a village in Purandhar taluka (Pune district.). He employed a simple, cheap and viable water harvesting technique and launched a programme of group irrigation in 1978 through people's participation in Purandhar block comprising 100 drought-prone villages. Thus was the Pani Panchayat born; it adopted four cardinal principles which have proved to be of vital significance.

First, the water must be shared equitably on the basis of half an acre per capita per family within the command area and not in relation to the size of land holdings. A family of five is, thus, entitled to bring 2.5 acres of land under irrigation.This is to provide benefit of a scarce resource to the maximum number of farm families, ensuring at the same time that this 2.5 acre irrigated farm will be enough for subsistence under a viable modern farming.

Second, the cultivation of sugarcane is barred on account of its very high water requirements. The object is to maximise productivity per unit of water rather than per unit of land.

Third, each beneficiary must contribute 20 per cent of the cost of the project, which normally works out to about Rs. 400 per acre. 40 per cent of the outlay is obtained as government subsidy and remaining 40 per cent is provided by the Pratisthan Trust itself.

Fourth, irrigation water rights are conferred on the farmer and not on the land; if the land is sold, water rights revert back to the Trust. The chief objective is to prevent land sales to wealthier peasants and outsiders and to build communities of sturdy farming families who are enabled thereby to rise permanently above thc poverty line.

There are a number of socio-economic, political, moral, educative, perceptual and integrative lessons going through the minds of the villagers as a fall-out of this amply successful organization.

The beneficiaries themselves administer and operate each project and maintain accounts.

The Trust has trained local youths and school dropouts with elementary technical and maintenance skills.

Farmers thus participate successfully in the *Pani Panchayat* programme.

With an investment of Rs. 5 crores, in a phased period, 25,000 acres of land will be irrigated under 600 schemes providing employment to 25,000 persons at the rate of one person per irrigated acre.

Cropping pattern will diversify to prop up horticulture, animal husbandry and a host of other new outlets. Labour intensity on the farm front has already increased.

Confidence is built up among the lowliest of the low, i.e. communities of cobblers, ex-criminal tribes and nomadic shepherds, who among others, have joined Pani Panchayat. A lowly widow could afford to threaten that if the government did not "sanction an electricity connection as soon as their percolation well was complete, the members including 22 women participants would march to Bombay."

The beneficiaries, including a village of cobblers, have raised their own funds, having independently decided to divert a part of the available water for piped water supply. What are the benefits ? Kitchen gardens and trees are coming out. The water tap has liberated the women from the routine drudgery, and hard work involved in fetching water, a daily four-trip business and improved their health. It has brought more education and income-generating side activities, all to be merely followed by a declining fertility rate.

There is evidence of reverse migration of textile and other workers from the Bombay slums. The push migration from the villages might be stopped and lead to a sound rural to urban migration situation. Verghese exhorts that "the future of Bombay is tied to the Naigaons of Maharashtra", and may be also of other cities.

The socialization of water (by consent, not by law) has created a basis for community building and organisation of the rural poor around an emerging local leadership. This combination of organisation and leadership provides an instrument for a purposeful and direct attack on poverty and poverty - creating situations, and a focus for motivation to accept and work for relevant modernization and meaningful change.

The *Pani Panchayat* plans to open an office at each project site and to set-up a land-water-manpower management institute to train a cadre of rural dropouts aged 15 to 17 in water conservation, surveying, lift irrigation, water distribution, crop planning, marketing and accountancy. The programmed turnout of 30 matriculates each year will be absorbed in its expanding and diversifying activities, such as manufacturing activities of products like hume pipes, pumps, processing of agricultural produce, all in a bid to retain the rural youths in the countryside.

Verghese rightly counts out a number of problems yet to be faced and tackled, as "every solution creates new problems": these problems are related to land-shaping, consolidation for improved land-and-water management, surplus land distribution to the landless, water frugality and conservation of water for common use, making compact blocks of irrigated land by exchange of individual plots, harnessing community action and cooperation in management of uplands and in processing and marketing operations, etc. (Verghese, p. 6). Who can tell, Indian masses are the deaf and dumb' millions, fatalistic, and change–resisting fools! Who created them so?

Banwasi Sewa Ashram and its Role

In a situation of social and economic change with rapid population growth, the poor elements of population are caught in a vicious circle. Being landless and unequipped educationally and technologically to adapt themselves to the changing situation, they are left uncared for. There are two alternatives open to involve them in the levers of change; (I) whether they should be organized to inculcate awareness and develop self-leadership so that they could take advantage of the opportunities and facilities provided by the government and other resource providers by fuller participation and assertion of rights. This process states as to 'how to combine change with relative social stability (Owens and Shaw, 1972, p. 2, 74, 126), or, (ii) alternatively, the poor should be organized to assert their rights and, if necessary, rise in conflict and confrontation with the status quo forces of the vested interests.

Whatever the course to be adopted, 'organisation of the poor' is an import vehicle of social and economic change (ICFTU-ARO *et al.*, 1975, p. 3; Chopra, 1981, p. 6; Shourie, 1980, p.6; Thorner, 1953).

The local power structure is to play a crucial role in the effort. If it is aggressive, exploitative, dominant and unchangeable, the organisation of the poor has to be very effective indeed to deal with heavy odds effectively. Experience of the government officials as well as of the voluntary agencies working in the field shows that the poor also have friends within the power structure. The political, social and economic groups which, have a vested interest in poverty, are neither as powerful nor as monolithic as may be imagined by some (Chopra, op. Cit., p. 6). It has to be made to respond to the needs of the underprivileged and allow them to reap the benefits of development.

The experience gained by the Banvasi Seva Ashram in the Sonpar region in Mirzapur District (Uttar Pradesh) amply corroborates the above note of hope and help through people's organization. This Ashram has been working in the area for about last 30 years, and one of its wings-AGRINDUS Family Welfare Project-was started in 1968 with a view to developing a consensus among the rural population for a small family norm through a comprehensive development programme. The Agricultural Finance Corporation of India has brought out a 167 page report in 1980 on the Ashram's work which speaks of the locally generated tremendous social and economic change and development in the area. The Ashram has taken up five villages in each of four blocks of the region for intensive development and in other 100 villages efforts have been limited to helping 10 to 15 per cent of the families.

Economic and Social Changes

The gains achieved in the project area showed that once the motivation is built up and people are organised and proper facilities given and made accessible to them, economic development and social change get on to their own wheels. It is with this objective that the people were organised and taught the lessons of self-development through community efforts in multi fields of life. Agricultural Finance Corporation reports (1980) that per capita income has increased by 75 per cent and 35 per cent of the families have been brought above the poverty line. Gross cultivated area has increased by a third, and intensity of cropping too has improved. Two hundred literacy centres have been opened and, unlike government operated schools within region, are functioning. There is tremendous 'impact on the health of the tribals and (has resulted in) reduction in mortality rate, simultaneously increasing the longevity of life" (quoted in Shourie, p. 6). In the hundred villages (out of regional total of about 400), the target for land development was exceeded by 37 per cent and in the five adopted villages by 45 per cent and for area under high yielding varieties by 36 per cent and 50 per cent respectively.

These developments have resulted through very small or micro projects, specially designed for individual families, for individual ravines and small irrigation projects like small tanks, terracing, introducing banana trees, mulberry, soyabean, new varieties of crops, training in animal husbandry, providing easily payable loans, building strong stone and locally made brick structures for housing, etc.

All this success has come about because the projects have been selected, executed and monitored by the people's own institutions: the *Gram Swarajya Sabha*, consisting of all families in the village; the *Kshetriya Gram Swarajya Sabha* at the block level, and the *Kendriya Gram Swarajya Samiti* for the project area as a whole. The entire work is done by the trained local people and the Ashram workers.

What social changes have accrued with these economic changes? The evaluation and survey of the works exhibit ample evidence of the changes occurring in the various social cultural dimensions.

People in general are aware of the power of awareness, locally generated leadership, participation and organization and the political pressure they could build up for their own benefit. They no longer want individual charity; they want funds for development for eliminating floods and droughts, for water and land development, etc. (Shourie, p.6). This attitudinal change in the minds of the rural, down-trodden, uneducated people is a mile-stone towards real development.

The way of life of the tribals and other lowly people is changing, not as much under the impress of *Sanskritization*, urbanization and industrialization or westernization going on in the region, as under the home-grown rural development or self-development programmes. Arun Shourie observes:

"Tribals who had only cut trees for centuries are now planting trees yielding mangoes, jackfruit, banana, lime and guava.... A population that only 15 years ago knew only slash and burn agriculture is now taking to one new crop after another, to one improved variety of each crop after another. People who lived off wild grass and flowers are now tending vegetable gardens around their houses. People who knew only to leave their animals free to roam in the forests are now stall-feeding them with fodder" (1980, p.6).

Tribals' level of consciousness about this worldly business and perception about the natural and environmental resources has undergone a significant change. The people of witchcraft, magic and nature worship (Prembhai, p. 19), who learnt to make damaged and eroded land flower before them through watershed management and planting of trees and soil conservation, have also learnt that "nature is not a god beyond their reach. Selecting projects, executing them, managing them, learning new skills, setting up and making new forms of social organisation have taught them that the money-lenders, contractors, liquor merchants (local officials and politicians) are not gods either" (Shourie, 1980, p.6).

How about the nexus of the liquor merchant-contractors etc.? A sustained campaign, especially by women, has led to the closure of 25 liquor shops in the area. The *Bagai* (a grass for rope-making) contract system has given way to the cooperatives of the tribals, who have got a small simple pedal-operated machine, multiplying the labourers' productivity by eight times. A.F.C. Report states that the numbers of families going to money lenders fell by 60 per cent and the number of families indebted to them by two-thirds, and the average amount to be taken on loan also dropped by one-third. The debt incurred for social obligations also fell by two-thirds and, for consumption, to a quarter and the average amount to a one-fifth. The rack-renting usury, the greatest social sin in the area, has been thus given the hardest blow. Money-lenders have abnormally lowered their interest rate on their own under the pressure of market forces. The community *Panchayat* is looking after the disputes. In 1979, 60 cases were filed against the Mahajans, who used to grab land and reduce borrowers to bondage or landlessness, and all except two were won. Actually, the lower power-structure is getting transformed, and reactions are so high from the vested interests that even the U.P. Assembly forum was used by the politicians against the Ashram activities.

The Banvasi Ashram's performance and that of similar hundreds of exercises being carried in India on small scale (Chopra) might seem to be a miniscule, a drop in the ocean, but it does suggest that if not the government, not the bureaucracy, not the politicians, but certainly under the pressure of the existential needs, growing population and poverty and the deprivation and squalor, the masses themselves might organize not for conflict *per se* but for positive change, by increasing their participatory assertiveness. Probably looking into this dynamics of change, Ashok Mehta had observed indulgently that "all these trends, which are an earnest for social change, cannot be thwarted, much less reversed."

Fellow delegates, I took rather a long time, but I hope that I have taken you a little to the real world around us, to get some food for thought and for a little activational stir – up, and agitation of mind as well. I thank you all for bearing with me for so long.

Shah Manzoor Alam
1928 -

Manzoor Alam is buried neck deep in the study of the Dead Sea Scroll. Scrutinizing the English translations of these Hebrew and Aramaic texts, Alam's aim is to decode the principles which unite religions that are contained in these works. It was a write up in Edit a newsletter of the University of Edinburgh in 1997 that led Alam towards the historical richness of these traditional texts. Identifying and creating a unique niche of work is not new to Alam .

When Alam joined as a lecturer at Osmania University in 1952, the department of geography was languishing in obscurity. It was a department tucked way out in the south and stood isolated from the heartland of geography which held sway in the north. Intellectually the university was impoverished, as two third of its faculty had fled to Pakistan as an aftermath to the partition of India . It is here that Alam built a department which the University Grants Commission recognized as a Centre of Excellence way back in 1978. This is not all, Alam is the founder of the Centre for Area Studies in 1982..Its objective to bring together the countries of Indian Ocean to a common platform for research was unprecedented not just to the State of Andhra Pradesh and the University of Osmania but to India as a whole. Invited to a vice-chancellorship of the University of Kashmir, Srinagar in 1984 was Alam's other arena where he displayed talent. In the exceptionally hot soup of political challenges which embroiled Kashmir valley, Alam introduced half a dozen new courses of study and revitalized many which had virtually gone defunct. His vision was not merely to guard chair, but to use his position in fostering close ties between Kashmir and the rest of India. A Talent Promotion Scheme where each winter vacation more than twenty teachers of the university were funded to tour and research in any part of India was a scheme whose goodness is still remembered. Laudable were his works with the World Bank from 1982 to 1997, that till date he remains a consultant in their file .

How did Alam accomplish all this? Alam had no intellectual mentor in India, he has a doctorate from the University of Edinburgh. Born on the first day of the year in 1928 in a small town of Ghazipur about 75 kilometers to the north of the city of Banaras, Alam does not hail from an elite family of political, economic or academic repute. It was from St.Andrew's College at Gorakhpur that Alam did his intermediate. Academics was not one of Alam's first career options, to commission as an officer in the Defence Forces was his desire. A graduation and post –graduation from the University of Aligarh in 1948, did not add feather to his cap. A short year as lecturer in an intermediate college at Jaunpur in 1949 and a term of teaching at the National Defence Academy were not pads for a launch of any sorts. Filled with pride and dignity, Alam is far from the type who networked or begged favors. What then was the chemistry to Alam's success? Innovative research in geography, is what catapulted Alam into the stage of spotlights.

Availing the British Council Travel Grant and the University of Edinburgh Scholarship, it was under the tutelage of Watson, chairperson at the department of geography, Edinburgh that Alam had completed his doctorate in 1962. Do the theories of Hoyt, Harris and Burgess on the urban evolution of America explain the morphology of Asian city was the interesting question Alam addressed in his doctorate . His results 'are truly penetrating, very revealing, and original contribution to urban geography' is what Wredford Watson writes in the preface of Alam's published thesis : 'Hyderabad – Secunderabad – a study in Urban Geography' in 1965. Alam's use of a mixture of theory, common sense and inferences drawn from data challenged the established models and led him to the conclusion that 'all cities are too much the children of their cultures to be alike, each speaks in a unique way of the history and geography of the region it expresses.' Studies on urban geography were not new to the academic landscape of Indian Geography, but Alam's work was a departure from the kind of urban studies which were prevalent in the country at that time. His research so stirred the academic community that Alam could not be ignored. Invitations of visiting professorship poured in from as far as the University of Massey at Palmerston, New Zealand, and the University of Macquarie at Sydney, Australia where he spent a year each in 1970 and 1974 respectively. The Planning Atlas of Andhra Pradesh – the first of its kind in 1976 in India, was Alam's next turf for success. Bringing together three diverse departments: State Planning Board of Andhra Pradesh, Survey of India and the University of Osmania the thrust of the Atlas held a strong message – administration can understand planning better through maps. The acclaim acquired through the Atlas invigorated Alam towards another unusual creation – the Indian National Cartographic Association in 1978 . It was Alam's brainchild. When Joy Dunkerley, the economist with the United States senate was in search of an anchor for her project on fuel wood in urban markets, Alam was an obvious choice. This paved the way to a series of projects on urban energy with the World Bank through 1994 to 1997. Writing five books, editing another ten and publishing fifty research articles — it is in the harvest of innovative works in geography that Alam reaped his bounties.

Creative people like sensitive species tend to retreat rather than adapt when the environment gets hostile . Even though nurtured with personal care when conferences turned more political than professional Alam preferred to limit his days of attendance. When political medling interfered with his vision of a vice- chancellor, Alam forwarded his resignation .

How does Alam peg himself ? Reticent and humble he attributes his works to the will of God. Little wonder that Alam has found another unique niche – to make alive the secrets of the Dead Sea Scroll.

Untitled

S.M. ALAM

Man has been interacting with environment right from the primeval stage of human development and continues to do so in this age of nuclear technology with greater vigour. The interpretation of this interactive relationship between man and his environment and its spatial expression has been the focal theme of geographers since the inception of geographical studies. With the advance of science and technology the frontiers of knowledge have expanded beyond the cosmic space and the geography of the earth has transformed beyond recognition, but geographers, particularly of India, are still preoccupied with discussions on dichotomies in geography, and the geographical syllabi in Indian schools, colleges and universities have not kept pace with the speed with which the geography of mankind has changed. Geography from school to the college level has remainded by and large gazetteer oriented and description in nature. The concept of village and neighborhood geography has not yet found a place in our syllabi in schools and where it has it is mere location oriented. It makes no effort to create an awareness of the village neighborhood environment and interpret to the very young mind the problems generated and make them inquisitive to look for explanations for the problems and seek their solution. It is the responsibility of geographers to inculcate in the young and receptive minds that the earth and its environment are crucially important resource which should be judiciously utilised and carefully conserved for the survival and benefit of the mankind. The post-graduate syllabi in geography need radical changes and a totally new outlook. It is time we give up text book approach to the teaching of geography and introduce research oriented courses in post-graduate classes. This naturally implies all the basics of the discipline, have to be completed, at a fairly advanced level at the undergraduate level. May I draw the attention of fellow geographers of the undergraduate syllabi in Economics, Political Science, Sociology, Botany, Zoology, Chemistry, Physics etc. which compared to geography are far advanced. Consequently graduates in these cognate disciplines have tremendous advantage over

---

9th Indian Geography Congress
Srinagar, 1987 December

geography graduates in the employment market.

An undesirable practice which is still being pursued in our post-graduate courses is multiplication of optional papers which have no bearing on the research of the faculty. As for instance in some of the university geography departments we do reach advanced level optional courses on oceanography, biogeography without any back ground of research with those who teach these courses. Naturally such courses will always be text book oriented based on the researches of others. The teacher will not be able to contribute his/her own share to the advancement of knowledge in that area of specialization. He will not be able to add anything new based on his own research experience and which the student cannot get from the prescribed text book. This type of course will not be able to excite the interest and imagination of our students. A teacher can impart dynamism and a new meaning to the course which is developed through his own researches. He will be able to share with his students his experiences of successes and failures, the methodology used by him and the analytical techniques applied. This sharing of research experience with the students relating to a specialised course will excite their research interest profoundly, will develop their critical faculty, and will help them to grow as competent researchers and scholars. This will save post-graduate teaching from being monotonous and unscholarly.

Geography, a science of spatial relationship should concentrate on explaining the changing geography of lands and people caused due to human and natural factors. We have very comprehensively covered in our geographical studies the adjustments made by man to his natural environment, but we have paid little attention to the changing political, economic and administrative policies which significantly influence man-land relationship. Can we explain the change in cropping pattern from paddy to sugarcane or from wheat to cotton or from dry crops to wet crops without understanding the market forces, the taxation and pricing policies, land tenure system and change in the water supply system for crops. The market forces can be both national and international. A decision to boost the export of quality rice and restrict that of sugar will be well reflected in the changing crop pattern from sugarcane to paddy. Similarly, the urban mosaic of India cannot be explained without an understanding of the transport network policy, industrial and power development policy, etc. of the State and Union Governments. The growth of cities is inevitably linked with the policies concerning the dispersal or concentrations. The decision of the Union Government to control the key sectors of economy such as steel industry, major power and irrigation project has given rise to a series of new settlements which perhaps might not have developed if their development had been left to private capital. Thus, in short we cannot explain the geography of region if we ignore the policy issues.

This is what geographers have been doing and consequently our analysis lacks the depth and penetration which other social scientists have acquired.

Geography is one of the most ancient disciplines, but in terms of development has lagged behind most of the social and physical sciences. These disciplines besides possessing a strong theoretical background have focused their studies to problems of life and society and have therefore made themselves more meaningful to the society. Geographical studies have too moved in this direction but not to the extent they ought to have. In order to stand on equal terms among the leading disciplines of knowledge we must focus our studies strongly to problems of life and society in order to establish firmly our social relevance. Some of the key problems which are of global concern such as the energy problem, environmental degradation , urban and industrial pollution, growing urban poverty and proliferation of slums etc. have hardly attracted the attention of geographers in India concerning the energy problem particularly in India. The indiscriminate use of firewood is a health hazard and also leads to wanton destruction of forests thereby causing soil erosion which makes the land sterile for growth of vegetation. We must look for the substitute of firewood which is also one of the inefficient sources of energy.

In the field of urban geography, geographers have made significant contribution in explaining growth and morphology of Indian towns or in explaining city hinterland relationship. Unfortunately, we are now overdoing it. Let us grow out of this growth and morphology syndromes and pick up the key urban issues for in depth analysis. As for instance we can examine and analyze the problems of metropolitan India. The metropolitan cities of India are acquiring the contrasting characteristics of prosperity and poverty resulting in the dichotomy of their economic structure and the growth of informal sector. The dynamism of these metropolitan cities attracts immigrants in large numbers which leads to proliferation of slums and low income generating jobs in the informal sector. The metropolitan cities are collapsing under the weight of their own development. They have therefore become the most vulnerable of the urban settlements.

The study of the location of industries is indeed important but more important are the consequences of industrial location on urban living. Industries have become the major source of pollution of ground and surface water and therefore constitute a major health hazard. Every major metropolitan city of India is a potential Bhopal and with the increase in the number of nuclear power plants the human civilization will be engulfed with nuclear volcanoes. All these developments have significant spatial consequences and should constitute major concerns of geographers. The geography of nuclear power plants should make a fascinating study.

With the advancement of modern technology the exploitation and development pattern of natural resources are being radically transformed. I would not be surprised if before the end of this millennia small villages and small towns will disappear and settlements will be attracted more towards the coastline closer to the sea bed resources which by then are likely to be commercially exploited.

The social geographers should critically examine the social consequences of technological developments. Technological transformations are likely to influence significantly the social contours of our established social order and may lead to the emergence of a new social system which will reflect not only a new pattern of social relationship between man and man but also between man and land.

The satellite system of communication provides geographers with the unique opportunity to re-emphasize the basic geographical theme of global interdependence, through it we should spread the message of the geography of international peace. No other discipline understands, appreciates and explains the global and international scenario as well as we do. For we geographers alone visualize the concept of one world in its global dimensions.

Before I conclude let me caution my fellow geographers that we are on the threshold of 21st century and we have to move in that century as a scientific discipline capable of responding to the challenges of the century. Geographers have to make a determined bid to stand on equal terms with other disciplines which are far ahead of us in their scientific researches, analytical techniques and applied orientation. We have to make a quantum jump in order to catch up with satellite geography.

May I conclude that the challenges of the 21st century should lead achievements of our discipline and its contributions to the development of society. Let us perceive and visualise in clear terms the directions and dimensions that we propose to lend to geography in order to emerge as a leading branch of knowledge and learning. We cannot do so in isolation of other disciplines for the 21st century be a century of interdisciplinary studies. The disciplinary barriers will have to be demolished for a scientific and objective appreciation of the problems of the 21st century. Are we ready to move in this direction?

Rajagopala Vaidyanadhan
1931 -

Vaidyanadhan has to his credit the interpretation of over one thousand aerial photographs and numerous satellite imageries. Yet focusing rapt attention to interpret an aerial photograph through the stereoscope is not Vaidyanadhan's main interest. He has documented his research in seventy articles, published in different geographical and geological journals. Today he is busy completing his book on the Geology of India. Yet hankering after publications is not a passion with Vaidyanadhan. He has led field visits to places as far reaching as Pahalgam in the north to Cape Camorin in the south, Bhuj in the west to Tezpur in the east. He has also conducted geomorphic mapping camps to train officers of the Geological Survey of India . Fieldwork alone is not a burning obsession with Vaidyanadhan. With patience and care he has edited the Journal of the Geological Society of India from 1992–1995. Editorial works too are not a fascination with Vaidyanadhan. For many years Vaidyanadhan has served as member of the governing body of the Wadia Institute of Himalayan Studies and has been an expert in committees of the Department of Science and Technology, University Grants Commission, Center for Scientific and Industrial Research. These he says are academic chores which are best digested in small dosages. As a rule Vaidyanadhan has stayed away from a variety of ships – principalship, wardenship, or vice-chancellorship. Despite a first class first in school and at the under-graduate and post-graduate levels, Vaidyanadhan did not opt for a career in the Indian Administrative Services. Taking decisions on the grounds of administrative logic was not his strong suites. What has then been the energizing force, which propelled Vaidyanadhan through an uninterrupted

innings of thirty-eight long years stay in the University of Andhra Pradesh,? 'Students' is Vaidyanadhan's prompt reply.

The answer discloses the secret of his being a teacher of established repute. Every year the Syndicate of the University of Andhra Pradesh selects one out of seventy odd professors for the Best Teacher Aaward. In 1983 in a grand ceremony held at Hyderabad, in the august company of the state chief minister, vice-chancellor and other dignitaries Vaidyanadhan's name was announced for this prestigious award. Vaidyanadhan was busy undertaking fieldwork with a group of students.The award was given in absentia, yet Vaidyanadhan's roster for the day had kept, in a way, the spirit behind the award alive. When the academic committee of the University of Andhra Pradesh proposed the inauguration of a department of geography, Vaidyanadhan was their first choice. Serving in the department of geology, it was not just the fact that Vaidhaynadhan's doctorate was on 'Geomorphology of the Western Cuddapah Basin' but more his reputation as a teacher, that had outweighed in his favour as an obvious candidate. A devoted teacher as soon as Vaidyanadhan switched from geology and joined the department of geography in 1973 his first task was to attend to the needs of students.

Today if the geomorphology lab at the department of geography of Waltair University, is proud to possess two hundred pairs of stereoscopes, two hundred fifty aerial photographs and a dozen imageries, a considerable share of the credit for this goes to Vaidyanadhan. Inviting experts from the fields of oceanography, climatology and hydrology to the department of geography, was Vaidyanadhan's way to inculcate an interdisciplinary culture of learning. More important than infrastructure was the judicious blend of geology and geomorphology which Vaidyanadhan grafted into the department of geography. Inspite of being a geologist for twenty long years, Vaidyanadhan never overlooked the fact that he was to service the needs of students of geography. Sensitive to the reality that most of the geography students belong to the humanities and not the science stream, Vaidyanadhan focused his attention on study of deltas, coastal and erosional surfaces where knowledge of geology is needed but only at an elementary level. Clarity, commitment and an ability to communicate is what made Vaidyanadhan a teacher of class. Focusing on processes rather than patterns, principles rather than description, a doctorate student of his summed up " with him one knows where one is". Locating oneself is after all a critical step in moving ahead. Combining the skills of the spoken word with the visual aids and verifying it with reality in the field soaked Vaidyanadhan's lectures in power. Most versatile were his 'ways' to teach the interpretation of aerial photographs and imageries.

Vaidyanadhan availed the Smith Mundt Fullbright grant to study photogrammetry and photointerpretation at the Ohio State University at Columbus, United States of America in 1959-1960, but it was more his gift of visualising flat features in a three dimensional perspective. To Vaidyanadhan there was no flat surface, all land had a concavity or convexity, and at times both. He went out of his way to train students to develop 'this eye'. Procuring aerial photographs in India is ridden with problems of secrecy and bureaucartic red tape. To override this barrier Vaidyanadhan took on ten research projects under the banner of different sponsoring agencies like the Oil and Natural Gas Company, Ministry of Defence and Department of Science and Technology, so that photographs were readily accessible. He personally organized visits for his students to the Photo Interpretation Centre, Dehra Dun, National Remote Sensing Agency, Hyderabad and Geological Survey of India, Calcutta. Students were the end users of his research. While Vaidyanadhan published in both geological and geographical journals he was careful to craft his papers according to the audience. The papers on structures, fractures and lineaments sought an outlet in geological journals while those on landforms, land use and applied geomorphology were directed to geographical journals. Nearly 50 per cent of his papers were written with students. Training and encouraging research scholars to publish, a hallmark of Vaidyanadhan is that he generously gave them credit. A check of his publications shows that the research scholar is the first author and Vaidyanadhan the second. Humility earned him deep reverence among his students.

To Vaidyanadhan, venturing far from his department was a colossal waste of time. A majority of his research papers are rooted within Andhra Pradesh. He explains that a juxtaposition of mountain, coast and delta in the close vicinity is ample opportunity to test processes and patterns and relationships of the physical world. Though he was born on 21st December, 1931, in the Kalia Kurichi village of South Arcot district in Tamil Naidu, most of his education and all his professional life has been spent in Andhra Pradesh.

A hallmark of a teacher is to continue learning and prepare for the 'next' class. Residing after professional retirement in 1991, in a small district town called Cuddalore, twenty-two kilometers to the south of Pondicherry, Vaidyanadhan a connoisseur of Karnatak music is fully engaged in learning to read and recite the Vedic shalokas and scriptures. With unflappable detachment so typical of many south Indian brahmins, he states: "I am seventy-one years of age, the average life expectancy in India is around sixty-two, I am living on a bonus and therefore preparing for the 'next world'." The sequential progression: facts, analysis and conclusion in this sentence alone epitomizes the teacher in him. All who join the academic profession – teach. But there are few teachers. Vaidyanadhan is one of them.

Whither Indian Geography

R.VAIDYANADHAN

I consider my election as President of the Ninth Indian Geography Congress as a token of recognition of the contribution made by my colleagues and young scholars in the Department of Geography at the Andhra University during the past one decade, particularly in the field of physical geography and application of remote sensing in geographical studies. I am conscious of my limitation, when I recall the distinguished senior geographers who held this position before me. It is with the confidence that I can draw on their sound advice and active cooperation from all the fellow members of this Association that I enter this office. A few of the earlier presidential addresses have drawn our attention to some of the lacunae in our curricula, research, professional competence etc., and have indeed suggested certain remedies as well. I wish to confine myself to some of the glaring inadequacies in us and draw your attention to possible corrective measures that can be taken in the light of certain actions already initiated by the government through certain institutions. I hope that these might set us thinking as to what we should do if we are to be an effective part of the Earth Science community in this country.

A layman, when he is sick, goes to a general physician, a financier with a desire to invest in mines goes to a consulting geologist, and another wishing to construct a mansion approaches an architect, whereas one with a lot of unaccounted money goes to an income-tax practitioner. In all these cases the needy seek the help of the appropriately qualified person and pay for it. Who comes to a geographer?

Well, then if our contention as geographers is that our discipline is not meant to solve the problems of individuals, but only that of a community or state, then what is the scenario? When dams are to be constructed, the engineers are called for, when pricing policy of agricultural commodities is to be decided, an agricultural economist is consulted, when an industry

---

10th Indian Geography Congress
Pune, 1987 December

is to be located a committee of economists and technologists are approached, when a chain of hotels is to be established, reputed caterers, management experts and tourist organisations are called in. Which community or state comes to the geographers?

Time and again we tend to remind others how important and all pervading is the subject of geography and how early geographers had thought and expatiated on so many issues that affect man and the land. We were the first to explore unknown lands, we were the first to study and document the distribution of life and materials on this planet, we were the first to evolve many hypotheses to indicate the relation between the man and his environment, we are the persons who can easily take a holistic view of many interdependent things that take place around us. It is all true. These things definitely give us a status to contribute to theoretical aspects of geography, which is equally desirable and necessary.

Let us have some honest introspection. Does this mean that geography had a useful role in the past, and has become archaic now, and is not required to be studied or practiced any more? Far from it. Fortunately, it is one discipline that can assist in the collection and analysis of data in a spatial frame better than any other discipline that has a spatial perspective. A geographer, if he is provided with all the necessary data, primary and/or secondary, can analyse them critically in the spatial perspective and his interpretation and synthesis may give a new dimension to the problem and also suggest its solution. Every school boy knows that the map is our main tool. However, with the rapid advance in tools and exacting requirements, successive generations of geographers have perforce to learn newer techniques to be really useful.

We have to reconcile to the fact that geography, upto a certain stage in the educational field, is a liberal art. But beyond it, it can be a utilitarian science only if high specialization is made in the sub-disciplines, which means extra knowledge to be acquired and effort put forth to deserve to be consulted as an expert by an individual or community or state. It is not unusual for us to lament now and then that our advice is not properly heeded, when we have so much to offer to the community and state! There are only two possibilities : either we really do not have anything worthwhile to offer or, if we have, we are very poor salesmen and have not either cared to or sincerely tried to impress the community of our worth, and it is therefore not surprising that we are not consulted. But yet there are cases where individual geographers, whatever be their specialisation – urban geography, regional planning, agricultural geography, population geography or geomorphology, are being consulted in specific cases and issues and their advice sought. Needless to say, this clearly indicates that it is not in the lack of potential in the sub-disciplines to be of use to the community, but in the overall inadequacy of equipment of the practitioner of the subject, particularly in our country, the fault lies.

Curriculum and Teacher

Distinguished geographers in India have over the past many decades time and again discussed and evolved syllabi to suit the needs of the different levels in the geography courses in the pattern of education. Unlike in other sciences, where the growth seems to be vertical as in a tree, with new branches spreading out, in geography it looks like a horizontal spread with cross-breeding with other related disciplines. Again, geography seems to have different facets to offer at different levels to a student and a scholar, and hence the practitioners of the discipline should be aware of this varying emphasis. Upto college level, under the present Indian conditions, geography can only be a subject which can impart knowledge of man's surroundings in all aspects, the area varying from a village to the earth as a whole. At the university level, in the interest of the students and the subject, concerted efforts need to be made to impart knowledge in depth in any one area of specialisation also, along with expertise in technical skills required for practicing that specialisation. This is not difficult and is being done in a few institutions across the country in a few sub-disciplines in geography.

Sponsored by the University Grants Commission, an attempt has been made recently to revamp the syllabi in different subjects for the undergraduate and post-graduate students in geography in colleges and universities in India. It can be reasonably hoped that provided the teachers in the colleges and universities extend their whole-hearted co-operation and implement and improve upon them as there is vast scope to do so - at least, we can have satisfaction that we are passing on to the students almost the latest in geographical thinking. But will our teachers take up this challenge and be themselves abreast in their specialisations?

It is learnt that a number of geography departments are being closed one after another in the United States of America. Since in that country even imparting education, to a large extent, is a form of private enterprise, perhaps the present community there feels that the students being turned out from these departments are not being trained in any skills or trades that will enable them to eke out reasonable living based on that knowledge. This has naturally upset the faculty, who are now equipping themselves in such of the applied fields where their knowledge of geography would serve as a basic input. A geomorphologist specialises in land use and resource analysis, an urban geographer becomes a town-planner, a population geographer becomes a demographer and a cartographer goes into an advertising agency, each of them learning new additional techniques and use of tools required to fit in appropriately in his new role. In the United States of America and the United Kingdom geographers are actively engaged as expert consultants in town and country planning organizations.

What is the situation in our country? One of our own senior respected geographer is of opinion that "there is no safer seat in the world than a chair in an Indian university or a position down the ladder, because no one gets checked out on grounds of academic non-performance". But then we should question ourselves, if such a complacency is for the good of geography, or for that matter any discipline in a higher academic institution? While I am not advocating the outright rustication of the incompetent, we at least have to develop a sense of moral accountability to the society in the profession we have chosen and the students we are entrusted with.

A vast majority of the students of geography get dispersed into walks of life unconnected with geography. This is true of many other disciplines as well, in India, and hence it is perhaps we do not shed any tears on this account. However, if only the teachers try to keep themselves abreast of the latest thinking and advances in their own sub-disciplines in geography and impart the same to the students, besides contributing themeselves to their chosen fields, a few more students may be really professionally employed. It is here that institutions of higher learning or those that have established a reputation for excellence, in certain sub-disciplines in geography , should come in and conduct special workshops for teachers. An attempt has been already made in this direction by the University Grants Commission, and one avidly waits to see the results of the same. If this is not done at all, there is the danger of teachers passing ritually on to their students now the same material that was handed over to them by their own teachers, decades ago!

Research

Most of geographic research in many sub-disciplines has been generally a post-mortem analysis, namely, studying the distribution of parameters in space and occasionally in time, and arriving at the possible mutual relationships. Whereas a novice in research in the earlier days used to be content with drawing a series of graphs of histograms to indicate the relationships between variables, the modern scholar talks about covariance, correlation, coefficient, regression, etc. Of course this is in the right direction and desirable, but it is often done unmeaningfully. Further,, individual scholars/teachers rarely stick on to a sub-discipline long enough to be able to master the subject and make original contribution. The bane of geographic research in India seems to have been the waywardness of a majority of the researchers. Hardly does one equip himself in one of the upcoming trends, whether it is urban geography, quantitative geography or environmental science, another wave from the West strikes him or gets generated from within the country by scientists in other disciplines, and he is right there so as not to be left behind; we hurriedly join that stream, to make our own limited contribution. This has perhaps not given us much time to project our own discipline to the extent it deserves.

There is perhaps a mistaken impression or phobia among a majority of students and teachers of geography alike in the country : that understanding of science-based sub-disciplines of geography like geomorphology, climatology, oceanography, bio-geography, pedology, hydrology, etc. requires a high level of proficiency in mathematics, physics, chemistry or biology. It is not so. There are so many areas even in these subjects where research can be done without a substantial background in any of these basic sciences, provided the objectives are clear, methodology correctly understood and techniques faithfully employed. These can be best seen in the papers in the volumes – "Applied Science and Development " and "Natural Resources and Development", published by the Institute for Scientific Co-operation, Tubingen, Federal Republic of Germany. True, a modern geographer may not be able to make a fundamental contribution in sedimentology or genetics or ecology just because he has studied geomorphology or biogeography or environmental science. But certainly one can amass a wealth of data on spatial relations among the land, water, soil, vegetation and last but not the least the man. This is something that must be dinned into the ears of every student of geography right at the college level in our country. The Earth Sciences and Mining Panel of Council Scientific and Industrial Research, while lamenting that very few projects were submitted, constituted a sub-committee to pin point specific fields in which geographers should be induced to submit research project. The chairman of the committee wrote personal letters to a large number of geographers to formulate and submit projects. The geographers should take full advantage of this opportunity.

Many of the modern users of aerial photographs - geologists, engineers, agriculturists, town-planners, archaeologists, etc. do not know that in the early days of the advent of air-photography it was the geographers who made substantial use of aerial photographs for preparing his base map, studying landscapes and deriving thematic maps. But as time passed on, the specialist scored a march over the generalist. To a limited extent today Landsat imagery and other data products of remote sensing are being used to map land use and natural resources by geographers trained in photo-interpretation. It is here that in India we must try to make substantial advances for our discipline with proper equipment and expertise.

There is one field in which, however, the geographers in India, particularly the teachers, are relatively very much ahead of their fellow earth scientists, that is in the number of published books. Whereas the enterprise and objectives are definitely laudable, the ultimate product ranges from good to very poor - particularly some of those from young post-doctoral teachers rushing their theses into print. It is necessary that this justifiable enthusiasm should be properly channelised in the interests of both the teacher and the subject. Similarly, one should realise that any work has always an added value if it contains data collected first hand from the field, though the quantitative analysis of secondary data may often look more modern and scholarly! Sometimes perusing through the papers in Indian geographical journals, one is apt to wonder if some of them are 'geographical' at all. I am aware that as geographers we have a very wide interest and link with many disciplines, but what is conspicuously missing in many of our researches now is that link. We have to establish this link and justify our expanding interests. Otherwise, it often tends to be a poor, substandard imitation of work carried out by specialists in those disciplines.

The Profession

I am not the first to voice the concern about the geographers having missed the bus, more than once, in finding permanent professional recognition for themselves in the higher policy-making bodies in the state or the centre. One redeeming feature however is that thanks to the certain individual efforts and also patronage from knowledgeable persons in government, certain institutions like the Census of India, National Atlas and Thematic Mapping Organisation have been in a position to do excellent work, projecting the professional capacities of geographers.

A certain degree of technical advance in cartography is discernible in the latest maps being produced by Survey of India. To this may be added the recent contributions of the geography division of the National Remote Sensing Agency. In certain institutions post-graduate students in geography specialise in closely related subject, for example, regional planning, and are in a position to contribute to the man-power requirements in certain integrated surveys. It is gratifying to note that some of the departments of geography in the country have brought out and are bringing out Atlases on different major themes, sometimes of states, with a wealth of information. This is a line of work worth pursuing by universities in the country. It is only through contributions of this kind that even the every existence of our profession will be known to the community.

The Association

A society or an association is created by a group of like minded persons to create a forum to enable them to work in unison in pursuit of their objectives. National Association of Geographers of India has also been created with many laudable objectives among which providing a national forum for promotion of geography is the foremost. We have been meeting regularly since 1980 and have been able to almost regularly bring out the journal of the Society, the Annals of National Association of Geographers, India. In these annual meetings many papers are read, some discussed and a few of them published. We do have commissions as standing groups representing broad areas of subdisciplines to organise activities. It is very easy to find lacunae in the conduct of many of these. For those I will only refer them to the Indian Geographical Union bulletin Vol. XXXVI, 1986, No.1-2 p., 35, wherein we note that international congresses also suffer from similar malady and hence we will do well to follow the remedies recommended therein to the extent possible.

One of the oft-quoted sayings in the recent past was that of the late American President, John F. Kennedy, who exhorted his fellow Americans not to think of what America can do for them but what they can do to America. It is now our duty, for each one of us, to realise our responsibility, as member of this association, however small the contribution may be, to upgrade the standard of all things connected with geography in this country, instead of hoping that perhaps someone from somewhere above will do all the needful. It is again only through societies such as these, that we can really voice the aspirations, achievements and requirements of the community of geographers to the proper authority.

Conclusion

Most of us are aware of the saying that justice should not only be done but also appear to be done. Similarly, geographers should not only be fully equipped to carry out different investigations connected with land and the man but also must actually carry out on their own initiative and show them as service to the community. We must ungrudgingly reconcile to the fact that our work can be more often only institutionally sponsored than commercially demanded. During the course of deliberations in different sections during this Congress, it is worthwhile to debate towards the end of each session what types of professional expertise can we really offer, and to whom and at what cost. It is not always necessary to have grandiose projects to impress the government or the society about the useful role that geographer can play.

Ladies and gentlemen, some of you may know that I am relatively a late entrant, about a decade and half ago, into the field of geography, though I have been an earth scientist since three and half decades. I crave your indulgence if my analysis appears to be less than just, but it is my conviction that we can really advance in our teaching, research and profession only if we correctly assess not only our limitations but also exert to improve our competence. Let us hope that successive years will see Indian geography making better impact on society at large through the sincere and honest efforts of its practitioners. Towards that end, I pray that let this Congress make its contribution.

Satyesh Chandra Chakraborty
1931 -

In a problem ridden world the ones who provide solutions are at a premium. Satyesh Chandra Chakraborty can provide solutions to problems. Among the type of issues Satyesh has tackled are water disputes of Bihar, Orissa and West Bengal, policy imperatives in Calcutta's Master Plan, designing expressways and priortising funds for different infrastructure. The spectrum of audience who have sought advice at his doorstep range from the Calcutta Metropolitian Authority, Calcutta Municipal Corporation, Reserve Bank of India, Tea Estates, Port Authorities, Fertiliser Complex, Mining Group, Pollution Control Board, and Solid Waste Managers. His address list of fifty-seven clients draws public and government concern from places far and wide. Though the state of West Bengal leads with a fifty per cent share, ten other states including Maharashtra, Karnataka, Kerala, Haryana, Rajasthan and Madhya Pradesh can be counted straightaway. Outside the shores of India Satyesh has attracted seekers from Middle East, Africa and the former Soviet Union. These buyers are not an easily satisfied lot. Many demand more than a pound of flesh. Take Georgia, a Russian Soviet Republic covered by a rugged Caucasus mountains. Its harsh climatic conditions would have daunted many, but not Satyesh. Nearing 70's an age when most are ossified, Satyesh learnt the state of the art technology like the geographical information systems to raise queries before reaching an appropriate management decisions may it be to lay a road or design a city health plan. A hefty pay cheque which customers use as bait is not the only temptation; the challenge to solve problems horns Satyesh ahead. In modern

parlance Satyesh could professionally be called a consultant. In traditional context the likes of him would be seen to possess a canvas of mind vast enough to comprehend problems and elicit solutions.

Satyesh possesses an under-graduation, post-graduation and a doctorate in the discipline of geography. Does he provide geographical solutions? The answer would be yes and no. Yes because he is a geographer and no because Satyesh is not only a geographer. He is a polymath. His interests cut across a variety of disciplines – sociology, economics, political science, social psychology, history, calculus and astrology.

Satyesh has a facile mind to learn, memorize and integrate a range of phenomena when drawing upon an interpretation. His special ken is at decoding processes behind patterns. Little wonder that the department of geography at the Presidency College could not hold him permanently or the University of Burdwan could not retain him for more than four years. An invitation to join the department of geography at the Delhi School of Economics was also put down by him. Satyesh chose to be a professor and chairperson at Indian Institute of Management, Calcutta where he served from 1974 to 1991. He did not take an extension of service, refused an offer to join the University of Calagary, on the contrary engaged full time in the private consultancy. That seventy per cen of his total advisory works fall in the leg of his private consultancy phase and he is on the rolls of many firms are proof to his credibility. Satyesh's ability to solve ticklish problems is backed by an almost hypnotic power to convince. His 91 research papers and two books cover a range of themes that defy classification. Satyesh, however, is at his best with the spoken word.

He has a passion to be heard. His thirty public lectures on issues like marine policy, strengths and weaknesses of cooperative workers, informal sector in India to Calcutta's urban space have seen more of an international podium. Three quarters of his lectures have been aired at universities and research centre like East-West Centre at Honolulu, Free University of Berlin, Dresden University Germany, University of Chicago, and the London School of Economics. A retinue at the Scandinavian countries have also been on his cards. Few who have heard Satyesh can escape the spell of his oratory skills. Borrowing a clipped British accent, through a dense haze of havana smoke, brick by brick Satyesh build his concepts and lays across his arguments. His words trap one and all. He is not a laden tree that stoops. His girth is strong and he bears his weight in apparent conceit. Yet he is not toffee nosed and bends backward to learn.

He not only secured a first class first in geography from Presidenc College but also bagged the title of Eshan Scholar for the highest rank in th faculty of arts. In his post-graduation he won gold medals all the way: for to rank in geography, for highest rank among the faculty of arts and for the highe rank in practicals among the science faculty. Though the University of Calcutta gave Satyesh honours, he reminiscences that his school days were the grand period of learning in his life.

Comilla, a town to the south of Dacca in Bangladesh, is the place where Satyesh was born on 3rd November, 1931. The transferable job of his father, who was an advocate in the judiciary of the British meant that Satyesh's childhood was punctuated by a dozen schools at different places. Far from feeling uprooted it built in Satyesh a resilience to cope with new situations. From the JBD ink tablets to the digitizing tables, for Satyesh technological, methodological or conceptual shifts have never been a barrier.

'Beyond the mountains there is a plateau, from where three mighty rivers originate, Lhasa is its capital –where is Tibet ?'- Satyesh recollects this as his first geographical question, but he affirms that the interest in natural sciences unbolted his keenness to study geography. Presidency College were years where the row of bookshops on the perimeter wall was frequented more eagerly than formal lectures. A heightened intellectual activity came to Satyesh at the London School of Economics. A joint supervision under Oligiviteee and Rawson for a doctorate was another strong impact.

Geography, Satyesh concludes has tremendous scope for being marketed outside academia, only geographers have to root their discipline in 'sense'. That he quips is not so common among the community of Indian Geographers. Since Satyesh has identified this problem – perhaps he should be the one to find a solution. It is time for him to plough back into the discipline that he has earned a lot from. After all, his talent to memorise and interrelate a range of disciplines, experiences and learning is what makes Satyesh a consultant par excellence.

Untitled

S.C.CHAKRABORTY

It is customary for the President Elect of the National Association of Geographers, India to address the Congress before assuming the charge of office of the President. For this Tenth Congress, this privilege has been given to me by you. I do not know how wise has been your decision to confer such an honour and assign such a responsibility upon me. But I do unqualifyingly acknowledge your presence here and your willingness to share my views today as a sign of kindness.

I shall not use this occasion nor my privilege as the President Elect to take a stock of what we as geographers have done in the past, what has been our achievement or where have we failed, although I believe that such retrospections are useful. I shall, instead, try to look at our future and speculate upon what our roles might be. If I seem to be drifting into a reflective mood, I shall only solicit your indulgence. This is unavoidable, as the impulses of time are inevitably carrying me towards the dusk of my active life as a geographer. Dusks like dawns are the moments of transition from one reality to the other, when one is tempted to reset the goals if the chance to enact the left behind is available once again. You should feel free to use my mood of this moment for any purpose that would give you comfort and confidence.

To help you catch my mood, I remind you of the seminal lecture that Professor C.D. Deshpande, the doyen of Indian Geographers, had delivered on January 6, 1988 at Pune. To honour the memory of Professor Nirmal Kumar Bose, he had conveyed his substantive desire in the very title of his lecture, which was to see geography in the service of common man. I had come very close to professor Nirmal Kumar Bose as a student and I believe that no better a homage could have been paid to him than this expressed desire of Professor C.D. Deshpande. I also wish to come to terms with the common man in India and to make our role as geographers appear meaningful to them.

10th Indian Geography Congress
Mysore, 1988 December

The common man in India has, however, posed a problem for me and, I suppose, for you also. He does not come to us with his problems. He does, of course, send his children to us if we happen to be working in a school, a college or a university. This he does possibly because of his judgment that the institutions that we belong to have the authority to confer diploma or degree. He also approaches us personally, if we happen to belong to a department in the government, for he knows that this department has been given the power to apply discretion to his advantage. I doubt whether the common man indulges in such interactions with us in response to our ability to behave like scientists. This doubt is given by the fact that we do not always utilise the full range of our freedom as scientists to design the contents of our tasks. Instead, we restrain our freedom often to enjoy the comforts of the task set for us by the institutions in which we have our respective placement. Our attachment to this comfort, this sense of well being, sustains a hiatus between us and the common man in India. The services that we offer, therefore, appear often peripheral to the needs of the common man.

I propose to go a little further than suggesting that the recluse that we have designed for ourselves shall continue to nourish us with comfort for a long time. I believe that prospects within the current pattern of our activities are rather meager. The basic reason behind this proposition is given by the fact that the common man is threatened in his effort to survive. If he fails, then all our possessions of scientific knowledge will also prove inadequate to let us survive. There are enough indications that the threat to survival of the common man has reached an alarming proportion. The facts are palpably staring at us.

We need only to look at the declining land-man ratio to realise our vulnerability as a society. In 1951, our total population was about 320 millions. It has increased to 658 millions in 1981. It would probably cross the billion mark by the turn of this century. Land and all non-renewable resources attached to it are finite in size. Per capita availability of these resources, actual and potential, is declining persistently. It decreased to half of 1951 by 1981. It is going to decline further. One does not have to be remotely Malthusian to sense the consequence of this very simple fact upon us and the common man. I do not wish to confine our attention to food alone. I refer to all aspects of our quality of life, which must decline as resources get depleted.

I should, however, raise a point of caution after having stated the problem. It is good not to engage in a task where one does not have competence. A problem of the kind that I have mentioned above has many facets. The way we have developed our expertise in science would not let us respond to all the facets of the problem with equal competence. It would be foolish to think otherwise. I should, therefore, request you to examine and select the specific facet where we can engage ourselves without sacrificing the rigour of our discipline. Unless we are careful about it, we shall only spoil our subject discipline without reducing the distress of the others. It would be unwise to go by popular beliefs.

Take for example, the general consensus about the need to reduce birth rate to tackle the problem of declining per capita resources. It is an agenda on its own merit. But can we as geographers act upon this agenda? I believe that we cannot act effectively, because the subject discipline of geography hardly equips us in this regard. As a man of the world, you may be knowing the technique of birth control. But as geographers, do you know how to get those techniques adopted by the larger society? You could certainly go out to persuade others about the merit of using contraceptives, which I suggest that we should all do. But this could be done by any one without getting trained in geography. The problem before us is to explore if there is any other facet of the problem at hand where the geographers can apply the rigour of their discipline to suggest some effective approaches. I believe that such facets do exist and that we have not given adequate attention to these in the past decades.

Let us recall our intellectual stances during the first two decades after independence. When reminded of the high rate of growth of population, we used to argue that economic development should be seen as the best contraceptive. This argument was based on the observed relationship between rising standards of living and falling birth rates as reflected in the instances of economically developed countries. But this was an act of arguing in the abstract because we did not examine the specific context of India to ascertain how the experience of the economically developed country was going to replicate. Please do not suspect that I am suggesting that we Indians are a peculiar society, an uncommon lot. On the contrary, as the different segments of the Indian society came to enjoy better standards of living their birth rates also declined. What we did not consider economic growth would spread across the diverse segments of our society. The segments which are yet to experience a better quality of life still maintain a high birth rate. One of the basic reasons behind this slow rate of growth of our economy is given by the smallness of the size and the poorness of the quality of resources that we had per capita to start with. The other reasons are given by the way we have failed to improve the quality of the given resources and to increase its quantum over these years. It is this facet of the problem that the geographers are competent to relate themselves to. I believe that we should be expected to suggest the ways and means of mitigating the harsh effects of declining availability of resource per capita in India.

Consider the Indian society, the major part of which is attached to land resource through agriculture. For them land is the capital stock to build upon. We responded to it by encouraging, sometimes actively and at other time tacitly, agricultural colonisation. Which is the other name of expanding the area under cultivation. Today our farms have stretched upto the valley crests, on the watersheds. Forests and natural pastures have depleted at an alarming rate without giving commensurate returns from their substitution by agricultural farms. We have created poor farms on land where the run-off of water was high and where irrigation could not be provided for. Bad land management was inevitable and erosion from running water increased.

According to the Society for Promotion of Wastelands Development, some 3 crore 54 lac hectares of wastelands in uncultivated areas of India suffer from water erosion. Within the non-irrigated cultivated area, according to the Society for Promotion of Wastelands Development, another 3 crore 82 lac hectares suffer from water erosion. If we add to it the other contributory factors like salinity and alkalinity or wind erosion, then the total wastelands of India would come to a staggering size of 9 crore 37 lac hectares, notwithstanding the declining quality of cultivated land under irrigation. The loss of soil from a vast area is only one aspect of the problem. It's consequence upon the drainage system, like channel choking and floods, is another aspect of the story. The two together bear an eloquent testimony of our proven ability to reduce the quality of land as capital stock.

Studies in the field of geography have shown that erosion accelerates when the cover of natural vegetation is removed. If depletion of soil through erosion was seen as a major phenomenon, then our approach should have been to get back the trees. We may recall that Dr. K.M. Munshi had initiated the "*Vanamahotsav*" (Programme to save trees) movement during the initial years of planning. But we had neglected the call. We did not organise popular movement for afforestation, neither did we examine what types of forests would the people require. Our emphasis went for other strategies, stimulated as we were by the dream of building an industrialised society overnight. Geographers had also joined the band wagon.

It would be wrong to claim that the aspirations for rapid industrialization was altogether wrong. If it becomes an objective to develop through increase of capital stock of the nation, then industries offer better opportunities to do so. Industries can produce many types of intermediate goods, which, if engaged as investment goods in the exploitation of other resources, can offer a lot of advantages in creating an efficient economy, in improving the quality of life. Whether we produced the right kind of investment goods for the other sectors of our economy is indeed debatable. We did produce fertilisers and pesticides. But the industry sector somehow went in for the production of consumption goods for the urban sector more than for the rural areas. This was seen as the preferred area at least by the private investors. The nation was divided in its appreciation about the importance of establishing inter-sectoral linkages for increasing the quantity or quality of available resources per capita.

As geographers we know that there is a limit beyond which the size of the basic capital stock in agriculture,that is, land, cannot be increased. The circumstances in India, however, gave us an opportunity to increase the quantum of agricultural land through the application of technology. Considering that rainfall is received in India generally in one season, use of land for raising crops was by and large restricted to that season only. The technology needed was irrigation. If perennial sources of water were created, then not only the uncertainties of rainfall could be mitigated but also the same land could be used more than once in year. The latter can be seen as a means of increasing the quantum of land for cultivation without extending the farms on the virgin land. The former attribute of irrigation could then be seen as contributing to improvement in the quality of the same capital stock.

Naturally, as a nation we laid our emphasis on developing irrigation facilities with the implicit idea that a large part of our geographical area could then be brought under forests. We may recall that the National Forest Policy of 1952 declared that about one-third of the total geographical area would be brought under for tests within the next 30 years. That target, we are yet to arrive at. We shall look into the reality of the forest cover in India after evaluating our performance in irrigation.

We, as a nation, had laid emphasis on the technology of gravity flow irrigation system. We did not opt for lift irrigation technology, because the country was short in energy supply. In the gravity-flow systems, mother earth supplies the energy for distribution of water free of cost. The shambles in which this sector of irrigation found itself is succinctly described by the Prime Minister of India while addressing the State Irrigation Ministers' Conference in July 1986. We quote...... "The situation today is that since 1951, 246 big surface irrigation projects have been initiated. Only 65 out of these have been completed. One hundred eighty one are still under construction ..... Perhaps we can safely say that almost no benefit has come to the people from these projects....The people have got nothing, back, no irrigation, no water, no increase in production, no help in their daily life. By pouring money out to a few contractors or a few contractors and labourers to build canals and may be Public Works Department to construct the dam, we are not doing our people a favour comes when the project is completed, when the benefits of the project start flowing".

The planners in India have naturally stressed the need for making further "massive investments" in the gravity-flow irrigation system to fully harness the untapped potentials to irrigate an additional area of 33.2 million hectares. At current prices, the required investment shall be of the order of 1,32,800 crores of rupees. To appreciate this staggering figure, we have to understand the meaning of "potential utilised" as distinct form "potential created".

When a conservation storage, the diversion structures and the distribution canals have been constructed, we know the size an orientation of the area that can be irrigated. This refers to "potential created". However, the smallest distributary canal might be delivering water at rates which are too high to permit good water management in the fields, that is, good husbandry. The Command Area Development programmes attend to this aspect of irrigation by way of inducing the farmers of command area to construct field channels, drainage outlets and to adopt the principles of regulation of flow of water and its management. The farmers need assistance to prepare themselves to do all these. The cost of "creating" potentials at current price is twenty seven thousand rupees per hectare. To "utilise" this potential, we need an additional investment of thirteen thousand rupees per hectare. It is worth speculating whether the kind of money required, that is, Rs. 40 thousand per hectare over 33.2 million hectares, for such a venture would at all be forthcoming. It is worth speculating whether there is any option to reduce the capital requirements. Naturally, it is worth speculating whether the manner in which such works are being handled do lead to conservation and improvement of our land resources. We, as geographers, have hardly looked into these issues.

Within the area where we believe that the potentials have been "created", the Command Area Development Programmes are yet to be fully implemented. To cover all such areas, we shall need additional investments. Till then, unregulated discharge from canals shall continue to take its toll through waterlogging and consequent salinisation of land. A look into the reality as obtaining in Haryana would reveal the essential features of the problem, which undoubtedly occur over more extensive tracts in the other provinces of India.

We are proud of Haryana as it supports a very prosperous agriculture. The farmers of Haryana have delivered the country by successfully engaging in green revolution. They are the enlightened farmers of India. Even here, more than ten per cent of the total area of the state has become wasteland. Five types of wastelands are found here. The processes contributing to their formation are still active. Sand dunes and sandy land cover about 4 per cent of the total area of the state and the processes responsible are operating within Haryana as well as over the adjacent states. Some 2.6 per cent of the total land have been severely affected by salinity and alkalinity and their formation is related to extension of irrigation in poorly drained area. With the rise of ground water table, the salts get deposited on the surface. This is also related to waterlogging, which has affected some 2 per cent of the total area of the state. Careless delivery of water in the name of irrigation coupled with seepage from canals are the major contributory factors. We should also mention that careless constructions of roads, canals, built-up areas of towns, etc. have disturbed and distorted the natural drainage systems leading to waterlogging. These are some of the aspects of the problems that we have created to deplete our capital stock of land through improper management of resources. These have initiated a few processes, which are likely to engulf more land unless effective measures are taken. Needless to mention, the processes contributing to the formation of wastelands in Haryana are also operating over many other states of India.

The above experience with Haryana reconfirms a general truth about technology innovation, which is that technology is basically a logical system and not exclusively a tool as a machine plant is. We may borrow the logical system, but not necessarily a given machine plant. Machines are designed to serve a purpose in a given circumstance. For example, a submersible pump-set is the product of a specific design intended to prove useful for lifting water from a falling water table within certain limits. If the water table remains stable, a simple centrifugal pump-set would prove useful by varying the designed capacities to suit the need. One can borrow a given machine plant after judging the suitability of the given design against the circumstances of the area of application, the purpose of use and the quantum of service required. This judgment is based on understanding the logic of the system that the design has endorsed. The innovators have to understand this logic. Quite often they are to be assisted. Otherwise, misuse shall follow to create more difficult problems for them. To get an idea on how such problems emerge, one has to look into the situation in Punjab.

Punjab is another prosperous state of India in agriculture. It recorded an yield of 20.7 quintals of wheat per hectare against an average yield of

12.54 quintals for India in 1972-73. This success was matched by failure in other areas. As a result of introduction of large-scale irrigation, salinity and water logging started reducing the area under cultivation to the order of some 57 thousand hectares per year in Punjab alone. The problem got practically solved through the introduction of rice in summer. But, it brought in a new kind of problem requiring a greater order of social engineering to deal with. The logic of rice cultivation should be examined to understand the nature of this new problem.

We know that puddling of soil is essential for rice cultivation. This increases the density of sub-soil in course of time to make it too high to be good for wheat. Such a problem is not faced in South or East India where rice follows rice. But in Punjab, wheat follows rice as the winter temperature is unsuitable for rice cultivation. For this state, the solution lies in growing rice under irrigation to be followed by wheat or gram without irrigation. This allows the leached soil nutrients under irrigation to come up through capillary rise in the soil without irrigation. This demands a discipline for crop husbandry which the farmers have to appreciate. It is difficult to develop such an appreciation unless the logic of irrigation technology gets interpreted in terms of the specificity of the reality obtaining in the region where innovation is intended.

Examples can be multiplied to illustrate how we have indulged in mimetic innovation without interpreting the logic behind the accepted technology. Management of resources is, therefore, out of joint with the prevailing environment. Its residual effect is continued depletion of both the quantity and quality of our basic capital stock, that is land. One may not, therefore, be surprised to observe that our investment for development have produced tardy returns. Even in Punjab and Haryana, the law of diminishing return from investment is showing its ugly head in agriculture. Since our discipline of geography is concerned with the changing relationship caused by human actions on environment, I believe that we have a major role to play as eyes and ears of the society in reviewing the impacts of technology innovation in our country.

The two examples given above may not be seen as if the problems are confined regionally. Those who live in other regions may not believe that they can escape the consequence of adoption of technology if done in an improper fashion. The success of green revolution in Haryana and Punjab has stimulated the dreams of the urban elites all over the country. They recommend the use of hybrid seeds of all varieties of crops to achieve success. These are indeed amazing products of science. But they never come alone. These are not immune to pests and need the application of pesticides.

Our industries are producing these. These chemicals certainly kill the pests, but also get into the body of the plants, where these are stored before entering our body as we consume the agricultural products. These are carcinogens.

Between 1974-80, from the different markets in the city of Bombay, samples of edible goods like vegetables, rice, fruits, milk, eggs, meat, fish, etc. were collected. Of the 995 samples analysed, some 573 or 58 per cent were found contaminated by organochlorine pesticides residues. Some 368 samples were found to contain residues of more than one type of pesticide. Some 203 samples contained residues in orders above the limit of human tolerance as laid down by the Food and Agricultural Organisation and the World Health Organisation in 1975. Since then research has further advanced and the limits have been revised downwards for many such chemicals. There is no reason to believe that the case of Bombay is exceptional. Like all other large cities, Bombay is also dependent on farms scattered over very wide regions. If these farms use pesticides, the rest of the society ingests it through the food chain.

I am not suggesting that we should refrain from using pesticides. I am only offering a cue, which is to admit the need for using pesticides that shall not leave non-degradable residues in our food chain. There are many such chemicals now available, which are not necessarily cheap. There are many varieties of plants which have germicidal and pesticidal properties and which can be grown easily in our country. Take for example, the case of *Neem* trees. These can grow on any type of soil. One can use *neem* leaves and oil cakes to treat the soil to remove the harmful pests. The oil is useful for making toilet soap, which are free from organometalics. The bark yields medicines to treat dermatitis. The wood is not attacked by termites. I can only add that *neem* is just one amongst many other plants which are useful sources of bio-degradable pesticides. These are members of our natural vegetation and can increase our national wealth, if properly raised. What is tragic is that we have neglected these and have preferred to borrow the final goods from abroad only to inflict irreparable harm to ourselves.

For the second time, we have come to note the importance of our natural vegetation. We have noted their importance in the context of arresting soil erosion. We have just now noted their importance in protecting crops and our life by way of giving us pesticides. There are many other ways in which the forests can be seen valuable to us. Our problem does not rest with lack of understanding. It lies somewhere else. Shrimati Indira Gandhi, while addressing the conference of the State Forest Ministers on Oct. 18, 1982 described our problem very clearly. We quote: "I have heard all the arguments of foresters that some kind of scientific management of forests is required and (that) the annual increment could safely be removed without affecting forests. This sounds attractive, but problems crop up when practices differ so much from concepts. In fact, decisions following the working plans have resulted only in annual felling of trees ...., exceeding the annual plantations or accretions".

Shrimati Gandhi's observation about the continued depletion of our forest wealth was confirmed by the National Remote Sensing Agency . From their interpretation of the satellite imagery, we came to know that in 1982 only 14.10 per cent of the total geographical area of India was under forests of different descriptions. This upset the Forest Survey of India , since their claim was that forests covered some 19.7 per cent of the total geographical area of India. The two organisations were asked to reconcile the mismatch in computation. The reconciliation was obtained by upward revision of the National Remote Sensing Agency data on "open forests' and mangroves and by including coffee plantations as forests. We know how "open" the open forests can be. We also know that by including tea plantations under forests one could further heighten self-deception. Nevertheless, the official figure for forest cover now is 19.52 per cent of India's geographical area.

In the above controversy another important dimension of the findings of the National Remote Sensing Agency somehow got lost. This organisation had used the Landsat imagery of 1972-75 period, applied the same technique of identification as used for the 1982 satellite imageries and discovered that the forest cover had gone down from 16.89 per cent in 1972-75 to 14.10 per cent in 1982. If this rate of decline is not contested officially, then we are to believe that by the turn of this century there shall be no forest cover in India, unless drastic steps are taken for large scale afforestation.

The problem with our programmes on afforestation is that we have not yet discovered the ways and means of meeting the contending claimants for forest resources. Even a cursory look at the users of forest resources would reveal how varied the claims are. We need timber for constructing houses, furniture, carriages and implements. We need firewood. Then there is the demand for fodder because we do not raise enough for our domestic livestock. The demand for paper-pulp producing vegetation is also there. We also collect leaves, berries, flowers, fruits, nuts, gum, roots and tuber from the forests. A good programme of afforestation should be able to meet all these demands. But the programmes that we have so far designed have been less than comprehensive.

In the earlier decades, the emphasis was on timber production and the natural flourishing of the undergrowths met the demand for fodder partially. The resource so created got depleted due to inroads, illegal so to say, of fuel collectors. The new programmes emphasised on meeting the demands for paper-pulp. The species of plants chosen for this purpose restrain the natural flourishing of undergrowths. So the inroads upon the earlier stands of trees have been intensified. As the timber producing forests are getting degraded as a consequence of such inroads, we are blaming the common man as delinquents. Then, we replant those tracts as quickly as possible with the species of trees that are suitable for paper pulp. Here the retarded undergrowths make inroads for fodder unattractive. The trees are full of sap, which makes poor fire wood. As a result, inroads for fire wood become unattractive. These grow quickly and thereby the internal rate of return becomes attractive. These are sold in bulk to big consumers. Therefore, the cost of reaching the market is minimal. The programme is attractive for investment. But the value premises on which this programme is based are atrocious, indeed. It denies the common man and his needs.

I believe, we have arrived at a state where one can easily discover how to use geography in the service of the common man in India. The common need of our society is to improve the quality of the land-based resources and to increase their quantity, if possible. These two objectives can be simultaneously met because there exists large varieties of useful resources within our environment which are yet untapped. Not all of these can be directly consumed by us. Some can assist others to produce the materials that we can consume. For example, the forest litter can improve the structure of soil and provide carbon as the basic body building material for the numerous soil bacteria which can convert the chemical fertilizer into plant nutrients to help us raise a better harvest. The trees can act as wind barriers to reduce the harsher effects of aeolian erosion and consequent loss of soil. Eucalyptus grown in swampy areas can improve soil drainage. Cotton grown in saline soil becomes a useful measure to improve the quality of land, because it can store large amount of salt in its body.

I am deliberately referring to vegetation as means to serve the common man. There are reasons behind it. In the first instance, the organised society has neglected the common man's need to have access to these resources. We have to mitigate such unkindness . Secondly, vegetation is a friend of the human beings. Plants hardly betray human beings. But to make effective use of these resources for the service of the common man, the geographers must define their task contents as also their boundaries very carefully. I propose to hint at the way this can be achieved without compromising the rigour of our discipline.

In the first instance, we have to monitor the geographic space with a view to identifying the areas where the available vegetative resources are proving inadequate to meet the needs of the local people. We have to suggest the ways and means to increase the stock that would appear meaningful to the local people. Otherwise, they won't participate in the propagation of forests or other vegetative resources. We have to act additionally to get the other facilities that our nation has created and which can be harnessed to assist the participatory programme. To give one example, we have to get the forest department maintain nurseries of desirable plants for distribution amongst the willing people. Government departments, set up for soil conservation works, can also be similarly mobilised.

From the content of the first task, it should be clear that success will depend on the choice of right type of species. The geographers need to recognise that they are inadequately trained about vegetation. But they should be humble enough to approach other specialists like the botanists and agronomist to learn about the behaviour of plants about how these grow, what are the critical elements of environment that stimulated their growth, what materials can we get from them, etc. This knowledge we can utilise to determine how much of land should be allocated to meet the total demand. I have seen that people care for such plants which give them not one product, but many. For example, the *neem* tree, as I have told you earlier, is one such. In Mexico and other Central American countries, the people take good care of a plant called mesquites . These give them fire-wood. These arrest soil erosion. These can grow on any type of soil. In addition, the mesquit beans give the people a lot of protein , which are eaten. Mesquites can be gassified to produce kitchen fuel and the residue gives good quality charcoal. Mesquites can grow well in India.

The contents of the tasks so far mentioned tell us that it is not enough to raise stands of trees. We have to apply technology to process the products to derive more useful materials and to find their application. Gassification of mesquit is one example. Application of oil cake from neem as fertilizer and for treating the soil is another example. To raise other varieties of plants between the rows of chosen varieties of trees is a third example. The point is to make domestication of vegetational kingdom a truly social art. It will take many years of patient explanation before our society shall learn the importance as well as the means of domesticating this wonderful kingdom of plants. .

Finally, the geographers should sternly handle the myths that are commonly shared about the utility or disutility of forests. For example, the myth that the forests lead to increase in rainfall has to be seen as an unverified claim. What the forest do is to increase the frequency of precipitation during the season of rains. Evapotranspiration keeps the humidity level of adjacent air relatively high to stimulate frequency of precipitation, but not necessarily in quantity. Trees retain soil moisture through their roots and by increasing humus through decomposition of forest litters. These also restrain run-off to some extent. We should rather say that these restrain soil erosion caused by run off. Above everything else, these give us carbon, which we need most.

There are other myths that we need to discover. For example, it is claimed that eucalyptus is the fastest growing plant. It is true in certain types of environment, but not everywhere. In dry land, *sisho* accumulates biomass faster than eucalyptus. Under sparing irrigation on alkaline or neutral soil, *subabul* grows faster than eucalyptus. But in swampy areas with acid soil, eucalyptus grows faster than either *subabul* or *sisho*.

Many other myths will be discovered if we try to look around with the eye of scientists. Our observations will be meaningful if we remember that our search is for using geography in the service of common man. I wish, I could engage myself in this task if only I had a chance to enact my life of the youthful days once again.

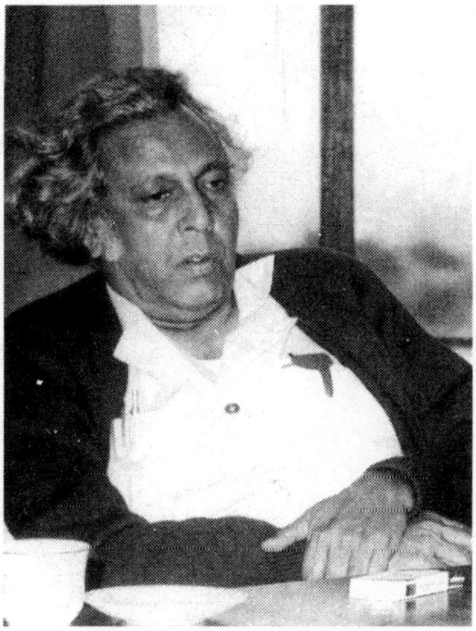

Moonis Raza died on 18th July, 1994

The grave is near the city of Boston, USA

His epitaph carries Aligarh on the map of India.

Regional Development as Eco- Development

M. RAZA

I am beholden to the community of Indian geographers for bestowing upon me the unique honour of having been elected as the President of the National Association of Geographers for the second time. I am greatly touched by this magnanimous gesture and accept the signal honour with humility. I take this opportunity of rededicating myself to the objectives of the National Association of Geographers, India – the symbol of the united endeavours of Indian geographers; and of promising to work, as its President, to coordinate the significant role of Geography in providing the much-needed spatial dimension to the development process and to sharpen its focus. I take this opportunity to pay homage and to acknowledge my debt to my teachers – Professor Qazi Saeeduddin Ahmad, Professor Mohammed Tahir Rizvi, Professor Syed Muzaffar Ali and Professor Nafees Ahmad – distinguished scholars who guided the destiny of geography on the sub-continent in the wake of our "tryst with destiny" and contributed to its advance towards self-reliant development.

Please permit me to share with you some reflections on two strains of geographical research which became important elements in the strategy for social transformation in two phases of our development and since independence which need to be now intertwined in a purposeful manner by the geographers of the sub-continent . The theme of regional development, rooted in two centuries of geographical research, was taken over in the post-war phase by regional scientist of diverse hues and the physical component was eroded almost completely away from it leaving the bare and barren stump of anthropogenetic processes alone. The second trend which has recently become important is rooted in the science of Ecology and tends to ignore anthropogenetic process altogether or looks at them only as instruments of eco-destruction. The science of Geography is the only discipline which has the unique capability to combine the two strains into a composite view of the planet earth and an integrated strategy

---

12th Indian Geography Congress
Delhi University, Delhi, 1989 October

for development. Regional development, in the final analysis, is eco-development.

A proper unfolding of this concept, both epistemologically as a model of the universe and methodologically as an analytical tool, has to contend with the continuing rigidities of the fragmented hierarchies in knowledge. While the social sciences have moved towards a certain degree of internal cohesion, the world of non-human nature is still alien to them, at best producing unnecessary noise in their sophisticated computer programmes. The agricultural economist would rather not dirty his hands with the soil, this nauseating residual in his regression model just cannot be wished away. The incapacity of the natural sciences to go beyond the rigid limits of their sub-systems is no less alarming. The internal integration of the natural sciences has at best produced the science of Ecology. In their just concern with the autotrophs and the heterotrophs, the ecologists tend to forget that Homo sapiens constitute a category qualitatively different from the other heterotrophs; that their explanatory system is incapable of accounting for the behavior of social man; that they are asking only limited questions and can, therefore, get only inadequate and partial answers. At best they recognize man as an element in the *man* and *nature* syndrome and have shown a unique incapacity to recognize the reality of *man* in *nature*. They fail to see that the rationality of man is as much natural as the irrationality of the monsoon wind, the *chernozem* or the xerophyte. The constraints, imposed by the complementary inadequacies of the social and the natural sciences, need to be broken. While the former cannot come to terms with the animality of man, the latter cannot come to terms with his humanity. Regional development, defined as eco-development, transcends this dichotomy. Please permit me to develop this argument a little further for your consideration.

Naturalisation of Man and Humanisation of Nature

A meaningful discussion on regional development calls for the generation of an adequate degree of clarity on the concept itself by clearing some of the ideological cobwebs, theoretical inanities and methodological inconsistencies which have accumulated around it during the last half of the century or so. The starting point of this odyssey of learning must be the categorical assertion that regional development is not a substitute for but the most effective form of and instrumentality for development. Its definitional attributes, therefore, flow from the universality of the noun which is the set and the specificity of the governing adjective, which distinguishes it from other sub-sets of the set. It is important to state this elementary position because some ideologues of the developed world have explicitly or implicitly taken the position that regional development is of particular *relevance* of developing societies to ensure the availability of the "basic minimum needs" with the help of "appropriate technologies" for the hewers of wood and drawers of water of the impoverished third world. Such a distorted view needs to be categorically rejected.

Regional development, as an integrated system of ideas, practices, methodologies and approaches, is definitionally global. It is based on the realization that the domain of the planet earth transcends the anthropocentric orbit of the world. This conceptual distinction is of the essence. While the world has been too much with us in the corridors of time, the mother earth *Gaia*, has been deeply wounded by the distortions of the injunction urging the Homo sapiens to "have dominion over the fish of the sea, and over every living thing that moveth upon the earth". While the concept of the world as the home of man has encouraged molestation and rape of the earth since the Neolithic times, the concept of the earth as the planet of life calls for harmony between human and non-human offsprings of *Gaia*. The new beginnings initiated in contemporary times have inexorably led us to a crucial element of the new *weltanschauung* – that of the earth citizen, the man in nature, who share citizenship in the republic of the earth with the rooted grass and the flying bird, the microscopic bacteria and the gigantic elephant, the thirsty sand dunes and the turbulent river, the mountain peak and the deep ocean. The restricted view of the world, with its frontiers as well as states needs to be replaced by the all encompassing view of *Gaia*- the mother earth of the solar family in the Milky Way of the expanding universe.

The most effective constraint in the received conceptualisation of this interactive relationship, which clutters clear thinking, pertains to the inability of current thought structures to break from the Cartesian dichotomies and assimilate as well as transcend the dualism between matter and energy, wave and particle, quantum and field, living and non-living, plant and animal or material and spiritual. The assertion of the monist view and a holistic approach should, however, not be mistaken, as Bokhim points out, "for a spectral oneness that yields cosmic dissolution in a structureless *nirvana*". To the contrary, wholeness comprises the variegated structures the articulations, and the mediations that impart to the whole a rich variety of forms and thereby add unique qualitative properties to what a strictly analytic mind often reduces to "innumerable" and "random" details.

The starting point of our advance towards earth citizenship must be the recognition of the unity of nature, a rejection of dichotomized models and the assertion of an essentially monist position. The fragmentation of the holistic into the realms of nature and culture or between the worlds of man and that of his non-human environment leads to a situation wherein each segment of knowledge ends up, in its own specifically sophisticated manner, with an aspectual, distorted, and limited vision of that which is definitionally total – dissected limbs of a cadaver being mistaken for the integrated, living, ever-changing system of interdependencies.

Regional development policies are rooted in the contemporary realization that the earth citizen, as a crucially important element of the eco-system, cannot conquer non-human nature but must learn to live in harmony with it within a system of interdependencies. Regional development should, therefore, be viewed as the articulation of qualitative changes in the geo-bio-techno-social complex of interdependent phenomena in such a manner that the quality of human life improves within the framework of the integrity of the eco-system. Regional development is, in this vital and fundamental sense, eco-development.

The concept of eco- development is based on the unity of the system of interdependencies through the mechanism of interactions between social man and non-human nature. The essentiality of man and nature is based on "man as a natural being and nature as a human reality". It is no doubt true that primeval nature is prior to man and continues to exist without him everywhere except on the micro-dot of a planet in the vastness of the universe. This non-humanized nature, which has not naturalized man, is of only marginal interest directly in the development process. Nature comes within the orbit of development primarily as a constituent element of social practice. Man interacts with nature through labour, transforms it and himself gets transformed in the process. This man, who makes himself in remaking nature, is the focus of eco- development.

The traditional division of the plant into the lithosphere, hydrosphere, atmosphere, and the biosphere would interest the geologist, the hydrologist, the meteorologist and the biologist, and they engage themselves in the study of each separately. However, when the alluvial fan in the Himalayan valley gets transformed into a system of terraces, when the mighty torrents are tamed to fertilize the thirsty earth, when a new crop rotation system is evolved to take advantage of short growing season, when a wrong grazing practice leads to deforestation, then the segments of the lithosphere, the hydrosphere, the atmosphere, and the biosphere get synthesized and transformed into the noosphere – the realm of cognized necessity. This is the realm of eco- development.

The noosphere – the sphere of man-nature interaction – may be viewed as a triangle of forces. Nature provides the base, lays down the limits of freedom and indicates the direction along which optimum appropriation through social labour is possible in the long run. Technology aids natural processes, brings them closer to human (and humane) purposes and thus extends the range of freedom. Institutions are either conducive to or restrictive on man-nature interaction – the former tending to replace the latter with every technological advance. It is this triangle of forces which is the primary concern of eco- development.

In such a eco- development context, the ecology- development contradiction is a false contradiction. The laws of nature not only impose constraints on but also point to the direction of optimal development. Ecology has to be saved from misdirected development, no doubt; but development has also to be saved from misdirected ecology. It is heartening to note that in the case of India as early as in the Fourth Five Year Plan, a fairly clear understanding about the relationship between ecology and development was discernible. It was stated therein; "The physical environment is a dynamic, complex and inter-connected system in which any action in one part affects others. There is also the interdependence of living things and their relationships with land, air and water. Planning for harmonious development recognizes this unity of nature and man. Such planning is possible only on the basis of comprehensive appraisal of issues- particularly economic and ecological.... It is necessary, therefore, to introduce the environmental aspects into our planning and development. Along with effective conservation and rational use of natural resources, protection and improvement of human environment is vital for national well-being. It is particularly important that long-term basic considerations should prevail over short-term commercial considerations; the social costs and benefits be used as the yardstick rather than private gains and losses."

Regional Development Revisited

Within the conceptual framework developed above , let us now critically examine the diverse trends emerging in Geography with respect to the theory and practice of regional development during the last decades. The seventies constituted a period of doubts and uncertainties with respect to the relevance as well as the efficiency of contemporary strategies for regional development. The latter had emerged during the days of hope in the development scenario during the fifties, the zone wherein the corridors of power impinge upon the cloisters of academia. Some of the seminal concepts as well as the sophisticated techniques associated with these strategies spread at the rapid rate and got established during the critical years of the sixties as a significant trend in the sphere of development planning. "Growth poles," "development corridors", or "core and peripheries" came to be quite often accepted as *mantras*, magical incantations, which would reconcile the contradictory pulls exerted in the development process by sectors and regions, growth and justice, concentration and dispersal, or area and people. This was particularly so in the context of the intractable problems of the developing world, wherein the open sesame of the growth pole strategy was hopefully expected to usher in an era of prosperity for the bulk of mankind. Notwithstanding the dogmatic optimism of the new converts to the regional approach, it was soon realized that it is erroneous to assume a free flow, diffusion, or propagation of growth impulses from the centre to the periphery, and of the fruits of development from the top downwards through the distorted allocation mechanism of the anemic market of the third world even under the impact of the initiating, sponsoring, or modifying role of the State. Without structural change, such a market could only operationalize polarization. This, in turn, led to the restriction of the home market and the consequent thwarting of growth itself. It follows from the above that, at least in the context of the developing countries, there is no essential contradiction between the demands of equity and of growth. Equity without growth is a stagnant cesspool, wherein only misery can be equitably distributed. Growth without equity leads to the accentuation of structural disequilibrium, and the chronic persistence of the low purchasing power of the mass of the toiling people constrains growth itself. The social concerns for the two can only be handled together, each sustaining and being sustained by the other.

The essential infirmities of the theories of regional development came to the fore through the experience of the seventies. The earlier milieau of hope gave way to a new questioning in an ethos of doubt and uncertainty. These questions were pregnant with immense possibilities. They led to new innovative approaches, whereby regional development theory was coming to terms with realities, particularly of the third world. New *mantras* like "rural development", "dispersed industrialization", "agropolitan planning", "labour additive appropriate technology", or "regional closure, autonomy, and the bottoms-up approach" soon replaced the growth pole symphony of the sixties. These constituted a step forward in the diagnosis of the chronic malaise of under development, but had serious limitations and inadequacies of their own which were essentially rooted in their dichotomous approach to development planning. Friedmann, the most ingenious among the new mandarins, attempted to remove the dichotomy by a feat of semantic surgery-implanting the head "agro on the body "politan", in the godly tradition of *Shiva* , who fixed the head of an elephant on the torso of a man to create the hybrid *Ganesh* of *Pauranic* mythology. Since casuistry, even of the most sophisticated type a la Friedmann, is incapable of removing structural bottlenecks. Let us look a little closer at the nature of these dichotomies.

Rural dominance in the third world can be properly understood only if it is traced to the transformation of these polities as raw material appendages of the metropolitan countries and as market for their manufactures. It is rooted in and is a symptom of the chronic disease of underdevelopment. In such a historical context particularly, the paradigms based on village versus city, rural versus urban, or agricultural versus industry, would and are perhaps intended to perpetuate the economic backwardness of the third world. These paradigms emerged from the demagogy of peripheral politicians wishing to hide the irrelevance of their platforms under populist slogans which were soon picked up by some ideologues of the developed world and were rendered more profound and sophisticated in the elysian heights of their ivory towers and presented to the innocents of the third world as the panacea for their ills. Experience in country after country has, however, shown that development is indivisible and cannot be fragmented along the rural-urban interface. It is undoubtedly true that the third world continues to be predominantly rural; and, consequently, any developmental strategy will necessarily have a strong rural base (to be distinguished from rural bias). It does not, however, follow that rural dominance in its population should be considered sacrosanct (as some kind of a sacred cow!) and, therefore, immutable; or that there can and should be a rural development policy parallel or in opposition to a regional development policy.

As in the case of the above, the inadequacy of the strategy of dispersed rural industrialization, as an important component of rural development, may also be demonstrated on the basis of both technological and spatial considerations. Agglomerated and dispersed patterns of industrialization are both, by themselves, partial and fragmented. Agglomeration, without dispersal, leads to the emergence of dysfunctional enclaves; dispersal, without agglomeration, leads to technological stagnation and debility. It is only the integration of the two along the rural-urban continuum that can lead to healthy regional development.

Likewise, increased emphasis on regional closure, autonomy, and the bottoms-up approach as elements of the new paradigm was positive in so far as it focuses on a crucial aspect of regional development which had not received the attention that it deserved in the past. It may, however, be stated categorically that this new approach was itself partial as well as one-sided. It was based on the erroneous understanding that autonomy gets strengthened at the cost of integration, or that the bottoms up approach renders top-down flows unnecessary. Experience has shown that autonomy and integration are dialectically united as simultaneous process in biological and social development. A higher level of autonomy is contingent upon a higher degree of integration; a higher degree of integration, in turn, can only be based on a developed and hierarchical system of autonomies.

Even such a general and cursory look at some of the essential dichotomies of the new paradigm is adequate to show that, while the questions raised during the seventies were relevant in the context of regional development theory as well as practice, the answers given to them could only partly provide the basis for an effective operational strategy, particularly in the developing countries. The essential inadequacy of these approaches lay in the fact that they look at regional development not as the most effective operationalization of the developmental process, but as an alternative to it-located, so to speak, "beyond development".

We entered the eventful eighties with a heritage of three decades of visions as well as confusions, the quintessence of agonies of many failures and ecstasies of many successes. It would be desirable to have a critical look at the conceptual frames, methodological tools, and planning techniques developed during the last thirty years, to discard the junk accumulated on the way and to sharpen the intellectual tools in such a manner as may help theoreticians and practitioners of regional development to face the nineties with a deeper perception as well as clearer understanding of, and a higher competence in handling problems of regional development, particularly in the third world.

While the new paradigm has yet to come up as a set of clear cut intellectual constructs and well defined methodologies, its emerging outlines may be identified as follows:

First : Recognizing the fact that the development proceeds within a triangle of forces – its apexes being located in nature, technology and institutions, the regional development strategy is essentially aimed at guiding its trajectory along the desired path so as to optimize development by transforming it into eco-development—saving ecology from development as well as development from ecology in this process.

Second : Development strategy, viewed as above, can be effectively operationalized only through the combination of the territorial division of labour with the sectoral division of labour in the national economy so that the "where" or location becomes as intrinsic an element of the planning model as the "what" or the sector of productive activity.

Third : The territorial division of labour within the national economy can be worked out in an equitable manner only on the basis of a critical assessment of the natural resource base of the regional economy within the framework of the national economy that is conceived of the nesting of fields within larger fields and wherein the comparative advantages of regional development in terms of its long-range consequences lead to optimal eco- development on the national scale.

Fourth : An analysis of the natural resource base of a region provides fairly clear cut indications about the production cycle, which would optimize the development of productive forces through a continuing system of outputs of a stage becoming intermediate products for the next till every unit of value-added has been squeezed out within the region itself.

Fifth : Once the elements of the production cycle have been identified in terms of their input-output linkages within the "introvert" regional economy, the problems of location and sitting of such productive force may be effectively handled by taking into consideration, on the one hand, the factors of the economy of scale , agglomeration and urbanization and, on the other, the factors of ecological concerns and the quality of life – the given dysfunctional and inequitous organization of space being thus transformed into a relatively more functional and equitable one.

Sixth : Since economies are increasingly becoming available on relatively smaller scales as a result of the micro-chip and bio-technology revolutions, space need no longer be organized in terms of large settlements becoming larger and eating up smaller settlements in this process or transforming them into their satellites; instead, the possibility has emerged of a number of settlements of various sizes existing together in meaningful relationship with each other within a humane and equitable system of settlements.

Seventh : Services of different kinds and of different orders in the same kind tend to coalesce – a high school, a primary health centre, a bank branch, a cinema hall, a fertilizer as well as high-yielding variety seed outlet, a developed market, a tractor repair station tending to coalesce in a *Qasba*, or a small town which serves as a nodal centre for the villages clustered around it.

Eighth : The location of productive forces, the emergence of service facilities of different orders on the scene in coalescence with each other and the provision of residential accommodation for the households engaged in the above transform structures of mortar and brick into the human habitat made up of a system of settlements of various orders linked together through input-output production relationships as well as nesting of lower order service functions into higher order ones.

Ninth : A territorial complex emerging on the scene in response to the processes described above is , on the one hand, bound together both internally within itself and externally with other complexes in national and international space through a transport network facilitating commodity and passenger flows as well as a communication network facilitating information flows.

Tenth: Regional development strategy gets operationalized by moving forward step by step from the territorial division of labour to the territorial complex of productive forces as well as service functions bound together and to other complexes of the national system by transport and communication network.

Regional Development and Rural-Urban Interactions

While the system of interactions among settlements of diverse orders constitute the basic mechanism for integrating space at the regional, national and global scale, special attention needs to be focussed on interactions between the two sub-sets of the settlement system – urban and rural. This is particularly relevant in the polities of the third world. Urban rural interactions constitute the basic links which unite diverse elements of the space economy into a functioning, dynamic and hierarchical system. The continuous process of the re-organization of space through the kaleidoscopic changes in the system of settlements is essentially a response to the changing character and level of man-nature interactions through which development proceeds. Looked at in this frame of reference, the changing spatial patterns of settlements reflect the dynamics of social transformation. The current fragmentation of the rural-urban continuum in India, as in most developing countries, is the direct consequence of the historical hiatus between the twin processes of industrialization and urbanization, between vertical shift within and horizontal mobility of the work force. Rural-urban interactions reflect inter-sectoral interactions and are essentially derived from the latter. It is only in this context that the rural- urban interaction acquire socio-economic meaning. While the form of the interaction is inter-settlement, its content is essentially inter-sectoral.

The vertical dimension of the system of inter-sectoral linkages, that are expressed as input-output matrices, finds its spatial manifestation as freight exchange between different category of settlements in the space economy. If the rural-urban interactions are symbiotic and not exploitative, the products of the primary sector would be shipped from the rural to the urban sector in the form of food and raw materials in exchange for wage goods and technological inputs into agriculture, which would be shipped from the urban to the rural sector.

Rural-urban interactions may be examined in the context of the structure of the economy through the analysis of migration flows. The Rural-Urban stream may be looked upon as the crucial link between the structure of the economy and the hierarchy of settlements. It is through this instrumentality that vertical shift in the work force is projected as horizontal mobility in space.

It is, however, crucially important in this context, to distinguish between urban accretion, on the one hand, and urbanization, on the other. The essential characteristics of accretion lie in the following:

(a) The Rural-Urban stream is not absorbed, by and large, into a corresponding expansion of the secondary sector in the urban area.

(b) The area of urban influence and its facilities is highly restricted and there is a sharp fall of their gradients.

(c) Huge conurbations tend to float in an ocean of rural backwardness.

Rural-urban interactions, as we have noted earlier, are also a function of the differing thresholds of the various levels of the hierarchy in the service sector. Services, depending on similar thresholds, tend to coalesce at the same level of the settlement hierarchy. The hierarchical system of the coalescence of services would be healthy and function in the interest of the development process if the catchment area and the area of influence of the coalesced services tend to coincide with each other. While the concept of the catchment area relates to upward movement, that of the area of influence relates to downward diffusion. Their coincidence reflects healthy and symbiotic relationship of the two processes in space. With the nesting of lower order catchment areas/areas of influence into higher order ones, there emerges a hierarchical system of reciprocal relationships which optimize the utilization of services equitably in space.

Rural-urban interactions may finally be studied within the framework of the modernization paradigm, wherein a progressive development of a system of cities is expected to lead society forward from distorted to balanced spatial systems, from partial to total spatial integration and from modernized enclaves to total modernization of national spaces. Viewed thus, the cities are centres of innovation and nodes for the diffusion of impulses of societal transformation. While stating this position, some scholars tend to ignore the fact that this is not a one way process. Like the Greek giant who got his strength from his mother Earth, the cities are rooted in the folk ethos and derive their basic sustenance and vitality from this relationship. Their capacity to be effective centres of diffusion is essentially determined by the strength of these roots. The tragedy of a large segment of the Asian continent lies in the fact that the cities have grown therein as alien "anti-bodies" in the organism and as centres of rootless and imported value systems. Rural-urban interactions in this sphere, therefore, tend to acquire the character of confrontation between sophisticated anemia and rustic vitality. To the extent that such a confrontation is replaced by a symbiotic relationship, to that extent alone the third world city would regain its capacity to influence the village and the entire national system of settlements would throb with sophisticated vitality.

India – Diversities and Disparities

In the context of a scientific understanding of regional development as outlined above, it is possible to enquire into the nature of regional stresses and strains that are threatening to strike at the very roots of Indian nationhood. India, with its sub-continental size and the chronological depth of its tradition, presents a spatially differentiated picture of development experience which enables scholars to abstract generalizations of significance in terms of inter-regional diversities as well as disparities with a view to utilize them in their analysis of problems and their formulation of policies relating to regional development.

The infirmity of the Indian nation state and the current tensions and strains in the Indian polity are essentially a function of the unfinished tasks of nation building and reflect the inadequacy of the strategies evolved since independence to correct inequities and distortions embedded in the Indian space economy during the period of colonial rule. Since these stresses have in recent years acquired alarming proportions and have been weakening the foundations of Indian unity and integrity, a united national response is called for to meet their challenges. Such a response, if it has to escape the quicksands of both chauvinism and separatism, must be based on a scientific analysis of the role of integration and differentiation in the development process.

Development is a process wherein integration and differentiation are dialectically united, being contingent upon each other. The unicellular amoeba is neither integrated nor differentiated; the complex human organism is both. Integration should be distinguished from homogenization. Unity within a system presupposes and lies in plurality, not in the negation of it. While homogenization is the function of the breaking up of identities and their fusion into synthesized products, integration is articulated through a multi-level and hierarchical system of interdependencies. Homogenization is, in fact, the antithesis of interaction. Just as one has not to be less of an Indian to be more of a man, one has not to be less of a *Tamil* to be more of an Indian. Integration is not fusion, differentiation is not fission. Differentiation should be distinguished from segmentation or secession. Plurality within a system presupposes and lies in unity, not in its negation. While differentiation is the unfolding of the process of specialization and definitionally strengthens the bonds of interdependency, the process of segmentation is based on the breaking up of these linkages. It follows from the above that the development process is based neither on integration without differentiation nor on differentiation without integration. It unfolds itself through the simultaneous integration of the differentiated and the differentiation of the integrated.

In the process of social – as distinguished from biological – development , differentiation may lead to the flowering of diversities and/ or the accentuation of disparities. The former should not be confused with the latter just because they are often accompanied by one another. Differences in initial resource endowment, largely of a natural character, lead to territorial specialization as well as division of labour through the utilization of resource advantage- comparative as well as absolute. These constitute the basis and substance of inter-regional diversity. Inter-regional disparity, on the other hand, is the function of the operation of socio-economic factors which do not permit a region to exploit the development potential of its initial resource endowments, its latent comparative and absolute resource advantages and is, therefore, comprised of factors which are essentially institutional, historical, socio-political and/or economic technological. Viewed thus, diversity is neither the basis nor the cause of disparity. Essentially, inter-regional disparity is a consequence of institutional constraints incapacitating a region from converting its initial resource endowments into economic resources, that is capital resources producing further resources. The relationship between diversity and disparity is, thus, mediated by the logic of the process of capital accumulation. It follows from the above that diversity and disparity are products of different socio-ecological processes, play contrasting roles in development and call for different operational strategies and policy approaches.

Diversities have evolved over millennia and constitute the basic material of which the Indian nation is made. Unity and diversity of India are not opposites which can grow at each other's cost. They are symbiotically linked, support and sustain each other. Any attempt to over-emphasize either of these would disturb the delicate balance. Diversities are not irritants to be gradually eliminated from the polity. Unity is not yoke to be thrown away in the interest of the liberation of subjugated "nations", "nationalities" or "homelands". Those who view India as a monolith and those who view it as a mechanical mixture of diverse elements put together by the British–both are in error and do not understand the characteristic feature of the Indian polity, that has made India what it is. They appear to be contradictory on the surface but they both strike at the unity and integrity of the nation. Indian is a unity in diversity; and we can ignore the characteristic feature only at great peril to ourselves.

The challenge posed by the accentuation of regional disparities is, however, highly disquieting and should be met by a forward looking policy of balanced regional development. The operationalization of the territorial division of labour along with and as a complement to the sectoral division would lead to regional specialization in productive endeavors through the unfolding of resource based production cycles and the maturation of economic regions. This would simultaneously and definitionally lead to the consolidation of the home market and the strengthening of inter-regional dependencies in the country. Differentiation and integration would thus proceed together within the developmental process supporting and strengthening each other.

In the light of the above, what should be our approach toward diversity and disparity in India? The flowering of cultural diversities within the framework of an Indian ambience is a positive feature reflecting its unity in diversity. Endeavours to "Indianize" Indians in the name of unity are as deplorable as efforts to carve out "homelands" or erode the Union. Regional disparities may, however, be considered to be the consequence of persisting attributes of underdevelopment and its minimization constitutes one of the key tasks of socio-economic transformation. It may, therefore, be asserted with some confidence that national policies should be directed towards the flowering of diversities and minimization of disparities within the national framework of integrated differentiation accompanying the development process.

Viewed in this context, the centralization-decentralization contradiction is a false contradiction. This is particularly true in the sphere of resource development. Let us take the example of water management. As long as *kutcha* wells are being used, management can be highly dispersed or "decentralized" – the household being the unit of decision making. But the system of Ganga-Kaveri connecting canals can be managed only by a strong Union Government. If the water of the north western rivers, which is mostly the snow melt of the Himalayas, were to be considered the property of the Punjab and the oil drilled at Bombay High of Maharashtra, regional as well as national development would be in serious jeopardy. Decentralization is not a *mantra*, and centralization is not a dirty word. Both are two sides of the same coin of development. There is some avoidable confusion in this regard due to the fact that the term "decentralization" is defined negatively - as being away from the centre, and not positively in terms of people's participation in the making of decisions that affect their lives, and enjoying the powers to implement them. If it is so defined, one arrives at the model comprising systems of inter-dependencies nesting into larger systems as their sub-systems, of fields within fields. The gravitation field of the moon is contained within the field of the earth, which in its turn, is contained within the field of the sun. These are not mutually exclusive and equivalent areas of influence but a multi-level and hierarchical system comprising sub-systems. The relative influence wielded by each in a given situation depends on the specificity of the specific conjunction. The sun is far more "powerful" than the moon, but the latter exerts greater influence than the former on the tidal phenomenon over the globe.

In the context of the approach as outlined above, it would be erroneous to reduce the complexities of the process of integrated differentiation in a developing society to the question of state-centre relations. Such a reduction would have some justification – at least on juridical grounds – if India would have been a federation. It is not. India is a union, not a federation of states. This distinction is of the essence. Sovereignty lies with the people of India, who have given themselves a constitution. The powers of the state or the *Zila Parishad* or the village *Panchayat* are all derived from the sovereignty of "we the people of India". In the case of a federation, sovereignty lies with the people of federating units and the powers of the centre are derived from the multiple sovereignties. The present debate on the relative powers of the centre and the state is, therefore, being carried on within a dysfunctional frame of reference. The complexities of the problems of integrated differentiation can be properly appreciated within the framework of multilevel system of autonomies and accountabilities – from the individual, the household, the village/town/city/metropole, the block, the district, the sub-state, the state, the zone to the nation and in fact to the globe and the eco-system. Each has its autonomy and is accountable in terms of its autonomy for only robots are not accountable and only slaves have no autonomy. It is thus that the unfolding of the process of integrated differentiation would be facilitated; unity would be strengthened in symbiosis with diversity; specialization would flourish in tandem with accountability. Let us hope that the people of India, who have successfully passed through many vicissitudes in history, will have the wisdom and courage to meet the challenges of the last decade of our century and move forward with confidence to the twenty-first.

On the occasion of the Eleventh Indian Geography Congress, dear colleagues, let us rededicate ourselves to this noble objective so that we may serve the cause of our discipline and enable it to play its rightful role in national development.

Vidhiparti Lova Surya Prakasa Rao 1917 - 1992

In a private room of the Medwin Hospital at Hyderabad was raised a unique appeal 'geographers in India must research if the downhill path of the discipline is to be arrested'. The words carry weight, for they emanated from a heartfelt anguish of one of India's grand-masters of geography – Prakasa Rao. On 22nd December 1992 a mourning filled the room as the frail gasping body ceased to breathe.

The talent for conceptual and methodological clarity, an analytical ability backed by a plethora of creative ideas is what distinguishes a master from the rest. Prakasa Rao had mastered the craft of the discipline of geography.

He was among the first Indian geographers to use factor analysis in 1954, almost a decade before Berry popularized this methodology in the United States of America. He questioned the critical role of small and medium towns in regional development two decades prior to such a realisation by the United Nations Development Agencies. Prakasa Rao evolved a composite index for groups of regionally differentiated characteristics and chose themes like the central places, role of growth poles and growth foci in propelling regional development for an in-depth inquiry as early as the 1960s. All this stand attestation in the court of originality. This is not all, the locational analysis of inter-urban patterns, the changing characteristics of the rural- urban continuum, and the reorganization of administrative units, all are ideas which can be traced to the prolific mind of Prakasa Rao. He did not simply broadcast ideas but had the intellectual grist to test and validate his hypothesis. Simplistic descriptive conjectures were disliked by him and he fuelled his analysis on rigorous quantitative techniques before formulating a conclusion. It is on the shoulders of applied statistics that Prakasa Rao identified ways of measuring centrality, investigating disparity and studying spatial structures. An early browse of the 'handbooks' of the Census of India convinced him of the limitations of secondary data and it is on the girders of primary data that Prakasa Rao rested his analysis. His relish for fieldwork is exemplified by the village level data for the study of Muzzafarnagar, the socio-economic questionnaire for the survey of Bangalore and the 1075 household interview schedules generated at Vijayawada. Drawing experience from the National Sample Survey, Prakasa Rao aimed at designing a spatial sampling frame to accomplish a regional-trend analysis. Selecting areas of study, which range from the micro to meso scale allowed Prakasa Rao to draw meaningful conclusions at the macro level. Furthering an original idea, applying a novel technique for analysis, identifying new methods of data collection was not the end of his research. A hallmark of a master is one who likes to present and arrange his results in a meaningful and near perfect manner. The map was Prakasa Rao's favorite tool for display and his adept skill at cartographic techniques gave him exceptional power to access designs and styles. The Atlas of the Urban Landscape of Vijayawada, as an example, exhibits a stylish combination of lines, shades and symbols whose insets and superimposed graphs lend an aesthetic quality to its twenty-four different plates. All masters sharpen their tools before they chisel their ideas. Prakasa Rao was no exception.

Born on 23rd February1917 in the town of Vishakapatnam on the west coast of India, Prakasa Rao was the eldest child in the family. His father served at a local post office and was honest to announce that his savings could only take his children upto the F.A. level; this is an education upto senior secondary school. So deep was Prakasa Rao's passion for education that he opted for a child marriage, pawned his wife's jewelry and paid his way to higher classes. It is often claimed that a true master will sell his shirt to learn! Completing his education at the C.B.M. Government School, Prakasa Rao enrolled for a Bachelor of Commerce at the A.V.N.College at Vishakapatnam. A course on economic geography in the curriculum seems to have turned Prakasa Rao away from commerce and towards geography. Completing his post–graduation in 1942, he plunged headlong to take on a doctorate from the University of Calcutta in 1950.

It was his apprenticeship at work rather than formal education which became a playground for testing ideas and techniques Prakasa Rao's fervor for innovative research made him pen articles on town planning, location of industries, scope and limitations of land use surveys as early as in the 1950s.

The assignment as editor of one of India's oldest publications, the Indian Geographical Journal, Madras gave Prakasa Rao additional advantage of access to the literary world. But deep at heart Prakasa Rao longed to expand his creative impulse specially in the area of urban and regional planning. His intention found manifestation. Prakasa Rao was selected to join the regional planning survey of the state of Mysore , under the auspices of the Planning Commission. Working initimately with Learmonth and Mahalonobis, Prakasa Rao's keen intellect outshone his peers and when the Regional Planning Unit was set up at the Indian Statistical Unit in 1956 he was appointed as its first director.

In the search to master a study, many masters become footloose. Prakasa Rao's spurts of dislocation from Calcutta to Madras back to Calcutta then to Hyderabad to Delhi and at last to Bangalore highlights - a soul in search of a perfect environment for research and study. Prakasa Rao could not retain himself in any institute for more than seven years. His stay at the Indian Statistical Insititute lasted for five years, he was professor at department of geography, Osmania University for an interlude of five years, and at the department of geography, Delhi School of Economics for only seven years. It was at the Institute for Social and Economics Change at Bangalore that Prakasa Rao spent another seven years. The Indian Institute of Management, Bangalore, was his refuge for the last four years of his professional life. A brief teaching assignment at the University of Syracuse and the ones in France and Germany were also trials of possible anchorage.

In the seven year periodicity of movement, Prakasa Rao's interactions with statisticians, economists, sociologists and those from the field of management fertilized his thinking and sharpened the tools of his inquiry. Though brief, each transit station reaped abundant benefits from the research led under Prakasa Rao's sharp eye. A Survey of Towns in Mysore at the Indian Institute of Statistics, the Study of Vijayawada and the Regional Structure of Muzaffarnagar District at the Delhi School of Economics, the Study of Bangalore at the Institute of Social and Economic Change in the city remain till date monumental pieces of work. Master's give back more than they take.

A pious and humble soul, Prakasa Rao did not want followers but original researchers. Prakasa Rao, a scholar who played the harmonium, and enjoyed the melody of Yedudi Menon's Violin, is no more. A fitting tribute to this grandmaster of Indian Geography is to heed the words of wisdom he voiced on his death bed.

In Search of Unexplored Themes

V.L.S. PRAKASA RAO

I deem it an honour to be elected as the President of the National Association of Geographers, India for the Rajkot session, December 1990. I would like to take this opportunity to share with you my thoughts on some of the unexplored themes in Indian geography. Indian geography has not lagged behind in exploring new dimensions: behavioural and welfare dimensions, environmental perception and location allocation models to mention a few examples. In this search for frontiers, geography should not lose its bearing and thrive on its branches like the famous Banyan tree of Calcutta Botanical Gardens. Geography as a discipline and profession should not become ethnocentric taking the 'GE' out of geography, to use Wooldridge's expression. Neither the man nor the environment, should be overemphasised and specialised, one to the exclusion or the neglect of the other. The training and even research programmes in geography at different levels and the neglect of physical geography partly reflect this ethnocentricity.

Natural Regionalisation

Natural regional framework constitutes the conceptual and analytical framework to understand man-environmental relationships. natural region-natural landscape- physiographic region- physical complex - 'geocomplex' - geographic zonality', land system, ecosystem: there is much more than semantics in these terms. This also brings out that there is no uniform nomenclature. Even the terms area, region and space are used interchangeably though there are differences in addition to common properties (Annexure 1). It is known that the elements of the natural region are diverse and inter-related :landform - climate-(hydrographic cycle and water balance) - vegetation- soil type- the units of data generation are different. Each element has a scale or hierarchic order ranging from the

13th Indian Geography Congress
Rajkot, 1990 December

site to macro-region: topographic 1:5,000 and 1:50,000 to chorographic 1:250,000 and 1:1000,000. It is recognised that hierarchies are based on significant elements and not on totality, and are not inherent in a landscape. How to match and integrate the differences in the unit areas and the scale / hierarchy between different elements taking into account their genesis and the associated processes. This is an unresolved question in spite of long tradition in the search for regions and natural regionalisation. There is scope for experimentation here in the different type areas.

In natural regionalisation there are other questions to be resolved. These relate to the very concept of natural region incorporating ecological dimension and resolving the semantic differences and methodological issues:

- macro and micro variables to be selected.
- unit of observation and data generation and mapping both secondary and primary(field) data taking into account the sharply contrasting physical environments and processes.
- the sample design to select type areas.
- the scale of the base map and the level of map generalization.

Earlier exercise in natural regionalisation of India needs to be reviewed, reinterpreted within an ecological framework and reformulated where necessary, taking into account the changes in the classification systems of different natural elements and mapping programmes of organisations like Geological Survey of India, Soil and Land-use Survey, Botanical Survey of India, Pondicherry Vegetation Mapping and taking advantage of the cartographic revolution including remote sensing, computerisation, compugraphics and geographical information system. It must be mentioned here that the potential of the toposheet supplemented by the geological map in natural regionalisation has not been fully tapped.

Regions acquire a fresh significance when they are subjected to scientific analysis on a continuing basis: time-space series. In this context, natural regionalisation is an unexplored theme particularly considering its utility in the planning of eco-systems and conservation of natural resources.

Weather Cycle Versus Crop Cycle

Indian agriculture is the gift of the monsoon, though monsoon determinism is partial in the areas of irrigation farming. This is in spite of remarkable advances in the fields of meteorology and agronomy. It is known that weather system is non-linear and atmosphere is global and explosive.

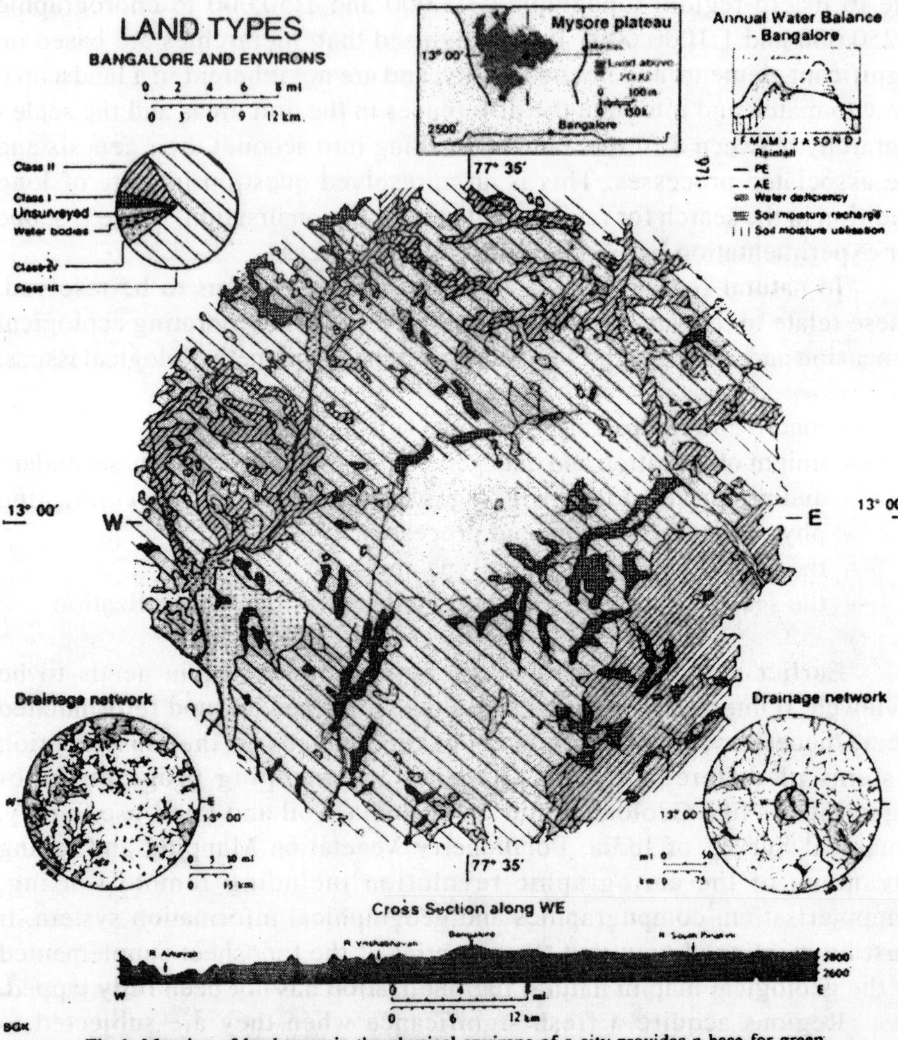

Fig 1. Mapping of land types in the physical environs of a city provides a base for green belting, natural landscape conservation and land-use zoning. The map is based on field reconnaissance, land capability maps of the soil and land-use survey (IAAI. Hebbal, Bangalore), SOI toposheets, and a generalised land capability map (1:250000).Rocky outcrops and water bodies are excluded for regrouping of land types. Relief profile along the 13 degrees latitude passing through Bangalore brings out clearly the profile of the Mysore plateau and the ridge (900 metres above msl) on which Bangalore is situated. The hilly and undulating terrain of the west with its rejuvenated stream netweork and close texturing, and consequently the sharp landscape profile stand in sharp contrast with the rolling plateau with its gentle slopes on the east (ref. insets : stream network and landscape profile). While the western landslope profile developed over the younger intrusives of closepet granites, the eastern profile developed over granites and granitic gneisses. Differences in lithology and rock types contribute to east-west differentiation in landscape profile, rejuvenated on the west, and mature on the east. Both in the western and the eastern sections, the best agricultural lands (Class I type) are in isolated patches located in the flat valley bottoms of streams and streamlets and tank ayacuts. (Prakasa Rao 1983. Urbanisation in India: Spatial Dimensions. p215. Concept, New Delhi).

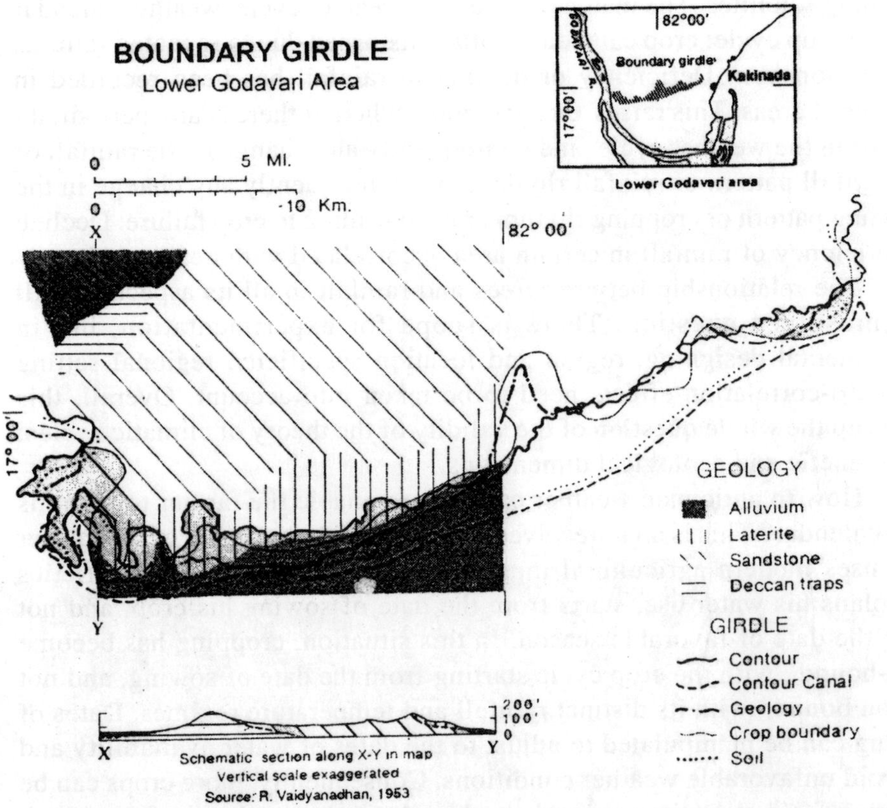

Fig. 2. Boundary girdle indicates an approximate accordance and a transitional area, a contact zone, between two mutually exclusive areal sub-classes. The sensitivity of the boundary girdle depends upon the sensitivity of the boundaries, both genetic (eg. contour canal, water parting) and derived (isopleth), the map scale and the level of map generalisation. Azonal elements (eg. geology) acquire significance in natural regionalisation when related to region forming elements (landforms and climate). The boundary girdle (ref. Fig 2) delineates the transition zone between the sandstone-laterite upland and the deltaic plain. The girdle zone is also an aquifer/artisian zone, which lends to its structural distinctiveness.

Data base : Field traverses, SOI toposheets and landsat imagery.

Source : V. Raghavaswamy and N.C. Gautam 1986. Application of remotely sensed data for the delineation of typological regions. NRSA Hyderabad.

R. Vaidynadhan 1953. Geology of Rajhamundry - Dwarapudi - Rajanagaram area : East Godavari. Personal communication March 1990.

It is this that defies the scientist in spite of his possessing the latest devices including satellites. The match between the weather cycle: weather calendar and the crop cycle: crop calendar is often disturbed due to repeated failures of the monsoon. Deficiency or decline in rainfall has been recorded in number of areas. This raises the question – whether there is any periodicity or shift in the weather cycle, and consequently any change in the rainfall or the rainfall pattern or rainfall rhythm, and consequently any change in the cropping pattern or cropping rhythm or even leading to crop failure. Decline or deficiency of rainfall in certain area is correlated with deforestation.

The relationship between trees and rainfall in all its aspects is still an unresolved question. There is scope for experimentation, but in experimental designing, region and location specificity, regional setting and auto-correlation effects need to be taken into account. Overall, this opens up the whole question of the validity of the theory of climatic cycles: both genetic and ecological dimensions.

How to anticipate weather calendar to enable the farmer to plan his crop calendar? This is an unresolved question. The crop cycle of the farmer who uses modern agricultural inputs and short duration hybrid varieties and plans his water use, starts from the date of sowing his crop, and not from the date of favorable season. In this situation, cropping has become time-bound , with the crop cycle starting from the date of sowing, and not season bound, with its distinct rainfall and temperature regimes. Dates of sowing can be manipulated to adjust to the dates of water availability and to avoid unfavorable weather conditions. Consequently, more crops can be grown in one climatic year and the length of the total cropping season increases without any intervening gap. This, in its turn, increases the demand for labour through-out the year and that with greater intensity of work. The traditional slack season is eliminated or its duration greatly reduced. This phase of modernisation in agriculture changes the cropping pattern, replacing the old pattern. In the Godavari delta, for example, earlier inter-season cropping of pulses (December to February) after the harvest of first paddy crop (December), and before the sowing of second paddy crop (February), a pattern evolved over generations, and confirmed by researchers as the best adjustment between the cropping pattern and the local climate-soil environment has now been replaced by a new pattern of cropping with the introduction of new varieties of paddy which can withstand the inhibiting winter weather conditions. Earlier, in spite of water availability in the Godavari canals during the period December to February, the second crop paddy could not be sown immediately after the harvest of first crop paddy due to inhibiting weather conditions. Only pulses could withstand these conditions, and hence they were sown (Refer Erogography Figures 3 & 4). The pattern of crop-weather calendar is different in the Tanjore delta with its dominant north-east monsoon regime and distinct rainfall type and variability, a climatic anomaly. In the rainfed area and unirrigated areas, the crop calendar is still closely tied to the seasonal weather calendar.

Farmers both in the irrigated and dry-farming areas resort to permutations and combinations in the cropping patterns partly based on the modern agronomic research and partly based on their own initiative and innovative urge, of course, taking into account the market forces. Inter-cropping, mixed-cropping and shifting- cropping patterns and better water management and moisture conservation are different practices and strategies adopted not only to increase yields but also to distribute risk and insure against the erratic monsoon. While some of the cropping patterns help in attaining production targets and also increase incomes to the farmers , some patterns are highly soil exhaustive and erosive. These require location specific and region specific corrective and monitoring, even if water is available and weather calendar is favourable.

Human Settlements

Human settlements can be viewed from different angies by different professional and research disciplines, and also by the people who live and work in them. Consequently, there are a multitude of dimensions and problems: physical, economic, social and cultural. The problems of human settlement have impact at various levels: global, national, regional and local and also within a settlement, that is, intra- settlement.

Human settlements are not passive and just physical variables in development and vary in population size, growth, functional structure and spatial patterns of distribution and linkages.

The size, structure and linkages are in a state of constant change, associated with economic, social and technological changes. Planning intervention through investment and development policies and location of infrastructure, and of course, political pressures and historical legacy, all have their due share in the development or differential development of settlements. Further, the uneven distribution of natural resource, endowment and human resources, and the uneven development surface lead to sharp variations in the distribution of settlements.

What is even more important, and which is a late realization, is the fact that human settlements constitute living environments: the habitats for the people with different socio-economic status, needs, attitudes, aspirations,

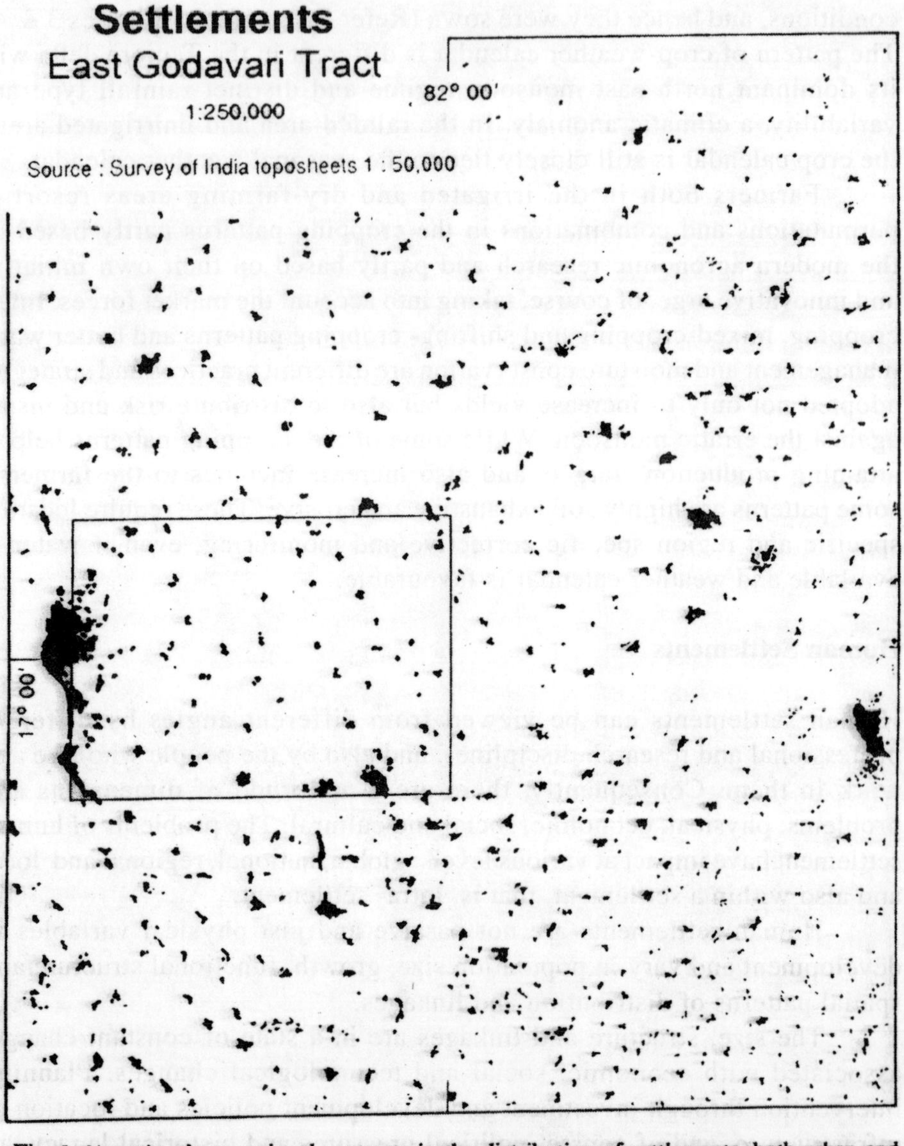

Fig. 5. Note the sharp regional contrasts in the distribution of settlements, both urban and rural : the size, density, and spacing of rural settlements and the associated patterns : dispersed (sandstone upland) and densely clustered (deltaic plain). Linear clustering is along the contact zone. The railway line, the highway and the canal (not shown in the map) follow approximately the boundary between the sandstone and the alluvium. In the landsat imagery, the sandstones and laterites have a light tone in contrast with the alluvial areas which appear relatively dark due to moisture and cultivation. (Vaidyanadhan. Personal communication March 1990). Fig 2 and Fig 5 bring out the significance of lithology, topography and rural settlement patterns in natural regionalisation. The missing correlates are drainage patterns, water bodies and landuse.

customs and, above all, their wisdom and perception. In this context, the quality of life of people living in the settlements, irrespective of their size and functional scale and regional / locational setting becomes a major issue in settlement planning. What needs to be recognized here is that objective and quantitative aspects like housing, health care, sanitation and income are not necessarily inter-related with the qualitative and invisible aspects like expectations, aspirations and satisfaction of those who live in the houses/ settlements. The house cannot be seen in isolation from the settlement, but must be considered as a part of a total spatial and social system, the whole landscape, more so in areas of dispersed settlement and where man is a part of the environment as in the case of tribals in the hill – forest environments.

Development strategies should be so designed as to give due weightage to both quantitative and qualitative aspects. One is tempted here to suggest working out solutions in consort with the local people using appropriate technologies. But people's participations have more of an ideological appeal. The challenging question is how to institutionalize peoples' participation in developing healthy living environments. At this micro and specific level, environment can be equated with housing, pollution, specially water, waste disposal and sanitation. Here, pollution is more because of social and living conditions than technological / industrial. Under housing, there is a package of services : water supply, waste disposal , energy use and location i.e., access to jobs, and infrastructure : education, health and shopping. While the income level of the occupant governs the size of the house, it is his occupation and the environmental setting that determines the functional and physical structure of the house. It is here that high technology and imported solutions and professed bias have been found to be total misfits to local situations. Innovative strategies even with simple and local technologies have to be thought of which require locations and site specificity. Housing has ceased to be just a product of brick and mortar and physical design. With increasing emphasis on socio-economic and environmental aspects, housing is interpreted as a process, changing with the socio-economic status and the aspiration of the people. Housing is both individual and institution based. Housing, both urban and rural, should be lifted from its brick and mortar and even welfare bounds to the status of a key industry, both labour intensive and capital / technology intensive, and take full advantage of its multiplier effects.

Dichotomising settlements into urban and rural, and a two tier classification : metropolitan cities, and intermediate and small towns only conceal the complexities in the settlement spectrum and the inter-related

RHYTHM OF EFFORT
(East Godavari District, Andhra Pradesh)

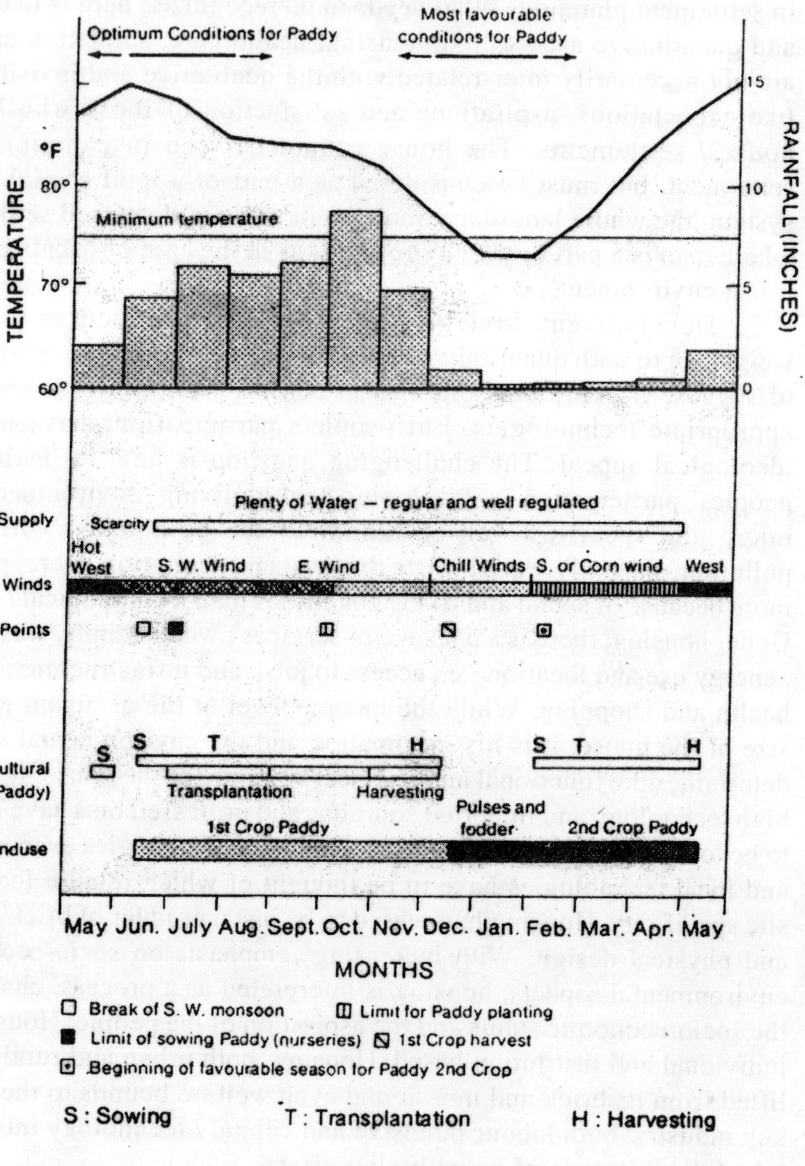

socio-economic system. This defies the unified concept of .the settlement system. This dichotomy is a function of the fundamental urban-industrial-metropolitan and agricultural dichotomy in development and sharp inter-regional and intra-regional socio-economic disparities. The hill-forest, the arid and the irrigated farming areas and the metropolitan areas and the associated settlement patterns are typical examples. Some of these areas have low population densities, small and medium size towns and villages, dispersed and inaccessible to transport and rooted in local resource use and development. Here, the linkage patterns should be appropriately planned, in the absence of which transport network tends to be imbalanced with more of extra-regional links and links with higher order settlement than with intra-regional and local links. Here, the overall problems is one of inability to sustain even minimal level of services due to the absence of the necessary population thresholds and also due to the very dispersed pattern of settlement.

Planning of human settlements requires scanning all along the spectrum. Absence of this or inadequate attention is a major gap in our settlement planning. There is even a gap in our knowledge on the structure and functioning of settlements in the interfaces (urban) that are emerging in the spectrum. We seem to know more about urban settlements and commuting patterns than rural settlements and commuting patterns. Much less we know about the temporal changes in linkage patterns. Likewise we seem to know less about settlements at the lower end of the spectrum: small villages, hamlets and uninhabited villages. Revolution in transport and technology, changing mobility and travel preference patterns of producers and consumers, consequent upon their changing levels of incomes, and no less, sectorally and administratively oriented planning and intervention, are disturbing and even destroying the earlier hierarchic system and linkage patterns. In the developed regions, intervening settlements are being bypassed within critical distance ranges by the higher and middle income groups, as their trips happen to be mostly multipurpose. The commuting and migration patterns in their turn change the system, more conspicuously in the areas where large-scale development and rehabilitation projects are located. This is to be expected, but disturbance is not taking place at all levels and in all regions; disturbance is minimal in the hill-forest regions, particularly in the core regions, and in some of the coastal zone environments. In some of the agriculture regions, higher order urban centres (primate cities) do not exist. Here, the regional scale and setting are important.

The settlement hierarchic system and the regional hicrarchic system

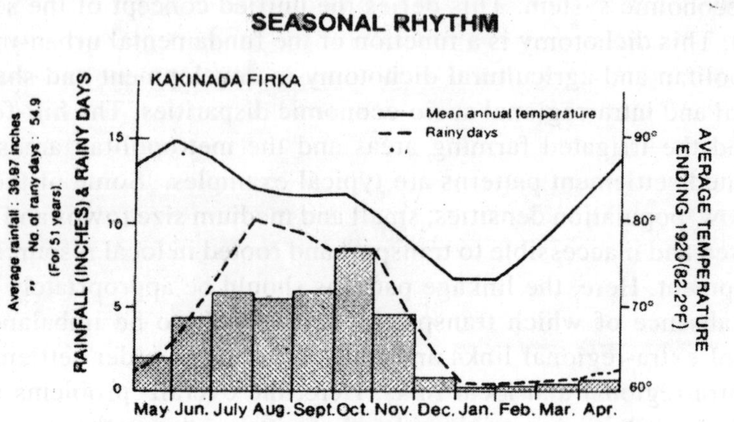
SEASONAL RHYTHM
KAKINADA FIRKA
Mean annual temperature
Rainy days
Average rainfall : 39.97 inches
No. of rainy days : 54.9
(For 51 years)
RAINFALL (INCHES) & RAINY DAYS
AVERAGE TEMPERATURE ENDING 1920(82.2°F)
15
10
5
0
90°
80°
70°
60°
May Jun. July Aug. Sept. Oct. Nov. Dec. Jan. Feb. Mar. Apr.

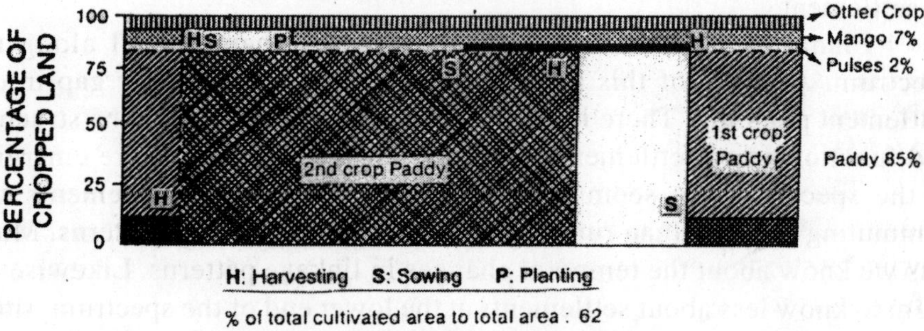
PERCENTAGE OF CROPPED LAND
100
75
50
25
0
Other Crops
Mango 7%
Pulses 2%
Paddy 85%
2nd crop Paddy
1st crop Paddy
H
S
P
H: Harvesting S: Sowing P: Planting
% of total cultivated area to total area : 62
% of net cultivated area to total area : 54
% of 2nd crop to total cultivated area : 13

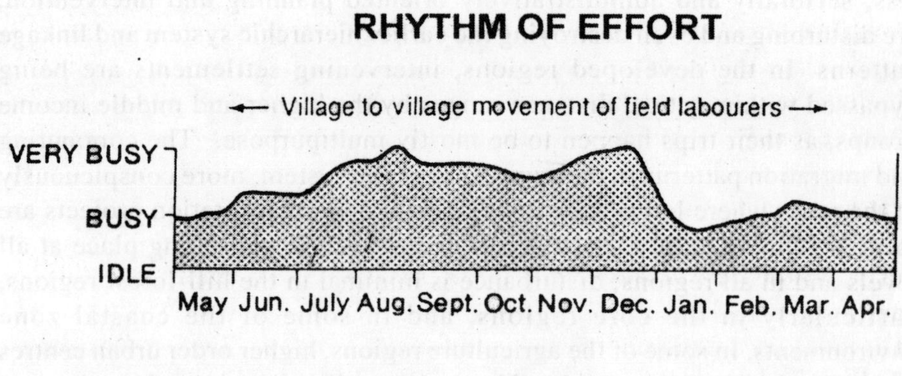
RHYTHM OF EFFORT
← Village to village movement of field labourers →
VERY BUSY
BUSY
IDLE
May Jun. July Aug. Sept. Oct. Nov. Dec. Jan. Feb. Mar. Apr.

are interdependent. At the higher levels in the hierarchic system, inter-city linkages are more important, and in the lower orders, urban-rural links are more important. The impact of the primacy (dominance and hence the shadow effect) of the metropolis can be reduced through regional development policies through counter magnets. Small towns and larger villages have the potential to function as service centres to the adjoining rural areas. These attributes of the settlement system need to be explicitly recognized in allocating investments for development of infrastructure, along with plans to provide economic base, which is necessary to sustain the infrastructure for better living. Economic base need not always be equated with industry, though even in the development of industry, the "tenet of appropriateness" (that is different types of industries in different sizes of settlement in different regional settings) should be the policy. Commercialisation of agriculture, if properly harnessed , could contribute to regional development. Though commercialisation is production and market based, it does not mean just that commercial agriculture economy implies an appropriate cropping pattern, processing units, market infrastructure, market and transport network, market-towns and villages including resource towns.

The inter-relationship between the settlement's functional structure and the structure of its hinterland is best reflected in the structure of resource towns : cotton towns, sugar towns, tobacco towns and silk towns to mention a few. A resource town is basically a product of its resource. The seasonal rhythm in hinterland dovetails with seasonal rhythm of its town. The town's functions are more oriented to its hinterland than to its neighbouring city. Linkage patterns, market channel structure, behavioural patterns of producers, consumers, intermediaries and agro-industrialists, all reflect the complex structure of settlements and hinterlands. Thus, there is an appropriate union of similars, an agricultural landscape in the making, distinct from the homogenous crop or crop combination region. But such a mono-economic landscape almost collapses when the supporting crop fails or when there is a shift to another crop as it happened in coastal Andhra when cotton displaced virginia tobacco leading to problems of adjustment and the consequent stresses and strains. But multi-sectoral and spatial jurisdictions and multi-level decisions lead to fragmentation of the landscape with the result, the plan and the people's expectation are distorted. It is this discardance between sectoral and territorial levels that poses a challenge to the policy maker, the planner and the administrator.

What is the type of institutional framework which will integrate the multi-dimensions association with the development of human settlement ?

How to integrate industrial land (both urban and rural) and housing policies, and policy instruments like industrial licensing and land-use-zoning ? How to integrate urban and rural administration? These are some of the questions which need operationally meaningful answers.

Viability of an Administrative Unit

The Planning Commission suggested even during the First Five Year Plan period , that it might be useful for state governments to review the size of the districts from the point of view of efficient administration and implementation of development programmes. Administrators of eminence made a strong plea for the radical rearrangement of administrative units on the ground that if the policy of provincial self-government was to succeed, it must be based on regional resource use and the identity of the people of the region. It is this identity which expresses itself in regionalism, which could be a destructive force degenerating into localism and sectionalism, or could be a constructive force with genuine neighborhood feeling, local patriotism and pride.

It is recognized that the size of an administrative unit, both in terms of its area and population, should be neither too large nor too small (Annexure 2). This is an elusive dictum. It is also recognised that the concepts of 'ideal size' and 'optimum size' of an administrative unit are myths. The concept of viable size of an administrative unit is, perhaps, more meaningful operationally. The concepts of homogeneity, centrality and viability, both administrative and economic, relating to a territorial unit are not mutually exclusive and static concepts. Homogeneity in regional resource structure, population density and distribution pattern, and level of development leads to the formulation of a unified development policy and operational procedures for administration. Though the smaller the area, the greater its homogeneity, the relationship is not precise, and much depends on the character of the terrain, distribution pattern of resources and accessibility to transport and communications.

Both the administrative centre and the administrator should be accessible to the people of the area. The area also should be accessible to the administrator. A central location of the administrative centre : district or taluk headquarters has the maximum accessibility potential and force of attraction, and is closest to all places linked to it. In terms of time and cost distances, peripheral location with convergence of routes is more accessible than the geometric centre without accessibility to transport network. A convergence of the geometric centre and the functional centre is possible where the shape of the administrative unit is compact. Even then, more often, due to historical legacy, there is more of divergence between the two centres. Thus, the shape of the administrative unit becomes an additional attribute to the geographical size of the unit area in measuring accessibility. Administrative viability is related to the size of the unit area, its population size and the number of sub-divisions. Here, population size is not just numbers only. The socio-economic levels of population and their political and regional consciousness, which could lead to cooperation or non-cooperation with the administrative machinery, tend to become more crucial factors than the size of the area and population. Even if the population size and area size remain the same, differences in the number of sub-divisions (talukas in a district and villages in a taluka) and the character of the area : irrigated, endemic drought, mining and industrial add to the administrator's workload, making the area non-viable for efficient administration. Thus, the area and population size of the unit area, the number of sub-divisions and the character of the area become the determinants of viability.

It must be mentioned here that whatever the territorial system one employs, it will soon in some respects become out of date because of changing regional structure, change in population size, socio-economic structure, mobility and people's aspirations and changing technology of resource use. This needs periodical revision of administrative boundaries, both at the district and taluka levels. In this context, as Professor Deshpande rightly observes in his supplementary note (Annals - National Association of Geographers, India, Volume 4, Number 1, June 1989, page 78 – 79), it would be necessary to recognise that the districts were formed under British rule largely for purposes of collecting land revenue and maintenance of law and order and administrative convenience. From time to time most of the districts were enlarged consequent upon territorial acquisition and administrative convenience. In the context of socio-economic planning and development most of these districts have become anachronistic territorial units. Consequently, in majority of cases, there is discardance between the administrative boundary and the boundary of the economic region. Discardance is maximum when the two types of boundaries cut at right angles, as it often happens when a district is characterised by sharply contrasting physical and economic regions : irrigated farming areas of delta-semi-arid upland areas of horticulture and grazing-sub-humid and humid hill-forest areas.

Discardance leads to conflict between the need for stability of the administrative boundary and the need for flexibility of the boundary which is needed to adapt to the very dynamic character of development and plan /

policy intervention. Even districts become non-viable units for purposes of planning resources like water and power. Even states become non-viable in such cases. Water and power grids, transport network and ecological boundaries cut across administrative boundaries. There are different regional scales or hierarchic levels. The question is how to match the cut-off points between different levels.

The significance of administrative boundaries also rests on the location pattern of central places and growth centres. The behavioural patterns, attitudes and regional consciousness of the people residing adjacent to the boundaries are of equal importance. In the rapidly developing regions and transitional regions, the edge effect of the boundary is neutralised. How to bring about the needed reconciliation or plan for a dual territorial system, one for administration and the other for planning and development? This is an unresolved question in regionalisation for planning. This problem becomes more acute now with the move for decentralisation, which is really democratic decentralisation with the district having the status of a third tier, next to the state. With the emphasis or over-emphasis on the development of local resources and potentials, local community needs priorities and local institutions with decision making powers to develop the district in accordance with the district priorities and needs, all local, promotes "localism", local autonomy for the district all tending to make the district more closed than open. This type of "localism" should not lead to a modified version of the type of Jharkhand or Chattisgarh or Telangana regionalism with its roots in historical-political factors and inter-district socio-economic disparities.

Viability of a district for efficient administration and development planning and the myth and the fact of administrative boundaries : this is an unexplored theme for research within a multi-disciplinary framework.

Annexure–1

Area – Region – Space

Expanded from Norton S. Ginsberg (1971), Area, Regions and Human Organisation, Regional Planning: 21st International Geographical Congress, Delhi, Ed. VLS Prakasa Rao *et al.*

Properties

1. Scale/Size
2. Location : absolute- relative
3. Structural Elements :

Land Form – Climate – Vegetation – Soil type – Land use and occupational structure – Settlement Structure – Population Structure Economic and social Infrastructure

4. Boundaries / Boundary Zones

---

5. Homogeneity
6. Centrality / Nodality
7. Regional and Settlement Hierarchy
8. Regionality / Regionalism

---

9. Open : Boundless – Directionless - Neutral – Noncontiguous

---

As a summation, a region has a scale, and an ecological connotation and has (1) a norm best expressed in its core (between two or more regions (cores), lies a transitional area / region). (2) a pattern of inter-regional linkages, and (3) a rank in the hierarchic system of regions. Regions are dynamic. Consequently some of the regional elements are transformed, some persist. New elements are added, and new region are formed and hierarchies change.

Annexure–2

1. A district with an area of more than 4000 sq. miles and a population of one million, and a taluka with more than 750 sq. miles and 150, 000 population were considered to be unfavourable for efficient administration and implementation of development programmes. Based on discussions with the Secretaries for Revenue, Planning and Development Departments, Government of Mysore (Planning Regions in the Mysore State: The need for Readjustment of District Boundaries. V.L.S. Parkasa Rao and L.S. Bhat. Indian Statistical Institute, Calcutta. 1960).
2. Area and population remaining more or less the same, a district with 17 talukas (Dharwar in Karnataka) has 70 per cent more paper work than a district with 10 talukas (Belgaum in Karnataka). A limit of 12 talukas is kept for a district. Non-recurring expenditure for a new district is estimated at about Rs. 2 crores of which 1 crore will be for medical and public health amenities. Recurring expenditure will be about Rs. 75 lakhs, half of which will be for public health. Non-recurring expenditure is estimated at 5 lakhs for each taluka, and Rs. 2.5 lakhs recurring. (Report of the One-Man Commission for the reorganisation of Districts and Talukas, Karnataka State, Government of Karnataka, 1975).

Laxmi Niwas Ram
1937 -

Ram lived in an exile of circumstances, which thwarted his intellectual talents to blossom to the fullest. Educated at the elite St. Xavier in Patna, the capital city of Bihar ,securing an unbroken record of first divisions from secondary, intermediate, graduation to post–graduation levels are test grounds of Ram's academic competence. Awarded the Patna University Merit Scholarship in 1956-1958 and the Patna University Gold Medal in 1958 cements this fact further. Selected lecturer at the young age of 23 at the department of geography, Patna University in 1960, securing a professorship at 1984 and the appointment as an acting vice -chancellor of the Patna University in 2001 demonstrate that Ram also rose many heights in an academic career. A flair for language, keen analytical ability and carefully cultivated articulation are his other assets. A personal collection of detective, science fiction and classics of the English literature remind us that Ram's avid interest in books extend beyond the geographical texts. He enjoyed carving sentences and weeding verbosity – can be seen from the 24 years he spent as editor, initially of the Indian Geographical Studies from 1973-1990, followed by the Geographical Perspective from 1990-1997, both journals of the department of geography Patna University. His consultancies in the capacity of member of the Master Plan for Patna and the Sone Command Area Development Authority are proof to his interests in the applied role of the discipline. Ram's efficiency to inspire and weld the spirit of team work is amply displayed in a number of chores that he took on. Ram recollects the spirit of cooperation he could instill in his fellow colleagues as

the chairperson of department and the president of National Association of Geographers, India to collectively bring forth a publication on a systematic geography of Bihar. Serving simultaneous posts as dean of Faculty of Social Sciences and principal Patna College he is one who dared to take on challenges. Ram reinitiated the mid – term examinations, which ,under protest of students had been abandoned for over 10 years in the Patna College. Though a doctorate in urban geography Ram holds the firm opinion that 'geography cannot be segmented into specializations - embracing an understanding of all its themes is the strength of the discipline.' Teaching a wide menu of courses in geography from cartography to physical , political to urban geography affirms that he put this belief into practice. The 30 doctorates he supervised also spill into themes as far ranging as settlement, political, industrial, agricultural, resource and urban geography. He does not also shy away from innovative experiments and has been on the advisory committee of a study in Bihar where the geographic information systems was an important tool for analysis. Cosmopolitan in taste, his hobbies range from tennis, photography to electronics. Residing in a sprawling haveli in the centre of the city of Patna, on whose perimeter he owns two dozen shops, speaks of opulence uncommon to most academicians in India.

Despite all the medals, ranks, skills and roles, Ram's intellectual merit outranks his performance. Most of his works are confined within the territorial limits of Bihar. All his education, all his 37 years of teaching, ninety per cent of doctorates he has supervised, his 4 research projects, 5 out of the 9 articles he has published, both his edited books, and the two chapters he has written in a book are on the state of Bihar. Despite the years of anchor within Bihar, why has Ram not been able to fulfill his very own professional desire to produce a geographical treatise on the State of Bihar.

Born in 1937 to a family of zamindars, the early death of his father, left Ram with a wealthy estate but also shackled him in a chain of litigation and chronic disputes. Though Ram's heart lay in the intellectual pursuits of the discipline of geography, yet the pressing demands of the court and the tax rooms snatched the peace of mind, a necessary precursor for creativity to flower. Ram however remains an optimist and says that the book "Geography of New Bihar and Jharkhand" will see the light of day. Circumstances make a person but a person can also create his own circumstances.

L.N. Ram delivered his Presidential Address extempore.

Padmanabha Doodhbhate Mahadev
1933 -

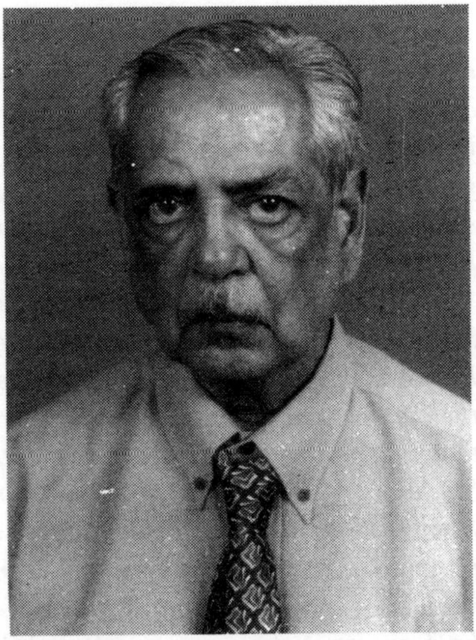

Carrying a near permanent demure tone and an unflappable temperament, it is difficult to comprehend the element of dissatisfaction that Mahadev harbors on his academic front. To all apparent observation Mahadev's professional career has numerous ingredients for satisfaction. He has successfully climbed the professional rungs from a lecturer to a professor at the department of geography, University of Mysore. To his credit is the supervision of ten doctorates, fourteen research articles in eight different geographical journals both in India and abroad. He has chapters in seventeen different books and has been author or co-editor in another eight books. As principal investigator he has undertaken four research projects, half of which have had a foreign funding. This is not all, Mahadev has attended over fifteen international conferences and has been invited on research or teaching assignments to several universities outside India. The Western University, Washington and University of Pittsburgh in the United States of America, Domaine Universitaire De Bordeaux, Talence in France, University of Kyoto and University of Hiroshima in Japan and the University of Groninger at Netherlands are all listed in his curriculum vitae. Besides the National Association of Geographers, India, Mahadev has been president of two other geographical associations : the Indian Council of Geographers in 1982, and the Indian National Cartographic Association in 1993. Over and above, Mahadev's self evasive and humble countenance has won him friends all around. Despite the mileage on many fronts, Mahadev's career trajectory is punctuated by signals of dissatisfaction.

Mahadev is among the very few geographers in India who has a double doctorate in the discipline. In 1969 the University of Mysore awarded him a doctorate, a short four years later he worked to get another degree from the University of Pittsburgh. Not only are both the doctorates in the discipline of geography, but both are on urban geography and both are on the city of Mysore. A single doctorate did not suffice and Mahadev's affirms that the one from Pittsburgh added a bit more to his wealth of exposure and experience.

A similar unease is noticeable in the professional shifts undertaken by Mahadev. After serving for a year as lecturer in the Alagappa College at Andhra Pradesh, Mahadev taught for five years at a college in Dharwad. He joined the department of geography, University of Mysore in 1964. After a decade of teaching and chairing the department, he moved to the Institute of Development Studies at Mysore as professor of Urban and Regional Planning and stayed on from 1979 to 1985. A brief stint for seven years and he reverted back to this parent department. The research themes he pursued also carry a search for a subject of interest. A knock down of his fourteen research articles show that half are on urban geography while the remaining relate to agriculture, settlement, industrial, cultural and environmental geography. His research projects too revolve around subjects which are poles apart–the impact of irrigation on settlement to rural health services to Japanese research on geography in India.

The years spent at the Institute of Development Studies, Mysore gave Mahadev a spring pad for travel, contacts and scope to widen his vistas of learning. Flushed with grants from the Ford Foundation, the Institute made it possible for Mahadev to organise numerous workshops as ones on locational analysis and research methodologies and attend the International Geographical Union held at Vienna and Paris in 1984. Visits to University of Ben Gurion in Israel, University of Groninger in Netherlands and the University of Hiroshima in Japan also fall in the time period when Mahadev was professor at this Institute. Despite all such benefits, Mahadev took a U-turn to go back to the department of geography at University of Mysore.

Mahadev recalls that the choice of selecting geography as a discipline for study also had no serious base . Born on 16th August 1933 in Coimbatore, his father's transfer as an employee of the government gave his schooling an itinerant character. Completing his studies at the Board High School at Chittoor, Andhra Pradesh, Mahadev joined the Presidency College at Madras to pursue his graduation and post-graduation. Throughout school or college no single subject of study caught his total fascination. If given a chance today, he would study anthropology rather than geography; nay, he would prefer to be an administrator rather than a teacher.

What is admirable is that despite a bed of internal uncertainites and strifes, Mahadev carried on his professional duties with pleasant ease. He never turned a cynic and never cast a caustic comment. A mild paralytic stroke today clouds his health. Yet, Mahadev maintains a compassionate composure. He exemplifies a noble learning of how a profession is to be pursued despite dissatisfying odds.

Sustaining Our Heritage

P.D. MAHADEV

Distinguished audience and fellow geographers, it is indeed an honour to deliver the Presidential Address at the XIV Annual Indian Geography Congress of the National Association of Geographers in the pink city of Jaipur. The honour is doubled when I see that the distinguished audience consists of a wide cross section of the fraternity of geographers; from the very senior geographers to the budding young ones waiting with their wings to take off.

My talk today would deal mostly with our heritage which we have inherited from our forefathers and to explore the means of sustaining it for posterity. I may not be able to cover this vast topic and may not come up with any tangible measure to sustain the heritage but I hope I shall be able to stimulate some new thinking on an issue which is of universal concern today.

Our heritage is sacred. This was realised by the Aryans who trudged their way from the wind swept Central Asia to this country which was diverse in every sense of the term, and they were the first to expound the theory that the universe was composed of five elements viz., the earth, the fire, the water, the air and the sky. The invaders were entralled by the majesty of the Himalayas, the perennial rivers, sindhu (ocean), the Ganga, the Yamuna and the other equally mighty rivers, the confluence of the rivers and oceans, the dense terai forests, the Sunderbans and the Dandakaranya, all of which abound in a variety of flora and fauna. Anxious to make use of them and also to preserve and sustain them for the posterity, they invested them with religious sanctity. The highest peaks were named as Gowrishankar, Kailash etc., the abode of Lord Shiva. Likewise, the rivers were declared sacred to prevent them from pollution and this message was given in the form of a mantra :

Gange cha yamune cheva godavari sarasvati
Narmada sindhu kaveri jalesiman sannidhikuru

Heritage consists of environmental, economic and socio-cultural dimensions. Let us see what they are and how we have treated them. Our

15th Indian Geography Congress
Jaipur 1992 December

environmental heritage dates back to historical times when inanimate and animate things were recognised as parts of a bigger system with specific roles to be played. The hills and dales were dotted with human settlements which served as meeting places and among them the central places were sanctified with a shrine so that no pollution took place. Also, environmentally and aesthetically, they remained as good as ever to sustain the interaction among the people and became places of sustained utility.

The five elements of environment as visualised by our ancestors were identified as gods and goddesses. Earth to them was *Dhartimata* or mother earth, air and wind were *varun dev* and the cosmos *Brahmand* presided over by *Brahma*. The flora was also held in high esteem as stated by *Lord Krishna* in *Geeta* "I am the *aswatha* or *peepal* among the trees" due to the special characteristics of the tree.

The question which looms large before us is : can we save the nature in all its glory ? Can we save the Himalayas and the Garhwal region ? Once the mighty Himalayas were layered sequentially by different species of trees at different elevation zones until the snowline beyond which was eternal snow and barren rugged rocks. But now, look at the Himalayas which once had dense forests and prowling tigers and other herbivorous and carnivorous animals (as described in Kalidasa's epic *Kumara Sambhava* in ancient days and Jim Corbett during the early part of this century) now stands naked, devoid of the rich flora and fauna which clothed it. There has been destruction of the natural heritage. In our greed and avarice, we have stripped naked the mighty Himalayas like *Draupadi* in the *Kaurava Sabha* where *Bhishma Pitamah* and *Dronacharya*, i.e. our elders who are custodians of our rich heritage and the intellectuals who are sentinels of our culture have remained mute spectators of this irreversible act. The government also, like the born blind *Drutharastra,* kept its eyes closed.

Perhaps nature would avenge itself some day if man continues his pillage unabated. The devastating floods and quakes are warning signals. With the soil eroded, agriculture has become less remunerative. The sacred rivers and their tributaries have already become sewers carrying the effluents. The holy rivers are no longer holy as they used to be. Instead of sustaining our heritage, we are saying good bye to it for some immediate gains which may cost us dearly in the years to come.

On the economic plane, the country is endowed with rich resources. There was a neat balance between environmental resources and population not only in the country as a whole but also in sub- regions. The densely populated areas in the coastal deltaic regions as well as in the flat river valleys were characterised by intensive grain farming whereas the densely vegetated and sparsely populated areas were marked by *Jhum* or shifting cultivation. The absence of mass production and mass consumption dispensed the necessity of concentrating population at selected points. The population was distributed more evenly in the subregions and hence there was an even distribution of small and medium sized towns. On the other hand, the present day witnesses not just population explosion, but more seriously population implosions in selected centres which become generators of toxic materials. Superficially, society may look affluent, but in reality, it can be called an effluent society.

From the time when each village was an entity unto itself, we have graduated to the globalization stage where any event in any corner of the globe has a telling impact on the unwary people elsewhere. This has brought about industrialization in some parts of the world and created a need for the chloroflourocarbons sinks. Now these sinks are sought to be located in developing countries where the development efforts to fulfil our basic needs are being curtailed. This is the right time to think of Gandhiji who outlined what a country's society, economy and ecology should consist of. Gandhiji might not have been a sociologist or an environmentalist in the strict sense, but he had a vision of India where nature and man lived as equal partners. Instead of man producing at a few places emitting pollutants, dehumanizing the urban folk and simultaneously impoverishing the rural folk, he advocated small scale production wherein certain values are treasured and preserved so that posterity's claim to a less distorted nature are not ignored. In other words, instead of encouraging points of prosperity in space for the benefit of a few of the present generation, we should strive for bringing about grassroot prosperity for the benefit of the vast majority spread over a vast area not only for the present generation but also for generations to come. As Thomas Jefferson aptly put it "The earth is given as a common stock for man to labour and live on".

The socio-cultural aspects of our heritage are distorted with the advent of the industrial revolution. The good old moorings of the people in their land and in the society have been cut off. A considerable number of people have migrated either to nearby towns or to distant places. In this process, they have lost their identity and their sense of belonging. They have taken up anonymity and have been overwhelmed in the sea of people. This has dehumanised them and what they would not be seen doing in their original homes would now become accepted behaviour.

In the present societal structure there has been a sort of vertical mobility of the people devoid of their firm grounding. This is the reason why several people feel alienated from their own kith and kin, their tradition and their heritage. People have no pride in their work resulting in indifference and sloppiness.

But what is sustainable heritage ? It is a heritage that lasts. Its specific concern is that those who enjoy the fruits of the past heritage today may not disinherit future generations of the earth's resources. To put it in a nutshell, the current generation should meet its needs without compromising the ability of future generation to meet their own needs. If we turn this into a policy, it raises fundamental questions about how to assess the well-being of present and future generations. What should we leave to our children and grand-children to maximise their ability to be no worse off than ourselves ? Considering what we pass on to future generations, we must take into account the full range of physical, human and natural capital that will determine their welfare and their bequests to their successors. The damage to the environment hurts people both today and will do so in the future - it provides additional grounds for rethinking of our measurement of progress, but this progress has its externalities. No doubt health, education and nutrition have improved by economic growth, but the environment is sometimes damaged by the growth. Usually, people suffering from the damage may be different from those enjoying the benefits of growth. They may be today's poor or they may be the future generations.

It is true that despite Darwin, we are not in our hearts a part of the natural process. We think we are superior to nature and are contemptuous of it. It would not be wrong to say that human ecology is deeply conditioned by beliefs about our nature and destiny, that is by faith. This is very evident in the case of countries like India and Sri Lanka. The western thought inherited from Judaism tries to make out that a loving and all powerful God has created light and darkness, the heavenly bodies, the Earth and all its plants, animals, birds and fishes. Finally, God created Adam and as an afterthought, Eve to keep man from being lonely. Man established a dominance over them. God planned all this explicitly for man's benefit and rule. As man's body is made up of clay, he is simply a part of nature. He is made in God's image. Hence, the Western philosophy can be called an anthropocentric thought. In contrast to the Eastern thought, the Western thought establishes a dualism of man and nature and insists that it is God's will that man exploits nature for his own ends.

On the other hand, the Eastern thought emphasises the harmony between man and nature. Traditionally, in our Indian heritage, man has inherited land as well as other natural surroundings from time immemorial. These things which he has inherited are meant to be safeguarded and utilised properly. There was almost an unwritten law that man should not destroy other living organisms indiscriminately. If he cuts a tree, he was expected to plant two in its place so that at least one would survive. There was almost reverence for nature and this stood us in good stead when the other advanced nations guided by materialistic view not only destroyed their immediate environment but also that of other countries over which they had undue influence. This has led to new ecological colonialism by which resources of some of the countries are siphoned off for the benefit of a few. Man has thus started living beyond his means and if he continues this way, the catastrophe is not too far.

Though the count down has begun, it is not difficult to make the environment sustainable if we follow the dictates of our conscience and not be blindly led by the economic animal in us and not assert the human arrogance over the heritagc which we have inherited. For this an integrated plan has to be drawn up. As a first stage, environmental dimension has to be built into policy making and not add it as an after-thought to get the clearance of the Ministries concerned. Further, land use has to be regulated to be in consonance with the time-tested land use pattern even if it means subsiding this act. In many cases the aggregate cost and benefit should not be the sole concern in developmental efforts but local damages have to be considered and assessed seriously. There should also be a realistic assessment of the trade – offs and efforts should be made to minimise it.

For this, developmental and environmental policies must be based on a comparison of benefits and costs and analysis. This will lead to the strengthening of environmental protection measures and consequently lead to rising and sustainable levels of welfare.

One of the ways to sustain our heritage is to create enough public pressure to convince those in power that survival is at stake and will remain so unless they get behind some really effective measures to deal with mankind's most pressing problem. The policy makers should realize that prevention of erosion of heritage is better than finding a cure. Environmental considerations cannot be divorced from geographic and socio-economic realities and the prevailing value system related to growth. In a developing society like ours, different flavour to ecology-based link between natural and social sciences is needed. To sustain our heritage and at the same time achieve development and higher quality of life for all people, there should be a reduction and elimination of unsustainable patterns of production and consumption.

Additionally, the government should enact environment friendly legislations. The environmental standards, management objectives and priorities should be reflected in the efforts of sustaining the heritage. In this context it should be pointed out that heritage, environmental protection and development are interdependent and indivisible. The Stockholm conference in 1970's and the Rio conference in 1992 have not only paved the way but have bound together the comity of nations to sustain their respective heritages for years to come.

What we do about ecology depends on our ideas of man-nature relationship. More science and more technology are not going to get us out of the present day ecological crisis until we find a new religion, a new ethos or rethink our old one. In this context, the profoundly ethical but seemingly primitive Gandhian spiritual autonomy of all parts of nature may point a direction. I propose Gandhiji as a patron saint for the heritage of India.

Shanti Lal Kayastha
1924 -

Daily in the wee sma' hours, a click- clack can be heard from the Akhnoor hut at Banaras. It makes two announcements - first the time on the clock is 4 a.m. and second Kayastha has set to work on his Olivetti machine. Perched amidst his personal treasure of about five thousand books and reports, a catalogue of photographs, slides and maps, it is clear that Kayastha's typewriter will never run out of facts, data and references. The map of his room is etched meticulously in Kayastha's memory and at a snap of a thought or a behest of a request he can pull out a reference or summon a report. Half a dozen cameras dangle from a nail on the wall, along with knapsacks and weather braving jackets. They tell us Kayastha is not an arm-chair geographer. Disciplined and painstaking work shouldered on extensive fieldwork are steps on which Kayastha has built his scholastic reputation. A tireless labor for geography has brought to Kayastha's doorstep – heavy duty works, eager students and scholars.

For nearly three decades Kayastha was the honorary editor of the National Geographical Journal of India, Banaras. Today if this journal has a reputation, it owes debt to the many hours of checks and rechecks sifted singularly by Kayastha. Many among his twenty doctorate students preserve their drafts or manuscripts as pieces of learning from their supervisor. Kayastha's five books, seventy published articles and over forty papers presented at various symposiums and conferences are a proof of his diligence. Rewards came to him in ways both bold and subtle. The National Geographical Society of India, Banaras conferred on Kayastha the prestigious Sardar Vallabh Bhai

Patel Medal in 1971; while a festschrift titled ' Geography and Environment: Issues and Challenges' is a befitting tribute by his students to their revered teacher. Little deterred to seek worldly awards, Kayastha maintains a steadfast commitment to any work he undertakes.

Kayastha has a virtually uninterrupted record of attending the Indian Science Congress from 1956 to 2001, an achievement considering that he never arrived at the meet without a written paper. He earned respect and was elected president of the geology and geography section in 1988. He is one among the only four geographers in India acquire this post. The International Geographical Union is another of Kayastha's favorable meets. Off the cuff, he can remember attending the ones at Delhi 1968, Moscow 1979, Karachi 1980, Tokyo 1980, Kathmandu 1983 and Sydney 1988. His presence earned him the full membership of the International Geographical Commission on Environmental Problems and corresponding membership of both the Working Group on Environmental Perception and the Commission on Population and Environment. Conferences and Congresses are only a spec in the life of a true academician. What is more enduring is the area of research. It is in the focus of research interest that Kayastha's persistense is best at display.

The region encapsulated within the towering Dhaula Dhar range of the Himalayas and the Beas, one of the five major tributaries of the river Indus, became Kayastha's unstinted preoccupation for over three decades. Nearly forty papers and one of his books is on the Beas Basin region within the state of Himachal Pradesh. The attraction for this Himalayan state holds his attention till date. Every summer Kayastha can be seen walking, observing and taking pictures in Kangra, Dharamshala and Dalhousie. More than half his album of photographs captures the river Beas as it flows through snow capped mountains. Kayastha's bonds with the Himalayas run deep and long.

Born in a small town of Kangra on 24th March 1924, Kayastha spent his childhood skirting dales and vales. Walking to the Dayanand Anglo Vedic High School at Kangra versed him with the "ways in a mountain." Perhaps it is Kayastha's idyllic attachment to the land and landscape that prompted the principal of the Government College at Lahore to advise this undergraduate student to elect geography as his majors in higher education. While pursuing a post- graduation at Aligarh, his association with late Muzzafar Ali ignited in Kayastha a desire to undertake a doctorate from United Kingdom. A letter of registration with Stamp at the London School of Economics in Kayastha's personal file is an account of dream and sacrifice. Kayastha opted to share the burden of rearing a family of nine brothers and sisters with his father, rather than take off on a personal rendezvous. A twist of destiny put Kayastha back into the lap of his first love – the Himachal Himalayas.

When Kayastha joined Banaras Hindu University as lecturer in 1948 and set to work for his doctorate these mountains were his only choice for study. He spent seven devout years conducting field work and assembling data in the region. Many crooks and crannies were scanned by Kayastha as his fieldwork spread in twenty-five villages across different habitats of the Beas Basin. Published in 1964, Kayastha's thesis was hailed as path breaking on many fronts. Most significant was the unit of study – a watershed. In the 1940s the concept of a watershed as a functionally unified system of study was little known to geographers in India. It was a chance meeting with A.T Morgan, president of the Tennessee Valley Authority, that stimulated Kayastha's imagination to choose a river basin as an area of study. Following perhaps Geddes', principle of ' place, work and folk' Kayastha's research titled 'The Himalayan Beas Basin: A Study in Habitat, Economy and Society' won immediate attention.

A consistent and vigilant eye witness of one region sensitized Kayastha to the changing environmental scenario and the menace of degradation and pollution in the Himalayas. The ecological deterioration in the mountains reverted Kayastha's attention to the widespread environmental issues across India and the earth as a whole. Kayastha is unwilling to take the credit of his role in popularizing environmental studies among geographers in India. He humbly acknowledges Gilbert White, emeritus professor at the University of Colorado as his intellectual mentor. Kayastha met White only twice; once in 1968 at the International Geographical Union Congress at Delhi, followed by a second meeting at the Congress at Tokyo in 1980, yet a stack of letters with Kayastha verifies the frequent exchange of news and views shared by the scholars. The introduction of a course on Environmental Geography in the curriculum of the department of geography at Banaras Hindu University and a series of public lectures on the interface between Environment and Development, Environment and Population, and Environmental Policies are planks on which Kaysatha acquired prominence as India's leading environmental geographer. Despite a faltering eye sight Kayastha has recently finalized a paper on 'Environment and Development: Crises and Conflicts'. Publishing a comparative account of environmental problems in countries he has visited is his next agenda.

From the crack of dawn to dusk, day in and day out it is the mould cast by discipline of hard work which drives Kayastha at the age of 77 to accomplish his journey ahead.

Environment, Development and Quality of Life

S.L. KAYASTHA

I am indeed grateful to the members of the National Association of Geographers, India for unanimously electing me as its President for 1994 and for asking me to deliver the Presidential Address at its XVth Geography Congress in Bhubaneswar. It is indeed an honour and a privilege to address this august gathering of geographers.

Kalinga, Puri and this great city of Bhubaneswar have since long nourished the higher intellectual and cultural traditions of the country.

Environment, development and the quality of life are interrelated. There is a need to have a perspective on environment and development. There is also a need for an appraisal of development and for such action that may bring equilibrium between environment and development, and thereby help improve the quality of life. In spite of numerous platitudes in professions, it is not so. The world is faced with environmental problems of mounting nature, situations of over development and underdevelopment, affluence and poverty, all of which detract from the quality of life. Development ultimately suffers, with the degradation of environment, but it is not so evident in the beginning. Degradation of environment also leads to reduction in the "Quality of Life". Evidently, development as measured by the Gross National Product alone does not by itself lead to improvement in the quality of life. It is 'therefore' imperative to look into the state of environment and development and examine measures that may help improve overall scenario and ultimately the quality of life.

To focus attention on these problems of environment and development, the United Nations Conference on Human Environment was held in Stockholm in 1972. It set an environmental programme for conservation and improvement and aroused much environmental awareness. But the development process also lead to serious imbalances, particularly between the developed and the developing countries. Sridhar Ramphal is quoted by Ambirajan (1992) "in the destitution of the third world countries and the over consumption of the industrial countries lie the seeds of all environmental problems". The Brundtland

16th Indian Geography Congress
Bhubaneshwar, 1993 November

Commission (1987) considers that many forms of development erode the environmental resources upon which they are based and environmental degradation would undermine economic development.

By any reckoning the industrial countries are directly or indirectly responsible for most of the environmental mess. Over 70 per cent of the current carbon emissions come from them. United States alone contributes 23 per cent of this. In 1988 the average per capita emissions of carbon from industrial countries was 3.36 tonnes, and from the rest of the world, it was just 0.45 tonnes (Tickell, 1991). Many types of human activities during the preceding decades have accelerated adverse impacts on environment, notable being deforestation, soil erosion, desertification, environmental pollution, global warming and climatic change, ozone depletion, ecosystem degradation, and depletion and extinction of several species of fauna and flora. This great energy crisis of the 1970's still reminds us of the energy crunch. Threat to fresh water is an even bigger issue. Unlike oil, there is no alternative to water. We simply cannot wait for a crisis (Grosvenor, 1993). Tolba (1988) views that the need for larger supplies of water may cause major conflicts in the next century. The changing character of human impact on environment is alarming. There could be meaningful cooperation between various countries of the world to share benefits of research and technology in such areas as environmental impact-assessment, so clearly enunciated by Munn (1979), in planning and management, pollution control, forest, soil and water conservation, flood control, water supply and sewage treatment, disaster-reduction strategies and community participation. Many such areas of meaningful cooperation emerge with the meeting of the minds that share common concern of environment and development (White, 1974, 1986; Clarke *et al*, 1969).

Development has strained the environment. The profligate use of resources of energy, water, land and forest by the rich, and to meet the needs of the poor, whose numbers are ever-increasing, is making environmental and developmental sustainability difficult. The concept of development should include the satisfaction of human needs in harmony with the environment and full participation of the people concerned (Sharma, 1987). Even though there is so much affluence and high consumption, yet there is no peace and happiness. Why with so much knowledge and skill, should things be falling apart. It is a matter of grave concern and calls for a closer scrutiny.

An appraisal of the national environmental problems and policies is of high significance and importance for the well-being of the country (Kayastha, 1986). Environmental degradation is causing adverse effect not only on the ecology of the life-support systems, but also on the quality of life. Large-scale exploitation of natural resources, notably the forest resources, urban-industrial development, growing population and unemployment, poverty and inequality have led to numerous crisis situations, notably the environment –development crisis (Kayastha, 1988). The official agencies in India are concerned about it. They have taken steps to formulate policies and enact legislation for environmental protection, although the hiatus between objective and attainment gives little scope for complacency (Tiwari, 1980) . The high importance of maintaining ecological balance to sustain life has long been known in India. When environmental and scientific truths are given cultural backing, they are easily accepted and assimilated (Pant, 1992). When nature is healthy, there is balanced circulation of elements, and of minerals, plant and animal kingdoms flourish. Good-life is impossible without good earth (Kaurance, 1992). During the British rule, there was excessive exploitation of natural and human resources, and a massive dislocation of space economy (Kayastha and Mukherji, 1979). This has been responsible for rapid environmental deterioration and deprivation. During this colonial stage the British used science as a colonial tool (Kochhar, 1992). This helped to accelerate exploitation. After independence much stress was laid on conservation and improvement of environment and many programmes were initiated. However, due to lack of location-specific planning and integration at various levels, and lack of appreciation of ecological constraints, resulted in ecodegradation (Raza, 1989). Due to land degradation, over 60 per cent area needs land conservation measures (Vohra, 1980; Agrawal *et al.*, 1982). No worthwhile sustainable development would be possible without integrating economic and ecological concerns in area development programmes. Urban and industrial growth is devouring good agricultural land needed to supply the food needs of a billion persons by 2001 A.D. Misuse, pollution and lack of integrated water management are responsible for the growing water crisis in the face of increasing demands for irrigation, rural and urban water supply and various other uses. There is an urgent need for a comprehensive water management policy based on a National Water Policy (Kayastha 1981). Deforestation is extensive and landsite imageries estimate a forest area of 10-12 per cent only against the national need of 33 per cent. So far, the National Forest Policy remains an unfulfilled dream. While the demands are increasing, the claims of net increase of national forest cover are not quite true (Forest Report, 1991). The task of eco-restoration would also involve reorientation of our policies and practices. Bock (1990) feels that time has come when the European silvicultural practices adopted in India by Brandis and Troup are abandoned. The ongoing disaster of deforestation is on account of radical transformation of resource-use that took place under British and became all the more entrenched after independence. Its highlight is the use of state power to systematically undervalue biomass, and more so the biological diversity, and organise its supply to the industry at highly subsidized rates. In this manner both nature and people suffer (Gadgil, 1989). We should call halt to such resource-use by the "The Iron Triangle" as the Americans call it, and empower the rural poor to take good care of the biomass resources of their local environments, enabling them to deploy their labour productively to the task of ecorestoration (Repetto, 1986, 1988). Nothing could be closer to the concept of 'Gramswarajaya' of Gandhiji than the creation of village ecosystems which are biologically diverse and self-reliant (Agrawal, 1986).

Dr. Bhabha considered the question of energy as critical to the problem of national development. "No power is as expensive as no power" was how he liked to put it. He even considered historical developments, as epochs in patterns of energy-use (Greenstein, 1993). There is a need for a energy policy with greater emphasis on renewable energy resources (Kayastha, 1981).

On account of ecological degradation, natural hazards like floods and droughts have become accentuated. In addition to huge losses and sufferings, these hazards destabilize India's national economy (Kayastha, 1983). It is an annual ordeal. Yet the government awakens to these problems when there is too much or little of water. There is lack of disaster planning and preparedness. It may be remarked that each place has its own distinctive combination of physical and human characteristics shaping the hazard to the extent to which it is vulnerable. The evolving interaction of people and environment in each place affects the opportunities and the costs that the rampaging forces of nature may reap. This enables geographers, as earth scientists, as well as social scientists, to make their distinctive contribution to the study of 'population, disasters and disaster-reduction strategies' are partners in the national endeavour of environment, development and the quality of life (Kayastha, 1991). Many techniques have been practised for minimising risks at the family and community levels, since pre-historic times. The historical approach to the management of uncertainty suggests three groups of strategies. Gilbert White's vista is not merely that of cutting of losses, but also of improving the quality of life in an uncertain world (Kates, 1986). Group I emphasizes 'strategies for eliminating risks' that include risk removal, avoidance and protection, that is, banning hazardous substances, siting towns on high grounds to avoid floods and tidal waves and strengthening foundations of buildings in earthquake zone. Group II emphasizes 'strategies for coping with known risks' that include learning, diversification, small construction, saving, self-sufficiency, ability to react rapidly to surprises, development of early warning systems and impact mitigation of disasters, that is, information retrieval, multiple crops, small dams, conservation, recycling and eco-development, adaptational, resilience, forecasting relief measures, etc. The third Group emphasizes 'strategies for coping with unknown', that includes all those measures given under coping with known risks, with emphasis on adaptive ability, and better forecasting systems. The word 'resilience' was first used in an ecological context by C.S.Holling (1978) to denote the ability of an ecosystem to return to a state of equilibrium after being severly stressed. It has been suggested that civilizations most vulnerable to surprise (least resilient) are neither the least-developed nor the highly industrialized. Instead, the most susceptible are those in transition, such as the developing countries, which are in the process of losing their traditional skills for dealing with environmental shocks (Burton, Kates and White, 1977). Even now, the subsistence farmers in semiarid regions grow quick ripening crops in preference to species that promise greater average returns, an insurance against drought that has been ravaging for several centuries. Such resilience is not only of value to rural agricultural societies, but also to urban societies, with respect to their resilience to environmental stresses. One of the scourges of development is pollution. It is the result of development without pollution control. Water and air pollution are now a menace in the large metropolitan cities of India like Delhi, Bombay, Madras and Calcutta. Delhi now ranks among the four most polluted cities of the world. In fact, as someone casually remarked, environmental and socio-political pollution threaten to ruin the natural and social systems. Water pollution is a serious problem in India and is responsible for many illnesses. Not many cities have sewage treatment plants and more than 50 per cent of the large and medium industries have not installed proper pollution control. Enforcement of the measures is another aspect. The essential needs of potable water, more housing, better transport, improved nutrition and healthcare, education and employment have to be provided in a rural-urban symbiosis (Khosla, 1974). There is a sort of destabilisation process in the compulsions of movement from unsustainable rural ecosystems to unsustainable urban ecosystems with about half the population living in the squalor of slums well below the acceptable standards of sanitation and health. It is not uncommon for government of developing countries with 70 per cent of their people living in the rural areas to spend only 20 per cent of their budgets there, leading to distorted underdevelopment (Moddie, 1988). Therefore, small towns have to be developed as nodal centres to stem the tide of rural-urban migration (Kayastha, 1989). The urban areas at present are a picture of squalor, smoke and stress, while the rural areas suffer from poverty, underdevelopment and social erosion. Development is needed for a better quality of life, otherwise, it would be a self-defeating process. Poverty is degrading to both man and environment. Nearly 40 per cent of the population of India is below the poverty line. The mighty Himalaya is showing signs of becoming ecologically an unsteady region. High population increase and haphazard development coupled with deforestation had led to the degradation of the fragile eco-system of the Himalayas (Kayastha, 1992). Agriculture being the main source of livelihood leads to the growing pressure of population on land, which varies from 179 to 1,270 persons per km2 in 1981, while the per capita availability of land has declined from 0.43 hectares in 1961 to 0.15 in 1981 (Kayastha, 1990). The government's decision to go ahead with Tehri Dam in a major seismic zone, reveals that the compulsions are based more on the needs of the people in the plains, than on the fate of the people in Tehri. In this construction of large dams, there has been submergence of large tracts of forests and good agricultural land, mostly in tribal tracts. Over the last 30 to 40 years, millions of people have been ousted from their homes for the sake of 'development'. They have been fired upon, arrested and forced to surrender their constitutional rights. Their only answer has been peaceful protests (Roy, 1993). No official study has been done so far on the total number of oustees from large dam areas, but the number, according to Indian Council of Social Institute, is estimated at 18.5 million persons, out of which hardly 4.6 million have been rehabilitated and that too somewhat unsatisfactorily. They have been scattered among hostile environments and populations. Similarly, in the case of mines, industries, wild-life sanctuaries and so on, the plight of oustees, largely tribals, continues to be appalling. At the cost of considerable environmental neglect and deforestation, these projects cater to the growing demands of industry and commercial agriculture rather than to the well-being of drought-affected areas or the poorer sections of society. Development should bring happiness, and not gloom to the people of the area. Asks a *Narmada Bachao Andolan* leader, "what kind of management is this which does not care for the lives of the people for the sake of development"? (Kapoor, 1993). The balanced development of both rural and urban areas, and of nature, economy and society, with the adoption and Indianisation of science and technology to respective needs, where the frontiers hold promise to help meet complex needs of nature and society in a sustainable manner provides a measure of much needed national scrutiny and national well-being (Khoshoo, 1986). Development should permeate the whole of our national life, all areas of endeavour and all regions, otherwise it will only accelerate disparities within the country, as indeed, it has done between the country during the last two hundred years. Development should be a liberating force and an ally of social equity. People cooperate when they benefit from the various development programmes and policies, and are inspired by exemplary devotion to the cause and country.

To deliberate on these issues, a United Nations Conference on Environment and Development was held in June 1992 in Rio de Janeiro. The participation by 103 heads of government gave it the official stamp. There were also many participants in various discussions representing 166 countries. The Earth Summit Agenda included five major issues, namely , the declaration on environment and development, principles of management, conservation and sustainable development of all types of forests, convention on climate change, convention on biological diversity, and agenda 21 – a non-binding action plan for environment and development. The conference defined a new model of global development cooperation based on ecological and economic considerations (Shah, 1992). To protect the American pharmaceutical industry, U.S. did not sign the biodiversity convention. Similarly, Malaysia blocked binding treaty on forests on grounds of national sovereignty. U.S. also rejected the binding targets on greenhouse gas reduction, and aroused much resentment. Actually, all attempts to cut down waste and emissions would ultimately trim fuel and utility bills. Japan is designing a century plan on environment and development. Germany is endeavouring to move to a trashless society. It is felt that those who do not pursue environmentally responsible development will be left behind gathering dust and smoke. Agenda 21 also faced opposition. It included programmes such as poverty-alleviation, preventing degradation of air, water, soil and hill areas, population pressure reduction, review of consumption patterns, debt liquidation, curtailing of military expenditure and diversion to development work, stopping of hazardous – waste exports produced in industrialized countries, saving of forest resources; all highly relevant to the promotion of sustainable development and germane to aspirations of developing countries; were either dropped or diluted. The financial commitments of the donor countries were not confirmed, but it is expected to be short of the need for switching over to less polluting technologies. Though India and the developing countries consume less than 15 per cent of the global chloroflourocarbons production and so are not responsible for the depletion of the earth's protective ozone layer, they agreed to join the Montreal Protocol to stress their role as environmentally conscious nations. India would need between Rupees 4,500 and 7, 500 crores ($ 1.5-2.5 billion) to completely switch over to non-chloroflourocarbons substitutes by 2010, provided financial and technical support is available from UN agencies and industrialized countries (Suresh, 1993). The global economy is rigged against both poverty alleviation and environmental protection. Treating the earth's ecological ills as separate from issues of debt, trade, inequality and consumption is like trying to treat heart disease without addressing a patient's obesity and high-cholesterol diet. There is no chance of lasting success (Postel, 1992).

The Human Development Report has advocated a three-pronged strategy for growth with human welfare. First, there should be more investment in people.

In South Asia, a paltry sum is spent at present. Secondly, small enterprises must be provided assistance so as to generate employment opportunities. Even in the United States, 50 per cent of the jobs were in small enterprises. And thirdly, the country must get into the service sector. The value of internatural trade in service was worth $ 1,000 billion, but the share of the developing countries was a meagre 5 per cent. Human development is an important aspect of the New World Order, in which markets have failed, governments have not managed to improve living conditions and the number of poor persons seems to be on the increase. The new slogan, therefore, would be, "Development for the people, by the people and of the people". Human development has to be the major concern of governance as well as the market relations. In South Asia, Gross Domestic Products grew at an average of 5 per cent during 1973-87, while the number of jobs grew by over 2 per cent. Obviously, technological innovations and market demand to cater up to 20 per cent of total income, have contributed to this trend. Decentralising governance, from capital cities to regions, towns and villages can be the best means of promoting participation and efficiency. An equity oriented regional policy strives to reduce regional disparities in socio-economic development. The long-term objective is to create in all regions adequately perceived conditions of life (Schatzl, 1993). An equalizing regional economic policy has the function of guiding mobile production factors into still undeveloped regions, and promoting the endogenous potential which exists there to improve the economic well-being. The final analysis, the response to this fundamental challenge to future will be rooted in the deepest motivations which spring from moral and spiritual values. The intensely competitive environment of modern economic life has subverted and distorted these value systems to very great degree. But they continue to provide a foundation on which can be built a new sense of belonging to a single universal community may though not replacing our national, ethnic and communal loyalties. This must be based on a new ethic of survival, a culture of cooperation, moving from "one earth to one world" (Strong, 1991).

The world in general is apt to forget its pledges and obligations in pursuit of its own interests. Historically, the pattern is roughly the same. In spite of the fact that the disastrous consequences of environmental degradation are better understood today, the world goes on its course as before. It seems that history repeats itself, but it does not teach (Kayastha and Juyal, 1979). The profit motive bordering on greed persists and calls the shots. Such is the case both in developed and the developing countries. The differences in the policies and programmes of various countries as between individuals, differ due to different perceptions (Lowenthal, 1972). Such perception if unrealistic, even though backed by political or industrial leadership could be attended by disastrous consequences. China's former leader, Mao Zedong, once declared war against 'sparrows' believing they were a pest and nuisance. This was halted after infestation of caterpillars, freed from predators, devoured the crops and enveloped even tress. Alaska too has declared war against wolves to boost population of Caribou and moose. Alaska's folly is the result of *theme-park mentality*, in which nature exists for our amusement (Gup, 1992). Nature cannot be cast in anthropogenic terms. To progress from nature's despoiler to its custodian, we must first redefine our place in and not over nature, accept the role of resident, rather than architect and resist the temptation technology affords us to mould a world responsible to our whims alone. But self-interest is apt to ignore environmental interest. As a matter of fact, any development should examine the best match between environment and development so that the ecological constraints are not overstepped. A plea is made for careful scrutiny of the Konark beach Resort Development Project that involves 2227 acres of Gadabangar reserve forest an Bulakhand Sanctuary, and the cutting down of 51, 788 trees (Satpathy, 1993). The Project area includes the World Heritage Temple of Konark, which should be best viewed in natural surroundings. The long-term environmental effects of the Konark beach Area Project should be looked into for impact assessment. Self-interest should not come in. It is also highlighted by Brundtland's mission to seek the support of Al Gore, the United States Vice President. She wants him to promise that America would not take punitive economic measures against Norway, which planned to defy an international moratorium on whaling (Linden, 1993). This comes from Gro Harlem Brundtland, who headed the World Commission on Environment and Development, so cherished in the report, *Our Common Future*. She got into the fix, because she needed the political support of the fishermen. This leads to what may be called the "First Law of Environmental Decline", that is, "the long term health of an ecosystem recedes in importance when the people are fighting over access to specific resources for their short-term economic gains". While people adjust to shortsightedness and compromise, nature only reacts. The results can be irreversible and disastrous, belying any rhetorical airbrushing. Environmental problems arise when the depreciation of nature is ignored, because it carries no price-tag (Mahabubul Haq, 1992). There are several models of sustainable development both for the developed and the developing countries, which put people at the centre of concern. But in actual process, this is often ignored. Loud emergencies like 'global warming' receive greater attention than 'silent emergencies' in developing countries , that affect the lives of many people. 133 million persons have no access to safe drinking water, and 2.3 billion lack access to sanitation. Of the 750 million persons who suffer from acute diarrhoeal diseases each year, 4 million die. 400 million lives of the world's children could be saved, if an additional $ 35 billion (about Rupees 75,000 crores) could be provided for adequate nutrition, clean water, basic healthcare and primary education, according to James Grant, Executive Director of United Nations International Children Emergency Fund (Grant, 1992). 35,000 children die each day from malnutrition and disease. This issue should receive serious attention; instead it is received with cold silence. The sum needed to alleviate the unnecessary loss could be provided by the developing countries themselves, without 25 per cent contribution by the developed countries. This amount is less than what the Europeans spend on cigarettes each year ($ 50 billion) or the Americans spend on beer ($ 31 billion). 'Social Darwinism' denies any empathy for the weak and underprivileged, and the South can look nowhere for support (Bidwai, 1992). Development must be shared in a spirit of interdependence and equity. While the South owes 'economic debt', the North owes 'ecological debt'. In the present state recession, economic survival takes precedence in the developing countries. The Uruguay round of the General Agreement on Trade and Tariff has threatened to undo what the Rio summit proposed, by treating environmental and social directives as covert trade barriers. The drive towards ever-increasing consumption must be abandoned in favour of commitment to sustainable development and long-term quality of life for all conspicuous patterns of high consumption, high income and high trade surpluses pose likelihood of greater conflict and violence. Simple living and non-violence are obviously closely inter-related. The optimal pattern of consumption production high degree of human satisfaction by means of relatively low rate of consumption allows people to live without pressure and strain (Krishnamurti and Schoettli, 1965) . However, such a transition presents a great challenge. Double standards create confusion and mistrust. There is obviously a mismatch between the policy of 'sustainable developed' for international conferences and of ''sustained growth' at home (Tickell, 1991). The International Union of Conservation on Nature defines sustainable development as ' improving the quality of human life while living within the carrying capacity of a supporting ecosystem (Naik, 1993). Sustainable development should keep in view the stability of the ecosystem. The closest ecosystem that may be sustainable are forests and agriculture (Mukherji, 1992). The much enthuse 'Green Revolution' has already reached a 'plateau', because it makes the ecosystem unsustainable. Swaminathan (1993) stresses that India needs to produce more keeping in view the ecology of the area. Soil fertility must be maintained, that is, agriculture must be made sustainable. Agricultural research should be more poor-oriented, women-oriented and nature-oriented. Sustainability can also be understood in a social sense, meaning a thriving economic and social order with productive structures and relationships, which ensure a fair distribution of incomes, power and opportunities, thus providing the basic for 'social peace'. Finally, sustainability is used in the sense of long-term carrying capacity of regions, where there is no negative impact on environment (Kuhnen, 1992). We need to have a national Committee on Sustainable Development that should function in coordination with the Planning Commission.

Sustainable development cannot be built on the foundations of inequality and exploitation. Gandhiji saw this clearly and remarked, "A small country like Britain needed half the world to industrialize. If God forbid, India should take to industrialization in the British fashion, would it not strip the world bare like locusts? (Alvares, 1992). Development cannot ipso facto mean human welfare. Words are only a means of expression, they can also be building-blocks of thought. It is, therefore, desirable to do some fresh thinking. "Development', 'growth', 'Gross National Product, etc. are used in misleading way often as buzz-words. Development should not only be sustainable and protective of environment, but it must also be humane. Development, while it presupposes growth, cannnot be reduced to mere economic development, and key to preserving nature is cultural (De Cuellar, 1992). A new kind of development – human, sustainable and shared is necessary. It can be built only on the basis of global consideration. All paradoxes arise because the spirit of cohesion and inter-relationship is not being recognized. Environment and development issues, if dealt with in isolation, make matters worse. Therefore, there is need to deal with them together. However, our universe is not being viewed as an integral part of the cosmic web; sea, forests, mountains and the vast populations of man, fauna and flora are not being considered as organic entities of this cosmic web. It is not fully appreciated that the affluence of the western countries is being maintained and enhanced by securing export of environment of developing countries and that consumption pattern in one part of the world are responsible for increasing deforestation, desertification and droughts in the other. The future is indeed bad news for the winners as well. The more sensitive among them are already wondering how long can they sustain their island of affluence in an increasingly devastated world (Lal, 1993). Remedies for most of the ills that afflict the world community as it is about to enter the twenty first century lie beyond the capacity of any one nation or region to dispense. Since they are transnational in character, effective cures can be undertaken only at transnational level . The world needs a new kind of leadership that builds the edifice of society on sustainability, equity and unity of mankind and helps to create a new landscape for life. Resources exist for reconstructing the world to bring about ecological and human equilibrium. It will need the support of all positive achievements of science and technology, and the cooperation of all to achieve this, and more, to further the quality of life of people everywhere. The environmental ethics and compulsions should unite us because few threats to survival are greater than those posed by the prospect of degradation of biosphere on which human life depends.

Ultimately, the purpose of all development is human welfare and the quality of life. The term 'Quality of Life' is generally used as a cliché. It is assigned different meaning when used by politician, the planner, the social worker, and the environmentalist, according to respective intentions and interests. It can also mean different things to different strata of society. By those, equating it with material self-sufficiency, it may have increased, but by other having to do with environment, social harmony and individual fulfilment, the quality of life has certainly decreased. The quality of life is not quantificable. It is a process, a relationship, a sense of belonging and a sense of wholeness, which is experienced and treasured. An individual's quality of life and its striving for it becomes a social quality of life, which can be reflected quantitatively in a way in terms of material and social well-being.

Can large growing populations live in harmony with nature and yet meet all their basic needs? At the risk of repetitions one may ask, can we live peacefully with dwindling resources? Are we moving in the right direction towards the goal of integrated, inter-dependent, shared world, that would promote peace and harmony? These are some of the questions that have been raised earlier to ensure sustainable development and human welfare. Economic development and sound environmental management are complementary aspects of the same agenda. Without adequate environmental protection, development will be undermined; without development, environmental protection will fall. More than 1 billion people today live in abject poverty. The next generation will see the world population rise by 3.7 billion, even if progress in reducing population growth accelerates. Most of these people will be born into poor families. Alleviation of poverty is both a moral imperative and essential for environmental sustainability. Economic growth is essential for sustained poverty alleviation. But growth has often caused serious environmental damage. Fortunately, such adverse effects can be sharply reduced, and with effective policies and institutions, income growth will provide the resources for improved environmental management. The environmental mistakes of the past need not be repeated. Today, countries have more choices. They can choose policies and encourage investments for efficient use of resources, substitution away from resources and the adaptation of technologies and practices that do less environmental harm. Such change will ensure that the improvements in human welfare which development brings are lasting (World Development Report, 1992). Though the poor developing countries were engaged in enhancing the quality of life of its citizens, they were also interested in global problems and international cooperation on the basis of basic self-reliance and equality of status (Narayanan, 1993).

Usually, welfare is measured in terms of Gross National Product, which is a measure of production, but not of equity, health and environment, security and fulfilment. Some international organisations, such as United Nations International Children Emergency Fund rank nations by infant and child mortality rather than Gross National Products Infant mortality rate cuts across belief systems. None of the oil-rich nations, that rank high in Gross National Products, has a particularly low Infant Mortality Rate. Therefore, there is no question of high quality of life. If the Infant Mortality Rate is any measure of the quality of life, then, taking into consideration the overall fall in the Infant Mortality Rate over the years, the corresponding improvement in the quality of life may be acceptable. Much more needs to be done, to provide the basic necessities for sustaining and nourishing every child in the world.

The United Nations Development Programme Human Development Report (1993) stresses people oriented development. Although the expenditure on defence has fallen, particularly in cold-war countries, yet in general, the peace dividends are not directed to development. World community has freed itself from the conventional concept of security which focuses mainly on military security. United Nations Development Programme's emphasis is on redefining security which focuses mainly on investing in people and empowering them to participate vigorously in the events and processes that shape their lives. Both the developed and the developing countries are trying to enhance the quality of life through investments in literacy, health and life-expectancy, and reduction in levels of poverty. Yet the task that lies ahead is formidable. Hundreds of millions of the poor in the developing countries continue to lead a sub-human existence. The report points out that people in rural areas are denied the opportunities for advancement available to the urban inhabitants. Worse, the process of development remains biased against women. There is a lot of unemployment. The developed countries can hardly afford to ignore these issues as they are as much as a victim of what the report calls the phenomenon of "jobless growth". The United Nations Development Programme index of human development places India 134th among 173 countries. The challenge that confronts our planners is greater than in most countries, particularly because India's economic reforms, which seek to accord a greater role to markets than hitherto, have yet to acquire a human face. The new economic policies have cast a greater burden on the poor, particularly in rural areas. To improve their living conditions, planners would do well to accept the advice of the United Nations Development Programme that the state must intervene to make markets people-friendly. The poor will not gain access to the markets unless the government reforms its credit systems, redistributes assets like land and creates visibly safe nets for the poor and those affected by sudden onslaught of competition. Apart from generous investment in education, job creation through retraining of workers and skill formation, encouragement to labour-intensive enterprises, public works programmes, planners will have to set up support-system for unemployed and the old, and malnourished children and women. The state will have to ensure basic health and education for low income groups as these are precisely the requirements which markets ignore. The human development index of Gross Domestic Product, income, education and health may not provide the true picture of human development as statistics cannot incorporate subjective factors like attitudes, values , wisdom, historical data and resource-constraints. The United Nations Development Programme itself has revised its original 1990 Human Development Index approach, and it appears to be an evolving concept. As a concept, the Human Development Index has no limit as human development is a process of expanding choices, and there can be many dimensions in which people can grow. Peace, stability and unity cannot be bought or coerced; they have to be nurtured by promoting a sensitivity to human needs and respect for rights and opinions of others. As the twentieth century draws to a close, it has become obvious that material yardsticks alone cannot serve as an adequate measure of human well-being. Even so basic an issue such as poverty has to be re-examined to take into account the psychological sense of deprivation that makes people feel poor. There seems to be an underlying assumption that an amelioration in material condition would eventually bring in its wake an improvement in social attitudes, philosophical values and ethical standard, but such axioms are hardly a faithful reflection of what actually get on in society. The unrelenting compulsions of those we already have, much to acquire more, has generated greater injustice, immorality and wretchedness than cumulative effects of the strategies of the severely underprivileged to better their lot. A narrowly focused materialism that seems to block out all consideration apparently irrelevant to one's well-bring finally blocks out what is in fact most relevant. During the "culture of contentment", which poses a challenge to the social and economic future of the United States, Professor John K. Galbraith has pointed out that the fortunate and the favoured are so preoccupied with immediate comfort and contentment that they have ceased to contemplate or respond to their own long-term well being. If the instinct to opt for narrow, short-term benefits can present significant threat to the continued prosperity and stability of a rich, industrialized state shored up by strongly established democratic institutions, how much more of a threat might it be to nations which have but recently embarked, rather unsteadily, on a grand adventure of free market economics and democratic politics? In a world which no longer accepts that "common" germs and diseases should be left unchecked to take their toll on the weak and defenceless, more attention should be paid to correcting "common" attitudes values that pose a lethal threat to humankind. Yet there is the hope that even a small light cannot be extinguished by all the darkness in the world (Suu Kyi, 1993).

It is easier to experience quality when one is not starving, or suffering from disease, when one can read and write and find a decent and satisfying job, when one's country is at peace, and when one has sufficient means to meet the average expenses of the family. However, nothing about high Gross National Product guarantees "Quality of life". American youth in their twenties do not consider material prosperity as a reliable yardstick of "good" life. On the other hand, the majority is for "rich" family life, have enough to help other, indulge in intellectual pursuits, make friendly relations with the people and lead a rich " spiritual" life (Mukherji, 1992).

The view is held that science and technology hold the panacea for all our ills. In his scholarly address, "Science and the Quality of Life" to the Indian Science Congress, Dr. Qasim (1993) also emphasized, "Nevertheless, I would like to address some important facts on the quality of life. A few decades ago the index of human activities tended to be measured by some quantitative indices, either by steel or energy consumption or per capita income or by economic growth rate. While these are undoubtedly useful in themselves, it is now being increasingly recognised, particularly during the recent past, that it is not enough to address issues of human life, merely in terms of quantitative number or economic growth, or per capita consumption. An overall improvement in the quality of life is in reality associated with the process of enlarging the range of choices of the community in terms of education, healthcare , income, employment, etc. The concept of quality of life is a holistic one, which encompasses not only the physical and economic improvements but also the social, cultural and even perhaps , political aspects of the community." This sums up the essentials. Science and technology, if properly harnessed, could ensure basic needs of food , water, housing and clothing. But again the main questions remain whether even if they are available can every one afford them? Therefore, the bounties of science and technology will mean nothing to the poor and the unemployed. As a matter of fact, poverty and hunger detract from the quality of life. While development is associated with improvement in the quality of life, it is also associated with the degradation on environment which leads to loss in the quality of life. Therefore, any improvement through science and technology for increasing development should not be at the cost of environment. Both poverty and illiteracy are in-fact "antiquality". Removal of poverty and illiteracy is a right step towards the means to improve the quality of life. Large sums of money are spent by the Planning Commission, various departments and state governments on projects to improve the lot of the poor, backward and illiterate people. How much it benefits the agencies through which this operates, and how much the poor, backward people, whose lot has not improved? It is a matter of serious concern.

Indian scientists ought to direct their energies to some of the thrust areas, which can help improve the living standards of the vast number of our countrymen. Professor C.N.R. Rao (1993), the eminent scientist, however, feels that it is not the scientists, but the whole approach towards science that is a major hurdle in the process of innovation, discovery, invention and development. More than the dwindling allocation of funds for scientific research, the attitude of the government sector is worrying. The scientific sector is today run by a bunch of bureaucrats and accountants, and they do not think we are good enough to be consulted about issues concerning us. In the name of liberalisation, today there are more controls and rules governing scientific research. If the situation continues like this, science will become extinct in the country very soon. Where is the high tech knowledge that should have come here after the economic liberalisation started? We have only got Pepsi Cola and Kentucky.Fried Chicken! How can Indian industry become competitive based on such foreign technology"? Science and scientific community should be treated with due regards as in other advanced countries of the world and provided adequate funds, so that scientists can play the role for which they are called upon at important forums such as the Indian Science Congress.

There are regions in all respects of development of the population in the country still in the grip of poverty. Lack of education, clothing, shelter, health-care facilities are still common. One of the possible ways to overcome this situation would be to adopt a change in life-style so that measure of quality of life may be possible for all. Science and technology should be applied in a manner that is soft on environment and high on production. In India , the quality of life has many dimensions. Science has struggled with human development provided some satisfaction of human wants, but not given a better, brighter self. Changes in the perception of science are becoming obvious. It is moving towards cultural dimensions, towards ecology, towards balanced development with nature. In essence, the quality of life is vitally linked with inner peace and much needed concept of optimum material needs. There is new convergence between religion and science, between matter and mind, between body and soul this is happiness, which is another name for a quality of life (Mahapatra, 1992). There is no doubt that quality of life depends not only on fulfilment of material needs, but also on personal and social fulfilment. It also depends on a harmonious equilibrium between man, nature and development.

Leading a qualitatively better life makes one creative and also equip one to benefit from the process of development. The ultimate means are the earth, the solar energy, the natural cycles that sustain and renew life and the ecosystems. These means cannot be created by man and or by science and technology. The ultimate ends are non-material and are non-quantificable. They comprise human happiness, harmony and fulfilment. The immediate means to achieve these ultimate ends need capital, labour, raw materials, energy and organization. Both the ultimate means and the intermediate means are finite, but the ends are not finite or limited.

In the 'culture of quantity', the 'culture of quality' suffers. It is postulated by scientists and economists that the simple extrapolation of present trends of increasing output is physically impossible and socially undesirable in the long-term future (Meadows *et al.*, 1975). A quantity cannot grow for ever. Such a system would be destructive of resources, environment and even society. An alternative is to aim at the quality of life. With the reorientation of life styles, population planning, rational use of resources, sustainable development, an environmental protection, equity and social justice, it should be possible to move towards a better quality of life. Wealth, education, research and many other things are needed for any civilization, but what is needed today is a revision of the ends which these means are meant to serve, which implies development of a life-style which accords to material things their legitimate secondary, and not primary place. The present logic of production is neither of life nor the society. It is subservient part of both. The destructive forces, unleased by it, cannot be brought under control unless the 'logic of production' itself is brought under control. It is of little use trying to suppress terrorism, if the production of deadly devices continues to be legitimate. Nor can the fight against pollution be successful, if the patterns of production and consumption continues to be of the scale it is today. The complexity and degree of violence which is becoming more and more apparent do not fit into the laws of the universe to which man is just as much a subject as the rest of the creation. Equally, the chance of mitigating the rate of resource depletion or of bringing harmony into relationship between those in possession of wealth and power and those without is non-existent, as long as there is no idea anywhere of enough being good and more-than-enough being evil (Schumacher, 1977). Environmental concerns will be the only meeting ground between the developed and the developing countries. That sense of survival will play a crucial role in re-uniting the world (Pitroda, 1993).

The questioning of conventional values by the young people all over the world shows the widespread unease with which our industrial culture is being viewed. Pollution must be brought under control. Population and consumption of resources must be steered towards a sustainable equilibrium. Unless this is done, civilization cannot endure. We must seek truth, goodness and beauty : *Satyam, Shivam, Sundaram*, as expressed so well in Indian culture. Each one of us can work to put our inner house, and the environment of concrete human action, the outer reality, in order, so that there is harmony and happiness, so essential for a good quality of life.

Half a century ago, it was not possible for us to view the planet earth as a whole, and understand its mechanism and interaction. Man now has the ability and the means to understand and integrate all, the human and ecological relationship for a better appreciation of their functioning. Harmony, interdependence and integration are to be viewed together. It is this responsibility of the present generation to make use of this integration and to maintain the quality of environment and enhance the quality of life. All endeavour in this quest for quality of life will be most rewarding. I would like to conclude with the following lines:

No equation can Divine the Quality of Life
No Instrument Record No Computer Conceive it.
Only Bit by Bit Can Feeling Men Lovingly
Retrieve It.

(Jerome Wiesner,
President, M.I.T., USA)

REFERENCES

Agrawal, A. *et al.* (1982), *The State of India's Environment*, New Delhi.

Agrawal, A. *et al.* (1986), *The State of India Environment*, II Report 1984-85, New Delhi.

Alvares, C. (1992), *Science, Development and Modernity*, Oxford University Press, New Delhi.

Ambirajan, S. (1992), *Partial prescription in world development, report, Frontline*, August 14, pp. 93 - 96.

Bidwia, P. (1992), *U.N. system after Rio - dismal prospects before third world, The Times of India*, July 7, p. 6.

Bock, M.N. (1990), *Restoring ecological balance: some suggestions*, *Yojana*, August 15, pp. 43 - 47.

Brundtland Commission (1987), *World Commission on Environment, Our Common Future*, Oxford University Press, New Delhi, XI, 1 and 2.

Burton, I. *et al.* (1977), *The Environment as Hazard*, London.

Clarke, J. *et al.* (1989), *Population and Disaster*, Basil Blackwell, Oxford and Cambridge, Mas.

DeCuellar, J.P. (1992), *Towards a new kind of development, The Times of India*, December 23, p. 10.

Forest Survey of India (1991), *Forest Report: Forest Cover in India*, Dehra Dun.

Gadgil, M. (1989), *Deforestation, Problems and Prospects*, S.P.W.D., New Delhi, pp. 1 - 44.

Grant, J. (1992), *UNICEF Report on State of World's Children*", Issued on December 17, reported in *The Times of India*, December 18, p. 8.

Greenstein, G. (1993), *A gentleman of the old school : Homi Bhabha and the development of science in India, Current Science*, Vol. 6 (2), January 25, pp. 121 - 128.

Grosvenor, G. M. (1993), *Water for our future, National Geographic*, Vol. 163 (1), p. 1.

Gup, T. (1992): *The world is not a theme park*, Time Essay, *Time*, Vol. 52, December 28, p. 62.

Holling, C.S. ed. (1978), *Adaptive Environmental Assessment and Management*, Chichester, U.K.

Kapoor, A. (1993), *Report on Narmada Bachao Andolan, The Times of India*, March 11, p. 3.

Kates, R.W. (1986), *Geography, Resouces and Environment: Themes from the Work of Gilbert F. White*, Vol. II, University of Chicago Press, Chicago, pp. 326-337.

Kaurance, I.K. (1992), *Life is impossible without good earth, J.G.S.I.*, Vol. 40(2), p. 88.

Kayastha, S.L. (1981), *An appraisal of water resources of India and need for National Water Policy, Geo-Journal*, Vol. 5, pp. 563 - 574.

Kayastha, S.L. (1981), *Energy problems of India*, In R.P. Chaturvedi *et al.* ed. *Socio-Economic Aspects of Energy*, Cortland, New York.

Kayastha, S.L. (1983), *Floods in India: a study of their occurrence, forecasting and control, National Geographical Journal of India*, Vol. XXIX (3 and 4), pp. 121 -141.

Kayastha, S.L. (1988), *Frontiers in Environment: Reappraisal of Environmental Problems and Policies in India*, Presidential Address, Geology and Geography Section, Indian Science Congress, Pune, Platinum Jubilee, pp. 1 - 36.

Kayastha, S.L. (1989), *Sustainability of metropolitan centres in third world countries*, In S.N. Singh *et al.* ed. *Population Transition in India*, Vol. 2, Delhi, pp. 327 - 333.

Kayastha, S.L. (1990), *Population pressure in Himachala Himalaya*, A. Ahmed *et al.* ed. *Mountain Population Pressure*, Vikas, New Delhi, pp. 27 - 55.

Kayastha, S.L. (1991), *Population, disasters and disaster-reduction strategies*, Professor N.K. Bose Memorial Lecture, *Geographical Review of India*, Vol. 53(1), pp. 1 - 14.

Kayastha, S.L. (1992), *Forests and ecology in the Himalaya*, In R.B. Singh ed. *Dynamics of Mountain Geosystems*, Ashish, New Delhi, pp. 26 - 39.

Kayastha, S.L. and B.N. Juyal (1979), *Man and Forest*, New Delhi, pp. 28 - 44.

Kayastha, S.L. and S. Mukheji (1979), *Spatial disorganisation and internal economy and development, Canadian Studies in Population*, Vol. 6, pp.45 - 61.

Kayastha, S.L. and S. Mukherji (1986), *Environmental policies in India*, In Chirs C. Park ed. *Environmental Policies: An International Review*, Croom Helm, London, pp. 223 - 258.

Khosla, A. (1974): *Population and environment in India's development*, In Ashish Bose *et al.* ed. *Population in India's Development, 1947-2000*, Vikas, New Delhi, pp. 45 - 56.

Khushoo, T.N. (1986), *Environmental Priorities in India and Sustainable Development*, India Science Congress, New Delhi.

Kochar, R.K. (1992), *Science in British India, I, colonial Tool, Current Science*, Vol. 63(11), pp. 689 - 694.

Krishnamurti, B.V. and U. Schoettli (1965), *Environment in India's religious and cultural heritage*, In J.B. Bandopadhyay *et al.* ed. *India's Environment, Crises and Responses*, Natraj, Dehra Dun, pp. 159 - 171.

Kuhnen, F. (1992), *Sustainability, regional development and marginal locations, Applied Geography and Development*, Vol. 39, Tubringen, pp. 101 - 105.

Lal, S. (1993), *The future is sad news: review article on Paul Kennedy's book, Preparing for the Twenth-First Century, The Times of India*, March 20, p.10.

Linden, E. (1993), *Will the system defeat Al Gore*, Time Essay, *Time*, No. 5, February 1, p. 56.

Lowenthal, D. (1973), *Environmental Perception and Behaviour*, Chicago University Press, Chicago.

Mahapatra, S. (1992), *The business of living and quality of life, Everyman's Science*, Vol. XXVII, Vol. 4 and 5, p. 78.

Mahbubul, H. (1992), *Human Development Report, U.N.D.P., New York*, Oxford University Press, New Delhi.

Meadows, D.H. *et al.* (1975), *The Limits to Growth*, Pan Books, London.

Moddie, A.D. (1988), *The urban apoclypse, Imprint*, February, Bombay, pp. 28 - 30.

Mukherji, S.K. (1992), *Sustainable development, Everyman's Science*, Vol. XXVII (4 and 5), pp. 115 - 116.

Mukherji, S.K. (1992), "Sustainable development", *Everyman's Science*, Vol. XXVII (1), March, pp. 1 - 2.

Munn, R.E. (1979), *Environmental Impact Assessment, SCOPE 5*, John Wiley, New York, pp. 1 - 190.

Naik, M.K. (1993), *Sustainability and the environment with special reference to food production in the semi – arid tropics, Everyman's Science*, February -March, pp. 11 - 13.

Narayanann, K.R. (1993), *Inaugural address, forestry forum of developing countries, The Times of India*, New Delhi, September 2, p. 5.

Pant, K.C. (1992), *Valedictory address*, In R.P. Misra ed. *Environment Ethics*, Delhi, pp. 137 - 143.

Pitroda, S. (1993), *Exploding Freedom: Roots in Technology*, Allied Publisher New Delhi, pp. 1 - 192.

Postel, S. (1992), *Denial in the decisive decade*, In L. R. Brown ed. *State of the World*, Norton, New York, pp. 1 - 8.

Qasi, S.Z. (1993), *Science and Quality of Life*, Presidential Address, 80th India Science Congress, Goa, pp. 1 - 13.

Rao, C.N.R. (1993), *Aesthetics, economics and status of basic sciences in India*, Symposium, Indian National Science Academy, New Delhi, Report August 4, *The Times of India*, August 5, p. 3.

Raza, M. (1989), *Regional Development as Eco-Development*, Address, 11th Indian Geography Congress, NAGI, October 3, Delhi University, Delhi.

Repetto, R. (1986), *Skimming the Water: Rent Seeking on Performance of Public Irrigation System*, World Resources Institute, Washington D.C.

Repetto, R. (1988), *The Forest or the Tree? Government Policies and Misuse of Forest Resources*, World Resourees Institute, Washington D.C.

Roy, S.K. (1993): "Drowned in the deluge of development", *The Times of India*, August 13, p. 8.

Satapathy, R. (1993), *Report on Konark beach report development, The Times of India*, August 20, p. 3.

Schatzl, L. (1993), *Regional economic policy in the growth countries of east-south-east Asia, Applied Geography and Regional Development*, Vol. 41, Tubingen, pp. 7 - 25.

Schumacher, E.F. (1977), *Small is Beautiful*, Radhakrishna, New Delhi, pp. 276 - 279.

Shah, S.M. (1992), *Towards sustainable development*, *Yojana*, Vol. 36, September 16, pp. 18 - 21.

Sharma, A. (1987*), Resources and Human Well-Being: Inputs from Science and Technology*, Indian Science Congress Association , Calcutta.

Strong, M.F. (1991), *For the ultimate security in survey of environment, 1991, The Hindu*, Madras, pp.11 - 13.

Suresh, N. (1993), *Report on environment and Montreal Protocol, The Times of India*, March 14, p. 12.

Suu Kyi, A.S. (1993), *Joyce Pearce memorial lecure, Oxford University, 1993*, Report, *The Times of India*, May 20, p. 8.

Swaminathan, M.S. (1993), *Agriculture situation in India*, Doordarshan Telecast of Interview, February 2, 8.30 A.M.

Tickell, C. (1991), *Prognosis for a planet, Geographical Magazine*, November, pp. 15 - 17.

Tickell, C. (1991), *Reaching for the Summit, Geographical Magazine*, October, pp. 14 - 18.

Tiwari, N.D. (1980), *Report of the Committee for Recommending Legislative Measures and Administrative Machinery for Ensuring Environmental Protection*, Department of Environment, Government of India, New Delhi.

Tolba, M. (1988), *Call to halt destruction of forests*, Report, *The Statesman*, New Delhi, March 17, p. 8.

U.N.D.P. Report (1993), *Human Development Report*, UNDP, New Delhi: Oxford University Press, pp. 1 - 230.

Vohra, B.B. (1980), *A Policy on Land and Water*, Department of Environment, Government of India, New Delhi, pp. 1 - 31.

White, G.F. (1974), *Natural Hazards*, Oxford University Press, London.

White, G.F. (1986), *Foreward, Nature on the Rampage: Our Violent Earth*, National Geographic Society, Washington, D.C.

World Development Report (1992), *Environment and Development, The World Bank*, Oxford University Press, New York.

Parmeshwar Dayal
1920 -

Among the handful of doyens in Indian Geography – Dayal stands apart as a legend in his own time. Conservative in manners, aloof in style and thoughtfully weighed in speech and action, Dayal commands outright respect. His prestige is based more on merit than position. Chairperson at the department of geography, Patna University for three decades, few among his colleagues can recall an incident or decision where Dayal faltered or stooped. Serving the cause of the discipline, Dayal's meticulous punctuality of being in office from ten to five set a culture of work. Though Dayal was not the founder of the department, yet as its first chairperson, he irrigated its various needs with a steel like gentleness. That many of the alumni of this department today occupy esteemed positions in India and abroad is a result of the high standards of education they had gathered at their alma-mater. If the department of geography at Patna today refers to a glorious past, the illuminating light goes to none other than Dayal.

Creating a disciplined atmosphere for teaching and research, Dayal fostered an exemplary solidarity within the department. Assured of a cooperative working spirit Dayal netted credos in numerous ways. Research projects from the Ministry of Defence , Planning Commission and the Indian Council of Social Science Research being one among the many. These paved way for the department to be recognized as the Center for Development Studies under the auspices of the University Grants Commission. He initiated and persuaded the inauguration of a number of departments of geography in Bihar. This earned Dayal additional respect. When Bihar formed its State Education Board in 1975, Dayal was its first chairperson. Among a string of his predecessors and contemporaries Dayal stands out as the first geographer to be honored with the position of vice-chancellor in 1975. It is different that he chose to resign within a span of two years rather than buckle under political pressure. A hallmark of an exalted person is discerned when he testifies that 'prestige is more important than post.'

Upholding integrity, a shower of positions aggregated towards Dayal. The Simmon Fellowship took him to the University of Manchester as a visiting lecturer in 1956-1957. He is among the four geographers in India who have has been elected as the President of geology and geography section of the Indian Science Congress. Diverse in expression was his association with Patna University: for eight years he was president of Patna Union Teachers Association, for ten years director, Indian Administrative Services Coaching Centre, for two terms principal of Patna College and for five years editor of the Transactions of the Indian Council of Geographers.

A fragrance about Dayal lingered at places he worked. This is evident from the experience at the University of Sri Lanka at Colombo where Dayal served as lecturer for a short 18 months in 1948 –1949. Repeated requests by Iver Jenning, the vice-chancellor of the University of Sri Lanka for Dayal's return did not meet with success. A visit to the University of Canberra, Australia opened another. set of similar opportunities. Dayal declined – Patna benefited. Patriotism too is a hallmark of the legendary.

Canons to the scholastic regard which Dayal drew is evident on page 984 – 988 of the Encyclopedia Britannica which carries a write up on the geography of Bihar authored by him. " Dayal's analysis of the correlation of soil, climate, topography and harvests of Bihar extremely interesting, unfortunately too detailed to summarize" a note by Spate in 'India and Pakistan: A General and Regional Geography' is another tribute to him. Cherishing quality over quantity, Dayal's list of publications are a modest, but meaningful number. Five out of the eight books authored by Dayal are texts. Simple titles like Commercial Geography, An outline of Practical Geography, Study of Modern Geography and one on Geomorphology give direct utility to school students and for those at the under-graduate level. Most books are in Hindi and thus confirm that Dayal gave priority to the grassroot needs of the discipline at the cost of his own research interest. Belonging to the traditional school of writing, Dayal had a disdain for the edited and co- authored works. Sixty per cent of his books and eighty-five per cent research articles are self authored.

Born on 15th August, 1920, in Bind village in the Nalanda District of

Bihar , Dayal's attachment to books all day long did not go unnoticed by his parents. When the day to finance Dayal's education to England arrived, the family dipped into its savings with a matter of pride. Stepping on an overloaded troopship which housed five thousand rather than its usual one thousand passengers meant that Dayal's journey from Bombay to Liverpool was far from pleasant. But for Dayal these were trivial concerns. The war ridden Britain where food was rationed and inflation ran amuck were also taken in stride – the London School of Economics, geography and a joint supervision under Dudley Stamp and O.H.K. Spate was all that mattered.

An event in history had taken a turn in 1947. When Dayal left, India had been a British colony –he returned to a free India. The enthusiasm to dedicate and work for the nation was on high ground. Dayal had a legendary mission: to build the discipline of geography on the home turf.

The Agenda for Indian Geography

P. DAYAL

I would like first of all to express my most sincere thanks to the members of the National Association of Geographers, India for unanimously electing me President of the National Association for 1995. I greatly value this honour and am touched by the confidence and trust reposed in me. At this moment I am reminded of my teachers of Patna and Aligarh - Professors S.C. Chatterji, Kazi Saiduddin Ahmad, S. Muzaffer Ali, S.M. Tahir Rizvi who along with Professor S.P. Chatterjee in Calcutta and Geoge Kuriyan in Madras steered the course of Indian Geography in those early years. I am also reminded of my teachers at the London School of Economics – Professor L.Dudley Stamp and O.H.K. Spate, both world geographers with immense interest in India, whose impact on Indian geography has indeed been profound and far-reaching. I owe a special debt of gratitude to them for the geographical insight and training that they provided and for their affection and generosity. We cannot fail to remember at this moment Professor Moonis Raza, the principal architect of the National Association of Geographers, India and its moving spirit until his untimely death a few months ago in the United States of America after a protracted illness.

Geography entered the portals of Indian universities nearly 75 years ago, the first undergraduate department being started at Lahore, now in Pakistan, in 1920, incidentally this happens to be the year of my birth, followed by Aligarh (1924) and Patna (1927). Aligarh Muslim University was the first to start post-graduate teaching in geography in 1931. The progress initially was slow and halting and by 1950, besides Aligarh, only seven more universities - Calcutta, Allahabad, Banaras, Agra, Punjab (Chandigarh), Madras and Patna had the distinction of starting post-graduate studies in geography. In the years that followed the initiation of planning. Indian geography witnessed a new upsurge and a sudden flowering with dramatic expansion in the number of university departments and use in the

---

17th Indian Geography Congress
Hyderabad, 1994 December

number of teachers and students with concurrent increase in research activity and publications. Geography has established itself as a university discipline and there is hardly any Indian university that does not have a geography department. Indian geographic research covers a wide spectrum with emphasis in agricultural geography and landuse, urban geography, population geography and regional development and the preparation of various kinds of maps and atlases. They have also involved themselves in the study of problems of development and environmental issues and in a variety of collaborative work with allied disciplines.

Even so, geographic research and studies would seem to suffer from certain obvious deficiencies. and imbalances, and a lot of conscious and cooperative effort is needed to bring it close to the status that geography enjoys in countries like the United Kingdom, Russia, Germany, France, the United States of America and some other countries.

The developments in German geography from 1952 to 1992 have been reviewed in a recent publication entitled '40 years after : German Geography, Developments, Trends and Prospects 1952-92', edited by Eckart Ehlers (1992). It is an excellent report of the trends in the major systematic fields and gaps in knowledge that need further research and is of great international significance in view of the importance of German geographical research. One would very much wish for a similar report on Indian geography to cover the entire period after 1950 to present a connected picture and detailed scholarly critique of the achievements and tasks, the strength and weaknesses and the trends and prospects of geographical studies and research in the country. I cannot think of a more appropriate organization than the National Association of Geographers to undertake such a task by involving the best scholars in the various branches of our discipline. The sooner it is done, the better it would be for the health and growth of the subject.

While the general and overall trend is one of steady progress, the last decade or so would appear to have witnessed a leveling off of this growth, and a standstill or plateau-like situation would seem to prevail and characterise both geographical effort and visibility. The general financial crunch in the universities resulting in cut in library, laboratory and field work grants, starting of post-graduate colleges without financial or academic support such as in Bihar the craze for doctorate degree without adequate preparation resulting in repetitions, stereotyped and sometimes even spurious work, the virtual collapse of the university system in some states, the blatant use of unfair means in examination have all taken a heavy toll of standards in many subjects. In geography the lack of funds have been a serious handicap in introduction of new techniques and equipment, and the problem has been further compounded by the retirement of a fairly large number of teachers who provided erstwhile leadership within a relatively short period of time. The governmental apathy and lack of adequate appreciation of the work being done by geographers has also been a contributing factor. You will, no doubt, be surprised to know that the Government of Bihar had recently decided to shut down the Centre for Development Studies attached to the Department of Geography, Patna University, on account of financial crunch in spite of the commendable work which it had been doing for the past several years.

It cannot, however, be denied that even under these difficult conditions, there are conscientious and dedicated workers who have found time and energy to devote to serious study and research and produce work of merit.

I would like to utilise this occasion to place before you for your consideration my views on some of the tasks which need our immediate attention and which deserve a high priority on our agenda if Indian geography is to move step in step with the advanced countries of the world and improve its academic visibility and enhance its social utility. The academic status of geography and its effective role in national reconstruction and international understanding are interdependent. Academic excellence will prepare us for a more meaningful and concrete role in economic and social development and active participation in the solution of problems of national and global concern will strengthen our academic base and enhance our prestige as an academic discipline. We have to pursue both these goals, concertedly and relentlessly. The applied side of geography to my mind is as important as its theoretical base. The two are not exclusive but complementary, each strengthening the other.

One of the first tasks would appear to be reorientation of our course of study to include more of physical geography to take care of the growing awareness about the natural environment and its sustainability. Our courses of study at the moment are too heavily tilted in favour of human geography, and physical geography occupies rather peripheral position in our programmes of study and research. This imbalance has to be corrected and a better balance struck between physical and human geography irrespective of whether we emphasise landscape – a real differentiation approach or man-environment relations type of approach. Enormous changes have taken place in the methodology and content of human geography providing deep analysis of the human variables in geography, aided by a highly sophisticated form of quantitative spatial analysis. Economic, social, cultural and psychological man figures so much more prominently than 'man on earth' in the conceptual framework of human geography that the ties between human and physical geography have received a severe jolt and have been loosened to such an extent that there appears to be hardly any need to relate human geographical research to the complexities and intricacies of the physical environment and the relevant environment variable. The concept of eco-system and eco- development and the unity of the system of interdependencies through the mechanism of interactions between social man and non-human nature (Raza, 1990), and the growing realization that man must learn to live in harmony with nature, call for a new perspective and a new understanding of the complex and dynamic environment and the inter-related and inter-dependent nature of all living things and their relationships with land, air and water; physical geography has thus come to assume a new meaning and new significance in man-land relationship, and has to be pursued as such. Physical geography as it is taught in our universities is mostly geomorphology, a list of climatology and very little of bio-geography. This internal imbalance in physical geography needs correction to include the totality of the environment and the spatial element in its make-up.

An integrated physical geography has been rediscovered under the name of environmental science largely by non-geographer. The contents of environmental science are identical with physical geography and the differences, if any, are confined to approaches rather than content. Fear has been expressed in some quarters that this may sound the deathknell of physical geography and physical geography may cease to be an integral part of geographical studies. Environmental science, born out of the environmentalist movement, emphasises three main problems of vital concern to the survival of mankind – population increase, quality of environment, and the decreasing supply of resources. Though man-environment theme is a vital part of the geographical tradition, geographers have stood somewhat apart from the environmentalist movement. Indeed , our concept of environment has been broader than that of the environmentalist movement. We see things within a spatially real framework. Land and its attributes, relative locations, networks and other spatial phenomena like climate, soils and vegetation are vital to the geographers as environmental elements, and so is the legitimate and necessary use of natural resources. Even so, geographers as a group have not taken the lead in the interdisciplinary study of environment and have preferred to leave the fields to be dominated by biologists, ecologists, engineers, with some interest shown in by economists, political scientists and lawyers. Whether physical geography reappears in its new garb as environmental science is immaterial so long as the problem is considered to be real and significant, and geographers are adequately trained in this area to be able to make worthwhile contributions for only then we can expect them to play dominant roles in environmental affairs.

Another item which should be high on our agenda is improvement in our cartographic interpretive and analytical tools and skills by provision of up-to-date quantitative techniques, aerial photo-interpretation and use of satellite imagery and geographic information system in our curriculum, fully supported by well equipped laboratory facilities and trained staff. This should be considered a thrust area upon which will depend in large measure our capability to produce studies which may be judged to be of high competence by the scientific community. Lack of funds may be a major constraint in the initial stages but it should not be difficult to build up the necessary facilities over a period of time with the financial support of the University Grants Commission and the other appropriate governmental agencies.

Quantitative revolution which started in the West in the fifties came to India about a decade later and the use of quantitative techniques is now fairly widespread among Indian geographers. On the whole this has had a salutary effect and has made possible more accurate measurement of phenomena and more sophisticated explanatory mechanism, but by no means has it led to any qualitative revolution and at its worst it has been used as mere embellishment to conceal lack of thought or judgement behind a façade of formulae and symbols a lot of sound and fury signifying nothing. This is being said not to decry the use of quantitative techniques by Indian geographers but merely to point out that quantification by itself is not geography. It is only a sophisticated tool and needs to be used wisely and properly. Unfortunately, there is sill dearth of teachers who are fully acquainted with its intricacies, niceties, and pitfalls, and many institutions do not possess the necessary infrastructure and staff to train students and to meaningfully employ quantitative techniques in research.

We are faced with the further new challenge of space technology and its application in geographical studies. It is most appropriate and timely that the 16th India Geography Congress is being hosted by National Remote Sensing Agency, Hyderabad, and the focal theme is Space Technology and Geography. Space technology has opened up a whole new field for data collection, mapping and geographical interpretation. Aerial photographs followed by satellite imagery in the recent past have made the task of the geographer vastly more easy and exciting, provided he equips himself with the necessary skills and expertise. Published secondary data usually take time to be available, and primary data collection is time-consuming, expensive, and beset with a number of other problems which affect its accuracy and coverage. Remote Sensing is a new and powerful tool for landform analysis and mapping of both the land form and land cover attributes including the functional uses of land, and can be used not only for landform analysis and land use assessment but also for monitoring dynamic environmental characteristics like vegetation cover, river behavior, flood-plain zoning, desert sand spread, landslides etc. The National Remote Sensing Agency has done highly valuable work in the mapping of forest cover and the identification of degraded land and wasteland (Planning commission, 1992) The School of Earth Sciences, Bharathidasan University, Tiruchirapalli, organised a seminar on 'Thrust areas in the application of remote sensing' in August 1990 which emphasised the role of remote sensing technology in landscape mapping, river systems, locating ground water and mineral deposits and for flood control measures and the application of remote sensing techniques in soil, forestry, agriculture, coastal zone and marine resources and environmental studies. Application of these techniques for surface water body mapping, surface water budgeting and ground water management and also for analysing temporal changes through multi-dated satellite data was presented by the National Remote Sensing Agency. It was also pointed out that Remote has got great potentiality in monitoring the salinisation in command areas, in forest inventory programmes, and also in crop area estimation. In neighbouring Bangladesh, the Bangladesh Space Research and Remote Sensing Organisation is headed by a geographer and geographers are playing a leading role in interpreting and using landsat imagery for thematic mapping and compiling land use inventories with accuracy and speed (Elahi, 1986). The use of satellite imagery supplemented with low-level aerial photography has been made for study of physical and biotic resources in Sudan and which has resulted in much time saving in survey, evaluation , planning and implementation stages (Wilson, 1979).These surveys have formed the basis of plans for the development of Southern Darfur almost in its entirety. The Centre of Studies in Tropical Geography, France, has made extensive use of landsat data and field studies for agroecological mapping of the dynamics of eco-systems and societies in Thailand, Malaysia and Venezuela (Racine, 1985). Interpretation of landsat imagery supported by field investigation in the Jaisalmer district of the Great Indian Desert by members of the Central Arid Zone Research Institute at Jodhpur have revealed some hitherto unknown, abandoned and lost courses of the former Saraswati river which may provide clues to the early settlements and the spread of Indus Valley civilization in the region (Ghose *et al.* 1979). These are just a few examples of the very wide application of remote sensing in geographical studies and research and in the effective management of natural resources.

Geographic Information System is yet another related area which has opened new opportunities for geographers. Together with remote sensing , it has helped raise the effectiveness and status of geography as the only discipline which can bridge the gap between physical and social sciences and provide the much-needed integration and synthesis.

It needs no gainsaying that for the effective implementation of the above programmes it would be necessary to draw more students and teachers with some training in mathematics. At the moment very few of our students and teachers possess even a modicum of mathematical background. Haggett has pointed out that among American students majoring in geography between 1960 and 1965 over 75 per cent offered mathematics as a supporting subject (Haggett., 1972). Even if 50 per cent of our students have a training in mathematics, it would make for vast improvement and inject new rigour and vigour in all fields of geography.

I would now like to draw your attention to the rather mundane subject of text books but one which constitutes a glaring weakness in our programme of university studies. There is a lamentable lack of good and up-to-date reading material on Indian geography for our university students and for those taking the State and Union Public Service Commission examinations. We search in vain for a comprehensive and up-to-date book on the systematic geography of India or the Geography of Indian Agriculture or the Industrial Geography of India or the Population Geography of India or even the Regional Geography of India. The revised edition of 'India and Pakistan' by Spate and Learmonth which continues to be most frequently consulted as the most authoritative work does not take us beyond 1967 and R. L. Singh's Regional Geography of India also dated 1971, India, Resources , Potentialities and Planning' by Ashok Dutt and associates (1973) and "India": Economic Resource Base and Contemporary Political Patterns" by Sukhwal are written essentially with the American student in mind. It is high time that we do something to improve this disgraceful and disastrous situation and take it up as a matter of urgent and serious concern.

There is also the need for state geographies which may highlight the physical, economic and human resources and the prospects for development , given the present position of economic and social realties. The state geographies will also enable us to understand the regional ethos, problems, and aspirations in a better way and help us to integrate them in the national matrix. The recently published, "India: a Regional Interpretation" by C.D. Deshpande (1992) is a refreshing addition, showing sensivity to identification of regions by people themselves with language as the main criterion but not mechanically based on the linguistic states. It is, however, a comparatively short study and provides only glimpses of the richness and variety of the Indian physical and cultural landscape. Regional cultures which have developed as ways of living in harmony with the regional milieu are alive and vibrant, characterised by solidarity and shared economic and cultural pursuits that cut across religions, communal and ethnic divides. Regional cultures as expression of cultural synthesis have immense potentialities for national integration if properly interpreted.

In Germany and Switzerland and other parts of Europe where geography is well developed, school children are taught about the environment, history and culture of their home regions through the medium of regional atlases of high level of cartographic craftsmanship. This makes learning about places a highly enjoyable and intellectually stimulating activity and develops a sense of respect for the environment , pride in one's home region and its traditions and love for the country of which the regions form a part. Schwartzberg (1981) has drawn our attention to the need for preparation of similar atlases for Indian high schools for bringing out the regional cultural diversity of India which, according to him, presents both an opportunity and a challenge to Indian geographers to make a worthwhile contribution to education, cultural enrichment, and to the furtherance of our discipline. Intelligently conceived, diligently compiled, and properly executed, with brief texts to supplement the maps, regional atlases can gain great respect for geography in India and enhance its usefulness. One will have, of course , to guard against the dangers of chauvinism and populism. The treatment of many topics will call for interdisciplinary effort and some will demand original field-work. Such an enterprise will instill in the students a sense of regional pride, contributing to rather than acting against a more encompassing love for the country.

Our research effort has been almost exclusively confined to India. While India has to be of necessity the main focus of our enquiry , we cannot completely shut ourselves from the rest of the world. In fact, one of the great attractions of our subject is the window that it opens upon the diversity and interdependence of the world and brings us face to face with problems that are global in nature or those that affect more than one country and which can be understood and analysed only against a larger canvas. To understand and solve many of our own problems, there is need for study of the developing world especially the developing countries of Asia and Africa, and to start with we may concentrate on our neighbors or other specific areas with which India has close relations. A first hand study and understanding of the problems of our neighbours is of the utmost importance and deserves a high priority as many of our problems have close links with them and can be seen in correct perspective only in relations to the countries that surround us. Then there are countries with whom we have close economic, cultural, and commercial ties, and academic contacts with them are likely to be extremely fruitful and rewarding. The educational needs of the subject also require specialists with first hand knowledge of specific areas. In view of the financial constraints that may come in the way, we may make a beginning with the countries of South-East Asia and West Asia as well as Africa. In fact, we should think in terms of establishing a full geographic documentation centre on developing countries with special reference to India as an active monitor of the dynamics of change in these regions of rapid economic and social change.

Even a cursory review of our research publications on India would show that we have tended to neglect certain very vital and promising areas from our enquiry. These include Geomorphology, Hydrology, Climatology, Bio-geography as also Historical Geography, Political Geography and Industrial Geography. Even though geography was guided in its early years by geologist geographers, this did not lead to great development of geomorphology or other branches of physical geography in India, like it did in Britain , in spite of the fascinating physical diversity of India. In view of the growing importance of the complex physical reality coupled with the need for comprehensive understanding of the physical resource base in eco-system based approach, it is imperative that this imbalance is set right at the earliest.

India provides very rich materials for the study of historical geography with its long tradition of peasant settlements, its ancient religious centres, and the routes of movement along the length and breadth of the country as well as the evolution of ancient, medieval, pre-industrial, and industrial towns. Historical geography needs impetus not only for the promotion of tourism but also for the widespread importance of a historical or developmental approach in the study of human affairs . In Political Geography, the geo-strategic importance of the Indian ocean, India's relations with its neighbours and better understanding of their mutual problems, interests and conflicts, boundary disputes external and internal, the phenomenon of increasing violence and crime and their relationships with caste, politics and unemployment, the need for national integration vis-à-vis regional aspirations, state union relations and electoral participation, the problems and perceptions of religious, ethnic and linguistic groups all present challenging subjects for scientific and perceptive enquiry and are of great practical importance.

Neglect of industrial geography by Indian geographers is rather intriguing, as industry has been perceived to be the main catalyst in our programmes for economic development. While there is great scope for technological and organizational changes in our agriculture leading to improved productivity and employment, it is generally recognised that there are far too many people on land than it can support, and diversification of our economy by the development of large and small scale industries is the only way of providing more avenues of employment and improving their economic condition. While large scale iron and steel, heavy engineering and heavy chemical industries offer little choice of their geographic patterns and are less labour intensive , there is a large group of consumer goods and processing industries in the sporadic and footloose groups which can be located in small towns and villages dispersed all over the country, fostering regional development. Such industries have large employment potential and have a strong leverage effect on commercial and service activities in their neighbourhood and cause minimum geographic migration of labour (Dayal, 1970).

The importance of changing technology, the development of new processes and new users of raw-materials for diffusion of industry have to be constantly borne in mind. Use of bagasse as a raw-material for paper has led to the development of paper factories in sugarcane growing areas. The technical advances have made possible the use of a variety of raw-materials for the cement industry – limestone, sea-sand, marl, lime-shell, blast furnace slag and calcium carbonate sludge, and have thus made possible a wide dispersal of the cement industry in India with a fairly balanced distribution or productive capacity in the different regions. (Dayal 1964).

It has been suggested that the most congenial and fruitful setting for new industrial activity is to be found in the small and middle-sized towns in the population range 20,000 to 3,00,000. These provide, as it were, the golden middle between the technical infeasibility of village centred locations and the obvious disadvantages of metropolitan centres with already a high concentration of industry and commerce (Dewas, 1965). Such an approach will make for maximum contact between agriculture and industry and will involve minimum geographic migration of population. Our knowledge about the characteristics of the towns of the above size, their administrative, educational, health and water facilities, power supply and transport connections, the size and character of local markets, the quantity and proximity of natural resources is however, extremely inadequate, and it is necessary to prepare a complete inventory of the salient characteristics of these towns.

Not infrequently industrial location represents the key to the whole process of planning, especially in the relatively backward and underdeveloped areas. The decentralised pattern of industrial development can be articulated through an efficient system of growth centres, functionally connected with industries in major cities on the one hand and the countryside on the other. The village and small scale industries, of course, occupy a special place in the strategy of labour-intensive industrial growth and are expected to have a higher growth rate than that of the manufacturing sector in the 8th plan.

Intimately connected with industrialisation is the question of adequate and sustainable power supply. Industry is the heaviest consumer of commercial energy in India and used more than half of the national commercial energy consumption. Energy production continues to lag behind consumption, and energy consumption is heavily dependent on imports of crude oil and production of petroleum products while domestic oil prodution continues to stagnate. Natural gas which can be used for power generation as well as for producing valuable chemicals is mostly flared at the moment. There is the need to restrict oil imports to a reasonable level and to stop the flaring of natural gas at the earliest. Only about 18 per cent of the hydroelectric potential has been developed and there is urgent need to accelerate development of this renewable energy resource especially for increasing power availability during peak periods. Some of the new decentralised renewable sources based on non-conventional technologies such as wind and solar energy, bio-mass and bio-gas have considerable potential. Coal and lignite are major energy resources available in the country but the coal industry continues to be beset by problems of low productivity and transport bottlenecks and the thermal power station by low generation levels. It is going to be a challenging task to meet the growing demand for energy and will call for massive effort towards utilisation of renewable sources of energy, with a major stress on conservation and efficiency.

Human development is of course, the ultimate goal of all planning, and it is towards this end that employment generation, population control, literacy, education , health, drinking water, and provision of adequate, good and basic infrastructure are listed as the priorities in the Eight Plan. All these have powerful geographical dimensions which geographers must explore and bring to light for purposeful use.

Geographers can indeed play a vital role in planning by their active participation in the preparation of various kinds of specialised maps (geographer's most expressive and effective tool) of land lineaments and its actual and potential resources based on data available from latest technology and the maps of population and its attributes in all its mutifarious aspects, maps for location of industry, for planning a more efficient system of transportation network or determination of hydroelectric and imitation possibilities. Secondly, he can assist in preparation of national and regional resource inventories which are absolutely basic to a programme of planned development. Thirdly, he can provide a regional framework for planning based on his understanding of the intricate inter relationships of the various components and their spatial distribution and the precise identification of backward areas and their potential (Dayal 1967). His sound knowledge of the ground realities for planning and the inter-relationships of the various components of the landscape qualifies him also for participation in the formation of policy and the work of coordination. Geographers who take up planning as a career may of course obtain further specialised training in urban and regional planning.

Unfortunately, the involvement of Indian geographers in planning till today has been only marginal, and a more determined effort is needed to make concerned agencies and the government is aware of the contributions that geographers can make to planning. Geographers have missed many an opportunity in the past and have failed to take their rightful place. Let them not miss it any longer, for now is the time to demonstrate their worth, capability, and relevance to tasks of national reconstruction by projecting the viewpoints of geography as a truly integrating discipline among the natural and social sciences, with a holistic understanding of social dynamics as well as physical factors in man-environment relationships. A wider appreciation of the eco-system approach to regional development, the emphasis on sustainable development (Blowers, 1993), and reduction in regional disparities provide a congenial atmosphere for the acceptance of geographical concepts and methods. Application of remote sensing techniques for land evaluation and computerised cartography have made possible rigorous analysis of the resource base and formulation of development strategies appropriate to different regions. Geographers should respond not by trying to fit Indian reality into a ready-made frame of hastily adjusted western models but by unhesitatingly taking up important questions of national and social concern which provide exciting fields of enquiry – communalism, violence and regional tensions, rural-urban migrations

(Gilbart, 1993) unemployment, poverty the doubtful success of rural development programmes, problems of the urban poor (Kundu, 1993) the scheduled castes, and women, child labour , health and nutrition (Gillespic and Mc Neik, 1992), the geographical implications of the new economic policy, industrial location, transport network, power supply, together with problems of deforestation and land degradation, utilisation of wasteland, implications of green revolution likely to be followed by the blue revolutions (Coull, 1993) the coastal and the hill eco-systems and many other problems. We should not be satisfied merely with the analysis of results of the policies but must also analyse the decision making processes and the political engineering for development, keeping in focus the spatial dimensions and the grassroot realities. This is bound to create greater public awareness about the work of geographers; about what geographers do and can do. But even more important than public awareness is the understanding, depth and realism in our own studies which can be achieved only if we sharpen our tools and techniques and improve our skills of mapping, analysis and presentation. Geography, said Mackinder (1921) 'Is inherently not an elementary but an advanced subject. It postulates both scientific and human knowledge' Wooldridge (1950), in his Presidential address to the Institute of British Geographers , spoke of what he termed 'the high calling of geographer'. Let us seek to be worthy of our claims in both teaching and research and the application of our knowledge to human welfare.

Geographers are interested in the earth's diversity and man's ingenuity in coping with the process of making a living. Our discipline teaches us to care about our terrestrial inheritance and the ways in which it is used. We must try to use our skills as best as we can, both to alleviate human misery and deprivation and to work for the conservation and stability of our country's and the planets eco-systems. Geography can do a lot to improve the lives of our men and women by its concern for better knowledge and the wise use of the earth's resources. We have new technical aids and many more people at work improving the theoretical as well as the scientific bases of our subject. 'The world of the future will have still more need of its geographers than the world of the past' (Wise). Let us reassert our faith in the long established themes of the subject-diversity of the earth's surface and the generosity of nature, human ingenuity in adapting the physical environment, conservation and the wise use of resources, the value of maps and field studies and geographical research into problems of social concern.

Let me once again thank you for the honour you have done me. I shall try my best to serve the cause of geography during my tenure. I have no doubt that the National Association will make every possible effort to improve the visibility of geography and to obtain for its rightful place in planning the development of our country.

REFERFENCE

Ahmad, A. (1985 and 1986-87), *ICSSR Journal of Abstracts and Reviews: Geography*, Vol. III (1 and 2), Vol. IV(1 and 2).

Blowers, A. (1993), *Environmental policy: the quest for sustainable development, Urban Studies*, Vol. 30, pp. 775 - 796.

Brown, E.H. (1975), *The content and relationships of physical geography, Geographical Journal*, Vol. 141, pp. 35 - 48.

Chatterjee, S.P. (1964), *Fifty Years of Science in India: Progress of Geography*, Calcutta.

Chatterjee, S.P. (1968), *Progress of Geography in India, 1964-68*, Calcutta.

Chatterjee, S.P. (1973), *A Decade of (1963-72) Science in India: Progress of Geography*, Calcutta.

Coull, J. R. (1993), *Will blue revolution follow the green revolution? The modern upsurge of aquaculture, Area*, Vol. 25, pp. 350 - 357.

Dayal, P. (1964), *Aspects of industrial location in India, Transactions of Indian Council of Geographers*, Vol. 1, pp. 1 - 12.

Dayal, P. (1967), *Geography and Economic Planning*, Inaugural Address, Summer School in Regional Development, Ravishankar University Raipur.

Dayal, P. (1970), *Regional planning and industrial location in India*, In K.N. Das ed. *Essays in Geography*, Bhagalpur University.

Deshpande, C.D. (1992), *India: A Regional Interpretation*, ICSSR and Northern Book Centre, New Delhi.

Dutt, A.K. ed. (1972), *India: Resource, Potentialities and Planning*, Kendal Hunt Publishing Company, Iowa, USA.

Ehlers, E. ed. (1992), *40 Years After German Geography: Developments, Trends and Prospects, 1952-92*. A Report to the International Geographical Union, Bonn, Deutsche Forschungsgemeinschaft and Tubingen: Institute for Scientific Cooperation.

Elahi, K.M (1986), *Use of Remote Sensing Techniques in Contemporary Geographic Studies in Bangladesh.* Paper presented at International Symposium on Traditional Geography, Modern Geography and Future Trends in Geography, Department of Geography and Applied Geography, North Bengal University, Siliguri, Darjeeling, December.

Ghose, B. *et al.* (1979), *The lost course of the Saraswati river in the Great Indian Desert: new evidence from landsat imagery, Geographical Journal*, Vol. 145, pp. 446 - 451.

Gilbert, A. (1993), *Third world cities: the changing national settlement system, Urban Studies*, Vol. (30), pp. 721 - 740.

Giliespie, S. and G. McNeill (1992), *Food, Health and Survival in India and Developing Countries*, Oxford University Press, New Delhi.

Haggett, P. (1972), *Geography: A Modern Synthesis*, Harper and Row, New York and London.

Hare, F. K. (1980), *The planetary environment: fragile or sturdy?, Geographical Journal*, Vol. 146, pp. 379 - 395.

ICSSR (1972), *A Survey of Research in Geography*, New Delhi.

ICSSR (1983), *A Survey of Research in Physical Geography,* New Delhi.

Karan, P.P. (1966): "Recent contributions to the geography of South Asia", *Chaiers de Geographie de Quebec*, Vol. 9, pp. 317 - 332.

Kumaraswamy, K (1990), *National seminar on thrust areas in the application of remote sensing, Geographical Journal*, Vol. 156, pp. 73 - 74.

Kundu, A. (1993), *In the Name of Urban Poor: Access to Basic Amenities*, Sage, New Delhi.

Lewis, J.P. (1965), *Quiet Crisis in India,* India Edition, Asia Publishing House, pp. 167 - 173.

Mackinder, H.J. (1921), *Geography as a pivotal subject in education, Geographical Journal*, Vol. 57, pp. 350 - 357.

Planning Commission (1992), *Eighth Five Year Plan, 1992-97*, Vol. II. New Delhi, p. 452.

Racine J. (1985): "The centre for studies in tropical geography, France" *Annals of the National Association of Geographers, India*, Vol. 5, pp. 63 - 65.

Raza, M. (1990), *Presidential Address, Eleventh Indian Geography Congress, Annals of the National Association of Geographers India,* Vol. 10, pp. 9.

Schwartzberg, J.E. (1981), *Regional atlases: challenge and opportunity, Annals of the National Association of Geographers, India*, Vol. 1, pp. 69 - 72.

Singh, L.R. (1980), *Recent trends in Indian geography*, Presidential Address, *Indian Council of Geographers.*

Singh, R.L. ed. (1971), *India: A Regional Geography*, National Geography Society of India, Varanasi.

Spate, O.H.K. and A.T.A. Learmonth (1967), *India and Pakistan : A General And Regional Geography,* Third Edition, Methuen and Company.

Sukhwal, B.L. (1987), *India: Economic Resource Base and Contemporary Political Patterns*. Sterling Publishers, New Delhi and Bangalore.

University Grants Commission, *Geography in Indian Universities*, New Delhi.

Wilson, R.T. (1979), *Recent resource surveys for rural development in southern Darfur, Sudan, Geographical Journal*, Vol. 145, pp. 152 - 160.

Wooldridge, S.W. (1950), *Reflections on regional geography in teaching and research, Transactions of the Institute of British Geographers*, Vol. 16, pp. 1 - 11.

Laxminarayan Sanna Bhat
1930 -

To swim snug in a swarm of ones own professional community may have been the desire but was not the destiny of Bhat. Though a popular professor of geography, author of thirteen books, forty-eight research papers in reputed international and national geographical journals, author in the First Survey of Research on Geography in India, member of leading committees which evaluate and assign projects to geographers, Bhat does not typify the typical academician in a university. His career bears out that even though positioned outside a department of geography one can build one's reputation as a geographer.

Joining as a researcher in the Regional Planning Unit of the Indian Statistical Institute at the age of twenty-eight, rising upto the rank of a professor at forty-five, Bhat spent thirty-two long years in this institute as a regional planner. Bhat belongs to the very small group of geographers in India who practice what they teach. The tenets of area and region for Bhat were not mere conceptual and methodological tools of reference for lectures in class room and critiques in reviews, they had to be used in the field, incorporated in projects and implemented through plans. The test of the region after all is in the use of it! Perfecting the cuisine of regional planning for Bhat has been a life time commitment. Almost all his research projects, eighty per cent of his thirteen books, sixty five per cent of his forty-eight research articles, four of the doctorates he supervised, majority of the conferences attended pivot around the theme of regional planning. Injecting more than just a flavor of geography into planning was an uphill task. The kitchen one must remember was crowded with economists, statisticians, architect planners and regional scientists. Yet today Bhat's works on regional planning find reference among all these social scientists, and his papers have been published in journals as far ranging as Economic Geography, Journal of Regional Science, Journal of Institute of Town Planners, Sankhya, Yojna apart from the geographical ones like the Annals of the National Association of Geographers, India and the Bombay Geographical Magazine. An office attached to the apex national body – Planning Commission, and member to the Economic Advisory Council, Government of Uttar Pradesh, Technical Advisor to the Regional Development Plan for Western Ghats, chairperson to Panchayat Resource Mapping Evaluations formulated by the State Planning Board Kerala, member of the Expert Committee on Regional Information System, Town and Country Planning Organisations, are all but tips of the iceberg to invitations and appointments Bhat has enjoyed.

With geography as a subsidiary subject in his Bachelor of Science and a focus on geomorphology and land use in the Master of Science, Bhat lacked even an elementary schooling on statistics and economics. His doctorate on 'Some Aspects of Regional Planning in India' dates to 1965, nearly seven years after he joined the Indian Statistical Institute. Serving as a lecturer at the Ruparel College of the University of Bombay, in the mid 1950s he taught the traditional subjects of the discipline which made no reference to planning. Despite all these limitations, Bhat was handpicked to join as a planner by the Indian Statistical Institute.

How did Bhat secure a foothold within the ambit of planning in India? Many would jump to the conclusion that when the regional planning movement swept through India's development plans in the 1960s and 1970s, Bhat was 'on the scene'. Others could add that the main advocate of regional planning and founder director of Indian Statistical Institute in India, Mahalonabis was 'known' to Bhat. These are however remarks from the lesser known, the more penetrative question is how was Bhat recognised or familiar on the scene. A simple brahminical outlook with the adage 'hard work pays' is Bhat's very lived philosophy.

Bhat was born on 28th August, 1930 in Holanagadde, a village so small that it did not even have a threshold to support a primary school. Kumta, a port town, the British had brought fame to, for the export of cotton, housed the nearest school. Along with his three brothers and a sister Bhat walked six kilometers each way to learn his ABC! Exploring different paths and observing the landscape en route became such a favourite past-time that Bhat began to frequently write 'travel accounts' that were published in the school magazine. A more lasting reward was his dissertation of the Master in Science. To the students of today this may seem a surprise – but the year long regional study in the Upper Panchagana river, a tributary of the Krishna, is what won Bhat immediate attention. It was the appreciation from Spate, his external supervisor for the masters dissertation that catapulted Bhat into the profession of planning. While laying down the blue print of regional planning, Mahalonobis would often consult Spate. When a team for an experiment with regional planning in India was drawn, Bhat was in the list. It is his work which earned him the Leverhulme Research Fellowship at the University of Liverpool in 1962 – 63. Hard work pays but needs continuous replenishment.

Surveys and planning atlas, resource and regional synthesis, and applying the concept of central place hierarchy for developing a region have been one among the many ways in which Bhat has imbibed the spatial element into planning. Research on Mysore in the south, to Karnal in the north, Ghats on western shores of India, and queries as far ranging as regional disparity, regionalisation and regional development have been Bhat's frequent points of inquiry. Visiting the planning departments at France, Germany, Denmark, Sweden and Soviet Union have been Bhat's ways to gain comparative insight into the merits and demerits of regional planning. Working in interdisciplinary teams sharpened his understanding of the role of a geographer in the planning process. Amidst his multifaceted works, Bhat did not abandon his duty to plough books and research articles to nourish the discipline of geography.

His publications are recommended in the curriculums of most of the departments of geography and students seek advice on a range of issues on regional planning from him. His forthcoming book 'Geography and Development Process: A Spatial View' to which he is adding the final editorial touches, is a much awaited text. That he did not belong to the comfort of a single department of geography has been a blessing in disguise. The discipline of Indian geography has many a faculty confined in university departments, geographers like Bhat are indeed few.

Geographical Perspectives and the Problem of Inequality

L.S. BHAT

Geography by its very definition is the study of earth as the home of man. Relationship between the earth and the man has been becoming increasingly complex over time because the surface of the earth itself has carried imprints of the man over time while the man himself has been undergoing transformation in the socio-cultural and economic pursuits. Hence, his imprints on the surface of the earth reflect sharp inequalities in the emerging features of the socio-cultural and economic landscape. The landscape approach as a synthesis of different but related elements that lend distinct personality to it has been unique to geography. Therefore, the subject is essentially inter-disciplinary in nature. Regional geography is considered as the synthesis or the end product of geographers' study of individual elements or structures of the region (physical structure, resource base-physical and human, urbanisation and industrialisation, movement of goods and people and so on). Regions thus identified are either topical (as in physical, agricultural regions, resource regions etc) or composite (integrated whole combing all the phenomena of an area examlpe: economic region or region as defined in regional geography). The latter are dynamic having district structure and interrelationship and hence they are hierarchic. These features of the region (or a system of regions) are best expressed in the evolution of a system of nodes ranging from the simplest or lowest level market centres and relatively small and isolated tributary areas to the more complex urban-industrial centres often forming axis or belts with overlapping and extensive areas of influence (example Bombay–Pune and Ahmedabad–Vadodara belts in the western region) This concept of evolution of regions through "man-land relationship" is best illustrated by the statement that "a formal region (example agricultural region or resource region) tends to become a functional region (market centres or nodal centres of different types and their tributary areas) and the emergence of functional region is the initial stage in the formation of economic region"

18th Indian Geography Congress
Jammu, 1995 December

Such a process of organisation of economic activities has built-in characteristics of spatial inequalities because the impact of nodal centres decreases with increasing distance, and this has been the basis for the construction of theoretical models of development by Von Thunen (1975), A. Losch (1954) , Christaller (1933) and applied by W. Isard (1960), Berry, B.J.L. (1967) and others. Even then a more uniform distribution of these locations having social facilities and amenities, infrastructure and economic activities leads to minimum disparities in levels of living and economic development within and between different parts of a country. Hierarchic clustering of social and economic inputs is implied in this concept. At the other extreme inequalities in the distribution of large urban-industrial centres lead to wide disparities in regional development within and between regions as the spatial organisation of most of the regional economies tends to be centrifugal. Hierarchically too, the urban-industrial centres acting as large nodes become top heavy with a large number of nodes (usually small towns and market place) at the lower levels having a very weak economic base. Progress of geography in both fundamental and applied studies is towards this aspect of the study of emergence of regions and regional differentiation which serves to explain the causes for regional imbalances in development. The concept of region has undergone changes from environmental determinism in the form and functioning of regions to man-made environment for which regional differentiation and characterisation of their positive and negative factors would be only the framework of reference in the initial stage of measuring inequalities. Towards minimising the ambiguity in the definition of the region in an inter-disciplinary context the term "space" is used as a neutral one so that introduction of spatial dimension to the sectoral-temporal development plan would be the common objective of different fields of social science which have space affinity, e.g. geography (geographic space), economics (economic space), and sociology (social or behavioural space). Also, the search for regional boundaries is less rigid and the regional boundaries, where necessary for analytical purpose are made co-terminus with the nearest administrative boundary to facilitate quantification of various elements of the regional structure and to understand and evaluate the spatial processes by applying appropriate quantitative and cartographic techniques of measurement of association among different elements (correlation, regression etc.) and areal variations in the extent of association among different elements (regional differentiation by using factor analysis, cluster analysis, discriminate analysis etc.).Mapping techniques have been complementary because the maps serve as "models of the real world" and help to understand the phenomena of contiguity as in the distribution of agriculture resources or discontinuities in the formation of 'core' areas of economic development and point to locations as spatial dimensions of industry and urban centres. Starting from qualitative and descriptive maps the trend has been towards preparation of maps to serve as analytical and prescriptive purposes (dynamic and problem oriented) in regional differentiation.

Geographers' Contribution to the Study of Inequality

Conceptual and methodological innovations in geography, as mentioned above, find their application in the following areas of research which have a bearing on the problem of inequalities.

Regionalisation

This has been an exercise in dividing areal units of higher order into sub-regions or aggregating small areal units into those of higher order based on homogeneity in the selected characteristics. This approach has been used both in systematic and regional studies. Prior to 1940's the objectives of regionalisation were mainly to provide a rational basis for the study of regional geography. Regional delineation was largely based on natural factors and the secondary data were used to understand the role of natural factors in the distribution of physical and human resources and the emerging patterns of spatial organisation of various phenomena (Spate 1954). As an extension of the study of regional geography to planning an attempt was made for the first time to identify a scheme of planning regions of the former Bombay Province and to identify the problems in planning. (Deshpande C.D.1948). The anomaly between regional and administrative boundaries was noted. A hierarchic scheme of regions of India (macro, meso and micro) was evolved by O. H.K Spate (1957) as a part of the study of regional geography of India.

Since 1950's there have been attempts in the delineation of planning regions of different scale—National, State and District levels. These studies emphasised the regional or spatial approach to planning using the concept of regional and locational hierarchy. The pilot regional survey of Mysore State (re-named Karnataka) conducted at the Indian Statistical Institute was a landmark in a systematic evaluation of the natural environment, resource base, population, patterns of urbanisation and industrialisation. Intensity and variation in the patterns of trade were analysed and a scheme of 21 planning districts grouped into 6 Divisions was proposed for the purpose of integrating the development plans from the micro level (Block and Districts) to the meso or State level (Learmonth A.T.A. and Bhat L.S.1968, Rao V.L.S.P. and Bhat L.S.1962). "That there is a lack of horizontal integration of sectoral plane formulated by different departments in isolation was brought out by these studies".

Emphasis on minimisation of regional disparities in development in the context of the national perspectives of economic development elaborated in the Third Five Year Plan served to re-orient their approach to regional studies conducted by geographers. While regional disparities in development in India were rooted in the historical and political factors operating prior to Independence, it was considered necessary to understand the cause for such disparities in development and to evaluate the resource base and its regional diversities as they necessitate formulation of development plans appropriate to the regional conditions. In this exercise, geographers have attempted delineation of major resource regions and sub-regions of the country using secondary data at the District level and the maps of natural resources prepared by departments of forestry, minerals and others (Rao V.L.S.P. and Bhat L.S. -1992, Planning Commission 1965). Agricultural regions were delineated identifying the core and peripheries of major crop associations. To evaluate the role of natural factors in agriculture, districts were grouped on the basis of similarities in the physical landscape and this regional framework compared with that of crop regions (Bhat L.S. *et at.* 1976). There have been notable instances in which inter-disciplinary exercises have been conducted in the study of regional variations in agricultural productivity and growth rate. This led to identification of dynamic agricultural regions of high productivity and high growth rate, and at the other extreme, stagnant regions of low agricultural productivity and low growth rate, (Minhas *et al.* 1965, Bhalla and Algh, 1979).

Impact of regional differences in agricultural serves to understand and evaluate the role of agriculture in organisation of other economic activities for balanced development of the regional economics. Identification of macro-economic regions by grouping diversified physical resources was also attempted using the concept of Territorial Power – Production Cycles on the model of the methods of economic regionalisation formulated by soviet scientists (Galina Sdasyuk and Sen Gupta p. 1968 and Bhat, CS *et al.* 1968). Delineation of economic regions by grouping linguistic states on the basis of complementarily in their economic regions and the resultant spatial organisation of economic activities within sub-region of such states is assumed to serve the purpose of spatial integration of the economy and reduction of regional inequalities in development.

Regional Disparities in Development

While regional differentiation and characterization of regions have a bearing on the problems of regional disparities in development, the problems of measuring the extent of regional disparities is a complex exercise of interdisciplinary nature. Geography in collaboration with statisticians and economists has contributed to measuring variations in levels of development and in providing regional interpretation of the observed patterns. There have been several attempts in the measurement of regional disparities in development from the national angle using states as regions for inter-state comparison. For more detailed analysis of the problems of development and under-development the district was chosen as the unit area for data compilation. Recognizing the inadequacy and limitations of the use of indicators such as per capita income and consumer expenditure, their studies used a variety of indicators ranging from the physical characteristics to the intensity and diversification of cropping pattern, agricultural productivity and growth rate, indicators related to urbanisation, industrialization and the occupational diversification. Techniques of working out composite scores ranged from adding rank scores of all the districts on each indicator to the application of principal component analysis (Berry B.J.L. 1966, Bhat L.S. 1973, Pal MN 1963: Dasgupta Biplab 1971, Kundu A. 1982. Arao Hemlata 1982, Mitra A. 1964 Sundaram K.V. 1983 Nair K.R.G. 1983). The results of these studies brought out the following patterns of development and disparities:

(i) The south-east region having important mineral resource (iron ore, coal, micro, etc.) and forests is marked by extensive area of underdevelopment with islands of economic development centered on Bokaro, Bhilai, Rourkela with very little impact on the surrounding region. The regions inherent limitations are its rugged terrain, low density of population mainly tribal and dominance of small and scattered human settlements, low levels of social facilities and amenities. The hierarchy of nodal centres is weak and distorted. The region comprises eastern Madhya Pradesh, Western Orissa, Chota Nagpur Plateau of Bihar and Chandrapur District of Maharashtra.

(ii) Contiguous but limited areas around major metropolitan centres have emerged as axes of developed areas and this pattern seems to be extending along major transport routes with little impact along the interstices of radial routes converging on them. There is dichotomy between major urban-industrial centres and small towns whose economic base is very weak. There are instances such as of the less developed Konkan area of Maharashtra where infrastructure development (e.g. construction of West Coast Highway) without complementary economic input has acted as counter to the growth of small towns which have come under easy access to Bombay and Panaji-Marmagoa areas (Deshpande C.D. *et al.* 1980).

Agriculturally developed areas in the Western Uttar Pradesh., Haryana and Punjab and the Delta areas of the Krishna-Godavari, and the Cauvery as well as the black soil Plateau of diversified agriculture around Kolhapur in Maharashtra and the Madurai area in Tamil Nadu are relatively developed. These areas have minimum variations in levels of development because of a more balanced development of a hierarchy of market towns and industrial centres.

Areas of poor agricultural productivity due to inherent topographical, soil and semi-arid conditions as in most parts of dry-farming areas of the Peninsular Plateau, are uniformly low in levels of development (example Telangana in Andhra Pradesh and Marathwada in Maharashtra). These areas are again conspicuous for the occurrence of small pockets of urban industrial centres without having their impact on the surrounding areas.

Whatever the limitations of the techniques of analysis the results of studies using states as regions do not permit us to arrive at such realistic observations of the variations in the regional structure and spatial organisation of the economy centred on a system of nodal centres and the emerging patterns of development and disparities. It is also apparent that vertical inequality among different sections of the society as well horizontal disparity are much less in the uniformly rich agricultural areas.

Micro-Level Planning

The geographer's contribution to planning at the District and Block levels as an exercise in introducing physical planning approach has been largely in the areas of the application of the concept of Central Places and Market Centres of Christaller and Losch (Berry B.J.I. 1969, Johnson, E.A.J.1965, Lalit Sen,1972, Wanmali 1976, Bhat, L. S. 1976). A large number of studies have not adopted spatial approach to micro level planning. The growth centre strategy advocated in the 1970's laid emphasis on ranking of human settlements on the basis of demographic and socio-economic attributes without paying adequate attention to factors that promote growth such as of the resource base and the patterns of development that would increase employment opportunities, income and buying capacity of the people. Some of the studies have used Block level data for district planning, and these being few in number do not reveal spatial patterns and variations unlike in the use of village level data. (Bhat, L.S. 1976, Rao V.L.S.P. 1976, Misra G.K. 1980 and Kundu A 1980).

Appraisal of the Studies on Inequality

The foregoing account of the contributions of geographers to the problem of inequality presents the fundamental view of geography as a spatial discipline, merits and limitations of the approach to the problem starting from descriptive account of regions, to regional delineation by qualitative mapping techniques and the application of quantitative techniques for the measurement of association among several phenomena and regional differentiation. This has enabled geography to focus its attention on spatial dimensions in national development planning in a multi-regional framework comprising different tiers of the political administrative work through which the planning process operates. Limitation of these studies stem from two considerations. Firstly, the traditional methods in teaching and research lacked logic and objective methods of explanation of the patterns and variations of the phenomena relating to the evolution of regions and the regional development process. Theories and concepts in regional development and disparities are inter-disciplinary and they are borrowed mainly from the experiences of the developed countries. Application of these theories and techniques by geographers has been in the majority of cases in isolation from other disciplines notably economics, sociology, demography, mathematics and statistics with which it is related. Regional economics is much less developed in India unlike in United States of America, United Kingdom and Europe and our pre-occupation with the preparation of highly aggregated sectoral temporal development models at the national level has not attracted specialists from these disciplines to work on the problems of spatial inequalities in development. Secondly, inter-state comparisons of the socio-economic structure or input-output tables do not bring out spatial inequality in a country of sharp regional contrasts which are more pronounced within states.

The concept of space or region which found its expression in the studies of sociologists and cultural anthropologists in the past does not seem to be popular with the sociologists of recent times who prefer to work at the "field level" (households or communities) without bringing in the spatial behaviour and regional consciousness of the inhabitants.

Secondly, while the techniques of analysis have improved the ability of geographers to study the regional patterns and variations, not all the studies of regional inequality can claim to be specific to the field of geography except in the interpretation of the observed pattern against the regional realities gained by way of the study of spatial patterns and variations through mapping techniques. Choice of indicators and working out composite scores of development have tended to be mechanical exercises and these have not been followed up by the evaluation of the relationship between regional disparities in development and the patterns of spatial organisation of the economy as mentioned earlier. This is a logical extension of such exercises of leading to the formulation of regional development strategies appropriate to different regions in a national framework. There are evidence that economic growth progresses more rapidly in regions adjacent to highly developed regions. While the measures for speedy development of less developed areas differ according to the nature of the problems inherent in them (example drought prone areas, hill areas., tribal areas and so on) the entire problem of regional disparities in development has been treated in the planning process as an adhoc programme for providing special assistance. With political overtones associated with the problem and emergence of parochial forms of regionalism, the studies on regional inequality have become more complex and require inter–disciplinary collaboration more urgently than ever before. Geography as a spatial and integrating discipline has a leading role to play.

In the studies on District and Block level planning the number of case studies conducted by geographers is large and increasing . Yet , a careful evaluation of the approach and the conclusions bring out the inadequacy of micro-regional surveys which should have preceded the studies on District and Block level planning. The essential aim of such studies should have been in the preparation of normative physical spatial development framework to be of use in identifying a shelf of development programmes that create durable assets and also serve to create employment both in the rural areas and the settlements chosen to be developed as "growth centres". The resource inventory which is considered basic to the District Development Plan is not adequately prepared using large scale topographical maps and other information. With access to more sophisticated and latest information through satellite imageries and computer, it should be possible to interpret these data in their spatial context.

Priority Areas for Inter-Disciplinary Collaboration

Regional Studies

Understanding the regional characteristics and choice of element that serve to differentiate regions need a sharper focus on evaluation of the social and behavioural aspects of the community for structural changes of the economy. Regional norms and co-efficients need to be built up to improve our ability to forecast rather than providing a static picture of the economy as is presented by geographers in their regional synthesis and economists in the input-output table. For this purpose there is a need to provide an analytical framework for undertaking regional studies and for regional differentiation which has a bearing on the problem of inequality.

Geography and the Problem of Inequality

The geographer's concept of homogenous regions based on such phenomena as natural environment, resource base, population and settlement patterns as well as the heterogeneous regions whose transactions are centred on nodal settlements of different hierarchic scale provides a spatial framework to understand and to evaluate the problem of inequality. For this purpose intra-state regions comprising groups of districts should be the basis for building up information systems on problems of inequality and for constructing normative development models. Geographers hitherto have attempted to build up spatial models of development only to understand the factors that have contributed to regional inequalities in development in the past and explanations of the phenomena related to future development example a modified colonial model of space economy formulated by Moonis Raza and Chattopadhyay (1975).

Rural Urban Integration In a Regional Framework

Dichotomy between rural and urban components of Indian social and cultural and economic structure needs to be understood in a regional framework. While geographical studies focus on the spatial patterns and variations there is a need to evaluate the interrelationship in a hierarchic system of spatial interactions.

Environment and the Problem of Inequality

The concept and analytical approach to environment have come under constant review and introspection in geography from environmental determinism to possibility in which the concept of ecosystem provides a better understanding of the dynamic aspect of man-environment. It is necessary to evolve a typology of such regions and to identify the key elements of man-environment relationship in the ecological regions which have a bearing on inequalities. Human response to certain innovations externally induced or internally motivated shows marked variations in the geographic space. Geography has overlap areas with some fields of physical sciences notably geomorphology, botany, climatology on the one hand and agricultural economics, sociology and cultural anthropology from social sciences on the other.

Study of Poverty

While poverty is acute in less developed areas, in terms of absolute numbers it is widespread.

Studies on regional inequalities in development carried out so far are inadequate in relating the problem of poverty with the nature of the development process. This is a difficult but challenging field of long-term research on account of inadequacy of data, field work and analytical approach. Yet, the strategy adopted for amelioration of poverty at the household level needs to be integrated in the exercises in Block and District level planning. Poverty is area specific and varies among different sections of the society within the same region. Hence, geography could contribute substantially by areal differentiation of the factors that accentuate poverty conditions because of the inherent limitations of the resource base–mainly agriculture, size and spatial arrangement of human settlements, and their attributes and the quality of the population (social, cultural and economic). Programmes of development could then be identified according to area specificity and the number of households chosen for poverty amelioration programme could be in proportion to the number of households in each area differentiated according to the characteristics that perpetuate poverty conditions.

The foregoing review of geography and the problem of inequality has attempted to highlight the strength and weakness of geography in its fundamental and applied aspects of understanding regions, regional differentiation and the problem of development and disparities. Research themes of inter-disciplinary nature cited above would need further modification and elaboration, identifying overlap areas with other disciplines in the problem of development and disparities in a spatial context.

REFERENCE

Alagh, Y.K. (1973), *Regional planning for industrial aspects of the Indian economy*, *Indian Journal of Regional Science*, Vol.V (2), pp. 147 - 166.

Alam, M. *et al.* (1982), *Settlement System of India*, Oxford and I.B.H. Publishing Company, New Delhi.

Berry, B.J.L. *et al.* (1968), *Spatial Analysis: A Reader in Statistical Geography*, Prentice Hall.

Berry, B.J.L. (1966), *Essays on Commodity Flows and the Spatial Structure of the Indian Economy*, Department of Geography, Research Paper No. 111, University of Chicago, Chicago.

Berry, B.J.L. (1967), *Geography of Market Centres and Retail Distribution*, Englewood Cliffs, Prentice Hall.

Bhat, L.S. and A.T.A. Learmonth (1968), *Recent contributions to the economic geography of India – some current preoccupations, Economic Geography*, Vol. 44 (3), pp. 189 - 209.

Bhat, L.S. (1973), *Regional Planning in India,* Statistical Publishing Society, Calcutta.

Bhat, L.S. *et al.* (1976), *Micro-Level Planning: A Case Study of Karnal Area, Haryana*, K.B. Publications, New Delhi.

Bhalla, G.S. *et al.* (1979), *Performance of India Agriculture: A Districtwise Study*, Sterling Publication, New Delhi.

Christaller, W. (1933), *The Central Places in Southern Germany*, Translated by C.W. Baskin, Englewood Cliffs, Prentice Hall.

Census of India (1971), *Economic and Social-Cultural Dimensions of Regionalisation*, Registrar General, India, Ministry of Home Affairs, New Delhi.

Dasguta, B. (1971), *Socio-economic classification of districts: a statistical approach, Economic and Political Weekly*, Vol. VI (33), pp. 1763 - 1774.

Desai, P.B. *et al.* (1969), *Regional Perspective of Industrial and Urban Growth*, Macmillan, Bombay.

Deshpande, C.D. (1947), *Western India – A Regional Geography*, Students' Own Book Depot, Dharwar.

Deshpande, C.D. *et al.* (1980), *Impact of Metropolitan City on the Surrounding Region: A Study of South Kolaba (Maharashtra)*, Concept Publishing Company, New Delhi.

Friedmann, J. and W. Alonso (1967), *Regional Development and Planning: a Reader*, M.I. T. Press.

Government of India, Planning Commission (1961), *Third Five Year Plan* Chapter on Regional Imbalances in Development.

Government of India, Planning Commission (1965), *Resource Development Regions and Divisions*, New Delhi.

Haggett, P. (1965), *Locational Analysis in Human Geography*, Edward Arnold, London.

Hashim, S.R. (1970), *Inter-regional linkages and economic regionalisation, Indian Journal of Regional Science*, Vol. II (1), pp. 11 - 20.

Isard, W. *et al.* (1960), *Methods of Regional Analysis*, John Wiley.

Indian Council of Social Science Research (1972), *Survey of Research in Geography*, Popular Prakashan Bombay, also subsequent volumes.

Johnson, E.A.J. (1970), *The Organisation of Space in Developing Countries*, Harvard University Press.

Kuklinski, A. ed. (1972), *Growth Poles and Growth Centres in Regional Planning*, Mouton, Paris.

Kundu, A. *et al.* (1982), *Indian Economy: the Regional Dimension* Jawaharlal Nehru University, New Delhi.

Losch, A. (1954), *The Economics of Location*, Yale University Press.

Mathur, O.P. (1973), *The problem of inter-regional disparities, Indian Journal of Regional Science*, Vol. V (1), pp. 81 - 100.

Mennes, L.B. M. (1960), *The Element of Space in Development Planning*, North-Holland.

Minhas, B. and A. Vaidyanathan (1965), *Growth of crop output in India, Journal of the Indian Society of Agricultural Statistics*, Vol. XVII(2).

Misra, G.K. *et al.* (1980), *Regional Planning of the Micro-level: A Study of Rural Electrification in Bastar and Chandrapur*, Indian Institute of Public Administration, New Delhi.

Misra, R.P. *et al.* ed. (1969), *Regional Planning Concept Techniques and Case Studies*, Prasaranga, Mysore.

Misra, R.P. *et al.* (1974), *Regional Development Planning in India: A New Strategy*, Vikas, Delhi.

Mitra, A. (1965), *Levels of Regional Development*, Census of India, Vol. I Part I A (i) and (ii).

Nair, K.R.G. (1983): *Regional Experience in a Developing Economy*, Wiley Eastern, New Delhi.

Pal, M.N. (1963), *A method of regional analysis of economic development with reference of south India, Journal of Regional Science*, Vol. 5(I), pp. 41 - 58.

Raafe, E.J. ed. (1970), *Geography: Survey of the Behavioural and Social Sciences*, Prentice Hall.

Rao, H. (1982), *Regional Disparities: Dimensions and Typology of Backwardness*, Institute for Social and Economic Change, Bangalore (mimeo).

Raza, M. *et al.* (1975), *Regional development analytical framework and indicators, Indian Journal of Regional Science*, Vol. VII (1), pp. 11-34.

Rao, V.L.S.P. and L.S. Bhat (1962), *Regional framework for resource development, Bombay Geographical Magazine*, Vol. 10.

Rao, V.L.S.P. (1964), *Regional Planning*, Indian Statistical Institute and Asia Publishing House, Calcutta.

Rao, V.L.S.P. (1983), *Urbanisation in India: Spatial Dimensions*, Concept, New Delhi.

Sengupta, P. and G. Sdasyuk (1968), *Economic Regionalisation of India, Problems and Approaches*, Census of India 1961, Monograph Series, Vol. I (8), New Delhi.

Sen, Lalit K. ed. (1972), *Micro-Level Planning and Rural Growth Centres*, National Institute of Community Development, Hyderabad.

Spate, O.H. K. (1954): *India and Pakistan*, Methuen.

Sundaram, K.V. ed. (1985), *Geography and Planning*, Concept Publishing Company, New Delhi.

Sundaram, K.V. (1983), *Geography of Underdevelopment*, Concept, New Delhi.

Singh, T. (1974): *India's Development Experience*, Chapter Two on Regional Growth and Disparities, Macmillan, India.

Wanmali, S. (1970), *Regional Planning of Social Facilities: An Examination of Central Place Concepts and their Applications*, N.I.C.D. Hyderabad.

Rameshwar Prasad Misra
1930 -

If an opinion poll is conducted to elect the most popular geographer in India today, Misra is certain to score very high. An index to his more than ubiquitous presence are a cupboard full of citations wrapped in those typical off-white shawls, while a wall mosaic could be created by the Fullbright Fellowship, Golden Jubilee Award of Mysore for best research publication, Scholarly Achievement Award from the Institute of Oriental Philosophy, Tokyo, the Bhoogol Ratna Award and the Gandhi National Fellowship bestowed upon him. The number of doctorates he has supervised are untraceable, and seminars and conferences attended by him are countless that his twenty page curriculum vitae ignores to make a note of them. May it be in the capacity of a nominee for selections and examinations or invitee to deliver lectures Misra's reach in the departments of geography extends far and wide in India. Other than geographers, Misra has led research teams of development planners, economists as well as regional scientists. Many among his fifty books find a place of compulsory reading in the curricula of the departments of geography in India. India's leading publisher of geography books confirms that he is an author whose books sell. How has Misra garnered popularity ?

It could be said that Misra's wide front of works gave him a high measure of visibility. After all from his first appointment as a researcher in the National Atlas and Thematic Mapping Organisation, Calcutta, reader in the department of geography, University of Mysore, founder of Institute of Development Studies, University of Mysore, vice - director of the United Nations Centre for Regional

Development, Japan, professor at the department of geography, Delhi School of Economics, vice-chancellor of University of Allahabad, chairperson of Gandhi Bhawan at University of Delhi, and consultant to United Nations Development Program in a number of countries, Misra's geographical locales of work have stretched far and wide .But more than the niche he occupied it is the method of anchorage that rewarded him immediate spot light.

Misra survives in a habitat of work not so much by adapting but by changing the environment. Introducing daring alterations, Misra captures immediate limelight. Take his appointment at the department of geography, Mysore in 1965, in a short ten months he overhauled the post-graduate department and launched a Centre for Urban and Regional Studies . Finding the department too 'small' to contain his ideas, in less than five years Misra set up the Institute of Development Studies. While the city of Mysore acquired one of its first meta-disciplinary institutes, for Misra it became a platform for interaction with other social scientists and a centre where novel programmes in name and style were created. One cannot dispute that a Master in Development Planning, Diploma in Environmental Planning as well as in Multi-level Planning, more so through correspondence, were unique to the Indian academic landscape in 1971. Inaugurating the inhouse journal of Regional Development Dialogue in a few weeks after appointment at the Regional Development Center at Nagoya is a similar case of Misra's ability to generate and implement new artifacts in work . As vice-chancellor of the University of Allahabad he succeeded in inaugurating department for seven new disciplines.

On a bookrack Misra's personal publications stand out in bold . He has a ten volume set on Contributions to Indian Geography, another ten volume series on Nagoya Regional Development, three volumes of Habitat Asia, and two volumes on Million Cities of India. The row does not end here for there are another two dozen books whose attention is not so much driven by bulk but by diversity in themes. Tackling a concourpia as vast as agricultural innovation to medical geography, rural area development to local level planning, third world peasantry to conflict resolution , environmental ethics to research methodology means that a greater catch of audience is added to his basket of popularity.

Overarching has been his advocacy in the growth pole as a paradigm of spatial development. Though an idea created by Perroux as far back as in 1955, Misra's staunch belief in the role of growth poles in sucking India out of its chronic underdevelopment compelled him to write on the theme of regional planning . It is no coincidence that twenty-three of Misra's books and double the number of his research publications are singularly devoted to the theme of regional planning and development. While these may sound as reasons for his wide acclaim, yet one should not forget that in the field of academics not all among those who gain appointments and write books and are honored attain popularity. Misra claims that "a compassionate understanding of events and people, success and failure, is of equal importance if one hopes to carry along a large following". His pragmatism has deep origins.

Misra was born on 5th September, 1930 in the village of Hanumanpur in the district of Pratapgarh in the state of Uttar Pradesh. At a high school of Kalakankar, the veteran Gandhian Naresh Bahadur Srivastava evoked in Misra the twin ability of compassionate understanding along with reasoning. Exposed to the writings of Marx and Gandhi it is under the supervision of his favorite teacher, that Misra learnt the first concepts of man and society. Thereafter, as a student at the University of Allahabad and a doctorate at the University of Maryland enhanced Misra's insight about the question of development and its wide ramifications. That hybrid learning is essential to comprehend the complex nuances of development, prompted Misra to take a double post-graduation: geography from University of Allahabad and economics from University of Agra. Even in the United States of America, he took courses on agricultural economics and sociology along side the doctoral work. More than the books, Misra's pragmatism was honed by the work he had done as assistant in the Lok Sabha Secretariat of the Parliament of India at the impressionable age between twenty-five to twenty-eight years. Travelling across the country with members of parliament, skilled his pulse about people and greased his efficiency to produce voluminous reports in short notice of time. His encounter with the parliament though, brief implanted a deep ambition to command and channel people into a field of work. Driven by understanding along with intellectualization, today Misra acquired popularity among geographers in India. In modesty he adds 'he is not gifted but guided'. What is his next forte ? At the age of 71 his one pending desire is to enter Parliament. The dynamism in Misra goads him to plunge into a study on Gandhi and establish a Gandhi Dham at Allahabad. Honoured the first Gandhi National Fellowship, by the Gandhi Smriti and Darshan Samiti. Misra is all set to edit a ten volume set titled 'Rediscovering Gandhi'. His latest research could take Misra nearer to an indigenous theory of spatial development, closer to a search for truth in life, or even head him straight to the house of Parliament in India. On any or all the three fronts, Misra's popularity is bound to increase.

Indian Geography: Problems, Challenges and Opportunities

R.P. MISRA

It is once in a life opportunity to be elected as President of National Association of Geographers, India and I feel a sense of satisfaction and elation that this opportunity has come to me at a time which, I feel, is momentous in many ways, and at a place which is so well known for natural serenity, human dignity, cultural authenticity and social solidarity. I am grateful to the Vice-Chancellor Professor B. Pakem, Professor R. K. Rai, Professor A.C. Mohapatra, Professor R. Gopalakrishnan and other members of the faculty of the Department of Geography, North-Eastern Hill University for inviting us to meet here to renew our contacts, to learn from each other and to exchange our thoughts and 'hearts' during the next few days.

Friends, geographers had always been interested in north east in general, and Meghalaya in particular. You are perhaps aware that the name of the State of Meghalaya was given by late Professor S.P. Chatterjee years before anyone could think of statehood for the region. The region which has Cherranpunjee must be the land of clouds (Meghalaya). Not only the nature, but also the people of this part of the country had always been of special interest to geographers, for it is here that man's relations and interactions with nature have been highly symbiotic. The concept of sustainable development was put into practice centuries before, and in my view, this region still provides the answers to many of the ecological and environmental problems we are going to face in the 21st century.

Only four years are left when we will enter the third millennium; this will also mark, in practical terms, the coming of age of National Association of Geographers, India. The Association which was conceived in 1976 will be 25 years old then. I call this meeting momentous because it is time for us to examine the direction in which we are moving and what type of Indian geography we are going to present to ourself and to our children when we enter the 21st century .

19th Indian Geography Congress
Shillong, 1996 October

In the next few pages, I have tried to sketch out the challenges and opportunities before us and to chart out a futuristic course of action which will enrich our discipline as well as the humanity with better understanding of the planet earth and the micro-spaces in which we live and die.

Unique Features

Craddle to Grave Subject

Geography is unique in many ways. It is a craddle to grave subject – from dust we come to the dust we go. There is no escape from it. The *Panch bhootas* of which all that exists on the earth created, are also the *Panch Bhootas* that constitute the subject matter of geography. To deny the importance of geography is to deny the reality. In fact, we not only study but also live and feel it. It is part of us whether we study it through a formal course of instruction or not. To ignore geography or to dilute its role in human life is brought with dangerous consequences.

From School to the University

Geography, later joined by history and mathematics, is a discipline which runs through all stages of education. It is a school subject as well as a research discipline at the highest level of education. There is a vast difference between school geography and university geography: and it has taken a long time consistent and creative efforts to level the two into an integrated whole. But the problems of integration continue and we will take up this aspect a bit later.

Link Between Science and Humanities

Geography is often called an integrative discipline. It recognizes, but does not accept the thesis that knowledge can really be divided into watertight compartments of disciplines. Disciplines are carved out to reach the bottom of the parts and not to snap the interrelations among them or to deny the unity of the whole. Geography offers the medicine of integration of all disciplines grouped as sciences and humanities. The medium is the "space". Space is not of inert phenomenon; it is a living and dynamic phenomenon. It is a reflection of what has gone on in the world in the past and, in turn, reflects on how humans interact with nature and among themselves. The image, the form, the appearance and the value of space depend less on natural endowment and more on humans. Which of the two have greater influence depends on how long the human occupancy of the space-physical and/or mental and with what motives and intentions has been.

For a geographer, sciences and humanities are two sides of the same coin and coin is geography. It is an influence on both the sides but it stands on solid ground of its own. It has interest in geomorphology, climatology, biology, physics, history, economics, political science and many other disciplines which impinge on the character of space and they impinge together and in conjunction with each other. This togetherness and enmeshing of a variety of forces to make the space what it is the subject matter of geography.

Unique Methodology

Geography has its own methodology. In ancient times, it emerged from chorographic description of new lands explored or visited. Slow means of transportation and communication limit the scope of exploitation of neighbouring regions. India and China met in southeast Asia; Indians and Arabs met along the Arabian sea coast. Then in sixteenth-eighteenth centuries Europeans reached almost every part of the world. Geography become a discipline of explorations.

Explorations provide new data on lands and peoples. Side by side, attempts were made to give quantitative measure of the things/places explored and to construct maps and charts. Cartographic depiction apart from chorographic representation and quantitative analysis continue to be the tools of geography. Exploration has now given place to field work and measurement to instrumentation, quantification and Geographical Information System, etc.

Focus on Sustainability

Sustainability appears to be a new perspective in development research and thinking. For geography, it is an old theme. When *Atharr Veda* (first millennium B.C.) said *Mata Bhumi Putro Aham Prithvyah*, it was the clearest enunciation of the concept of sustainability. This concept was, by and large adhered to during the agricultural era in essentially rural civilizations. Urbanisation, whether in Mohenjodaro and Harappa or Rome and Mesopotamia or in the great Andies of present day Latin America did break this rule of thumb and became one of the major causes of the death of many civilizations, but these were aberration rather than rule. It is the urban-industrial era which began in an incipient way in the seventeenth century which threw this age-old principle of human survival and development over board.

As if to prove the superiority of this civilization, geography and its tools were bent backwards. Much of the agricultural world was colonized by Europe;

environmental determinism, and it's off-shoots like possibilism and probablism became tools to demonstrate the superiority of Europe, while the colonized peoples struggled to adhere to ancient rule of symbiosism.

Problems Facing Indian Geography

School Geography

Indian geography has kept pace with the changes which have taken place in the discipline the world over, but the progress in different sub-fields has not been uniformly distributed. In terms of spatial spread of the field, India has done fairly well and the progress continues even though slowly and haltingly. But there are areas of concern too.

One of the major problems encountered is the identity of school geography: "complications arise from the nature of geography itself" (Williams, 1976,8). Should geography be taught as an independent subject by geographers or it should form part of social studies? If we go back into history and nature of geography, we cannot but agree with Kirk (1963, 357) that modern geography was created by scholars, trained in other disciplines, asking themselves geographical questions. Geography as an academic discipline, therefore, was one of the earlier 'Integrated Studies'. It was also true at the school level. Geography to claim its repute to be in school was presented as an integrated subject: The early attempts at introducing an integrated course stemmed from the struggle to introduce geography into secondary school — (Williams, 1976,8). Integrated studies stand as a dual reminder to geographers of the prolonged and continuing quest for a stable subject identity and of early days when the subject itself was a low status ingredient of integrated courses. The changing philosophies, pedagogies, and content orientation of geography are symbiotically related to its presentation, acceptance and status as a subject (Goodson, 1996, 72).

Geography got recognition as a part of school curricula after the First World War. Soon, it was pressurized to link with history. Mackinder (1913) was a leading protagonist of this combined subject, although in an address to geographical Association he feared that history may make in roads into their classes, in the same way as geologist, a couple of years earlier, entertained fear of geography. He advocated the teaching of geography and history as a single subject, not in the primary school but in the upper half of elementary education and lower half of secondary education.

Mackinder's arguments in favour of integration were clearly limited to a view about geography's aspiration as a school subject.

How are children going to use their curiosity by taking up a subject ? That is an academic idea. A special subject will be taken up by a few scattered people as a hobby, but the vast majority will increase their knowledge not by the study of any definite subject, but by reading this and that cheap books, by reading the newspapers, by talking with friends and by seeing what they can when travelling.

For a vast majority what is important is not to send them out with the rudiments of history as such and the rudiments of geography as such in their minds, but to send them out with some sort of orderly conception of the world around them. Whether a fact is historical or whether it is geographical matters not one straw to them.

"It does perhaps matter to those who are going to increase the knowledge of history or the knowledge of geography, or who are to be specialised teachers of those subjects, who are going to prepare for examinations in those subjects" (Mackinder, 1913, cited in Williams, 1976, 5-6).

Not everyone agreed to Mackinder's view. In fact, the opposition to his concept of Integrated Subject later snowballed. His contemporary Unstead (1913) offered an alternative view of geography as a school subject and said:

"What is a subject? It is an organized body of knowledge, the different parts of which naturally hang together, and I think in practical teaching it is well to develop it as a whole in geography, the facts to hang together, children can see relations, they may get the sense of proportion if they have the thing treated as a whole".

The above view was endorsed by Geographical Association in 1919. Geography, they argue, is a unique combination, "a balanced subject with a unity of its own and many claim" to contribute in a unique fashion to an education which aims at the appreciative interpretation of modern world." (p. 18).

After the War, the Ministry of Education (1919) saw geography and history as the most relevant of the traditional subjects as far training for citizenship was concerned. And noted that the best way to teach these subjects was as part of social studies but many teachers continue to teach them historically through the centuries or geographically through the regions (Ministry of Education 1949; Williams, 1976, 62-3).

In 1950, Royal Geographical Society's Education Committee (R.G.S. 1950) stated frankly that social studies would destroy the value of geography as an important medium of education and hence was concerned with its spread in schools.

"An attempt to study a group of subjects together introduces such complexity that children cannot see any general pattern or gain a clear and memorable educational experience. The geographer is well aware that knowledge is whole, but makes no apology for dividing it into separate subject for the purpose of learning. History and geography, for example, are distinct branches of study, and each is recognized as having a unique contribution to make to the intellectual equipment of the educated citizen of today. But these contributions are different and cannot be made unless the recognized content and characteristic method of presentation of each subject are preserved" (cited in William, 1976, p.82).

Indian educationists, following the British and American trends, introduced geography as part of social studies in school. Although attempts were made by Indian geographers to balance the curricula by not defacing the unique place of geography in social studies but the way social studies is taught in Indian schools is depressing. Teachers knowing nothing of geography, teach geography. And since geography is more difficult to teach than history, it is often the neglected subject. Most schools have only one teacher in social studies; he teaches both history and geography.

Geography as an Academic Subject

Geography finds an honourable place in almost all universities in India both at the graduate and post-graduate levels. Over 70 per cent of the colleges offer geography as an elective. School geography has gone through a series of problems (some of which will be discussed in later sections), but it remains, along with history and mathematics (arithmetic and geometry in junior primary) the first charge, quality of text books, too, have improved but India has a long way to go before it can give geography a rightful place in school curricula.

On the research front, too, Indian geography has made some notable strides. Quality of M.Phil and Ph.D thesis in some universities comparable to any good university in the world is poor. But we have, still, to go a long way. A large number of universities in the country are not even concerned about the deteriorating quality of research. It may appear harsh but we cannot ignore the fact that a great majority of Ph.D. theses produced in the country in the field of geography are unbecoming for our discipline. It is partly because we are not training our research students in research methodology and partly because the supervisors are unacquainted by modern nuances of research.

The National Association of Geographers, India has some role to play in this regard. We cannot allow this situation to further deteriorate. The future of geography as a research discipline is at stake. Some commissions of National Association of geographers, India have done excellent work. Should we not have a commission to prepare report on the studies of doctoral research and the steps to improve the situations for our consideration next year?

From its position as a low status integrated school subject in the early twentieth century, geography has progressed to a broad acceptance as a high status university discipline. However, the subject continued to be plagued by its image "as essentially for school children and by the idiocyncratic interpretation of the subject emanating from the universities, particularly in respect of field work." Thus, despite the acceptance of the subject as a university discipline with academic rigour, within the universities themselves the status of geography remained low, until about 1960's. Its status went up with quantitative revolution heralding greater rigour in analysis. But many geography departments in India took advantage of this new trends and remained content with the old choreographic approach to geographical research.

Challenges and Opportunities

Indian geography faces a number of challenges in years ahead. These challenges come from outside as well as from within. I intend to sketch out a few of them.

Crisis of Paradigm

I believe that Indian geographers have not yet even begun to explore the history of Indian geography. The ecological concepts enunciated by our forefathers in regard to man-nature relationship can offer us new ideas for theory building. Symbiosism, which our ancients advocated, is now getting recognition from all over the world. It offers the base for a new paradigm. Had we explored this concept more deeply, we could have presented an alternative to determinism, possibilism, and probablism. There are many other ideas contained in our *Sanskrit literature* which are geographic and highly relevant to the present day world.

There exists a paradigmic crisis in Indian geography. It is obsessed with Darwinian theory of evolution and urban-industrial civilization. Our culture is based on 'GIAN THEORY' of evolution and rural-agricultural civilization. Mahatma Gandhi was the latest of our great men who advocated a new civilization different from the industrial civilization which we have come to believe to be the latest stage in the evolution of human society, even though its human and environmental consequences are so very apparent and clear. How many geographers in India have given any thought to this ?

Landuse Planning and Food Security

Indian geographers have kept themselves aloof from the societal problems, distancing geography from society. In general, there is tendency to be encyclopaedic. Let me illustrate this with just four examples of post-independence Indian geography.

India's arable land resources are double of that of China, but its food production is less than half of China's. One, and perhaps the most important reason for this is the total absence of landuse planning—a field which has always been of special interest to geographers. Geographers made signal contribution to landuse planning in Europe, America and even China. Here in this country the government ignored the geographic imperatives of agricultural development and proceeded on irrigation projects, chemical fertilizers etc. to usher in Green Revolution. This revolution offered only short term, though very significant relief. Now the agricultural production has reached a plateau and may even decline unless landuse planning is resorted to on a massive scale.

Unfortunately, much of the geographic studies on landuse are highly descriptive telling which land is being used for what purpose. What is needed is studies on land potentials and the uses that they should be put to and identification of areas where land is being used unscientifically and against known ecological principles. Need for scientific land use planning using the past and present data, and keeping in view the future population pressure and the imperatives of environmental reconstruction, requires no emphasis. We have now new and more reliable sources of data (satellite imageries), but we are reluctant to utilize them as we observe from Ph.D. thesis on landuse produced in recent years.

Our land resources are depleting fast and population is rising equally fast. Availabilities of land for agriculture is declining; percentage of land under irrigation is also declining, and food production has come down by six million tonnes last year. For the last eight years, we had good rainfall and droughts were limited to just 10 per cent of the total area. What will happen if this 10 per cent increases to 20 or 30 per cent? We will be hand to mouth again.

The Association should try to revive the landuse studies in geography and petition the Government of India (relevant departments) of dangers ahead and the way land resource planning can be carried out in the country.

Social Development

Two aspects of social development, apart from spatial distributive justice, have always attracted the attention of geographers i.e., education and health. Professor Moonis Raza, Dr. S. Nuna and other colleagues have done a good work in the field of education. There is a whole sub-field of geography of health (medical geography) where meaningful contribution have been made by several Indian geographers. But the distance to be covered in both these areas is, still, pretty long.

Geographic principles of micro-level planning for educational development have been in currency for quite sometime. Kothari Commission had used these principles to plan elementary education. Geographers have, however, limited their attention to distribution of educational facilities and achievements. How to plan for educational development so that maximum number of students benefit from the investment of scarce resources. Networking of institutions for mutual learning and support has also been ignored by geographers. The foundations for such works have already been laid through atlases of various educational norms. More can and should be done in this direction. We should, however, move out of the atlas syndrome to planning for educational development with special emphasis on local and regional needs and educational facilities and contents.

Assessment of educational needs, locality and regionwise is another dimension that should claim interest of geographers. How to make education relevant is a question of vital importance. Should geography wait for encroachment from the newly conceived environmental studies to become alive of its responsibilities?

Medical geography is another field of considerable importance. It has four main aspects: (1) spatial distribution of health conditions and health facilities, (2) spread of health practices, practitioners and diseases; (3) environment and health, and (4) use nature as the doctor. So far only the first dimension has received the attention of geographers in India. The spatial diffusion of communicable diseases like cholera, Aids, chicken-pox etc. have yet to be taken cognizance of. The causal relationship between physical environment and health, too, has not received adequate attention. And the studies conducted have been highly generalized and chorographic. The last aspect which I call, geo-medicine is of great practical significance to geographers. How to use the gifts of nature, the food, the mud, the water and the air to treat diseases and maintain good health.

Let me dwell on geo-medicine in some more detail because it has the potential of making our society minimise, if not eliminate diseases, and also of creating hundreds and thousands of job opportunities for geographers. Nature care or naturopathy iÿ an old system of treating diseases. It uses natural resources like soil, water, plants and herbs, etc. to treat diseases. If we combine environmental geography and naturopathy and provide a base of ecology and biology, we get geo-medicine. If we offer a two-year postgraduate diploma course to those who have graduated with geography, we can carry geography very close to the hearts of the people and offer new opportunities to our graduates. I have run such a course successfully and proved that geography can become an important instrument in making our country healthy.

Environmental Studies

Environmental science studies is emerging as a new discipline. It is being taught at the school as well as university levels. At the school level, it is essentially geography but it is so presented as if it is something new. If this situation continues, the day is not far off when geography will be taken off the school curricula. It will be replaced by environmental studies.

Geographers have, therefore, to be watchful of the curriculum development in primary education in different states of the country. Geography is in danger of being replaced by environmental studies, thus doing immense harm to the citizenship education. Instead, geography should broaden its coverage to include environmental studies and the new text book should reflect this adequately to give to environmental issues.

Environmental impact assessment, environmental audit, environmental budgeting and environmental accounting have not even been touched by geographers. Environmental law is another field which has been completely neglected. All these are important partly because they are concerned with natural resources, and partly because they help us in resource planning and management. How can we teach or research on resource management without having understanding and knowledge of the methodology of resource assessment and accounting?

Environmental laws permit or restrict natural resources uses. All disciplines study laws relevant to them except geography. Indian geographers have not made any noticeable contribution to conventions and international or national laws governing the use of resources-land, water, forest, wild life etc. In my view, environmental or natural resource laws should constitute a course at post-graduate studies in geography.

Regional Planning

I recall the days when our efforts to use geographic principles to spatial planning in the sixties were not very welcome. Although regional geography has been the end product of our discipline, we did not venture in the field of planning and development. At first, geographers started studying the spatial structure of development. Regional planning remained the domain of professional physical planners (town planners). While at Jawaharlal Nehru University, further progress was made in the field of regional development studies. Mysore department of geography became the centre of regional planning initially following Geddes's valley section principle. The pioneering work done by late V.L.S. Prakasa Rao had its imprints on this effort and a new Institute of Development Studies came into being in 1970's, managed by geographers, economists and physical planners.

The work done in Jawaharlal Nehru University and Mysore has remained incomplete. Not much progress has been made in theory, methodology or explanation, although ecological and environmental problems have now emerged boldly, nothing substantial has been done to incorporate these concerns in regional planning.

How to incorporate ecological and environmental concerns and issues in multi-level regional planning exercises have yet to be demonstrated. This naturally requires, apart from other techniques, practical knowledge of Geographical Information System and Land Information System. How many geography departments are really equipped for this ? How many geographers have training in this field ? Apparently, we are lagging very far behind others even though Geographical Information System has geographic trade mark.

Another example will illustrate our reluctance to develop geography as a field of great societal significance. Take the case of watershed management. The whole concept of watershed is geographic. The idea that watershed at the micro level is an ideal unit of land use, occupational and human settlement planning is an old one. The valley section of Geddes is built on this idea. What is the contribution that we geographers have made to watershed planning and management? We have limited ourselves to showing the drainage system on maps (adopted from toposheets) and then telling without scientific analysis of potentials, what crops can be grown.

Urban Geography

Urban geography is the most developed sub-field of geography. Literature on various aspects of urbanization, urban system and individual cities is copious. Indian geographers can congratulate themselves for the amount of quality work done – urban geography is being taught in practically in all universities of the country and the number of Ph.D. theses in this field is perhaps the largest.

A critical mind, however, cannot fail to see any similarity in these contributions. Our paradigm of thinking and theoretical foundations are not Indian. They are western. The conclusions derived in the West are often faithfully used by us to stress that urban pattern emerging in India will follow the one we notice in Europe and America. We except our country to be without villages in some distant future. India will be fifty per cent urban by 2015, eighty per cent by 2050 and so on. We rarely see a difference in the urbanization process in the West and in India.

Some seventy years back, Mahatma Gandhi said that India should not industrialize itself on the lines of the West. To industrialize a tiny island kingdom (United Kingdom), the resources of the much of the world were denuded. What will happen to the world when a country like India (at that time with 300 million people) follows suit. Industrialization and urbanization go together. That is why he promoted the idea of decentralized production. Now it is realised that India can urbanize and industrialize itself on Western lines only by inviting calamities like the ones we see in cities today.

Half of the population of Delhi lives in the slums. Can we offer to bring more migrants to cities? We need to think of new models and structures of human settlements. India need not be urbanized through large cities. Can we not think of our villages becoming tiny citilets so that people prosper wherever they are? That is what Mahatma Gandhi suggested. His concept of oceanic circles has to be picked up by geographers to evolve new theories and concepts of decentralized planning and development.

Nature of migration to cities has changed a lot during the last one or two decades. We have used only migration data produced by the Census of India. Micro-level studies, earlier common in geography to assess migration stream, are now rare. Much of our urban studies are based on census data; hardly ten per cent of them emerge from field studies. Is it not surprising that no city in India has yet been subjected to urban base study, not even a small city of 10,000 population?

Other Fields

It would be rather too lengthy an essay to touch each branch of geography. I must, however, mention that the neglect of physical geography (geomorphology), climatology and bio-geography in particular) has done a lot of harm to our field. It is now the time to lay stress on these disciplines and get students with geology, biology, and physics/chemistry background to our Master and Ph.D degree programmes. Unless we have geographer scholars in these fields, it will be difficult to contribute substantially to environmental studies, eco-development, resource analysis and management,.agricultural, medical and social geography.

Concluding Remarks

Friends, the above are a few of the strengths and weaknesses of Indian geography. I have deliberately laid emphasis on weaknesses, for events like the Indian Geographical Council are the right occasions to introspect and evaluate ourselves so that we can do better in future. Other branches of geography and cartography, too, need new directions and orientations. The sample given above is only indicative, not exhaustive and final. Let us discuss some of these in the sessions of the Indian Geographical Council and learn from each other during these 3-4 days.

Information technology has changed a lot more. Changes are in the offing. Geography has nothing to lose from it. It stands to gain for it will provide us new data and facts for which we have been looking for centuries. But our tradition of explorations must go on. We can have satellite imageries of whatever is physically present on the surface of the earth, but there is no instrument which can scan minds and hearts of the people. Fortunately or unfortunately, it is the minds and hearts of the people which give rise to geographers on the surface the earth.

We are on the threshold of a new era in geographic teaching and research. The next century is the century of integration, wholism, sustainable development and humanism. We are passing through difficult times, there is light in darkness, as there is life in death. A new world is taking shape. Let geographers be participants in the creation of this world. Let us change our ways and pick new threads to unfold the inherent potentials of geography.

Let me now close by digressing from the main theme to appeal to your hearts. Friends, geography is a discipline of unity and integration—unity of science and humanities; unity of man and nature; union of space and people. Let us try to make our discipline a discipline of unity and love. Let our departments/institutions be examples for sister departments, and let us individually try to be true human beings. We cannot be perfect, but even a step forward will make our discipline richer and our society better.

REFERENCES

Council of Geographical Association (1919), *The position of geography, The Geographical Teacher*, p. 10.

Goodson, I.F. (1996), *Becoming an academic subject: patterns of explanation and evolution, British Journal of Sociology of Education*, Vol. 2, pp. 163 - 180.

Mackinder, H.J. (?), *The teaching of geography and history as a combined subject, The Geographical Teacher*, Vol. 7.

Ministry of Education, UK (?), *Citizens Growing Up*, Pamphlet No. 6, HMSO, London.

Royal Geographical Society (1950), *Geography and Social Studies*. Mimeograph Prepared by the Committee.

Unstead, J. (1913), *Discussion on Mackinder's paper, The Geographical Teacher*, Vol. 7.

Williams, M. (1976): *Geography and the Integrated Curriculum*, Heinemann, London.

Aijazuddin Ahmad
1932 -

Ahmad does not belong to the band of human beings who are easy to comprehend, condense and pen. It perhaps is a truism that simplicity is elusive. In his journey as an academician Ahmad's commitments have been intense, perhaps a bit too emotional to be in tune with the academic ethos prevailing today in the portals of universities in India.

Born on 12th January, 1932 at Firozabad in the agrarian lands of western Uttar Pradesh, one day Ahmad's family received a packet wrapped in the one million map of the United States of America. While his father, an employee in the British Department of Revenue found the contents urgent, to the ten year old Ahmad the wrapping paper was a delight. Developing a love for maps, a book on the world deserts, bought with bargained care from a local kabadi shop, instilled in him an urge to know the world beyond his little world. Early in life he resolved to learn and research about the world - if geography became a natural choice, the department of geography at Aligarh was the logical destination. Carrying the flag of being India's oldest department of geography and close proximity from home were added attractions. Housing one of the finest collections of geographical journals and books if the Seminar Library was his favourite refuge, it was the fervent intellectual activity in Aligarh which kindled Ahmad's instinct to delve into the causes of wide scaled disparities and continuous human suffering. While vigorous discussions and heated debates became forays for geographical thought it is in his most private moments that emotions gave birth to poetry and prose. Recording the pains in life, Ahmad's profuse publications in Urdu literature and his geographical contribution cannot be divorced. Gifted with a literary flair, imbibing an understanding of spatial concept, writing was Ahmad's true academic companion in years to come.

When formal education saw an end with his doctorate in 1962, Aligarh was quick to offer Ahmad a lecturership. Whereas the carefree days of student life had kept Ahmad in Aligarh for eight continuous years, a sense of being stifled drove him in 1972 to the more "socially relevant" geographical research promised at the newly established Center for the Study of Regional Development of the Jawahar lal Nehru University, New Delhi. Outgrowing the charm that the book on desert had cast on his childhood with the completion of a doctoral thesis on 'Human Geography of the Indian Desert', Ahmad also discarded teaching the course on the arid zone when he fled to Delhi. The core of his interest at the Centre revolved around social geography which embraced not just perspectives on historical geography, regional development and planning, but drew heavily from critical geographical thought. An authorship of a dozen books like Social Structure and Regional Development, 1993, Muslims in India, 1993, along with sixty research papers in national and international journals, capture Ahmad's reflections on different social dimensions. The precipitate of his ideas over a quarter century of teaching and research at the Centre find culmination in his recently published book titled 'Social Geography of India', 1999. He now hopes to add a companion volume on 'Critical Social Geography of India' which will address issues of minorities, caste and tribe.

Gifted with powers of exceptional literary thinking gives most of Ahmad's publications a high rank among quality and not only won him fellowships to the Union of Soviet Socialist Republics, Academy of Science and the Fullbright, United States of America, but it preoccupied him as editor for leading journals in India. He was editor of 'the geographer' (1964-1972) honorary editor of Indian Council of Social Science Research, Journal of Abstracts and Reviews: Geography (1981-1988) joint editor and editor of the Annals of the National Association of Geographers, India (1982 to 1994). Few geographers in India can boast of holding the editorial office for such long years as Ahmad. Loyal to the tradition of student-teacher relationship, few would also know that Ahmad was worker and ghost writer in a number of research projects and papers published under joint authorship or even without claims to a name!

Ahmad's critical insights though a boon for intellectual work, became a bane when targeted at mediocrity, which pollutes the pool of scholarships in India today. Ahmad could comprehend the social dynamics of a complex society like India, but ironically his ability to deal with the people and processes of his professional environment were beyond his skill. The result: more critics than friends fill his balance sheet of the day. But then, who said popularity was the dominant measure for scholarship.

It is often stated our intentions mirror the world outside. Scholarly passions kept at bay any offers of administrative and management posts. Freed from the mundane routines, Ahmad had ample time to indulge in interests of the finer arts of wide reading, classical music, and travelling. Learning from the kaleidoscope of his life experiences, Ahmad hopes to one day write his memoir as a geographer in India. Though the idea is still at an embryonic stage, when complete it would be a blend of realism and idealism punctuated where prose fails with Ahmad's very own lines of poetry.

Fifty Years of Geography in India and Abroad

A. AHMAD

I take this opportunity to place on record my deep sense of gratitude to the Executive Committee and the General Body of the National Association of Geographers, India for honoring me by electing as the President of the National Association of Geographers, India. For a modest teacher of geography, like me, it is a rare honor indeed. I am greatly beholden to the community of geographers in the country for vesting their confidence in me and assigning me the challenging task of leading the National Association in these critical years, transitional to the twenty-first century, a period when the entire nation is in a state of ferment. In fact, the clarity for long-term goals has been blurred by the compulsions of an insatiable desire to appropriate the immediate gains by whatever means they can be achieved.

This responsibility has been assigned to me in the Golden Jubilee Year of India's Independence. Even though this adds an extra feather in my cap, it adds to my responsibility immensely. It reminds me of the role geographers were expected to play in the stupendous task of nation-building. It reminds me of the glorious achievements which became possible through the dedicated service of stalwarts like C.D. Deshpande, George Kuriyan, S. M. Ali, S. P. Chatterji, V. S. Gangadharan, V.L.S. Prakasa Rao, S.M.T. Rizvi, M.B. Pithawala, Kazi Saeeduddin Ahmad, M.L. Chhibber and Nafis Ahmad. This galaxy of names on the Indian skies on the eve of independence shone continued to guide us like beacon lights from decades. It also reminds me of our glaring failures, the missed opportunities and the great betrayal that followed.

In this Golden Jubilee Year of our Independence, it is my most cherished duty to pay my homage, our homage, to the countless men and women, sons and daughters of India, who fought for the cause of India's independence. They sacrificed their comforts of life to enable us to live in freedom and with dignity, holding our heads high as an independent nation, free from the shackles of slavery, poverty and misery. While we became politically independent, economic

---

20th Indian Geography Congress
Thiruvanthapuram, 1997 December

independence seemed to be a distant goal. In fact, we created our own ruling class which eventually came to be ruthless and no different from the British and a bureaucracy worse than the British. These two elements within the higher echelons of power collaborated to enslave the multitude of Indian people who slided down the poverty line decade after decade. With every day that passes the grip of chains is becoming tighter and tighter.

Today geographers have a responsibility to stand up and point our grey areas in our national endeavour, to enlighten our students not only on their rights but also on their duties towards the nation. Geographers have to contribute their might to the unfinished task of nation-building, by training their students to undertake meaningful research committed to the task of nation-building, painting a vision of unified India where differences of color, caste, creed, community, region or language were irrelevant and were to be forgotten in the name of the one-ness of the Indian nation. They have to generate model research to bridge the gap between the developed and the under-developed regions of India, between the privileged and the lagging sections of our population, between the *dalits* and the haves in the ranks of the upper castes, between the male-dominated ethos and the gender equality. Model research is equally urgently needed in the area of social well-being to minimize the yawning gaps in nutrition, proneness to sickness, literary attainments, employment, social networking and access to basic existential amenities, particularly in cities.

While commenting on the state-of-art in India geography, an eminent geographer commented that in order to find a place in the sun, 'Indian geography must become human and humane, must become Indian in character'. He also stated that the bogey of relevance, prima facie, hinges upon the simple questions: relevant to what, relevant to whom? How do we define relevance? He dismissed relevance as an ideological stance. Interestingly the scholar never used the term social relevance. The word social is alien to the lexicon of this school of thoughts. It is not enough to say that Indian geography should become Indian. What vision of India do you have in mind? In the words of Ramanujan, 'there is no single Indian way of thinking, there are Great and Little Traditions, ancient and modern, rural and urban, classical and folk. Each language, caste and region has its specific world view. So under the apparent diversity, there is really a unity of view point a single super system'. What is that super system? Is India better understood by exploring the spirit of place, the Hindu vision of sacred space as Rana Singh puts it? Or are there other ways of looking at the mystique of the place? Where do you go after having come to know the spirit of place ?

When somebody says that Indian geography should become Indian, perhaps the underlying idea is that instead of aping the west it should bank on its own instinct of perceiving the Indian reality with the Indian eyes. Frankly speaking, this issue is irrelevant to the departments of knowledge. There cannot be an Indian physics, although there can be a history of physiucs in India. Similarly there cannot be an Indian astronomy, although one can examine the Indian contribution to astronomy or astrophysics. Disciplines are not to be Indianised or Russified, or Anglicised or Frenchised, Keralised or Tamilised. Taxonomy of knowledge does not proceed along country lines. There is a universal unity of disciplines. Therefore, there is no sub-altern view of geography unless otherwise the idea is to confuse the issue and get lost in the mythology of paradigms. What is specific is not only specific, it also helps in understanding the generic, because the generic expresses itself through the specific.

The question of social relevance will continue to be central to the very existence of the disciplines in the decades to come. No scientific discipline will be allowed to grow sufficiently if it does not subserve the primary interest of human kind. Geography, in my opinion, will be an academic redundancy if its value as a utilitarian discipline is not generally recognized. Who will throw money on trivialities ? O.K. I agree, that information on the basic elements of geography should be collected and disseminated. Himalayas lie on the north, Indian Ocean on the south. Calcutta is situated to the east-northeast of Mumbai. The State of Kerala lies on the west coast of India, Sri Lanka to the south and east of the Indian peninsula. This cape and bay, peak and valley, plateau and the trough geography will be like the alphabet. Everybody has to learn it. Will you continue to teach the alphabet at all levels of education from primary to the graduation ? At some stage somewhere you have to make your students conscious of their responsibility towards society and make a meaningful use of the alphabet they have learnt. It is this usefulness which will decide what place you occupy in the family of disciplines, central or peripheral. The process of marginalisation begins when it is generally perceived that you are a useless lot. If more geography is done outside the geography departments then geographers will be the last people to be consulted on any thing under the sun. It is time to think why we have lost ground to geology, to meteorology, to environmental science, to economics, to social anthropology, to digital cartography? This is just to mention a few areas of the lost academic space.

The primary task before us is to inculcate a sense of social responsibility in our students who come to us in the pursuit of knowledge. The new geographer in the making should spend his/her energies not on trivialities but on the significant social problems which can acquire new meaning if analyzed with the tools of geographical analysis within the frame of time-space continuum. The sense of social responsibility should grow from an animated and positive concern for the ailments of the society.

This new approach to social priority and geographical research has its own demands. Tremendous information gaps exist in our understanding of the social reality in India today. We do not have any data along the space scale on the prevalence of economic inequality as revealed in the mal-distribution of the means of production and an unequal share of the different segments of population in the natural resource endowment; on the regional variations in land inequality, land relations, tenancy systems; the processes leading to the land alienation; on the proportion of our population unserved or partially served by such social amenities as schools, hospitals, maternity clinics, drinking water and so on; on the regional and ethno-lingual, or caste, variations in the level of schooling; on inequalities in the educational opportunities available to the different categories and classes of Indian people. The new agenda for geography is to throw a force of dedicated researchers in the field to generate this knowledge and thus helps the emancipation of the deprived, the down-trodden and the under-privileged section of our people.

The need for change in the criteria of social relevance arises not from a philanthropic anxiety over the persistence of such social problems as poverty and squalor, it grows out of a sense of belonging to the people, particularly the classes who toil in the fields and the factories and contribute the fruits of their labour for continuance of all research activity. We owe a debt to them and can pay it back only by reorienting our research to their immediate needs. Let us minimize the parasitic tendencies which geographical research has acquired in the past and make it an instrument of social awakening and tool of social reconstruction.

Reminiscing on geography's past and present may not be a very pleasant exercise, particularly if the audience is predominantly Indian and the subject-matter is geography as we know it in India today. Such occasion may be fruitful if the purpose is constructive and a healthy stock-taking of the achievements and failures of generations of teachers and learners of geography in the South-Asian sub-continent. Particularly, the effort may be useful if it is made with the eye on the future. Such exercises may be highly valuable if they culminate in introspection and reconstruction for better future. But if the community of geography is not prepared to agree to this introspection, the whole effort may crash down into pure acrimony.

The implicit idea behind this project is innocent both in spirit and purpose—an exercise in intellection, in conceptualization of achievements or otherwise of a tradition of geographical pedagogy and research as it evolved over the decades since the Buttler Geography Department was established at the Aligarh University in 1927. This incident itself was quite late in the history of the discipline if one looked at this development in the global context—one hundred and nine years after the first chair of geography was created at the University of Berlin. The tradition as it was handed to us was indigenous but not Indian. Aligarh's primacy is unquestionable, although the late appearance of academic disciplines on the Indian horizon could be attributed to the causes which explain under development in all spheres of life—economic, political and social – the causes which led to the submission of the Indian genius to an alien intellectual tradition.

The heritage of geography as we are familiar with is a mixed bag of hopes and expectations as well as shattered hopes and disillusionment. Any comment on the state of the art may raise many eyebrows. It may be branded as outright prejudiced or purely euphemistic, or both. Judgements in such situations may not be always free from biases from which an individual point of view suffers. For a pure critic nobody is above board including the critic himself.

The state of the art of a discipline like geography may not be described in a vacuum, detached from the social milieu or the political environment in which intellectual development is promoted or thwarted. In the development of a body of knowledge, individual contributions lead to the creation of a climate which is more important than individuals. The objective conditions of existence which characterize the academia at a given point of time in history define the outer limits within which individuals function, set their goals, spell out the dimensions of their commitment to the cause for which they stand. All this contributes to the work ethos. The younger colleagues and students are likely to imbibe the ethical values as demonstrated to them by their seniors. Ethics may have a theory, but its best manifestation is in practice. The ethical values are systematically replaced by a variety of functional mercantilism if politics replaces the academics. Conditions such as the growing political nexus between the academics and the lower order functionaries within the institution help in the erosion of the moral authority of the teacher. Then the teacher ceases to be an example to be followed. More importantly, the teacher may also crave to become a lower order functionary. He might prefer to ape the ways of his superiors in the hierarchical order or local bureaucracy. If he fails to do so, he may be in the endless race for professional promotion.

I am dwelling upon these issues because they are central to the theme for our discussion. The climate that the prevailing conditions create may be conducive or detrimental to the process of intellectual development, including the development in the geographical academy.

The farther you go to explore this question, the more disgusting the exercise becomes. The experience gained over the years show that departments of teaching and research have developed as fiefdoms. Individual initiative and freedom were curbed under the domineering authority of a departmental leader.

Specialisms were born or made to die at his or her will. Despite the unhelpful conditions that prevail, departments acquired specialties as a quick recollection would show—Aligarh in agricultural landuse and nutrition, Banaras in urban and caste morphology, Madras in economic, Calcutta in regional, Delhi in human, Saugor in physical, historical and cartography, Andhra in geomorphology and climatology, Chandigarh in population, Pune in regional, urban, geomorphology and environmental studies, Baroda in settlements and political, Mysore in regional planning, Jawaharlal Nehru University in social and regional development, Kurukshetra in agriculture and so on. Growth of individuals as well as sub-fields suffered from hereditary problems, and a second line of descendants was never easily traceable.

In my estimate geography in the South-Asian sub-continent suffered from individualism and adherence to the feudal values which led to incurable genetic diseases. While systematic and regional geographies were talked and discussed in classrooms and departmental seminars, open debates on the country-wide scale were never conducted mostly because of groupism that permeated the body academic of local geography. Regional or local leaders organized themselves in groups with parochial tendencies, jeopardizing the chances of emergence of a collective leadership or an all-India platform. Associations of geography as well as journals launched by them had a regional, even local character, symbolizing diversity without an over-arching unity. An all India geographical association grew from the ashes of this divisive history, but crashed down in just over a decade, leaving behind traces of a still surviving feudal order satisfied with its propertied ownership of the ruined association. If one man's exit meant so much of devastation, who would commit the folly of reconstruction ? Writing, brilliant pieces of writings poured out from individual pens but they did not lead to the rise of schools of thought. Serious geographies of India were written but not by locals. Regional monographs may be exceptions to this general rule. For example, Deshpande's Western India, Inayet Ahmad's Bihar and Moonis Raza's half-finished Valley of Kashmir were landmark contributions. City geographies such as on Banaras and Hyderabad were ably documented. So were the studies on Mysore state.

Recalling this part of history is not necessary, although it is not relevant if we want to fix responsibility and mend our ways accordingly. Over the years we have lost ground in many areas that were dear to us and were due to us. Our grip on physical geography and environmental studies has loosened. There are departments without geomorphologists or those having a grounding in physical geography. One inevitable consequence is that our students do not get necessary scientific training in the study of environment and its elements such as rocks, geomorphological process, depositional and erosional history, palaeoclimatology, climate and weather factors, soils and field studies of pedogenetic process, hydrology, floral and faunal elements, forest ecology, agronomy and the like. Exceptions apart, expertise did not develop in many of these areas: no laboratories were established. In this context, the current emphasis of Geographic Information System and remote sensing equipment appears crazy. First, the theoretical basis has to be created before you can build the methodological nuances.

In sum, while geographers were the first people in the world to develop comprehensive and integrated knowledge of environment, the current upsurge in environmental studies and the related ecological issues took place without our involvement. It is not that the things that the geographers were supposed to do were not done. They were done by more informed and alert social and environmental scientists. Planning Commission depended on economists for evolving a scheme of agro-climatic regions of India. In regional perspective planning, infrastructural or transport studies conducted by the Planning Commission, geographers rarely figured.

Geographical metaphor today reflects a state of epistemic pluralism with all the streams of thought which represented different stages in the development of theory since 1950 existing simultaneously, although with varied degrees of intensity. That the geographical tradition is pluralistic is undisputed. What is not understandable in the geographical academy of the Third World is the distance between the multiple theoretical positions taken by the practitioners of the subject and the prevailing social reality. The urge to receive the currency of paradigms in circulation is so great that often the gap between the ground reality and its portrayal in theory is completely ignored. This epistemic pluralism is evident in the continuance of all schools of theory—abstracted empiricism, positivism, humanism, behaviouralism, structuralism and post-modernism. While the western economy seems to have made a big leap forward into the age of post-modernity, the lagging sections of the community in the east and the south are still striving to recognize the social and political meaning of the processes of modernisation. In a way, they have not yet experienced modernity. By implication it would mean that most of us are grossly unprepared to share and appreciate the intellectual concerns of the protagonists of post-modern metaphor. This is not withstanding the fact that the academic development in India is highly fragmented, spatially as well as temporally. The few centres of eminence which had so far managed their affairs with efficiency are gasping for breath. In common parlance they are facing a financial crunch, which I believe is artificially created. Among other things this has hit library purchases, filling of faculty position and other renewal programmes. This has obviously resulted in stunted growth or even stagnation. In the immediate hinterland of these so-called centres of eminence, there may be campuses which still carry with them an Indianized version of the nineteenth century legacy. So while time passes, it does not leave its imprints on the sands that it trods gleefully. While the time passes the environs do not change. The psychological distance between the two poles is often so great that each of the adherents takes a special pleasure in remaining enconsed in a philosophy of mutual exclusivity. Even otherwise there is no dialogue either between or among them, partly because of material limitations or psychological inhibitions. But above all, the language in which a dialogue can be conducted has itself been drowned in the babel of tongues all around.

One outcome of this history of development is the division of the academic space between the westernized elite's and the backward-looking masses inhabiting the hinterland. There is a need to bridge this gap as there is a need to minimize the unevenness in the process of development. The situation calls for rethinking on the question of language in which the dialogue is to be conducted.

Luckily, so far we are concerned, post-modernity is miles away and many among us may be unconcerned about its epistemological implications. But that may be unrealistic as the implications are dangerous both at the philosophical plane as well as in practical terms.

Modern geography has a rationalist position which determined its epistemological basis. With the changing conditions in the global context that rationalist project supposedly failed making scientific positivism an undesirable quality. It was widely felt that with these changes in the objective conditions, a pluralist relativism was inevitable. Such a situation was noticed in the wake of the receding tide of quantification. It was further accentuated by the changing world economic and political order in the post-perestroika, post-cold war scenario: the socialist block crumbled and the world political system succumbed to a state of unipolarity: the unchecked expansion of the capitalist formation across the globe with market economies rejecting the prospects of planned, socially equitous development beyond any hope of redemption: penetration of the trans-national capital and the attendant technologies of the western cultural vantage into the little economies of the Third World countries promoting consumerism: and the rise of a television generation which takes pleasure in short spans of ecstasy. Seen in the context of this background, Livingstone's reminder is worth repeating:

'The prestige of scientific precision is gone only to be replaced by a delight in ambiguity, an uncertainty that only seems confirmed by the experimental research of the quantum physicists: consistency is neither possible nor desirable and the different styles can be juxtaposed in playful ways; the idea of texts revealing author's intentions, or indeed these being an authorial self at all, is being subverted by deconstructionist literary critics; and the architectural functionalism or Le Corbusier's modernist movement recedes before pastiche and nostalgia.'

The pursuits of scientific observation and enquiry have been relegated to mere fetishism. What used to be a concern for realism has been replaced by relativism. Subaltern view points have been glorified to the extent of becoming an obsession. A subject cannot be observed accurately by an outside culture and an outside representation may be rejected as patently imaginary and false. Subjective viewpoint is perhaps the best viewpoint. Description has acquired thicker ethnographic idioms (for example, women's issues can be studied more accurately by women only).

The construction of geography of post-modernity is yet not clear, although geographers have been forced to review and restate their position in the midst of growing confusion. Broadly speaking the first major encounter with post-modernity was snagged by David Harvey himself as early as 1989, who conceptualised the post-modern situation as an outcome of advancing capitalism. The all round confusion that the post-modernist geographies created forced among other Derek Gregory and Edward Soja to plead for rethinking the history and genealogy of geography. Soja's work on post-modern geographies was subtitled as 'reassertion of space in critical social theory'. Whether these attempts at reassertion would help geography regain its lost position in the centre stage of contemporary social theory is still an open question. But the fact that the geographers are making systematic attempts towards spatialisation of social theory is itself indicative of the future direction of geographical discourse.

We may discuss this issue further citing the arguments that Soja advanced in support of his veiwpoint. Soja lamented the subordination of space in social theory recognizing the period 1820-1920 as critically important one in this squeezing out of geography from the 'competitive battleground of theory construction.' To quote Soja,

"By the end of this period the ascendance of a historicism of theoretical consciousness had reached such heights that the possibility of a critical human geography was made to appear inconceivable if not absurdly anachronistic to generations of Western Marxists and critical social scientists."

In his view, the isolation of modern geography and geographers from the production of social theory was well advanced by 1920. 'For most of the next fifty years, geographical thinking turned inwards and seemed to erase even the memories of earlier engagements with the main streams of social theorization'.

A quest for the causes of this 'involution' in the history of social theory may engage many geographers like Soja but not be easy to locate. A trip around Los Angeles reassures him of the future potential of post-modern geographies. Whether these similar voyages into urban and rural landscapes will replace historicism by spatiality is difficult to perceive at this juncture. We may only end up with a new phase of geographical poetics. In Livingstone's view, 'post-modernism's celebration of difference, of juxtaposition, of fragmentation, has further reasserted the importance of the specific, the local, the place bound' (page 344; cit. Derek Gregory, Edward Soja).

One may agree with this viewpoint giving due weightage to Livingstone's argument that classical foundationalism is in bad shape and better be given up for dead.P We have no option but to live with the positivist geography, Marxist geography, Islamic geography, structurationist, Christian geography, a people's geography, and on and on' (page 345). There may be further additions to this pluralistic catalogue such as Hindu geography, Gandhian geography and so on.

The real issue confronts us is rediscovering in the post-modernist idiom a spatialised ontology with spatialisation (the organization of space as a social product) emerging as the programme for reconstruction.

It may appear futile to reiterate my already stated position that intellectual and epistemic development in any discipline is rooted in the social theory. In the theory of knowledge, ideas develop in the course of social experience and not independently. The point is that there is a social theory which helps in the interpretation of the phenomena and in the process gets reinforced by the development of knowledge of the phenomena. When German thinkers like Humboldt, Ritter or Ratzel and Richthofen were talking of the unity of nature within the frame work of the earth visualized as an organic whole, they were expressing the epistemic need for the unity of nature and man (humans) within the global system. They were paving the way for the eventual ascendance of European civilization as a leader of humanity. There was socially felt need which prompted the European maritime powers to discover and explore the farflung parts of the world, although many of these newly discovered areas had already been discovered and explored by the adventurers in the oriental civilization. Or, for example, when Hugh Robert Mill described geography as 'a sternly practical' pursuit, he was perceiving geography as a vehicle of European ascendance over the rest of the world. The nineteenth century brand of European geographical epistemology was designed as to make geography to subserve the 'interests of nationalistic self-absorption.' In the words of Livingstone, "the reason was simple: geography to him (Hugh Robert Mill) was absolutely essential for our well-being, and even for the continuance of the nation as a power among the states of the world.' Moreover, it afforded "an important clue to the solution of many problems affecting the mutual relations of land and people, and lightening the course of history, anticipating the trend of political movements, indicating the direction of sound industrial and commercial development."

As European experience shows, knowledge of the world grew under the shadow of a social theory. But when paradigms, evolved in an exotic environment, are carried across the civilisational boundaries, they are likely to become irrelevant socially and historically and appear as epistemological curiosities. Our search for growth poles, or for the hierarchical ordering of settlements based on their functions in isolation of the mode of production appeared as irrelevant as wonderful. Here was a theory and a planning strategy handed down to us in complete oblivion of the political economy of development and the administrative convenience of the ruling elites. The point is that there has to be a social theory to justify the passage of ideas and methodologies into the classroom. It is a pity that geography in this part of the world could afford to live with this dualism for so long. Whether it is environment determinism or pure environmentalism, western philosophies have grown in the pursuit of socially felt needs and they can not be accepted uncritically. Their transference to alien environments would be hazardous.

This debate necessarily leads to the relationship between the level of social development and the pedagogic tradition. What you teach in a given situation may have political underpinnings. What you do not teach may be more important than what you teach. Our accumulated experience is that the tradition of omission may be the artifact of political conceit. In essence, it may be more conspiratorial than accidental. In societies of the Third World, where contradictions characterize economic and social development, any reconstructionist approach in geography will have to be grounded in the theory of social casualty, interactive space between the people and their environment, natural and social, is articulated through social processes determining the concentration or disposal of forces of production and the distribution of social surplus. The geographical theory will have to be interwoven with this most cautiously. The geographical explanation should redefine its position by discarding the tradition of bi-polar relationship between natural environment and people in favour of a new theory of social causality, where a social formation and not the environment plays a key role. The need for recognizing this socio-spatial dialectic is most urgent. What the geographers should do is to recreate consciousness of the need for the 'interpretation of human spatial organization as a social product'. This realization would call for a new urge for restructuring curricular programs along the new lines leading to the rejection of much of what may be turned as geographical obscurantism.

Kavasseery Vanchi Sundaram
1929 -

On 18th August, 2000 under the umbrella of geographers was launched the first consortium of earth scientists in India. It was christened as the Bhoovigayan Vikas Foundation. The occidental and oriental flavour in its name perhaps heralds the spirit of its common search for sustainable life styles and sustainable development from two different worlds. Sundaram is not merely the founder chairperson but the moving force behind this professional non- government organization . At the outset he had carried a triple mission – celebration of the Earth Day with a pledge to work for a sustainable future, honouring the Bharat Ratna as a life time achievement award to an eminent geographer and initiating the first geographical museum in India.

By August 2001, all the three objectives were met. Earth Day flagged, the Bharat Ratna Awards given, and a 350 acre piece of land cordoned for an earth museum. In a few months, Sundaram has achieved what many geographers long talked about– he has created a scope for the foundation of an Institute of Geographical Studies. The event unfolds two features: one Sundaram has exceptional determination and second his devotion to geography is in an exceptional niche. The uniqueness comes to the fore when one realizes that in his younger days, Sundaram had been skeptical about pursuing geography as a discipline of study. He spent all his professional life in the company of non-geographers. He never taught at any university department of geography. He never supervised a master of philosophy or a doctorate on this subject. He was a lecturer in the Alagappa College of the University of Madras from 1951–1958. When he resigned from its faculty, he was twenty-nine. It was in 1998 that he was elected as the President of the National Association of Geographers, India. After fourty years, at the age of sixty nine, Sundaram re-established connection with his own community. He exemplifies a return of the native.

Sundaram's sojourn of fifty hectic years of professional life involved him in national and international agencies across India and countries of Europe, Asia and Africa. He was one of the first geographers to be appointed at the Town and Country Planning Organization, Delhi in 1958, an office he served for fifteen years. The next fourteen years he rose the ranks from Joint Director to Joint Adviser at the Planning Commission. In the decade of the 1990s Sundaram globe trotted as consultant under the banner of United Nations and other international organizations like United Nation Centre for Regional Development, UNESCO, Food and Agricultural Organisation and Centre on Integrated Rural Development for Asia and the Pacific. In geographical parlance, Sundaram has scaled in his career from the micro to meso upto the macro realms. His mission in life was to deliver the tenets of planning within a spatial context.

The event that propelled Sundaram to discard academics and move to the applied domain of planning was a traumatic one. After an extended village level fieldwork in the Cumbum valley, Sundaram was in the throes of finalizing his doctoral submission when the authorities of the university informed him that a thesis cannot be accepted from a college with an affiliating status. The administrative mess frustrated Sundaram to the hilt; dumping his thesis,he resigned from teaching and joined the newly created urban planning authorities at Delhi. Following the postulates of the central place theory, through an extensive survey of 368 villages, Sundaram drafted the rural development plan for Delhi. When the Town and Country Planning Organization was formally inaugurated in the capital in 1955, Sundaram was absorbed without hesitation. The First Master Plan of Delhi, Regional Plans for Rajasthan Canal, Dandakaraniya, South – East Mineral Industrial Region and many others had Sundaram as a member of their team. Gaining valuable experience when the Planning Commission advertised the post of geographer- planner Sundaram had few competitors. It is with this apex planning body of India that Sundaram evolved and matured as a regional planner.

From centrally planned schemes, to multilevel planning,.to decentralized planning, Sundaram dished out projects and led study teams. The critical lesson he learnt was that the efficacy of a regional plan needs to be bolstered by an effective training of the officers who finally implement the objectives. By the end of the 1980s the climate of thinking was focused on how to remove bottlenecks to achieve equitable spatial development. Sundaram specialized in the role of translating goals into reality in the area of rural development. The innovative training modules which he designed attracted attention from international development agencies. Sundaram's wisdom seasoned on issues of regional planning and his backhand understanding of situations in the field made him a much sought after consultant with the United Nations. Over a dozen prestigious assignments stud his professional life from 1987- 1995. Forwarding a voluntary retirement to the Planning Commission, Sundaram spread his advice on issues of regional planning. Many areas of development in countries like Nepal, Bangladesh, Thailand and nations of Sub - Saharan Africa hinges on the manuals and plans spelt by Sundaram. Seventeen reports, many running into several volumes and over 120 technical papers decorate the bookshelves at his residence in Delhi. After a profession, remote and distanced from the mainstream of academics, how was Sundaram able to Return as a Native?

Born on 30th November, 1929 in Calicut to an orthodox Brahmin family which was overtly conscious about education meant that Sundaram inherited the pulse for a literary life. It is no surprise that after a jilted affair with a doctorate, Sundaram nursed back his wounds only after he acquired a Doctorate of Literature. To comfirm the path breaking research of his thesis the university seeked reviews from over a dozen different referees . It is this collective praise that metamorphosed into a Doctor of Literature, the first of its kind given to any social scientist by the University of Mysore in 1977. The experience in planning forever kindled in Sundaram the desire to pen his learning. His book Urban and Regional Planning in India was published in 1977. This book is his jewel in the crown and won him the Nullfield scholarship for post doctoral work at the University of Cambridge in 1978-1979. By the end of the 1990s Sundaram had written eleven books and twenty-seven chapters in different books. The tenor of his work is evident from the fact that nearly half the books and ninety per cent of his articles are authored by him alone. He does not dabble superficially into themes is proved by the fact that a major share of his publications square on issues of regional planning and development alone. Sundaram's publications find multiple entry in the curriculum of leading departments of geography, and serve as valuable reference on courses of development and planning.

All along as Sundaram soared the skies to become a national and international consultant on regional planning, he did not forget to nourish with books and publications, the roots of his discipline geography. Launching an elaborate blueprint of the Foundation for Earth Science Development is Sundaram's exceptional contribution to geography. His return is more than welcome !

Sub- National Development and Underdevelopment

K.V. SUNDARAM

I feel highly privileged to be elected as your President for this 20th Congress of National Association of Geographers, India, which also coincides with the terminal year of this millennium. I accept this unique honour with humility and express my deepest gratitude to all of you for this magnanimous gesture shown to me. I take this opportunity of rededicating myself to the objectives of the of National Association of Geographers, India, the symbol of our united endeavours. I also take a pledge that during the tenure of my Presidentship, I shall try to serve the cause of Geography; as best as I can, to promote our discipline in touching greater heights of performance and achievement, both in the academic sphere as well as in the applied areas of planning and development.

This meet at Gorakhpur is significant for the National Association of Geographers, India for more than one reason. Firstly, we are meeting in the "heartland of Indian Geography" that is, Uttar Pradesh, and secondly in a Department of Geography, which is one of the largest producers of Doctorates in our discipline. Thirdly, our meet is at a sacred place in our country. From all angles, this is an appropriate venue for us to rededicate ourselves to the cause of our discipline. We are also meeting on the 50th year of our Independence, and perhaps 75 years after the first Department of Geography was inaugurated in 1924 at the Aligarh University. The present occasion, therefore, seems to be an appropriate time to look back and reflect, to look ahead, and project a vision, mission and strategy to chalk out our line of action for the future.

The Changing Times

We are living in extremely exciting and changing times. The 20th century, which witnessed major technological, economic, social and political changes is about to end, and we are witnessing the dawn of a new millennium. This new

---

21st Indian Geography Congress
Gorakhpur, 1998 December

millennium is likely to be more transformational, radical, innovative and challenging than any other century in the past. It is almost impossible to predict the shape of things to come. At the same time, it is feasible to see an opaque picture of the future. We may definitely predict that the new millennium would be qualitatively quite different. The pace of change will be phenomenal and exponential. When Alvin Tofler wrote his book, "The Third Wave", he had conceptualised a 'global village', which seems to be becoming a reality. The evidence of this change is what we are witnessing today: weak trade barriers, efficient telecommunication linkages, greater cultural and scientific exchange and rapid communication systems. Rapid growth of all disciplines and fierce competition among them, to make themselves more and more relevant and useful to the economy and society of the future, may be visualised in perspective.

The Challenges to be Met

At this stage, the competency levels required of all disciplines have to be quite high. Information and knowledge would be the hallmarks of progress. Obsolescence and incapability to cope with such progress will spell the doom of any discipline. We will surely witness a 'churning' in all sciences, who will be literally scrambling to improve, adapt and adjust themselves to the pressures of a changing globally integrated economy. It is needless to say that our discipline too has to respond to such changes with alacrity and make several adaptations. While we must make our own pathway for the next millennium, one thing is clear. That is, our discipline has to become qualitatively more different, scientifically more sharp and fully equipped with more modern tools and techniques, with the ability to compete effectively with other social sciences. We must seriously think about the question of the strategic change involved here and how to materialise it in the quickest possible time.

Let us look at this issue from a different angle; let us ask the question: What kind of geographers do we foresee in the next millennium? What attributes and what qualities do we expect in them? In my own imagination, I see the future geographers transformed into totally information-technology-based and more multi-disciplinary knowledge-based people, who will have the world at their finger tips. They will be doing not merely teaching related jobs, but more and more planning and policy oriented jobs. They will be the leaders and constant learners, continually adapting themselves to the change, sharpening the tools of their discipline to the new ways of perceiving and thinking about the world, and working out new ideas and solutions to tackle, what the Club of Rome has called the "world problematique", which is a complex web of economic, sociological, ecological and political problems. The scale of the very many human interventions on the earth that supports us is now so great, that we find ourselves faced by a series of threats: nuclear warfare, the population explosion, the food problem, the energy crisis, the degradation of natural resources, unsustainable development, pollution, and so on. Each one of these problems is complex enough in itself, but then it turns out that it is only one aspect of, as it were, a "Total Problem", in which all aspects of man's interference with the world's natural systems are interrelated. To find appropriate solutions to this "Total Problem" or the world problematique, individual disciplines have to increasingly collaborate with other disciplines. This is only to underline a point that geographers in the new millennium have to be more and more interdisciplinary oriented. They have also to use more and more modern techniques to find solutions (Quantitative techniques, Geographic Information System, Remote Sensing and other techniques). I have, however, touched on only one aspect of the "strategic change" desired to move into the next millennium. The issue is more complex and there are many other requirements to be met. Each one of us has to think more deeply on this subject. I therefore leave this for the present as open-ended.

The State of the Discipline

As is customary in all annual meetings of professional bodies, let me commence my address by taking stock of the state of our discipline at this point of time and by outlining our role in the emerging future scenario. As I look back at the nearly half a century of my professional career, which I may characterise as less narrowly geographical and perhaps more interdisciplinary, I find that it roughly coincides with the rise of, what may be called, the "modern geography", with the discipline breaking its traditional shackles and becoming more quantitative, applied and inter-disciplinary in character, with numerous additions to its techniques and research methods. The "tree of geographical knowledge" has grown both at the core and the margins, as witnessed today by an increasing number of geography departments offering numerous specialisations of the subject.

When I was a student in the late forties, hardly 5 or 6 branches of the discipline were taught. These were primarily the philosophical and the basic dimensions of the subject, which included Historical and Political geography, the Physical basis of geography, Human geography, Regional geography and Cartography. The specialisations were limited. Today, new dimensions have been added, which are in thematic and technique-oriented specialisations. The thematic specialisations encompass, a wide variety of subjects such as Urban geography, Industrial geography, Development geography, Medical geography,

Population geography, Agricultural geography, Eco-geography, etc., and the technique-oriented specialisations include, Quantitative geography, Remote-sensing, Geographic Information Systems, Rapid appraisal techniques and computer Cartography and its applications.

Thus, today the diversification of the discipline is indeed mind-boggling. For instance, the Department of Geography at Delhi University lists 37 courses in its prospectus. I guess that it must be the same with other geography departments as well. This is indeed a welcome trend. At the same time, we have to be cautious that in this race for specialisation and quantification, the philosophical and the basic dimensions of the discipline are not neglected or under-rated, as any intelligent inferences or interpretations that we draw from these analytical branches of the discipline, must be rooted on a strong base.

Apart from this diversification, if we take other parameters of growth, like increase in the number of geography departments in our universities, the current number of professional geographers in the country, the number of Doctorates turned out in the geography departments, the number of professional journals available to articulate our research findings etc. we get the impression, that the growth has been indeed quite phenomenal.

According to Dr. Anu Kapur in her recent book on "Indian geography: a Future with a Difference", with only 5 departments of geography at the time of our Independence, there has been a four-fold increase at the end of the 1970's. In 1996, their number has increased to 67. With only 3 Doctorates before 1947, the number has grown to 1026 in 1990. The acceleration in research activity is particularly marked after 1960. The number of geographical journals has increased from 7 before 1950 to 54 in 1993. The role of geographers has been not merely in the academia, that is, teaching in the schools, colleges and university departments, but also in the applied areas of the Census, Organisation, National Atlas Organisation, Survey of India, Social Science Institutes, Planning Organisations, and Defence and Administrative Services. It is estimated that there are 15,000 to 20,000 practising geographers in the country. Although 80 per cent of them are engaged in education, the opportunities in other professions are expanding. An organisation like the National Atlas and Thematic Mapping Organisation, which alone employees about 450 geographers, has made impressive contributions. Similarly, the few geographers who have been able to occupy senior positions in applied fields, have succeeded to some extent in improving the visibility and image of the discipline in research and policy-oriented areas. This trend should increase and continue. The Centres of Excellence in our university departments are growing. I am an optimist and I see only expanding horizons and no shrinking opportunities.

The SWOT Analysis

However, a relevant question in our present context is: With what weaponry and tactics are we entering into the 21st century to face its big challenges? Perhaps a SWOT (Strength, Weakness, Opportunity and Threats) analysis may give us some partial answers to this question. Trying to be as objective as possible, I present a SWOT matrix as follows:

Strengths

(i) Strong presence of the discipline in the academia.
(ii) Well established departments of Geography with new specialisations and technique-oriented skills.
(iii) A large student community, which is enthusiastic and eager to make a mark in applied areas.
(iv) Ability to deal with a number of issues within the spatial dimension.
(v) Ability to integrate the physical as well as the social dimensions of problems.
(vi) Professionalism with special capabilities for cartography, Geographic Information Systems techniques, Remote Sensing, and Area Studies.

Weaknesses

(i) Inadequate leadership.
(ii) Absence of a committed and skilled workforce.
(iii) Attitudinal constraints coming in the way of collective teamwork.
(iv) Trappings of repetitive and low performance research.
(v) Slow assimilation of new social science field techniques into geographic research.

Opportunities

(i) Globalisation with greater trans-national exchange opportunities.
(ii) India's emergence as a sourcing base for many innovative activities.
(iii) Large potential for research contributions in the country for Regional/Area studies, studies on population and natural resources and sustainable development and micro-level planning.
(iv) Exploration and expeditions into little known areas.
(v) Opportunity for policy planning studies, particularly at sub-national and sub-state levels.

Threats

(i) Competition from other social science disciplines.
(ii) Competition for technical perfection and Business professionalism in view of customer's emphasis on quality and just-in-time delivery.

On the whole, what this matrix shows is that the opportunities before us are galore. Our potential strengths reinforce our optimism and enhance our confidence limits. We should be safe, if only we develop our core competencies to their fullest potential. The weaknesses are those that can be remedied with a force of will, and the threats are nothing unusual, and in fact, common to all disciplines. In any case, they have to be surmounted with courage. If only we stand united, we will be able to overcome all these challenges. Nothing is more important than the unity and integrity of our profession at this juncture. I therefore, appeal to all geographers in the country to come together, swell our ranks and make our apex professional organisation-the National Association of Geographers, India-strong and dynamic, so that our professional interests will be best served.

The Economic Reforms and the Changing Spatial Structure of our Economy

With these preliminary remarks, I now come to the main theme of my address, which is "Sub-National development and under development". Let me first take up the issue of development, which has undergone yet another 'paradigm shift' in recent years. In the wake of adoption of the stabilisation and structural adjustment programme in mid-1991, India has introduced sweeping changes in its economic policies, covering almost every aspect of the economy. Some have termed these reforms as a U-turn in the policies. (Khusro, 1993). In this context, the Government's accomplishments have been mainly in two directions these are:

(i) The dismantling of the licensing system that governed industrial and trade decisions; and
(ii) The opening of the economy wider to foreign trade, along with a favourable shift in our attitude and a major shift in the policy towards direct foreign investment.

Reforms in other areas have been relatively slow. With political will, they are expected to pick up in due course. Since our focus is on sub-national development, we may pose a question relevant to spatial dynamics, which is one of our professional concerns. That is: What is going to be the impact of these economic reforms on regional and local development ?

The answer to this question has to be necessarily based on an analysis of the trends of the changes in the spatial structure of our economy since independence. In the colonial era, economic activities were mainly centred around the major ports of Bombay, Calcutta and Madras, leading to a geographical division of labour between these segments of the dependent colony and the metropolitan economy of the imperial power. This has been described as 'enclave economy', with the port towns, the plantation areas and the mining areas constituting the 'enclaves', and the rest of the country relegated to the position of "a hinterland of primary production". After the attainment of Independence, changes in the regional structure of the economy and consequential modifications in the geographical division of labour took place. During the 50's and 60's, a major thrust was given to industrialisation, based, on the premise that heavy industry was fundamental to rapid growth and for a self-reliant and self-generating economy. This led to the setting up of capital-intensive industries and power projects in the public sector, using modern technology. Some of the major industrial projects, which are resource based were located near the source of raw-materials, which happened to be the industrially backward states of Bihar, Orissa and Madhya Pradesh. But many of these giant projects became merely another set of "enclaves", which built up no positive and interdependent relationships with their hinterlands. On the other hand, they positively disrupted the traditional culture and the economic and social life of people in the immediate neighbourhood. Thus, this rapid industrialisation strategy led to certain adverse oonsequences of "geographical dualism".

At the same time, developments undertaken in the agriculture sector led to three major types of changes:

(i) Vast increases in irrigated areas brought about by the large multipurpose and irrigation projects;
(ii) The intensification of agricultural production; and
(iii) The intensification of agricultural specialisation within the physical zones and states.

All these changes were expected to act as important 'region forming forces', triggering off the development of an internal territorial specialisation and the forging of economic linkages among regions. However, the capital-intensive, multipurpose and irrigation projects failed to build up utilisation capacities, leading to poor returns in the capital invested on them. Similarly, the green revolution strategy, pursued vigorously during the late 1960's and 1970's, accentuated the regional disparities, by benefiting the elite class of farmers and certain preferred locations only. Thus, the spatial structure of development in India in the early 1970's revealed an uneven growth pattern of a "localised" and "patchy" character in the interior. The growth processes were certainly penetrating into the interior, but in an uneven manner. This is typically characteristic of the way development spreads in an underdeveloped country and a gradual closure of the 'regional gap' ultimately results. This expansion is not like how oil spreads on water, but through a leapfrogging and infilling process. The spatial structure of the Indian economy was typically following this growth trend and was moving forward on a 'point-line-network' principle. In course of time, given a favourable policy environment , it would have continued in this progression, and perhaps significantly promoted growth in backward areas to close the spatial gaps in development.

Since industrialisation is one of the basic determinants influencing the spatial pattern of development, we may examine how the present policies will be influencing the location and growth of industries in the country. During the pre- economic reforms period, incentives were offered by the central government for the dispersal of industries in backward areas in the form of concessional finance, Central investment subsidy, central transport subsidy and some special backward area development allowances. Another scheme intended to encourage industrial dispersal was the one of 'freight equalisation', according to which the prices of certain critical industrial raw materials like cement, steel and coal were made uniform at all locations. Collectively, these incentives constituted the "equilibrating mechanisms" of our industrial policy.

Besides the central incentives, state governments in turn, have also been offering several incentives to attract enterprises to the backward areas. After the new economic reforms were announced, the industrial incentive schemes have undergone lot of changes in their content. The central investment subsidy has been withdrawn. The freight equalisation scheme has also been done away with. Thus most of the 'equilibrating mechanisms' have virtually disappeared. Some studies on the trends in industrial dispersal and the performance of the incentive schemes revealed that the backward areas in the developed states have proved to be more attractive for industrial investment than those in the backward states, emphasising the importance of the infrastructure element, as the crucial determinant for the siting of industries. Based on this finding, the industrial policy shifted to a "growth centre approach", during the eighth plan, which implied that investment concentration will be in and around better developed areas with assured infrastructure. Added to this, the liberalisation and globalisation policies are attracting several transnational corporations into the country with their external investments. The location and spatial configuration of these investments will be determined by the transnational corporations in their own global interest and we would have no choice but to accept the resultant outcomes. This makes it very clear that it is difficult to manipulate the location of external investments and mould development according to our own desired pattern, dictated by a regional policy of accelerating the development of backward areas. Professor Gopal Krishan's recent analysis of foreign direct investments in India has already pointed to this trend of concentration and polarisation (Gopal Krishan, 1998). He has also pointed to the emergence of some grassroots level imperatives, which may perhaps counteract these trends. I shall elaborate this point later in this address.

Special Area Development Programmes

Apart from the incentive programmes for industrial dispersal, the implementation of some special area development programmes has also been a major strategy in our plans to overcome the backwardness in some selected problem areas. These include the programmes for the hill areas, the drought prone areas, the tribal areas, the north-east region, the irrigation command areas, the border areas and the desert areas. These are specific regional programmes.

The backward area development strategy adopted here is one of 'transition growth', which means initially making a deep dent into the diagnosed critical problem of the area, and gradually enlarging the effort in definite progression, along a 'development continuum'. Such transition should be characterised by continuity in the philosophy and approach to the problem of development and consistency in the use of the policy instruments devised for the purpose. The transition strategies must be pursued long enough in a graduated manner and large enough in scale and magnitude, to effect the desired pattern of change. The transition should also be conceived as a time-bound phase. In our context, the temporal perspective may be construed as a period ranging from ten to fifteen years. During this period the crucial bottlenecks to progress and the barriers to development must be identified, and these should be overcome through the various means elaborated in the plan. Thus planning for successful transition growth would require the economy to be carried through a succession of growth phases, in which more and more advancements will be ensured. Each emerging phase of development will be conditioned by the growth accomplishments in the preceding phase. A realistic development strategy must, therefore, ensure continuity in policies, approaches and programmes and must ensure that the present is linked to the past and then to the future. No hard and fast generalisations are possible concerning the evolution of backward areas during the transition phase of development. But certain ideal-type directions of structural change, that modernisation involves, may be outlined to compare and take stock of the progress of development.

While operationalising a backward area programme in accordance with this strategy, the allocation of development funds is crucial. They should be progressively stepped up until development gets saturated in the area. If we look at the Indian experience, this has not really happened, as continuity and acceleration have been sacrificed midway. Some components of the backward areas programme, like the Drought Prone Areas Programme, Tribal Development Programme, Small Farmers Development Programme, etc. have already been phased out and incorporated into the Integrated Rural Development Programme. Currently, these individual area programmes are showing diminishing trends in overall allocations. If we look at the year-wise allocation of special central assistance to a backward area programme like the hill area programme for instance, the static nature of allocations, and hence of developmental back-slide, is revealed. With such a regressive trend in the pattern of allocations, the 'take-off' stage for backward areas is an illusion and a mirage. From an envisaged goal of the development of underdevelopment, we seem to have slipped to a reversal of this policy. These are: the underdevelopment of development. It is clear that the central government, in its pre-occupation with macro economic adjustments and in meeting the obligation of international debt repayments, does not have either the time or the resources to tackle, at its own level, the problem of regional disparities within the country. In this situation, the regional and local areas will have to mainly shoulder the burden of development on themselves and take the major initiatives in this regard. For enabling them to do so, democratic policy reforms, involving decentralisation and devolution of functions and powers to the local levels, with their parallel ideas of local resource mobilisation, people's participation and "development from within", are quite relevant.

Revitalisation of Panchayats

Thanks to the enactment of the 73rd and 74th constitutional amendments in 1992, and a later one to extend their provisions to the Scheduled Areas in the country, a new era of revitalisation of Panchayats, conferring powers of enfranchisement, empowerment and planning for their areas has been ushered in. This historic change, with its local imperatives, has also its great implications for pushing developments in backward areas. The constitutional amendments now provide for :

(a) The preparation of area plans for economic development and social justice;
(b) The implementation of schemes for economic development and social justice, as entrusted by the state Government; and
(c) The constitution of a "District Planning Committee" to consolidate the plans prepared by the Panchayats and the Municipalities in the district and to prepare a draft development plan for the district as a whole.

While for (a) and (b) the legal provisions to be made for the devolution of the necessary powers and responsibilities have been left to the discretion of the state governments, the task envisaged under (c) that is, the constitution of the District Planning Committee, is mandatory under article 243ZD of the Constitution.

These constitutional provisions mark a significant departure in the *Style, Stance* and *Substance* of planning The "Style" refers to the democratic and participatory character of planning. "Stance" refers to the "people doing and government supporting" a 'two-way planning process' and "Substance" refers to the programme and project components informed by the goals of growth, equity, stability and sustainability (Sundaram, 1997). It has injected a new conception of a multi-level planning process, cutting across the three layers of the local level and finally integrating into the State Plan. In the new context, such planning is both a democratic and technical exercise, as well as a management and negotiation process, to obtain the maximum benefits of development to the local population. The institutions at the local level can now exercise a micro-strategy of development, most appropriate to their areas and tackle their community and area problems by evolving a more effective local level planning. Thus, the utilisation of funds in rural areas will gain in terms of local relevance and specifications. If such local level planning is effectively accomplished, it can go a long way in reducing developmental disparities and countering uneven development.

The state governments are now struggling to operationalise area planning on these lines at the different local levels. The progress, however, is slow and halting, as capabilities for planning are lacking at the local level. For devolving plan funds from the state to the local levels, each state government is devising its own criteria. The degree of relative backwardness of districts is an explicit criterion in this inter-regional allocation of funds. If effective planning based on local area analysis could be simultaneously undertaken, keeping the goal of narrowing spatial disparities in view, a lot could be achieved towards closing the regional gap. However, with various constraints operating, which I shall not elaborate here, democratic decentralisation is passing through a phase of "teething problems". As no general allocation formula can adequately tackle the problem of entrenched backwardness, a few state governments have devised some innovations. States like Gujarat, Maharashtra and Tamil Nadu have provided for a District Equalisation and State Equalisation Fund to provide grants to backward villages and districts. All state governments should emulate this example. The central government should also consider a similar measure in the interests of distributional equity for the country as a whole.

Changing Relationship Between Growth and Inequality

The central government cannot absolve its responsibilities towards the backward areas on the plea that it would pull down the overall growth rate of the country. This was the traditional economic thinking, which is now being questioned. The Human Development Reports of the United Nations have now established that the countries which actively promoted human development had also enjoyed higher rates of growth. Thus, the economic thinking on the relations between growth and inequality has started changing. A number of empirical studies made towards the end of 1980's and 1990's, based on much wider empirical evidence than Kuznets ever used, showed that there was no unequivocal relationship between growth and inequality. For some countries, inequality increased with growth; but for many others it did not; while in a few countries, a reduction in inequality was accompanied by rising growth. These empirical findings have led the proponents of equality to plead for appropriate policies that would redistribute incomes without adversely affecting growth.

Geographer's Contribution

The new wave of democratic decentralisation in the country, that is, the Panchayat Raj renaissance, offers an unprecedented opportunity for geographers to contribute their skills to the development of the country. Since the recent constitutional amendments have emphasised area planning at the local levels, area studies at the village, block and district levels have become basic and fundamental. As a discipline, geography has been traditionally identified with 'Area Studies'. Physical geography and regional geography are important cornerstones in this context, as they help provide the physical and cultural base for area planning. I have heard some general comments that, of late, there has been some decline of interest in both physical geography and regional geography. These negative trends, if true, must be corrected. The application of geography to area studies will provide the cultural and area-specific dimension, which I believe is essential, if planners are not to make the mistakes of over-generalisation and false universalism, which have affected many a development plan. Geographers with their ability to recognise various development phenomena and interrelate them in space, should be able to contribute significantly to some aspects of planning at all the three area levels, these are: Village, Block and the District.

Here, I would like to underline the words "some aspects", which has its connotation for the specific expertise which marks our special forte in the applied area of planning. I am here reminded of a word of caution, which Professor Satyesh Chakraborty sounded in his presidential address to the Tenth Congress of the National Association of Geographers, India in 1988. I quote from his address. "The way we have developed our expertise in science would not let us respond to all the facets of the problematique with equal competence. It would be foolish to think otherwise. I should, therefore, request you to examine and select the specific facet where we can engage ourselves, without sacrificing the rigour of our discipline" (The quote ends). I am not going to elaborate in detail all those areas where our discipline has its relevance in these changing times, except to hint at one or two possibilities.

One of the areas would be in constructing meaningful "area profiles" for all levels of planning. Let me not hide the fact that geographers have already made excellent contributions towards the relevant concepts and methodologies for going about this task. Starting from Professor Deshpande's excellent regional study on 'Western India' and Professor Learmonth, Prakasa Rao and Bhat's 'Regional Studies' in Mysore state, we have now a galaxy of eminent publications by geographers. As illustrations, I would cite Professor R. P. Misra and R.N. Achyutha's book on Micro-level planning, Professor Bhat's excellent case study of North Kanara District and Professor H.S. Sharma and Srikumar Chattopadhyaya's latest edited book on "Sustainable Development—issues and case studies". To this, I must add the three books of Professor Neela Mukherjee on "Participatory Rural Appraisal" for field techniques. Building on the guidelines available in these contributions, let us now assist the revitalised Panchayats to come out with meaningful area plans at their levels. In all these exercises, let our creativity come into play. Let us avoid stereotyped and repetitive patterns of research, which once characterised our academic efforts in the past and let us allow many variety of flowers to bloom. In this way, we will be able to make significant contributions when the world is talking about alternative models of development.

I may perhaps point to one more area of relevance where geographer's contribution could be of significance at this juncture. This is in providing some technical assistance to the District Planning Committees, which.have been now mandated constitutionally to prepare integrated rural-urban Plans for the district as a whole. In this context, the analysis of rural-urban linkages and interactions, studies on population carrying capacity and food security, inter-block disparities in development, application of remote sensing techniques to the identification of problem areas, as well as computer cartography and its numerous applications to development problems will be quite relevant. I may add that geography, which is really the "Science of Environment", can richly contribute to analysing issues in sustainable development, which are of world-wide concern today.

Restructuring Our Course Curriculum

While making these observations, I have, however, a feeling that our academic training is not matching the requirements for the type of transitional development processes, which are underway in our country. We should, therefore, restructure our course curriculum in accordance with our changing times. In this context, one of my suggestions to you is to incorporate "Area Development" as a compulsory sub-branch of our discipline. It is my earnest desire that our students should develop all those skills, which will make them reality-oriented, environment-sensitive, globally adaptive, professionally innovative and vision-driven qualities which will render them capable of pro-actively responding to the increased uncertainties of our times.

The Development of Underdevelopment: From Vision to Action

Ladies and Gentlemen, before I conclude, let me revert back to the theme of underdevelopment and outline an agenda for the future. At the end of five decades of planned effort, the results show that, atleast so far as the backward areas are concerned, we stand where we were originally in relation to the comparatively more developed areas. The "Big Bang" approach implied in the Mahalanobis model, with its prospect of the "trickle down process" of development, however, failed to materialise. Instead of resulting in spread and multiplier effects of growth, it only encouraged the "back-wash effects" While some large projects are, no doubt, necessary to lay the foundation and trigger off industrial development in the country, so far as the backward areas are concerned, we need to conceive a strategy, by and large, within the framework of democratic decentralised institutions, empowered to plan and implement local development schemes. Such schemes will be of three kinds these are: Production-oriented, Infrastructure-oriented, and Welfare-oriented. The 73rd

Amendment of the Constitution has made this development possible through the revitalisation of the Panchayats, organised in a true multilevel framework. With reduction of disparities in development at the local level as one of the major goals, a new paradigm of planning is emerging, which is expected to spread the development impulses spatially outwards. Some of the essential features of this paradigm could be:

Firstly, stretching the production potentials of the area (that is, Village, Block, and District) to the maximum through "chain effects", "circular flows", or "economic circuits", by consciously adopting a "selective spatial closure" strategy. Thus, all production surpluses would be recycled within the local areas themselves, thus increasing local incomes. This is an aspect of, what German geographers have called, "the strengthening of the auto-centric and auto-dynamic forces of development". The establishment of appropriate "economic circuits" in the local area is an essential feature of this strategy. Thus "Economic-circuit analysis" is important in this context.

Secondly, a wide dispersal of small local resource-based industries with appropriate technology in 'punctiform' locations in the rural areas, thus consciously adopting a spatial strategy of "decentralised concentration". It should be emphasised here that much could be achieved in the rural areas by implementing some "little ideas", requiring only small investments by private entrepreneurs. I am reminded of the three "bullet points" emphasised in management literature, which runs as follows: "Little ideas" get little respect; Big ideas get all the attention, resources and applause. But the best ideas start out as little ideas and grow into big ideas. This is only to emphasise the importance of "localism" in development through small local-resource-based industrialisation as a graduated effort. I have elaborated this idea at some length in my Professor Prakaṣa Rao memorial lecture delivered during last year.

Thirdly, adopting what Professor Misra has called, in a highly philosophical essay contained in his recently edited book "Million Cities of India", as the "Micropolitan approach" to rural development, to siphonoff concentration, stress and pollution from big cities and foster the evolution of a pleasant countryside and help evolve a congenial spatial organisation of settlements in a central place hierarchy. Professor Misra's "micropolises" will be small "nodal townships", supplying vital inputs to the villages and helping to process and market the output of the villages within and outside their ranges.

Fourthly, encouraging, what is called "development from within", a concept which I elaborated when I was serving in the African countries as an International Civil Servant. I found that no other solution was possible for the Sub-Saharan African countries, plunged in a deep debt crisis as the consequence of a "dependency syndrome", induced by the World Bank and International

Monetary Fund loans. The "development from within", a basically Gandhian idea, is essentially a "bottom-up approach", through encouraging "capillary effect" in rural communities, by invigourating indigenous institutions as well as establishing some new community-based organisations to perform different functions. These have been called "Polycentric institution", which will catalyse development activities in the rural areas. There could be a variety of such institutions, each tasked with some particular function or responsibility. Building such institutions constitutes, what has been termed as creating "social capital". The origin of this notion of "social capital" may be traced to a French philosopher Alex de Toquiville, as early as the late 19th century. The time has now come to operationalise this idea by creating a variety of people's institutions, which may include social groups, economic interest groups, user groups, cooperatives, Voluntary Action Groups, Natural Resources Management Interface groups and so on. In this way, development responsibilities will be decentralised among the people of the village, contributing to maximum people's participation.

Fifthly, working through a strategy of "Graduated Pragmatism". This implies the idea of a "developmental sequence" in the development of backward areas, which has to be engineered through time, in distinct phases of accomplishment, constituting a stepped approach. It is the same as the "transition growth strategy" operated on a 'Point-Line-Network Principle', to which I have already referred in my address.

Ladies and gentlemen, the five-point-agenda for backward areas development at the local level, which I have proposed here, is neither utopian in conception nor impossible of accomplishment. In our changed economic and political circumstances, may I say that there are no options; such a strategy is being thrust upon us as a "developmental imperative". May I also add that it infuses some "hope in the midst of hopelessness", by handing over the planning and development function into the hands of the people and making them responsible for their own development. They are now free to avail of the technical assistance necessary for this purpose from any competent source—government technocrats, the academia, consultancy organisations, enlightened Non-Government Organisations, etc. Thus our role is clear. If you examine this agenda carefully, you will find that there are several action points, which are well within our competency levels. I, therefore, commend that this agenda be woven into our tapestry of action for the future.

Ladies and gentlemen, I have spoken long enough and perhaps tried your patience. I now wish you all a happy new year, which beckons us with beautiful opportunities, and invite you to join me in getting started on a journey into "fresh woods and pastures new". As a Chinese proverb says "Every journey starts with a single step". And may I add that every single step that we may take is sure to lead us to innovative activities that will enhance the status, prestige and glory of our profession.

REFERENCES

Kapur, A. (1998): *Indian Geography, A Future with a Difference,* Allied Publishers Limited, New Delhi.

Bhat, L.S. (1987), *Strategy for Integrated Area Development: Case Study of North Kanara District (Karnataka),* Concept Publishing Company, New Delhi.

Deshpande, C.D. (1948), *Western India: A Regional Geography,* Students' Own Book Depot, Dharwar.

Krishan, G. (1998), *From Centralised Planning to Liberalised Economy,* (Mimeo).

Khusro, A.M. (1993), *The U-turn in India's development strategies*, In U. Kapila ed. *Recent Developments in Indian Economy with special reference to Structural Reforms,* Part I, Academic Foundation, Delhi.

Learmoth, A.T.A. and L.S. Bhat (1960-1962): *Mysore State,* Vol. I and II.

Misra, R.P. and R.N. Achyutha (1990), *Micro-Level Rural Planning: Principles, Methods and Case Studies,* Concept, New Delhi.

Misra, R.P. and K. Misra ed. (1998), *Million Cities of India,* Sustainable Development Foundation, New Delhi.

Mukherjee, N. (1993), *Participatory Rural Appraisal, Methodology and Applications,* Concept Publishing Company, New Delhi.

Mukherjee, N. (1995), *Participatory Rural Appraisal and Questionnaire Survey,* Concept, New Delhi.

Mukherjee, N. (1997), *Participatory Appraisal of Natural Resources,* Concept, New Delhi.

Rao, V.L.S.P. and L.S. Bhat (1960), *Planning Regions in the Mysore State,* Indian Statistical Institute, Calcutta.

Sharma, H.S. and S. Chattopadhyay, ed. (1998), *Sustainable Development: Issues and Case Studies,* Concept, New Delhi.

Sundaram, K.V. (1997), *Report of the Working Group on Decentralised Planning and Panchayati Raj,* Government of Tamil Nadu, Chennai.

Sundaram, K.V. (1997), *Decentralised Multilevel Planning: Principles and Practice- Asian and African Experiences,* Concept, New Delhi.

Gur Bachan Singh
1936 -

A lure for travel, penchant for photography and hospitality, the bold steps of approaching authorities and desire to experiment and lead typifies Singh as a person. His long innings of teaching for thirty-five years was nourished by his love for the land and people in rural setting. Tilling his research with first hand experience drawn from the background of a farmers family, his work on agricultural geography reached its zenith through ten years of labor and over ten hours of daily toil in the 'Agricultural Planning Atlas of Punjab'. While the inspiration for this atlas was instilled by Coppok, his doctoral supervisor at the University of Edinburgh, what adds novelty to Singh's atlas is the dense descriptive material in narrative and tabular form, in both English and Punjabi. His innovative bilingual methodology made the atlas a model for different states of India. Winning Singh praise and recognition, it proves that even a single solid piece of research can be most rewarding.

Territorially, Singh is deeply rooted in the soil of Punjab. His entire education was in Punjab and he was chairperson of the department of geography at Punjabi University, Patiala. All his twelve books and research papers are on the state of Punjab, eighteen out of the thirty-eight conferences and seminars attended and fourteen out of the twenty-one honors or posts conferred on him are from the state. Three doctorates and twenty master of philosophy which he has supervised also belong to this land of five rivers. Except for the years he spent at Edinburgh, United Kingdom with the Lamb Fund Award 1973, all his span of education was drawn from Punjab. Singh was born on 2nd August, 1926 ,to an agricultural family of Ganaur village in the district of Gujranwala, now in Pakistan Punjab. More than a mere affection for a place of birth, Singh's addiction for Punjab stems from the fact it is one of the most prosperous and rapidly progressing state of India .The opportunities it provided to Singh as a geographer were far and wide .

A practical man, early in his academic career Singh tried to solve academic problems. Identifying the pressing need of geography texts in Punjabi at a young age of twenty-seven he translated books on diversified fields of geography such as, World Geography, Physical Geography, and Economic Geography of India. His textbook on Social Studies in Punjabi, for the fourth and fifth standard remain a model text for nearly four lakh school students under the Punjab Education Board. As Member of Punjab Flood Control Board, Border Area Technical Committee and President of the Punjab Heritage Society his advice on various issues found applied value. On his suggestion tuneets were constructed along certain key locations along the river and the fact that floods played less havoc in these areas proved that geographical solutions are sustainable. Compiling a four volume 'Encyclopedia of Punjab Heritage' is Singh's latest passion. Capturing through the lens the deteriorated condition of monuments in seven districts scattered over Majha, Doaba and Malwa regions of Punjab, Singh hopes to draw the attention of policy makers towards the restoration and conservation of these sites.

Retirement days are often times of wanting to relive life, while it is a truism that much of it remains a fantasy, the realm of academics can provide another chance. Today Singh is giving a new shape to his Atlas. It was just two days after retiring from the department of geography, Punjabi University, Patiala that Singh delivered his Presidential address, "Green Revolution: Gains and Pains" at the 21st Indian Geography Congress, held at Nagpur in 2000.

Despite a track of nearly a half dozen presidentships in different societies and associations, like the Association of Punjab Geographers, Punjab Heritage Society, and Kalgi Dhar Gudwara, one of NAGI he claims was indeed a prized honour . He insists that the presidentship of NAGI was a call from the divine, yet his continuous involvement with NAGI stretches for twenty long years since early eighties. His curricula vitae records his presence in the third, eighth, sixteenth, twentieth, twenty first and twenty second Indian Geography Congress. Each Congress was a landmark in his life. At the third Congress held at Centre for Regional Development, Jawahar lal Nehru University, New Delhi, he had his first hand encounter to see, hear and meet some of the famed Indian geographers. His Atlas received an academic release at the eighth Congress held at Srinagar. The sixteenth Congress held at Hyderabad conferred on him a

citation for his distinguished and outstanding contribution in the field of agricultural geography for his illustrious career for the cause of promotion and development of geography. He was elected President at the 20th Congress held at Gorakhpur. Though his role as President of the National Association of Geographers, India was a pot of brewing frustrations and dreams, Singh's life as a geographer blends the happy light hearted mix of work and pleasure.

Green Revolution in India: Gains and Pains

G.B. SINGH

I am highly grateful to all members of the National Association of Geographers, India (NAGI) for kindly electing me the president of this great association of distinguished geographers of India, at the 20th Indian Geography Congress held at Gorakhpur last year. I greatly value this honour and am touched by the confidence and trust reposed in me. At this moment, I am reminded of my great teachers at Panjab University, Chandigarh-Late Professor O.P. Bharadwaj and Professor G.S. Gosal and at Edinburgh University (the United Kingdom)-Late Professor J. Wreford. Watson, Professor J.T. Coppock, Dr. D. N. Mac Master and Dr. A.J. Crosbie with whom I worked as a student. I owe a special debt of gratitude to them for the geographical insight and training that they provided and for their affection and generosity.

I laid down my office as professor in Geography from Punjabi University, Patiala, only two days back-the last day of the last century. I am very thrilled and consider myself very fortunate that I shall be shouldering the responsibility to serve this esteemed association of distinguished geographers at the outset of the New Millennium. Must I say that I shall put my head and heart into the efficient functioning of this association. But this will be possible only with your kind cooperation and help which I am sure will be forthcoming from all of you in abundance.

The man we have amidst us this morning, Dr. M.S. Swaminathan, has become a symbol throughout the world for the potential for improvement in agriculture that does exist in India, indeed, in most developing countries. When I was to choose the subject for today's address, I being a student of Agricultural Geography, naturally wanted to have one with which Dr. M.S. Swaminathan, and most of you, are very closely associated. Hence, I opted to share my few thoughts with you on the topic 'Green Revolution in India: Gains and Pains."

22nd Indian Geography Congress
Nagpur, 1999 December

Green Revolution In India : Gains And Pains

The term "Green Revolution" coined and used for the first time by William Gaud – the administrator of U.S. Agency for International Development in a speech before the Society for International Development, Washington in 1968. In his speech he glorified the dramatic increase in yield and production in major cereals like wheat and rice triggered through the development and large-scale adoption of semi-dwarf high-yielding varieties.

The Green Revolution became a reality in India too in late sixties, especially in states like Punjab, Haryana, Western Uttar Pradesh, and parts of Tamil Nadu, Maharashtra and Andhra Pradesh. In these states, a combination of factors like use of High Yielding Varieties, irrigation, mechanization, land reforms, consolidation of holdings, credit facilities, and other related rural infrastructure helped them in taking the lead. Once the benefits of the new technology became known, others followed suit.

Green Revolution *per se* did not occur overnight, in fact it was the result of a culmination of a process which began as early as the first quarter of the 20th century, though initiated much earlier. To understand and know the mechanics of "Green Revolution" one has to go back in history to delineate its course.

Pre-Independence Scenario

Prior to Independence in 1947, India was largely a region of self-sustained villages in which traditional agriculture, based on centuries of experience, was more a way of life than a business. Most essentials were home produced and outside needs were limited. Most of the goods produced were also consumed locally. The trade was limited and most exchanges were in kind or in services. Income distributions were unequal, but significantly the disparities were relatively modest. Communal property rights existed. Production was on a small scale and traditional methods were used. All these imposed a low ceiling on accumulation. Farming was carried out on a crop share basis and hence there was a general incentive to work together for a good crop. Good harvest meant benefit to all.

Because of the continuing pressure of population, India had to maintain a high level of cultivation. About 45 per cent of the geographical area was under plough. Food crops occupied 75 per cent of the sown area. Non-agricultural land occupied about 15 per cent of the area and the prevalence of traditional and primitive techniques of farming accounted for about 7 per cent of culturable waste. Of the total cultivated area, 80 per cent was sown every year, leaving 20 per cent as fallow. The high incidence of fallow was largely a reflection of rain-dependent farming. Irrigated land comprised about 16 per cent of the cropped area, but by methods which were largely inefficient and inadequate and designed simply as supplementary provision. Consequently, only a small proportion, just over 11 per cent of the net sown area was sown more than once. The intensity of cropping was just 111.

The typical response to increasing demands was to expand the cultivated area rather than to strive for increased productivity. In the traditional agricultural pattern both seasonal and perennial crops played a part, with diversification emphasized rather than specialization of a limited range of crops. Inter-cropping was also more characteristic than cropping in pure stands, cultivation by wooden plough was almost universal and the cropping practices customary. Fertility was largely maintained by keeping the land as fallow, by green manuring, and, within limits, by using cow dung and composite manures. In general, the peasant approached agricultural production with the aim of minimizing risk rather than ensuring maximization of production of profits. In the wake of increasing population, many methods of land and water management which were sustainable were no longer sustainable. There was a total stagnation of agriculture.

The British Colonial rule began with drought and famine in Bengal in 1770 during which one third of the population of the province perished. The Colonial period also ended with great Bengal famine of 1943 in which over three million people died of hunger. Between 1770 and 1880 as many as 27 serious famines were recorded. Between 1850 and 1900, 20 million lives were lost in about 20 famines (India's population including Pakistan and Bangladesh then was 300 million).

In such a grim situation, the serious shortages of foodgrains started to be felt in late 1920's. The British Government realized the urgency of the matter and hence planned some programs such as colonization of new areas to overcome these shortages. The process of agricultural change in India has its roots as far back as the colonization schemes of Punjab and Sindh, introduced during the British Period in response to food shortages being experienced in the country at that time. With the main aim of increasing foodgrains production, the first two canal colonies, Sohag Para and Sidhani in Punjab (both now in Pakistan) were started as early as 1886-88, the major breakthrough came with the establishment of the larger canal colonies of the first quarter of the twentieth century. The colonists in the Punjab colonies came largely from the farming communities of the Central Punjab and most of them were peasant proprietors. These colonization schemes achieved tremendous success and Farmer (1974) described them as "...the classic achievements of the British administration in the Punjab, where colonization was indeed on the grand scale. For the Punjab Canal Colonies eventually covered 2.2 million hectares of land, almost all of which had been previously waste or subject only to nomadic pastoralism or occasional catch-cropping. Nothing on the same vast scale has so far been achieved in Independent India, ... It was, of course, the construction of great irrigation channels that enabled the colonists to bring the previously arid or at any rate semi-arid *doabs* of the Punjab under plough". "....they [the Canal Colonies] formed the greatest achievement in colonization....; and that they were in various ways the model and the inspiration for schemes of colonization, past and present, in the present territory of the Indian Republic". To these farmers "these colonies provided a training ground for the adoption of irrigated farming, improved seeds, implements and cultural practices, while for the planners and researchers, they were testing grounds for the modernization of agriculture" (Singh, 1975 : 334).

These colonies clearly demonstrated that given the will and skill of the people involved, the so-called 'Vicious circle' of tradition and backwardness can be broken. The local inhabitants who were opposed to any change in their traditional ways of life, and who were very hostile to the new settlers in the beginning, were finally convinced of the benefits of the new economy, and were converted 'from a lawless nomad into an industrious agriculturist' (Darling, 1947 : 123).

To promote research and extension, the establishment of the Indian Agricultural Research Institute in 1904, the Indian Agriculture Service in 1905, and the Indian Council of Agricultural Research in 1929, were highly commendable steps at the time. Other programs included the enactment of The Co-operative Credit Societies Act – 1904, and consolidation of holdings through Co-operative Consolidation Societies in 1920. "The Grow More Food Campaign" launched during the Second World War received an additional fillip during the Bengal Famine in 1943. "Although these programs had a very limited impact on the total economy at that time, they helped in educating the people about the need and urgency of the improvements as well as providing the foundations for the development of the institutional and structural framework of the post-Independence network or research, extension, education and credit. Indeed, the general impetus of these was carried forward into the post-Independence period" (Singh, 1975 : 335).

Post-Independence Scenario

In the wake of partition of the country in 1947, the food situation was further aggravated: (I) general food shortage was witnessed in India, since the surplus food growing areas were transferred to Pakistan; and (ii) about five million people became destitute refugees as a result of transfer of population and they had to be fed and rehabilitated. Out of these, 2.7 millions settled in Punjab and were largely agriculturists (46.7 per cent). Thus the first five years of Independence (1947 – 51) marked the transitional period when the old efforts were consolidated and new thinking crystallized. Within this period the government of India decided that drastic economic changes are essential for survival. It also decided to design and implement programs for planned economic development within a socialist society.

In order to overcome the inherent disadvantages and ultimately improve the food situation in the country, India launched a massive program of rural reconstruction through five-year plans and other allied projects. Consequently a significant progress was achieved in the face of many stressed and strains – internal as well as external. From the stage of 'deficiency' in 1950 to that of 'self-sufficiency' in 1970's and finally 'surplus' in 1980's is an achievement in which Indian farmer, planner, researcher and administrator can take a lot of pride and which they all richly deserved.

Pre-Green Revolution Phase

This phase began with the launching of the First Five-year Plan in 1951, whose main objective was "to initiate a process of development which will raise the standard of living and open out to the people new opportunities for a richer and more varied life". To strengthen the pace of development, the Community Development Program was the first of its kind and was launched on October 2, 1952. This was followed by the National Extension Program a year later. These were aided self-help programs, planned and implemented by the villagers with government technical guidance and financial assistance. The major concern was the expansion of agricultural production and the growth of subsidiary occupation which were the necessary foundations for the development of social welfare services in rural areas. Another strategy of agricultural development was carried through by creating a new development unit called 'Block Development', and the whole country was divided into blocks. Efforts to improve agricultural production during the first plan were concentrated on building up the institutional framework. The Second Five-Year Plan sought to extend the process by taking a fresh look at the whole background and by attempting to make up for any deficiencies. The coverage of Community Development Blocks was extended during this plan and their administrative structure was further strengthened. In September 1956, a new Ministry of Community Development at the national level was created to give further impetus to the Community Development concept. The Third Five-Year Plan marks the beginning of induced agricultural change. Having realized the inadequacy of the Community Development Program in achieving the desired results, a new extension approach 'Intensive Agricultural District Program' based on the recommendation of the Ford Foundation team of specialists, was launched in the country in 1961. Another important feature of this period was the establishment of Agricultural universities in the country, which provided a sound base for teaching, research and extension. Complimentary to Intensive Agricultural District Programme, another program 'Intensive Agricultural Area Program' was introduced in 1964-65. This program concentrated on specific crops.

The success achieved through these programs, coupled with the will of the government to introduce new innovations and the ready willingness of the farmers to accept them (only in few states initially), resulted in increasing use of fertilizers, pesticides, new seeds and implements. Mechanized, self-controlled, and assured supply of irrigation water through the use of power-operated pump-sets and tube-wells greatly changed the face of agriculture. The creation of Agricultural Price Commission in 1965 highlighted the need for more rational price policies. During this period, increasing efforts were also made in the much ignored subjects of soil conservation and water management. This period also brought into focus various elements of the evolving agricultural strategies for the ensuing periods. These included the interaction of various improved agricultural practices as a package, the time-saving techniques in response to increasing labor requirements due to multiple cropping, increased demand for better roads, markets, storage and other related facilities.

Human element played an equally important role in ushering the Green Revolution. The most important linkage in the early stages of the Green Revolution process was indeed provided by the 'refugee farmers' who migrated from the canal colonies of the west Punjab (Pakistan) and were largely settled in Punjab. Some of them, sure of their success, moved to the new areas where canal irrigation was recently introduced. These were largely canal-irrigated areas of the border states such as Haryana, Uttar Pradesh and Rajasthan. These farmers had a long experience (40 years) of irrigated farming and were more progressive than their local counterparts. This may be called 'relocation diffusion' process which emerged largely as a historical accident and although not recognized at that time, this proved to be the most significant development of the period. Thus they acted as catalyst in the transformation of agriculture of those areas where Green Revolution became a reality in the years to come.

During the Pre-Green Revolution phase (1950-1970), total cropped area increased from 131.9 to 165.8 million hectares. The corresponding increase in Net sown area had been from 118.8 to 140.8 million hectares. Significantly the area sown more than once doubled. Culturable waste declined from 7 per cent to about 5 per cent of the geographical area. Non-agricultural land also declined from about 15 per cent to 13 per cent. Net area irrigated rose from about 16 per cent to over 20 per cent. The consumption of fertilizers also enhanced considerably.

In response to these developments, the output of all agricultural commodities had gone up by 22.2 per cent, giving an annual rate of growth of 4.2 per cent during the First Five-Year Plan. A similar increase of 21.7 per cent in output was achieved in the Second Five-Year Plan, which accounted for 4.3 per cent annual increase. The trend sharply reversed during the Third Plan. The output declined to 7.4 per cent with an annual rate of increase over 1 per cent. The production of food grains had risen by 27.4 per cent, giving an annual growth rate of 5.3 per cent during the first plan. The second plan recorded an increase of 18.9 per cent with an annual rate of growth of 4 per cent. In the third plan it came down to 11.5 per cent with an annual rate of 1.9 per cent. During these 15 years, the increase in foodgrains production alone was 34.1 per cent, giving an annual rate of 2.6 per cent.

During this phase, the area under foodgrains increased by 1.5 times, while production increased by 2.3 times (Table 1). This obviously reflected improvement in yield component, which along increased by 1.6 times. Two crops, rice (35 per cent) and wheat (20 per cent) accounted for more than 55 per cent of the total foodgrains production. The improvement in yield of both wheat and rice signaled encouraging trends. As a consequence the production of wheat almost quadrupled and rice doubled. The acreage under pulses more than doubled and production went up by 2.5 tonnes. Oilseeds acreage and production almost doubled during this period. Per capita availability of food also enhanced from 145.7 kilograms. In 1951-52 to 201.0 kilograms. In 1970-71. Despite these gains the imports of foodgrains also rose from 3.93 million tonnes to 10.34 million tonnes to 10.34 million tonnes during 1951-52 to 1965 (Fig. 1.). It, however declined in later years.

The efforts in this phase had largely been concentrated on improvement of infra-structure, setting up of institutions for genetic and allied research, creating credit facilities, marketing structure, providing better implements, better breeds and seeds, providing irrigation and above all improving the human resource. More areas were brought under plough. The strategy for increasing agricultural production largely remained acreage-dominated rather than yield-dominated, even though the improvements in yield had signaled an upward trend.

Fig. 1

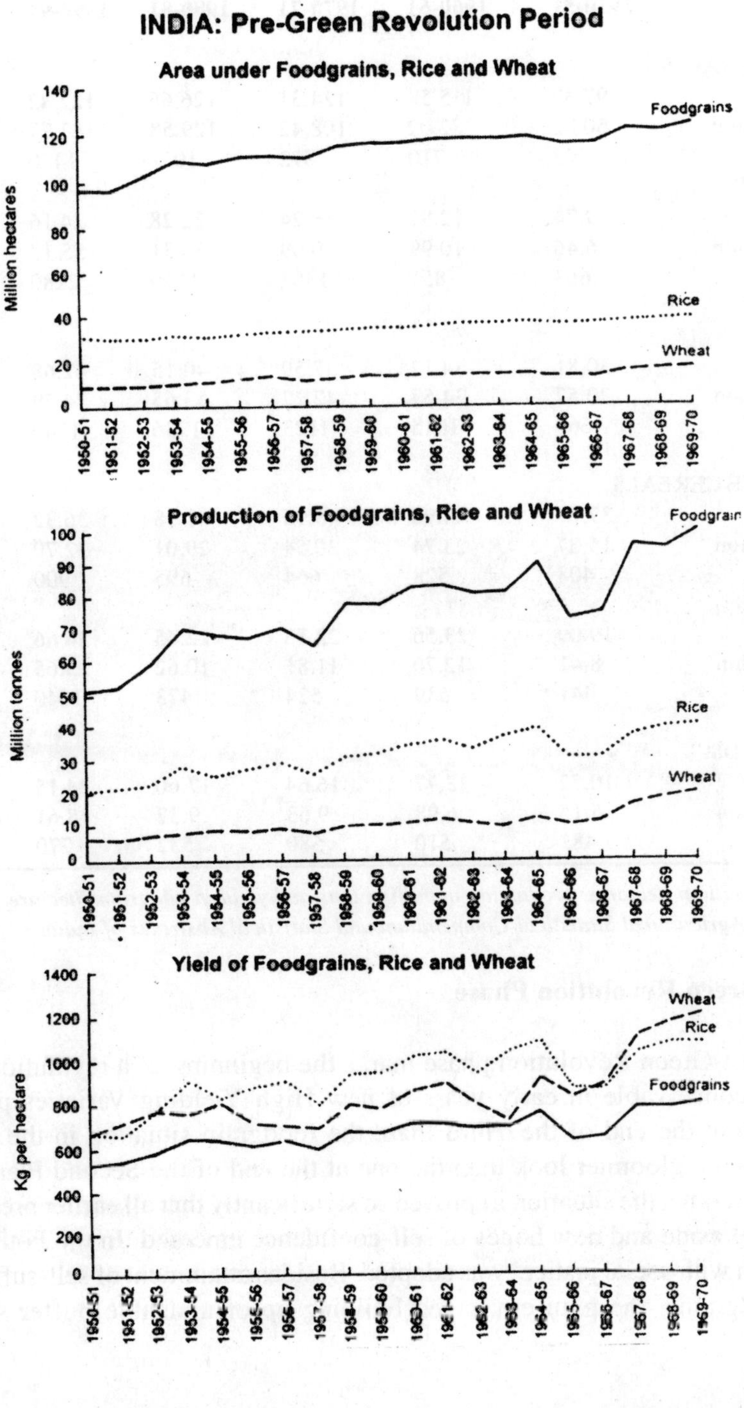
INDIA: Pre-Green Revolution Period
Area under Foodgrains, Rice and Wheat
Million hectares
Foodgrains
Rice
Wheat
Production of Foodgrains, Rice and Wheat
Million tonnes
Foodgrain
Rice
Wheat
Yield of Foodgrains, Rice and Wheat
Kg per hectare
Wheat
Rice
Foodgrains

Table 1: Area, Production and Yield of Foodgrains and Oilseeds in India

Year	1950-51	1960-61	1970-71	1980-81	1990-91	1996-97
FOODGRAINS:						
Area	97.32	115.58	124.31	126.66	127.82	124.51
Production	50.82	82.02	108.42	129.58	187.77	199.30
Yield	522	710	872	1023	1470	1601
WHEAT :						
Area	9.74	12.92	18.24	22.28	24.16	25.93
Production	6.46	10.99	20.09	36.31	55.13	69.27
Yield	663	851	1307	1630	2280	2671
RICE:						
Area	30.81	34.12	37.59	40.15	42.68	43.30
Production	20.57	34.57	42.22	53.63	74.29	81.31
Yield	668	1013	1123	1336	1740	1879
COARSE CEREALS :						
Area	37.67	44.96	45.95	41.18	36.32	32.10
Production	15.37	23.74	30.54	29.01	32.70	34.24
Yield	408	528	664	695	900	1068
PULSES:						
Area	19.09	23.56	22.53	22.45	24.66	23.19
Production	8.41	12.70	11.81	10.62	25.65	14.46
Yield	441	539	524	473	1040	623
OILSEEDS:						
Area	10.72	13.77	16.64	17.60	24.15	26.81
Production	5.15	6.98	9.63	9.37	18.61	24.96
Yield	481	510	580	532	770	931

Area in million hectares, production in million tons and yield in kilograms/hectare.
Source: Agricultural Statistical Compendium and Statistical Abstracts of India.

Post-Green Revolution Phase

The Post-Green Revolution phase marks the beginning of a revolution which was inconceivable in early years of new High Yielding Varieties package. Though at the end of the Third Plan, the foodgrain situation in the country presented a gloomier look than the one at the end of the Second Plan, in the years to come, the situation improved so significantly that all earlier predictions were set aside and new hopes of self-confidence emerged. In the Fourth Plan 'growth with social justice' was adopted. Besides attainment of self-sufficiency in foodgrains, the plan envisaged building-up of a sizable buffer stock of foodgrain and stoppage of concessional food imports. In the Fifth Plan, emphasis was laid on bringing more area under High Yielding Varieties. For the first time it was recognized to cover dry farming areas alongwith irrigated one on a large scale. The Sixth Plan followed almost the same pattern. In the Plans which followed the thrust had been an all round development.

As result of these concerted efforts, more area was brought under cultivation, about 4.7 million hectares were added between 1970-1990. Consequently cropped area increased from 165.8 to 185.5 million hectares, an addition of about 20 million hectares. Area sown more than once almost doubled. Culturable waste declined further accounting for less than 5 per cent, while non-agricultural land comprised less than 13 per cent of the geographical area. The irrigation potential of about 90 million hectares was created by 1995-96. The increase in fertilizer consumption was indeed phenomenal. It increased from under one million tons to over 14 million tons in 1996-97. The acreage under High Yielding Varieties witnessed an increase from 2 million hectares in 1950-51 to 72 million hectares in 1996-97 (Fig. 2). During the Fifth and Sixth Plan period, almost one third of the total cultivated area was consolidated, though in some States it was completed as early as 1967-68. There was an overall improvement in related infrastructure, distribution of quality seeds, and other inputs. Above all, assured market with remunerative prices further helped this process of development to grow in all its dimensions.

By all standards, the production of foodgrains in 1983-84 was an outstanding achievement. The total production exceeded 150 million tons, leaving far behind the plan target of 142 million tons and the previous record of 1981-82 over 133 million tons. This not only re-affirmed the nation's confidence to become self-sufficient in food, but also enhanced the nation's chances of becoming an exporter of food. The Ministry of Agriculture, Government of India, described these developments "as the ushering in the Second Green Revolution" with distinctive features. It was labeled as "completely Indian in its strategy as well as ideology". It also had the distinction of adding a new chapter of agricultural development with states like Bihar, Madhya Pradesh, Orissa, Uttar Pradesh and West Bengal contributing over 60 per cent of the increased production of 22 million tonnes over the previous year.

Sixth Plan envisaged a growth rate of 3.9 per cent for all foodgrains. The achievement in four years was 4.34 per cent, rice 3.92 per cent, wheat 6 per cent and pulses 3.7 per cent. A significant program was the launching of a pilot project in 51 selected blocks of Assam, Orissa, Bihar West Bengal and eastern parts of Madhya Pradesh and Uttar Pradesh as the forerunner of special rice production program to be taken up in these states during the next plan. It

Fig. 2

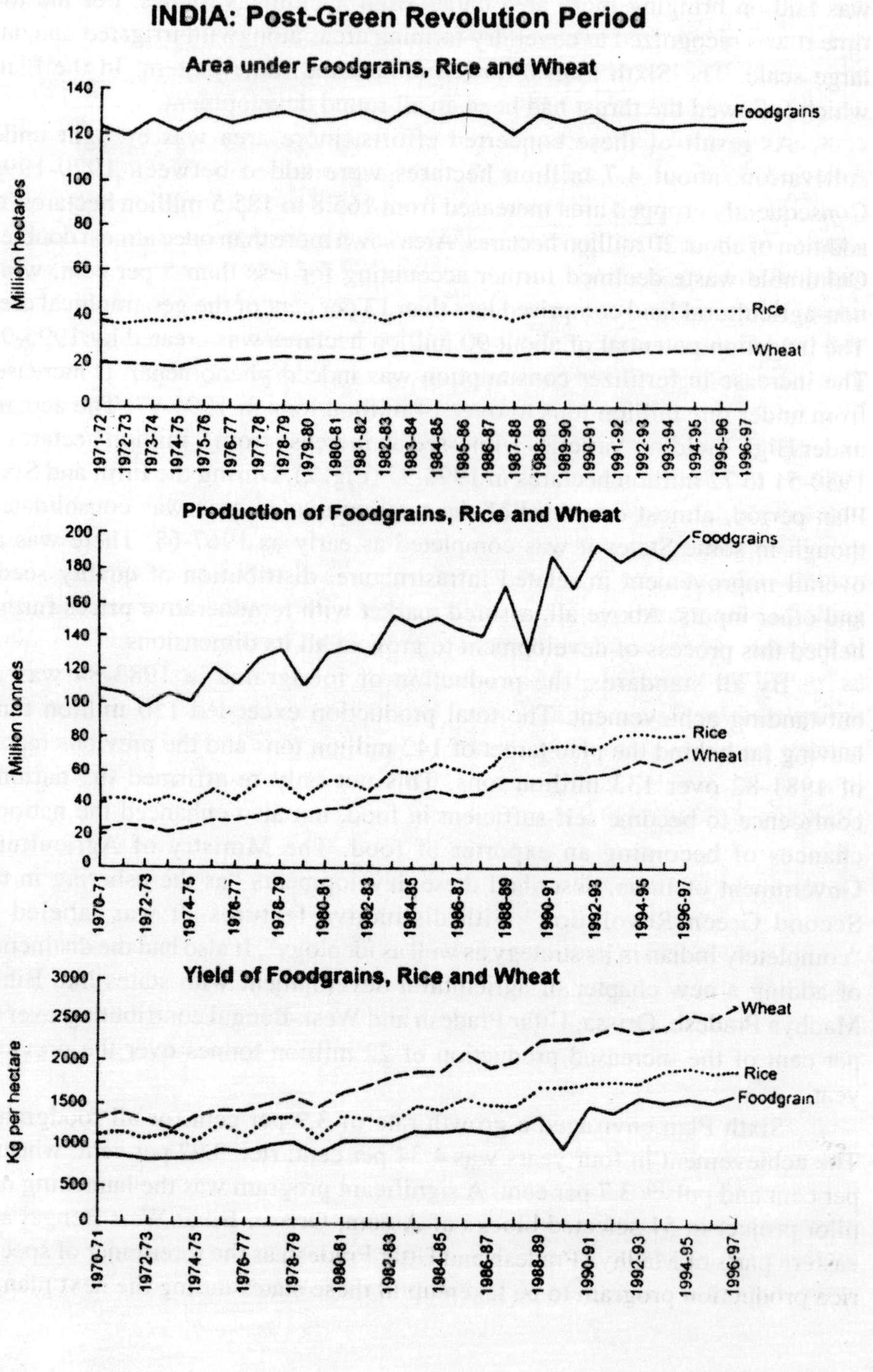
INDIA: Post-Green Revolution Period
Area under Foodgrains, Rice and Wheat
Million hectares
Foodgrains
Rice
Wheat
Production of Foodgrains, Rice and Wheat
Million tonnes
Foodgrains
Rice
Wheat
Yield of Foodgrains, Rice and Wheat
Kg per hectare
Wheat
Rice
Foodgrain

may be remembered that the productivity in these states was below the national level but potential was considered to be high. The record production was reflected in the procurement of grains for central pool. The procure of rice and wheat in 1983-84 reached a new high of 117.13 million tonnes. During the first decade of this phase, production of foodgrains increased at a rate of 2.28 per cent, acreage by 0.38 per cent and yield by 1.88 per cent. In the decade which followed, foodgrains again registered an increase by about 47 million tonnes, from 129.6 to 176.4 million tonnes. By 1996, it touched almost 200 million tonnes. Wheat, during these three decades increased its production by 2.5 times and doubled its yield. Rice almost doubled its production and yield by over 1.5 times. Since Independence, total foodgrains production increased by 4 times, and productivity 3 times. Wheat production had a phenomenal increase-more than 10 times and its yield quadrupled. The oilseeds increased its production by 5 times, doubled its yield and acreage by 2.5 times, an encouraging trend. The situation of pulses – the main source of proteins-was discouraging. It increased its production by 1.7 times, acreage by 1.2 times and yield by 1.4 times (Table 1).

This period not only consolidated the gains accrued as a result of efforts made in the pre-Green Revolution phase, but also added and multiplied these gains into the present phase. Green Revolution thus caused a qualitative change in the food and agricultural situation. The Pearson Report described this change as 'one of the authentic marvels of our times'. "Never before in the history of agriculture has a transplantation of high-yielding varieties coupled with an entirely new technology and strategy been achieved on such a massive scale, in so short a period of time and with such great success", observed Borlaug (Randhawa, 1984).

Gains and Plans

A long list of gains and pains accrued from the Green Revolution can be appended. But since most of them are common place and well known, I would like to enumerate on a few of them which are more relevant and deserve our immediate concern and attention.

The Green Revolution has imported regional, intra-regional and inter-crop disparities. It has also produced serious imbalances in crop production, distorted crop patterns, and increased fluctuation in yearly agricultural output. It is true that it has increased the degree of inequality between perennially irrigated areas and those which are rainfed. It is also true that it has tended to increase the gap between the rich farmer and the small farmer. I would also agree that it has weakened the position of a marginal farmer and the agricultural laborer. It is again a fact that the Green Revolution has not helped reduce poverty and generate employment at desired levels. Overall degradation of environment has also emerged. The state and the central government are also accused of making institutional subsidies and cheap credit facilities available to a relatively more accessible rich farmer than to a small and poor farmer. It has also eroded the traditional social and political fabric of our society. But then all this was bound to happen when societies change and re-shape their destinies. These disparities are a part of the process which augment development. The fact of the matter is that despite these disparities, every section of the society-rich or poor, agricultural laborer or a small farmer-have gained in terms of better living and life styles, though the gains are tilted towards the affluent. But let us also admit that it has helped significantly and not permitted the poverty and unemployment to grow in proportions which were otherwise expected.

One of the serious concerns of today is that the food consumed by an average Indian falls short of calories and proteins required for healthy growth of the body. Consequently one-fifth of the Indian population is chronically malnourished. We have to strive and take cognizance of this at priority to achieve the desired level of calorie intake and make food management system efficient as advocated by Swaminathan (1977) "the most efficient agricultural management system will be one which gives the maximum calories of food energy per every calorie of cultural energy used in the production process" (Drieberg, 1977).

The pain of all pains is that most of the food including cereals, pulses, oilseeds, vegetables and fruits are pesticide-contaminated today, which is directly contributed by the Green Revolution technology. Long back the Insecticide Act 1968 was formed when a large number of deaths occurred in Kerala due to pesticide contaminated wheat which has been operative there since 1972. "Pesticides are still continuing to affect the energy systems and nervous systems in the animals [and human beings]. They are disrupting the micro-structural integrity in the tissues causing cancer and congenital malformations" (Joseph, 1991). People's exposure to these chemicals was measured in sample meals both vegetarian and non-vegetarian. Vegetarian means showed a mean Dichloro Diethyl Trichloroethane and Benzene Hexa Chloride level at 107 and 20 milligrams while the non vegetarian meals showed levels of 141 and 23 milligrams. A study of human milk samples showed mean level of 1.15 parts per million (ppm) and 4.62 parts per million (ppm) of Dichloro Diethyl Trichloroethane and Benzene Hexa Chloride respectively. These pesticides have been banned or heavily restricted in the U.S. and many other countries but are being produced in India. This indiscriminate, widespread promotion of pesticides is disastrous not only in our country but in all the third world countries. Another dangerous chemical Aldrin which is banned in the United States of America, the United Kingdom, Hungry, Netherlands, Mexico, Italy and many other countries is freely used in India. We infact imported 121 metric tonnes of Aldrin in 1983-84. There are many more which are eating away the health of our people. We have to control them and save our coming generations from various deadly diseases.

On the positive side, the Green Revolution has made available a greater capacity to produce. It has stimulated the institutional infrastructure development which is reflected in increase in number of tube-wells, network of roads including village link roads, expansion of regulated markets and foodgrains storage facilities, electrification of villages, increasing access to health, education, and drinking water facilities. It has also helped in slowing down migration from rural to urban areas. Tractorization has promoted multi-cropping and generated great demand for unskilled, semi-skilled and skilled labor. It has generated a host of subsidiary occupations in the rural areas. Moreover, the small farmers, instead of leasing their land to others, now enjoy the benefit of custom-ploughing by owners of tractors and keep the entire produce for domestic consumption and meeting other obligations.

Green Revolution has helped in a big way in improving the quality of life of our people. People have become more conscious of balanced food and nutritious diet. Consequently there is a rapid increase in rural prosperity which is evidenced from the possession of household goods including electronic gadgets and other amenities of life. It has also led to a sharp rise in aspiration levels of the people and they investing in good houses, in education of their children and in creating other comforts of life.

India's biggest achievement is self-sufficiency in foodgrains despite the fact that population has shot up from 359 million in 1950-51 to 845 million in 1990-91 (now 940 million). This obviously has saved millions of people from starvation. The very fact that now we have a sufficient buffer stock to off set the negating effects of floods, droughts and other calamities is indeed very satisfying.

Future Challenges and Strategies

The problems of future growth in agriculture will be more difficult and complex: (i) the present existing technology has almost reached a plateau in its potential for agricultural growth; (ii) the number of months to be fed are increasing, (iii) declining trends of productivity; and (iv) there exists a limited scope in acreage expansion. Therefore the future growth in agriculture must come from : (a) new technologies which are not only "cost-effective" but are also in conformity with natural climatic regime of the country; (b) technologies relevant to rainfed areas specifically; (c) continued genetic improvements for better seeds and yields; (d) data improvements for better research, better results and better and sustainable planning; (e)bridging the gap between knowledge and practice; (f) judicious land use resource surveys, efficient management practices, and sustainable use of natural resources.

There is ample scope in increasing foodgrains production in country by improving the present yield levels as the gap between potential yield and actual yield of various crops is high, ranging between 30 to 300 per cent (Biswas, 1992). There is a large scope for improvement in most crops. Rainfed areas which constitute a large proportion of area under cultivation are the future hopes. The improvements of yield in these area can enhance production to a great extent. It has been estimated that untapped yield potential of rainfed lands is in the range of 200 to 400 per cent (Kumar, 1992). The overall yields in India are much lower than many other countries of the world. China for example produces on an average 5727 kilograms of rice, 3179 kilograms of wheat and 1475 kilograms of pulses per hectare as against India average yields of 2691 kilograms, 2117 kilograms, and 553 kilograms per hectare respectively. These gaps can be narrowed down in the years to come. The second Green Revolution is destined to occur in the rainfed areas of the country. From these hard facts one can easily conclude that there exists a great scope in increasing the foodgrains production for meeting our domestic needs and outside obligations in the years to come. There is nothing to be sad about and we must not be complacent in our efforts.

In my optimistic note I must say that the Green Revolution is a reality and it is going to sustain itself in one form or another. We have successfully set aside the gloomy predictions of 1960's, and we are bound to set aside any discouraging predictions of 1990's. Must I re-affirm that the Green Revolution has neither gone pale nor yellow or brown, it is still green and will remain green. To make it greener, we all have to jointly and individually strive for more.

REFERENCES

Biswas, B.C. and Chanda, T.K. (1992), *A comparative analysis of agriculture and fertilizer scenario in India and China, Yojna*, Vol. 36 (12).

Chakarvarti, A.K. (1973), *Green revolution in India, Annals of the Association of American Geographers*, Vol. 63 (3).

Darling, M.L. (1947), *The Punjab Peasant in Prosperity and Debt*, Oxford University Press, London.

Drieberg, T. (1997), *Good farm management vital to economy*, *The Tribune*, May 2.

Farmer, B.H. (1974), *Agricultural Colonization in India Since Independence*, Oxford University Press, London.

Farmer, B.H. ed. (1977), *Green Revolution?*, The Macmillan Press, London.

Frankel, F.R. (1971), *India's Green Revolution: Economic Gains and Political Costs*, Princeton University Press, London.

Joseph, K.B. (1991), *How safe are pesticides*, *Yojna*, Vol. 35 (10).

Kumar, N. (1992), *Fertilizer management: focus shifts to rainfed area*, *Yojna*, Vol. 36 (12).

Randhawa, M.S. (1984), *Breakthrough in wheat*, *The Sunday Tribune*, May 27.

Singh, G.B. (1979), *Transformation of Agriculture*, Vishal Publications, Kurukshetra.

Gopal Krishan
1940 -

Gopal Krishan's urge to learn is insatiable. Experiments to experience, as a leader or follower, pursuing a single or multiple theme, specializing in one or generalizing from numerous areas, for him the fire to expand the vistas of knowledge have neither a route nor a routine. The familiar tag GK – an acronym which friends and students use interchangeably to address him as a person or one with General Knowledge probably bears complement to his personality. Teaching to research to consultancy, projects to plans to peoples programs, articles and books, book reviews to atlas and blue print for a geographical museum are a part and parcel of his work. Placed at regional to international universities, president of India's largest geographical and cartographic associations, interacting amidst economists, sociologists, architects, environmentalist and planners, GK's work is a dense mosaic of uncommon diversity. From green revolution to rural transformation, regional disparities to regional identity, rural – urban relations to pricing of urban water supply, hill towns to our national borders – GK's search spans a great variety.

His academic canvass is akin to a modern art painting. Transgressing bounds or boundaries the umpteen colors, shapes and form defy a ready made or simple caption. Careful observation decodes a heartfelt message: to make geography a more relevant social science.

GK's impulse to learn and search for relevance is manifest in the evolution of his research. Inheriting a legacy of population studies from his mentor at the department of geography, Chandigarh, he was quick to realize that research confined to the census of teeming millions would be meaningful only if integrated with an understanding of the development process. This explains his alert decision to take on development studies in the 1980s. In his interest for issues of development at the regional and national level, he squared urban as the microcosm for analysis and application. Population, development and urban studies are the dominant strokes of his brush. By a design of accident all three themes have a near equal, one third slice of his 103 research papers. What is remarkable is not sheer numbers, nor the themes but the fact that no area of his research was abandoned as the range of his interest expanded. His canvass though diverse is deftly welded in unison.

An enthusiastic learner, he galloped to first class grades and won himself ranks and scholarships all through school, graduation and post-graduation. His outstanding scholastic acumen attracted attention and at the age of 22, he was drafted in the department of geography, Chandigarh, Panjab University. Nestled at the base of the Jakhoo hill, it is in the non-elite and down to earth DAV School of the Himalayan town of Shimla that GK's desire to learn was kindled. Reticent and recluse by temperament, books are a retreat that offer a lot and demand little in return. To enroll in the Indian Administrative Services had been his first dream. Teaching was a second career option for GK. The tryst of fate and the joy of being appointed as lecturer so young, within ones own alma mater, anchored GK to the Department of Geography at Chandigarh for a life time. Despite his 38 long years in teaching, the pent desire to 'service' needs of the country and interact with 'administration' compelled GK to step out of his academic camp. Yoked by the force to 'learn and apply' his career is a zig-zag where the path at times leads to centers of learning while at others to those of application.

Invitations to teach and research gave GK prestigious appointments not only in India as the Professor of Regional Planning at National Institute of Urban Affairs, Delhi but also in leading universities overseas. The young scientist exchange program took him to Liverpool University, Indo – British Seminar to a number of leading centres, while it was an award from the Royal Geographical Society, London that gave him the opportunity to be part of the University of Cambridge. As a guest professor he visited Bemidji State University in the United States of America, University of Bremen at Germany and University of Pecs in Hungary.

From these experiences GK brought home many nostalgic moments and fond friendships. Bonds were fostered with Prothero, Toth, Chisoholm, Chorley and Bahrenberg, among others. Specially pleasing for GK was the degree of Doctor of Science conferred by the University of Pecs, on the millenium celebrations of Hungary as a nation in 1996. Perhaps more than these tangible benefits are the fertile ideas which GK carried back. Interactions with Chisholm at Cambridge for example had strengthened his interest in administrative geography. GK wanted to push administration as a separate branch of study in geography in India. His failure to meet success in this direction was perhaps less to do with the traditional mind set of geographers in India and more with the fact that Gk himself was unable to produce a valuable and simple text for easy reference on the theme ! The desire to embrace realms larger than that of the university thwarted the publication of such a text but on the flip side enriched the centers of application where he took an assignment.

A member and consultant to Punjab State Planning Board, National Institute of Urban Affairs, Human Settlement Management Institute, Central Tibetan Administration , and taking projects sponsored by diverse organizations like Indian Council of Social Science Research, the Institute of Rural Management,Anand, University Grants Commission and Chandigarh Administration allowed GK to research and take findings to people whom he thought could act upon them. His book on 'Underemployment in Rural Punjab' gained wide currency. Another among his diverse ventures: 'Inner Spaces – Outer Spaces of a Planned City: A Thematic Atlas of Chandigarh', serves as a crucial compendium in research, media and administrative decision.

It is these diversified experiences and assignments with a range of universities , disciplines and institutes that brim Gk's bag with 103 research papers , 19 projects , 9 books , 3 monographs, half a dozen book reviews, and supervision of 10 doctorates and 22 masters in philosophy . Working in meta-disciplinary groups is what strengthens GK's belief that research is spruced when worked in a team. It is little wonder then that half his research projects and a quarter of his publications are co- authored works . That his research papers span 14 different journals, both national and international, speaks volumes of the breadth of his themes and range of quality .

Within this dizzy pace of consultancy and publications GK's true love remains the department of geography at Chandigarh. The tenor and diversity of his contributions spill into administrative duties. Advocating artfully the merits of their department to the University Grants Commission, Gk and his colleagues were able to attract the much sought after prestigious Special Assistance Program from the University Grants Commission not once but for a second term . Under the umbrella of this programme, GK as co-ordinator, not only refurbished the department with the state of the art machines, but enthused a vortex of activities like seminars, workshops and invitations to visiting faculty to enrich the corporate life of students and staff.

Ever filled with plans, he is all set to roll the ball as chairman of the editorial committee for Fifth Survey of Research in Geography under the

auspices of the Indian Council of Social Science Research. Perhaps closer to heart is his dream to consolidate his learning into a book titled, 'Sustainable India: A Geographical Perspective'. To conquer domains and soar new heights of excellence- Gopal Krishan's urge to learn does sustain.

Development, Environment and Decentralized Planning

G. KRISHAN

When a search was on for the next president at the last National Association of Geographers, India Conference at Nagpur, I am told they were looking for a person with diversified geographic interests, having a multidisciplinary exposure, and enjoying regular interaction with the government agencies and research institutions. It seems that they were essentially setting an agenda for Indian geography. The implicit concern was that our discipline should enrich itself further by working on innovative themes, strengthen itself by cross-fertilisation of ideas from related disciplines, and extend its scope into policy making. I felt overwhelmed when I was identified for the purpose, unanimously. I am immensely beholden to the National Association of Geographers, India fraternity for according me this rare honour. It will be my sincere endeavour to come up to its expectations.

I deeply cherish the venue of this conference, Dharwad. Most enchanting are its serene surroundings, a spaciously laid out university campus, and a placid life style. In Karnataka's context, it is antipodal to the super-metro of Bangalore in both location and disposition. It offers a site in the nature of a *tapovan* (a place for meditation) and this augurs well for our deliberations.

The past presidential addresses, from such a venerable pedestal, represent the distilled wisdom of our most distinguished geographers, who steered Indian geography from time to time. These reviewed the state of our discipline as it had been evolving, defined the tasks that lay ahead, and indicated the strategies toward their accomplishment. A mosaic of their ideas is presented below :

- The regional scenes of ecology, society and polity were going to be more complex in future. This called for a higher level of competence on the part of geographers to comprehend, describe and explain the emerging scenario. Indian geography must sharpen its reflexes by way of immediately responding to new challenges.

23rd Indian Geography Congress
Dharwad, 2000 December

- We must find as to why we lost the initiative in taking up themes or methodologies which were inherently geographical in nature. These included, in particular, ecological studies, geographic information systems and regional planning. Other disciplines and professions took the lead. We simply followed.
- New millennium should be visualised as an opportune time for reinventing Indian geography. We must have a clear perspective of the spirit and purpose of our discipline. A blend of theoretical and empirical dimensions of any theme should manifest itself in our research work fieldwork must be our forte.
- Indian geography should be guided by the tenet of social relevance. It must improve its visibility and make its presence felt. It must be in a position to assert that 'this only I can do' and others should acknowledge that 'yes, this you only can do'.
- Indian geography should concentrate more on those themes in which we have greater competence. These include eco-development, area studies, regional development, public policy and geographic education, among others. The future professional scope of our discipline lies primarily in the promotion of geographic information systems. A sound base of cartography is a must for the purpose.

Indeed, the evolved scene of Indian geography resembles a polycyclic landscape. It displays a coexistence between geographies belonging to different eras. The best and the rest go together. For some, Indian geography is a saga of continuous achievements and consolidation; for others, it leaves much room for its improvement.

Here, we pose a set of fundamental questions. What form should the Indian geography acquire to be more authentic in our context? Which issues in terms of paradigm or methodology or content are involved? How to convince the lay person that geographical knowledge, cartographic techniques and spatial perspective are central to day to day life of any one? How to impress the policy makers, planners, and administrators that geography has an indispensable role to play in the scheme of things? How to achieve all these imperatives?

It will be appropriate here to recapitulate the virtues and inadequacies of our discipline. The greatest strength of geography lies in its eye for spatial diversity and instinct for regional synthesis. It has the ability to offer multi- rather than mono-factor explanations. It can claim a special expertise in the conduct of fieldwork and practice of cartography. It has a place of eminence as an applied profession. Some soft dimensions of our discipline may also be noted. It is obliged to be all inclusive, hence less deep, it is not that rigorous in training, hence less specialised, it is polite by temperament, hence less activist. The real challenge lies in capitalisation of our strong points, and labouring on for making up for our inadequacies.

The theme of the Conference has been announced as 'Decentralised Planning, Environment and Development'. It may be more logical to deal with matters in reverse order. We may first have a view of the development scenario, discern its impact on environment and reflect on the role of decentralised planning for managing the evolved situation. Most notable is the fact that all the three components of the theme are multi-disciplinary in nature. This is a matter of gratification as well as caution. While it represents versatility of our discipline, on the one hand; it also poses a challenge for demonstrating our specificity, on the other.

Development Scenario

It is often not appreciated that India set in motion four simultaneous revolutions of democracy, socialism, secularism and planned development soon after independence. A federal structure with a unitary bias was seen as the best answer to the question of regionalism; a socialistic pattern of society as a basic condition for eradication of poverty; secularism as a necessary response to the issue of ethnicity; and planned development as an effective strategy for not only raising the standard of living of the people but also for removing regional imbalances. Indeed much of the reality of emerged India can be attributed to the nature of its democratic polity.

The theory and methodology of Indian planning has been evolving over time. The complexion of the process at any stage was determined by compulsion of the internal situation, lessons drawn from past experience, and nature of the international aid and advice, including pressure. Food, employment, productivity, and equity have been the core concerns. A faith in desirability of the state's role, in the form of public sector production, provision of services and goods, and subsidisation of essential items persisted for long.

The outcome of India's planned development is a mixed bag. On the credit side, the country can take pride in achieving self-sufficiency in food; expanding, diversifying and dispersing its industrial base; containing the inflation rate at a level which is one-half of that in developing countries; attaining a high level of capital formation; reducing poverty ratios; and spreading the development process spatially. On the reverse side, its rate of rise in income level has been two-thirds of what was envisaged, its agricultural performance has been weaker than that of Sri Lanka, Pakistan, and Indonesia, and its industrial advancement lags behind that of Malaysia, Thailand and Brazil.

Striking regional disparities glare one in the face on the development map of India (Figure 1). It is a strange situation wherein the geographic heartland or core is weak and its shell or periphery is strong. The country's outer regions, coinciding largely with the coastal areas, are more developed than the interior mainland. Another notable feature is a comparatively higher degree of development in the former British provinces than in the erstwhile princely states. Tribal areas, barring the Christian ones, have generally remained in the backyard of development due to their relative isolation. Fortunately for the country, 'the regional disparities in India are not along the ethnic or subcultural lines, and there is nothing like the north-south polarisation one finds in western countries'. If anything, India has a relatively more developed west and less developed east. Its north-south characterisation is more on cultural than on economic lines. All this is opposite to what is described at the global level.

Some newly emerged spatial contours on India's development scene may also be noted. First, there is a kind of corridor development along the national highways as also along the trunk railway lines connecting Delhi, Mumbai, Calcutta and Chennai, with each other. Second, the sharp development distinction between the former British administered areas and the erstwhile princely states is getting blurred. Third, the state capitals are emerging as vital centres of diffusion of development around; a role which was confined to only port cities of Calcutta, Bombay (now Mumbai) and Madras (now Chennai) during the colonial days. Fourth, all the Union Territories and smaller states are recording faster rate of development. Fifth, urban-rural disparity is of the lowest order in areas distinguished by commercial agriculture, such as Punjab, Haryana and Kerala. Sixth, emigration zones are prospering while out migration areas are stagnating. Finally, some incongruity between the economic and the social development cannot be missed. Punjab is much ahead of Kerala in economic terms but the two find their placement reversed on social parameters.

The development discourse in India has coined a kind of characterisation of various states. Punjab is credited for its Green Revolution and agro-based industry, Kerala for human development and decentralised planning, West Bengal for land reforms and poverty eradication, Gujarat for dairy cooperatives and entrepreneurial environment. Maharashtra for pro-business ideas and employment guarantee schemes and Andhra Pradesh for promotion of information technology and e-governance. On the other hand, Bihar (erstwhile), Madhya Pradesh (erstwhile), Rajasthan and Uttar Pradesh (erstwhile) are lumped together as BIMRU states (Bihar, Madhya Pradesh, Rajasthan, and Uttar Pradesh)! Such sticky stereotypes have gained currency over time. How far are these apt or justified? Can we call Madhya Pradesh and Rajasthan sick when their performance on rural development and primary education is highly commendable?

Fig. 1 : India Development Level 1991

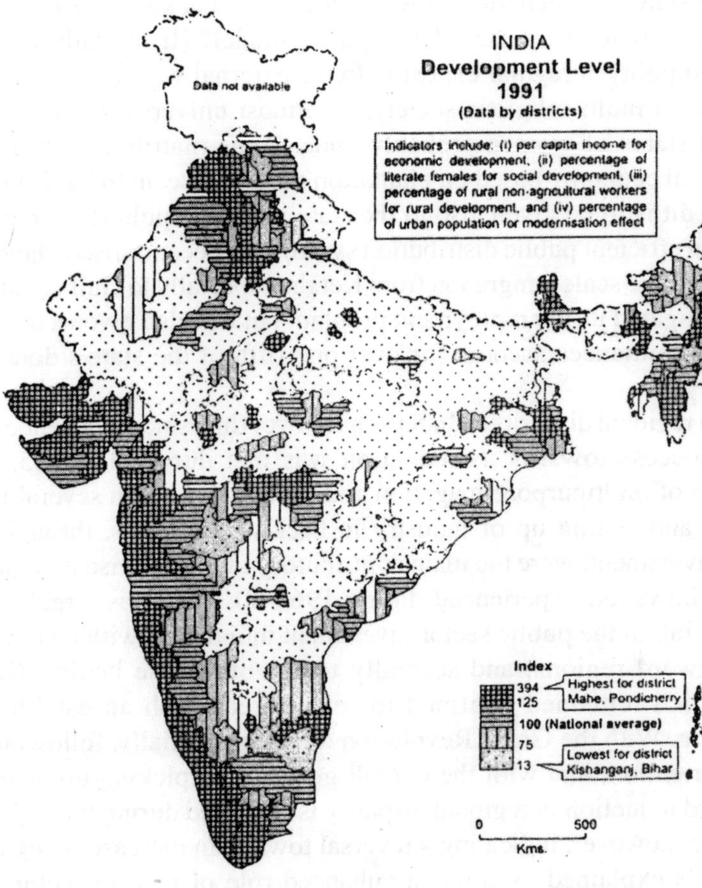

Is Orissa outside the so-called BIMARU (Bihar, Madhya Pradesh, Rajasthan and Uttar Pradesh) realm when its poverty ratio is as high as that of Bihar? Goegraphers may undertake serious research to test the validity of all such popular perceptions and deconstruct untenable myths.

An indepth analysis of the development performance of various states is imperative. Some illustrations will be in order here. Why did Bihar remain poor despite richness of its physical resources? Its backwardness is perhaps rooted in a higher order of structural inequality, political compulsion and administrative failure. Equally critical has been the negative role of resource –

population imbalance, high frequency of devastating floods and gross inadequacy of infrastructure. One has to figure out whether the aggressive casteism in the state has been the cause or effect of its backwardness.

How did Kerala emerge as a development model? Historically, a stable and enlightened polity, a regular exposure to the external world by virtue of a coastal location, a multi-religious society, an almost universal literacy base, relatively high status of women probably under some matrilineal influence, and a commercial economy based on plantation crops, all seem to have made a grand mix. Credit is to be given also to the state's welfare policies, including land reforms, an efficient public distribution system and decentralised planning. More recently, a large scale emigration from Kerala, especially to Gulf countries, has not only mitigated its unemployment problem but has also given a boost to the economy. Remittances account for over one-fifth of the state's domestic product.

How did regional disparity in India behave over time since independence? Some initial success towards its reduction was met during 1947-65. The implementation of multipurpose irrigation and power projects in several parts of the country and setting up of industry in backward regions, through the public sector investment, were the main contributory factors. A rise in regional disparity was, however, experienced during 1965-80. This was largely due, first, to a sharp fall in the public sector investment in industry with its adverse effect on backward regions, and secondly to the otherwise benign Green Revolution which remained confined to select areas with an established irrigation system. With the Green Revolution diffusing spatially, following an extension of irrigation, and with the overall growth rate picking up, a slight tendency toward reduction in regional disparity is observed during the eighties. The nineties are, however, indicating a reversal toward an increase in regional disparity. This is explained by a much enhanced role of private sector, and preference of the multinationals for investment in more developed parts of the country under the new economic regime. On the whole, the public sector did render spatial justice but its operational efficiency left much to be desired.

Why was the hue of the Green Revolution brightest in Punjab? This seems to be the outcome of adoption of a right sequence of policies. These included consolidation of landholdings, extension of irrigation and reclamation of wastelands for agriculture, provision of agricultural services as well as inputs, supply of power, construction of village-link roads and promotion of agricultural credit societies. The rural base of the political power, coupled with dynamism of its peasantry, facilitated the success of this Revolution.

How do the Indian states differ in terms of disparity within? Is any intra-state disparity a function of their physical size or development level or social structure or ideological orientation? Kerala is noted for the lowest order of internal disparity while Bihar lies on the other extreme. Broadly speaking, disparity within is more pronounced in large, less developed states, such as Uttar Pradesh, Andhra Pradesh, Madhya Pradesh, in addition to Bihar; modest in large, but relatively developed states, such as Gujarat, Maharashtra and Karnataka, and low in small developed states, such as Punjab, Haryana and Himachal Pradesh, besides Kerala. The internal disparity finds positive relationship with the physical size and negative one with the development level of various states.

A kind of directional bias is manifest on the development map of various states. For example, the north is more developed than the south in Punjab, but the picture is in reverse in Karnataka, Kerala and West Bengal. The east is more developed than the west in Haryana but the opposite is true in respect of Madhya Pradesh, Maharashtra and Uttar Pradesh. Locational advantages, coupled with matters of politico-economic history, seem to be at the base of such intra-state contrasts.

By now, there is considerable research evidence on factors underlying the development differential among and with various states of India. In contradiction to the popular belief, this variation is associated more with investment by private sector rather than by public sector. As much as 72 per cent of the gross fixed investment in the country is in private sector and the remaining 28 per cent in public sector, both at the central and state levels.

Even otherwise, the picture pertaining to public sector investment in the low income states is not encouraging. Per capita devolution of funds by the central government to them was less by 18 per cent in comparison to that to high income states; per capita transfers through the all India financial institutions or priority sector credit facility to them were just one-fifth of that to high income states. The location of central public enterprises in backward states did not succeed in generating the desired spread effects for lack of requisite transport facilities around. It follows that the public sector investment is necessary but not a sufficient condition for development of backward areas.

Contrary to popular notion, political power does not automatically lead to economic vigour. Notably the four low income states of Bihar, Madhya Pradesh, Rajasthan and Uttar Pradesh account for 38 per cent of the seats in the Lok Sabha while the high income states of Punjab, Haryana, Gujarat and Maharashtra are represented to the extent of 18 per cent. Most of the prime ministers of India hailed from the above mentioned four low income states. These have no reason to complain of any political neglect or discrimination against. Reasons are to be found perhaps in their own systemic failure.

How far was the development process in various states affected by the degree of homogeneity of their population? An empirical analysis reveals positive, though modest, relationship between the cultural pluralism and development level on this count. In relative terms, the role of religious heterogeneity has been of the highest order, followed by that of regional (migration-generated), and linguistic heterogeneity. Religious and linguistic pluralism in India seem to have produced more of complementarity than conflict in the domain of development.

How did the caste composition of various states impact their development process? There is some evidence to suggest that the states, such as Punjab, Gujarat and Maharashtra, which have been under the politico-administrative control of middle castes, performed better than others, such as Bihar and Uttar Pradesh, where the divide between the upper and lower castes is sharp. Things were relatively better in states, such as Tamil Nadu and Karnataka, where this conflict had been resolved at an early stage in favour of lower castes. Likewise, the states with a socialist bias, such as Kerala, made a greater thrust in human development while others with a strong competitive ethos, such as Punjab, scored higher on economic front. Persistence of feudal tendencies in states such as Bihar, Uttar Pradesh and Orissa had dampening effect on the pace of development process.

To what extent were the Backward Area Development Programmes, which have been a sterling feature of the Indian planning strategy since the Fourth Plan (1969-74), successful in achieving their objective ? A doctoral thesis, being pursued at our department, found that as many as 412 districts out of the total of 466 in 1991 in India, were declared as backward under at least one such programme. No less than 207 districts were categorised as fundamentally backward, being prone to droughts or being desert or hilly in physical disposition. Also, 288 districts were declared as industrially backward. The number of socially backward districts, by way of having a relatively high proportion of schedule tribe population, was placed at 185. Several districts were covered by two to five programmes. The overall impact of these programmes has been assessed as just modest. Why has this been so? It seems that our bureaucracy does not have the requisite skill to implement area-based programmes. Such programmes were implemented on the pattern of sectoral ones. Available funds often get distributed, in some form, among target populations in place of getting invested in beneficiary-oriented development projects.

As such, the development performance of various states can be ascribed to their strength of physical infrastructure, quality of human resource, ethos of policy formulation and efficiency of governance. As geographers, we may find out as to which kind of territorial arrangements provide the most effective base for the play of these factors. I reckon the designing of appropriate spatial organisations for development administration as one of the most critical tasks for geographers in India. They should recommend the optimal size and configuration of states, districts, and blocks, and all such spatial units, so as to minimise the cost and maximise the benefit of our development process.

They may reflect over a related issue as well. Are backwardness and development two different commodities or do they lie on two ends of the same continuum. If the latter is true, then why is development measured more often in economic terms such as standard of living or per capita income and backwardness in social terms, such as status of women or percentage of literate females? An answer has to be found for the popular tendency of perceiving development as economic and backwardness as social.

Environmental Issues

The development-ecology debate continues unabated. Modern development is seen as causing an immense damage to ecology. Eco-fundamentalists insist on moderating the pace of development. There is a natural reaction from the developmentalists. They point out that development alone builds a capacity for taking care of ecology. The argument offered is that some ecological problems, such as disease and dirt, decline as the development process proceeds. Some problems worsen initially but subsequently take a turn for the better. A phase of scientific afforestation may follow an earlier one of deforestation. Some problems do persist even at a high level of development. Air pollution, caused by emission from cars, thermal plants and industry, is one such case.

A golden mean between the two extreme positions is represented by the concept of sustainable development. Its basic message is that the wheel of development must move on, but it should advance within the supportive capacity of an ecosystem. Hence, the real issue is 'not of containing development to save ecology but of managing ecology to promote development'.

What is the scene of environmental degradation of India. Around 45 per cent of the country's geographical area is estimated as suffering from soil problems caused by erosion, water logging, and salinity/alkalinity. Hardly 20 per cent of the country's geographical area is under forest cover against the desired percentage of 33. No less serious is the contamination of water resources, both surface and subsurface. The ambient air quality in most of the cities has deteriorated drastically over the years.

Historically, environmental degradation was of a distinctly higher order in provinces which were under the colonial rule. Deforestation, in particular, was more typical of zones located in proximity to presidency capitals such as

Calcutta, Bombay and Madras primarily to meet the needs of ongoing construction; of localities where tea or coffee plantations were laid out, and of regions where dense populations started growing fast. The colonial power had the need, greed and technology for the massive exploitation of natural resources. The princely state territories escaped such an evil effect, by and large. Natural resources were exploited only to a limited extent in their case. Situation changed significantly after independence. Environmental degradation became rampant in and around developed pockets, which included areas marked by intensive irrigation or large scale mining, or thermal plant location, or industrial concentration. Slum localities represented bad ecology in urban places. Implications of any degraded environment, be it in the form of deforestation, or desertification or water contamination, or air pollution, for human life must be identified and analysed.

Some pertinent questions in research methodology may be raised here. Which are the most appropriate indicators for assessing the ecological health of any area ? Which are the quantitative measures of sustainable development ? Which arrangements best represent the concern of the state for environment ? This is what may be termed as 'eco-environmental, or green accounting'.

The ecological status of a region is to be assessed through both positive and negative indicators. The first group may include : (i) per capita forest land, (ii) percentage of households living in pucca houses and having access to safe water, toilet facility and power supply, and (iii) percentage of households using gas/electricity as cooking fuel. The second group could cover (i) percentage of land area prone to flooding or drought or soil erosion or waterlogging, (ii) per hectare excessive use of chemical fertilisers and pesticides in respect of agricultural land, (iii) proportion of settlements/localities subject to mosquito/ pest problem; (iv) percentage of urban population living in slums, and (v) frequency of reported cases of asthma, malaria, and dysentery. The former calls for conservation strategies, the latter for remedial measures.

Sustainability indicators have two dimensions. The first one pertains to the repair of ecological damage that has already taken place, and the second represents the efforts made to upgrade the prevailing quality of a region's ecology. As such, indicators would include: (i) percentage of total budget allocated to environmental items, such as forest, treated water supply, soil conservation, and pollution control, (ii) per capita land under recreational use, such as tourism sites, playgrounds, gardens and well-kept open spaces, (iii) percentage of land under national parks, wild life reserves, and bird sanctuaries, and (iv) per capita rise in direct income from natural resources and (v) decline in gini co-efficient of income distribution.

By comparison, it is easier to assess the state's seriousness in addressing the issues pertaining to ecology. Indicators, for the purpose, could include : (I) percentage of total budget allocated to environmental items, such as forest, treated water supply, soil conservation, and pollution control, (ii) per capita land under recreational use, such as tourism sites, playgrounds, gardens, and well-kept open spaces, (iii) percentage of land under national parks, wild life reserves, and bird sanctuaries, and (iv) per capita expenditure on sanitation. This list of indicators, as in other cases discussed above, is simply indicative and not exhaustive.

A few words on the quality of geographic research on environmental issues in India will be in order here. Such exercises are often based on textbook material rather than on solid data, use macro-level phraseology to describe micro-level situations, and focus mainly on disaster cases oblivious of some grand experiments in environmental management. The real difficulty in carrying out such exercises lies in non-availability of requisite data. Ecological studies have an inbuilt time dimension; thereby these require longitudinal information. This adds to the enormity of the task.

Decentralised Planning

Decentralised planning is a strategy which aims at achieving progress, prosperity and habitat quality through involvement of local level representative institutions. A great confidence is placed in the efficacy of the local communities in finding solution to their problems, in making optimal use of resources, in evolving an efficient delivery system for services and in improving life conditions, in general. In India, decentralised planning stands for planning at the district, block, and village/town levels.

Of course, the interest and competence in planned development at successively lower spatial scales would mature only with the passage of time. In India the initial thrust was to work out national level development projects through an unhindered utilisation of natural resources. This was soon followed by intensification of the development process at the regional or state level. A need was subsequently felt to take the development process to local level. By that time, the inadequacy of the national and state levels to take care of local level issues had been exposed. Meanwhile the capacity to plan at the local level had also been built.

It is well known that the seed for decentralised planning was sown right in the First Plan (1951-56) through the Community Development Programme. The Fourth Plan (1969-74) is said to have taken a strong stand in favour of this style of planning. A firm base, however, was provided by the Constitution (seventy-third Amendment) Act, 1992 and the Constitution (seventy-fourth

Amendment) Act, 1992. These gave a legal status to decentralisation of governance at the *panchayat (village) and nagarpalika (town)* levels, respectively. It is, however, worthy of recall that the idea of local self-governance for development had taken shape in the erstwhile princely state of Mysore where, as early as in 1874, 'local fund committees' were constituted in every district to take up construction of roads and subsidiary works.

What is decentralised planning expected to do ? Perspectives differ. Often its primary task is defined as filling of the spatial gaps in distribution of infrastructural facilities in consonance with hierarchy of settlements. Others opine that it is meant to achieve self-sufficiency by delimiting territorial production complexes in the spirit of agropolitan development. Still others view it as an instrument for solving local level problems, such as floods, soil erosion and deforestation, or for optimising the use of local level natural resource base, including land, water and vegetation. For geographers, however, the 'designing of location specific development projects' is the real task under any scheme of decentralised planning.

Decentralisation essentially involves substitution of the macro-space by micro-space, of the government by communities, and of bureaucracy by democracy. It calls for a precise delineation of functions and powers at the local, regional, and national levels. Its preconditions include a political ethos which has a faith in devolution of power, a populace which is educated and aware of its rights, and an infrastructure which is dispersed and adequate. Decentralisation is an integral part of good governance.

For that matter, one of the critical measures of good governance is the degree to which functions, powers and financial resources have been devolved to local authorities. This can be objectively assessed from the percentage of state funds earmarked for the purpose. The development seal of the local authorities can be judged from the proportion of devolved funds that they could actually utilise. Also, the regularity with which the local level elections are held and frequency with which local bodies schedule their deliberations can also be quantified for assessing their commitment to decentralisation.

Some research questions call for geographic attention. How have various states performed in respect of decentralised planning? Why Kerala has been the most successful while Bihar has much to lament for ? What has been the outcome of such differing situations ? Hardly any systematic study is available to provide authentic answers.

An additional question pertains to the kind of spatial unit which is optimal for decentralised planning. Is it a district or a block or a village/town? Or is it a watershed or a city region or a *patwar* circle (the basic unit for delimitation of the assembly and parliamentary constituencies). No less than 10,000 watershed development projects have been launched in India since 1 April 1995 as a part of the Drought Prone Area Development Programme. These are assessed as a grand success. Decentralisation of programme administration and community participation have been highlighted as the main contributory factors. The spatial picture of success is, however, highly uneven. Gujarat has made impressive gains than Orissa, Bihar and Uttar Pradesh. Andhra Pradesh is credited for being far ahead of all other states in the implementation of such projects. How do we explain all this?

Still another research challenge for geographers, in the field of spatial planning, pertains to the utilisation of common lands in villages and government lands in towns. These are the spaces which offer a grand scope for their orderly development. Needless to add that geographers owe responsibility for preparing detailed blueprints for their optimal utilisation.

The Mission Ahead

In fitness of things, India has chosen to promote simultaneously two decentralizations: economic and political. The economic policy seeks decentralisation in favour of the market; the new political programme entrusts greater powers to *panchayats* and *nagarpalikas*. The first is in response to global compulsions and the second to local imperatives. There is a streak of irony in the scheme of things. While the hitherto centralise economic planning worked essentially for spatial decentralisation of development process in the spirit of federalism and democracy, the new economic policy may centralise development at more advantageous locations. One does hope that the policy of decentralised governance counters any tendency towards such polarisation. Geographers must keep analysing this synthesis as it evolves in spatially varying forms.

The challenges which India faces include an unabated fast growth of population, an impaired ecology, the fragility of social fabric on questions of religion, caste and region, the inadequacy of federal polity and constraints inherent in the transition to a new economic order. There is a spatial variation in each case. There are success stories at the regional and local level as also the scenes of dismal failure. Geographers may document both, by areas make an indepth analysis in each case and draw meaningful messages. Success stories are to be replicated spatially.

The tenets of social justice, economic federalism and optimal resource utilisation call for a reduction in regional disparities without slowing down the growth in the relatively developed areas. This is possible through stronger boost to the development process in backward areas. Such a positive discrimination should not mean merely an injection of heavier doses of financial resources but also an improvement in management of their development process. The latter task will be greatly facilitated if the existing administrative organisation of space is reformed to meet the requirements of development planning. This amounts to recasting the administrative map of the country. Bigger states may be subdivided into smaller ones. The same applies to bigger districts within states. Geographers must contribute the finest of their skill in carving out of such spatial organisations.

Let me conclude by way of a call for some geographic meditation and an enunciation of a personal benediction. We may introspect as to why Indian geography could not acquire an identity of its own ? Why was it overtaken by other disciplines in cultivation of certain themes, such as ecological studies, or promotion of some latest methodologies, such as Geographic Information Systems, which are akin to the very nature of our discipline? Why could it not perfect a specialism that could go as a direct input into policy formulation? Why did it not correct its persistent internal imbalance in favor of human geography vis-à-vis physical geography? Why were we not that successful in demonstrating the utility of geography to society at large? Honest answers to such questions will enable us to delineate the operational parameters of our mission ahead.

And, as far as my prayer goes, it is for the fulfillment of the agenda which my esteemed predecessor presidents set for Indian geography. Let their goals be vindicated as attainable. Only then shall we have an Indian geography of our vision.

As the new century unfolds ,
The need of the hour,
Is a collective response,
To the Voice of Concern.

Anu Kapur

Select Bibliography on Indian Geography

Ahmad, Aijazuddin (1996): *Progress in Indian Geography*: 1992-96, Indian National Science Academy, New Delhi.

Akhtar, Rais ed. (1998): *Contemporary Approaches to Indian Geography*, APH Publishing Corporation, New Delhi.

Ahmad, G.M. (1952): "Geography as a Social Science", *Geographer*, Vol. 5., No. 2, pp. 14 - 20.

Ali, S.M. (1961): "Applied Geography, A Proposal for the Establishment of Departments of Applied Geography in Indian Universities", *National Geographer*, Vol. 4, pp. 1 - 5.

Ali, S.M. (1966): *The Geography of the Puranas*, People Publishing House, New Delhi.

Association of Indian Universities (1940 to 2000): *Bibliography of Doctoral Dissertations*, Annual Volumes.

Association of Indian Universities (2001): *University Handbook,* All India Universities House, New Delhi.

Bagchi, K. (1976): "Role of Geographical Societies and Journals in National Development", *Geographical Review of India,* Vol.38, No. 3 pp. 215-220.

Bhardwaj, S.M. (1987): " Toward an Indian Geography Agenda", *National Geographical Journal of India,* Vol. 33, pp. 327 - 334.

Chakraborty, S.C. (1987): "Contemporary Directions in Geography and Our Options in India", *Transactions*, Institute of Indian Geographers, Vol.9, No.2. pp. 1- 8.

Chatterjee, S.P. (1964): *Fifty Years of Science in India: Progress of Geography,* Calcutta.

Chatterjee, S.P. (1968): *Progress of Geography in India*, (1964-68), Indian Science Congress Association, Calcutta.

Concept Compilation (1982): *Who's Who of Geographers in India,* Concept Publishing Company, New Delhi.

Das, H.P. (1972): "Teaching of Geography as a Science Subject in Schools", *Geographical Review of India*, Vol., No. 1., pp. 93 - 96.

Deshpande, C.D. (1983): "Discovering Indian Geography", in R.P. Misra ed. *Contributions to Indian Geography: Concepts and Approaches,* Heritage Publishers, New Delhi, pp. 11 - 14:

Deshpande, C.D. (1991): Indian Geography in 2001 A.D., in Jaymala Diddee ed. *Recent Trends in Indian Geography*, Rawat Publications, Jaipur.

Dickason, D.G. (1992): "Geographic Research on India: Contributions from the United States", *National Geographical Journal of India*, Vol. 38 pp. 147-158.

Diddee, Jaimala ed. (1991): *Recent Trends in Indian Geography,* Rawat Publications, Jaipur.

Dikshit, K.R. (1995): "The Growth of Physical Geography, the Indian Scene and the Agenda for Future", *Transactions*, Institute of Indian Geographers, Vol. 17, No. 2, pp.145-163.

Dikshit, K.R. (1999): "Paradigm Shifts in Geomorphology ", *Transactions,* Institute of Indian Geographers, Vol. 21, No. 2, pp. 89 - 104.

Dikshit, R.D. (1984):" The Changing Professional Concerns in Geography: A Review ", *Geographical Review of India,* Vol. 46, No. 1, pp. 1-15.

Dutt, A.K. (1996):" Place of Geography in Ancient India", *National Geographical Journal of India,* Vol. 42, No. 1 & 2, pp. 1-8.

Ganguli , B.N. (1959) : " Role of Geography in Economic Development " , 1959, *Indian Geographer,* Vol.4, No 2,pp 10-13.

Gosal, G.S. (1989): *Report of the Curriculum Development in Geography,* University Grants Commission, New Delhi.

Krishan , G. , Sharma, H.N. , and Kapur, A. (2000): *Report of the Task Force on Indian Geography,* National Association of Geographers , India. New Delhi.

Indian Council of Social Science Research (1973): Social Science in India: A Report Retrospective, Vol. II, *An Abstract of Social Science Statistics,* New Delhi.

Indian Council of Social Science Research (1972): *Survey of Research in Geography"*, New Delhi.

Indian Council of Social Science Research (1972): *Survey of Research in Physical Geography"*, New Delhi.

Indian Council of Social Science Research (1979): *Second Survey of Research in Geography*, New Delhi.

Indian Council of Social Science Research (1984): *Third Survey of Research in Geography*, New Delhi.

Indian Council of Social Science Research (1999): *Fourth Survey of Research in Geography,* New Delhi.

Kapur, A. (1998): *Indian Geography: A Future with a Difference,* Allied Publishers, New Delhi.

Karan, P.P. (1966): *"Recent Contributions to the Geography of South Asia"* Chaiers de Geographie de Quebec, Vol. 9, pp. 317 - 32.

Karan, P.P. (1992): " Development of Geographic Thought in India", in R.L. Singh and Rana P.B eds. *The Roots of Indian Geography: Search and Research,* Banaras Hindu University, Varanasi.

McKay, D.V. (1943): Colonialism in the French Geographical Movement 1871 - 1881, *Geographical Review,* pp. 214 - 232.

Mookherjee, S. (1979):" New Direction in Geography", *Transactions,* Indian Council of Geographers, Vol.6, No 1. pp. 23.

Mukerji, A.B. (1991): "What Ails Indian Geography?" in Jaymala Diddee ed., *Recent Trends in Indian Geography,* Rawat Publications, Jaipur.

National Committee for Geography, Calcutta(1968): *Directory of Indian Geographers* .

Nag, P. (1992): "Role of NATMO in Promoting Indian Geography", *National Geographical Journal of India,* Vol. 38, pp. 301-310.

Prakasa Rao, V.L.S. (1953): "Geography and Social Studies in Secondary School Education", *Indian Geographical Journal* Vol. 27, No. 3 & 4, pp. 82 - 86.

Reddy, N.B.K. (1989): "Indian Geography: Tasks Ahead", *Transactions,* Institute of Indian Geographers, Vol. 11, No. 1, pp. 31 - 32.

Roy, B. K. (1992): "The Census Contributions to Indian Geography", *National Geographical Journal of India,* Vol. 38, pp. 283-300.

Schwartzberg, J.E. (1983): "The State of South Asian Geography", *Progress in Human Geography,* Vol. 7, No. 1, pp. 232-253.

Shafi, M. (1952):"Geographical Research in India", *Geographer,* Vol. 5, No. 2., pp. 33 - 41.

Shafi, M.(1970):"Applied Geography in India", *Geographer,* Vol. 17, No. 1, pp.1 - 3.

Shafi,M. (1984): *Country Report: Trends in Geographical Research in India:* 1980 - 83, 25th International Geography Congress, Paris.

Singh, J. (ed.) (2000): *"Progress in Indian Geography:* 1996 - 2000", A Status Report prepared for the 29th International Geographic Congress, Seoul, Korea.

Singh, L.R (1996): *New Frontiers in Indian Geography,* Allahabad University, Allahabad.

Singh, N. and B. Sangwan (1999): "Challenges in Geography: Teaching and Research", *Transactions*, Institute of Indian Geographers, Vol. 21, No. 2, pp. 85 - 88.

Sinha, B.N. (1986): *Trends in Geographical Research in India*, Indian Council of Geographers, Bhubaneshwar.

Sircar, D.C. (1971): *"Studies in the Geography of Ancient and Medieval India"*, Motilal Banarsidas, Delhi.

Spate, O.H.K.(1956):"Modern Geography and its Meaning for India", *National Geographical Journal of India*, Vol. 2. No. 4., pp. 175 - 185.

Stamp, L.D. (1946): " The Progress of Geographical Education in Indian Universities", *The Indian Geographical Journal,* Vol. 21, July - September, pp 126 - 128.

Sundaram, K.V. (1997):"The Interface of Geography with other Disciplines, Society and Government: A Feasible Approach", *Annals of the National Association of Geographers,* Vol. 1-2, pp. 138 - 145.

Survey of India (n.d.): *Historical Records of the Survey of India,* Vols. I and II, 1900-1930.

Thakur, B. (1994):"Indian Geography: Development, Trends and Prospects", *Transactions,* Institute of Indian Geographers, Vol. 16, No. 1 pp. 67-85, No. 2 pp.177-

Tickoo , C (1980): *Indian Universities : Historical Comparative Perspective,* Orient Longman ,Ltd , New Delhi .

Universities Grants Commission (1968): *Geography in Indian Universities,* Report of the Review Committee, New Delhi.

World of Learning (2001), Europa Publication Limited, London, 2000.

Wright K.John (1960): The Field of Geographical Society, in G. Taylor ed. *Geography in the Twentieth Century: A Study of Growth, Fields, Techniques, Aims and Trends,* Methuen, London